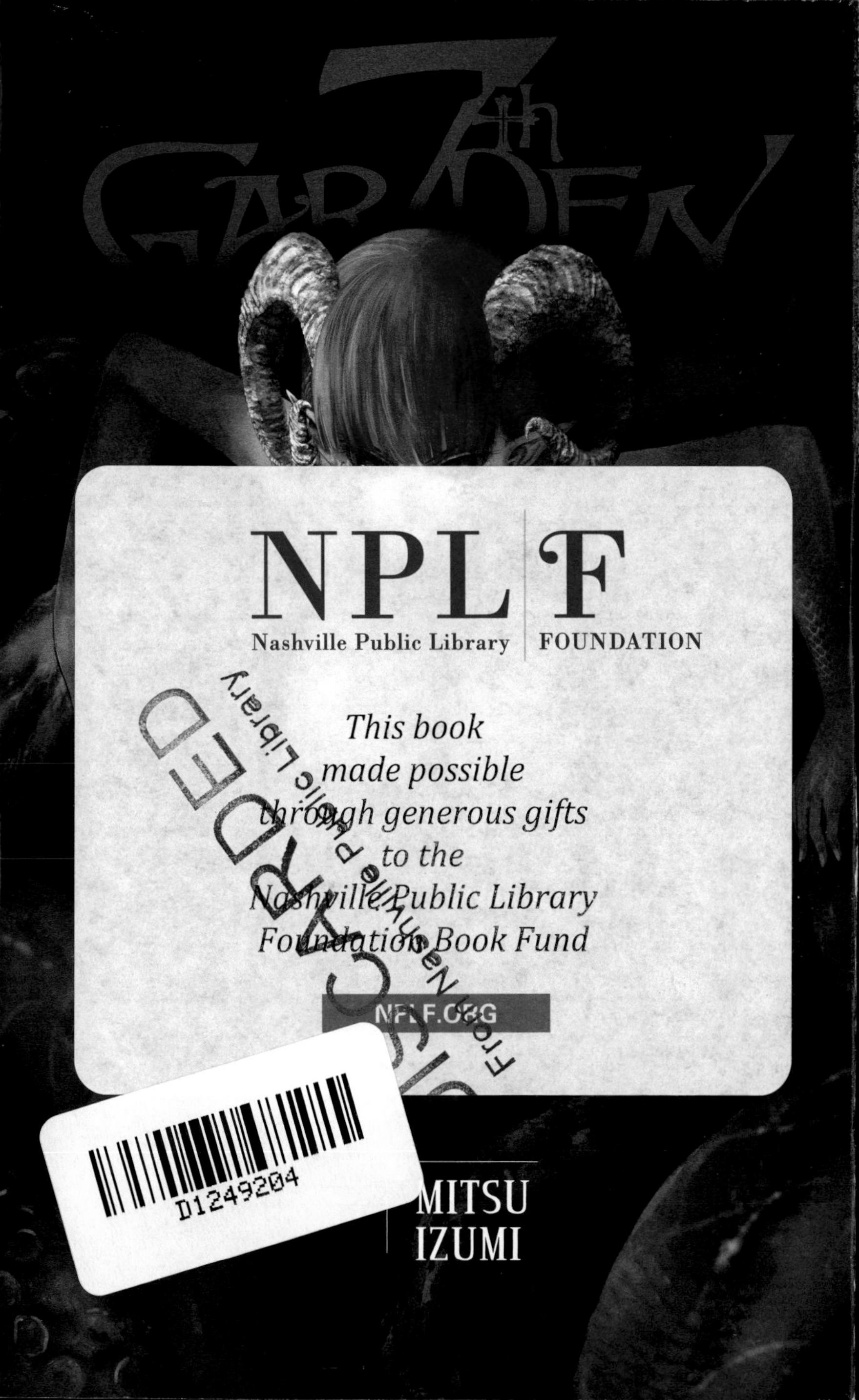
7th GARDEN
MITSU IZUMI

The Sixth Angel...

*...pruned the vegetation with hatchets
and shears...*

...and created a land for people and livestock.

7thGARDEN

CONTENTS

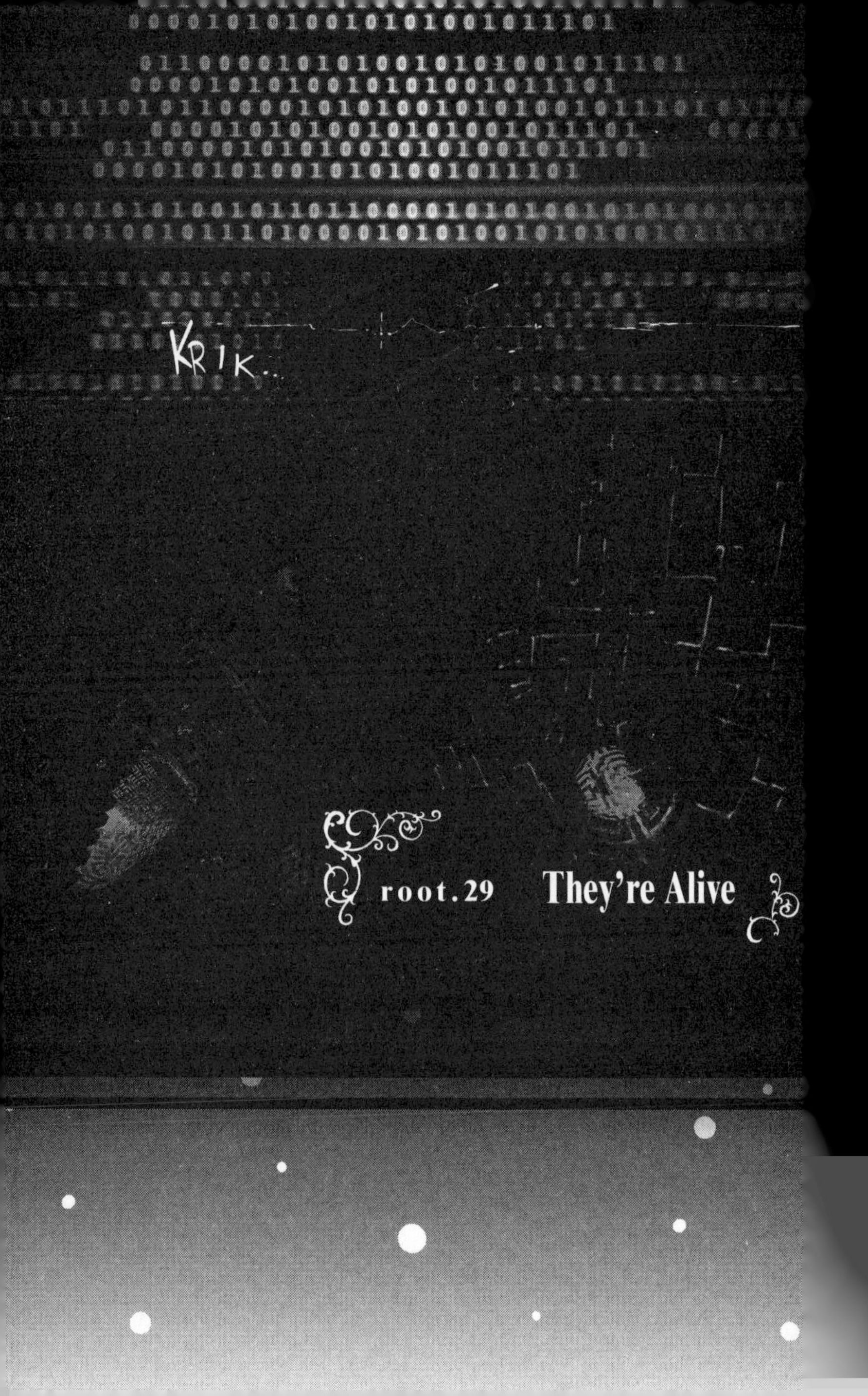
KRIK...
root.29 They're Alive

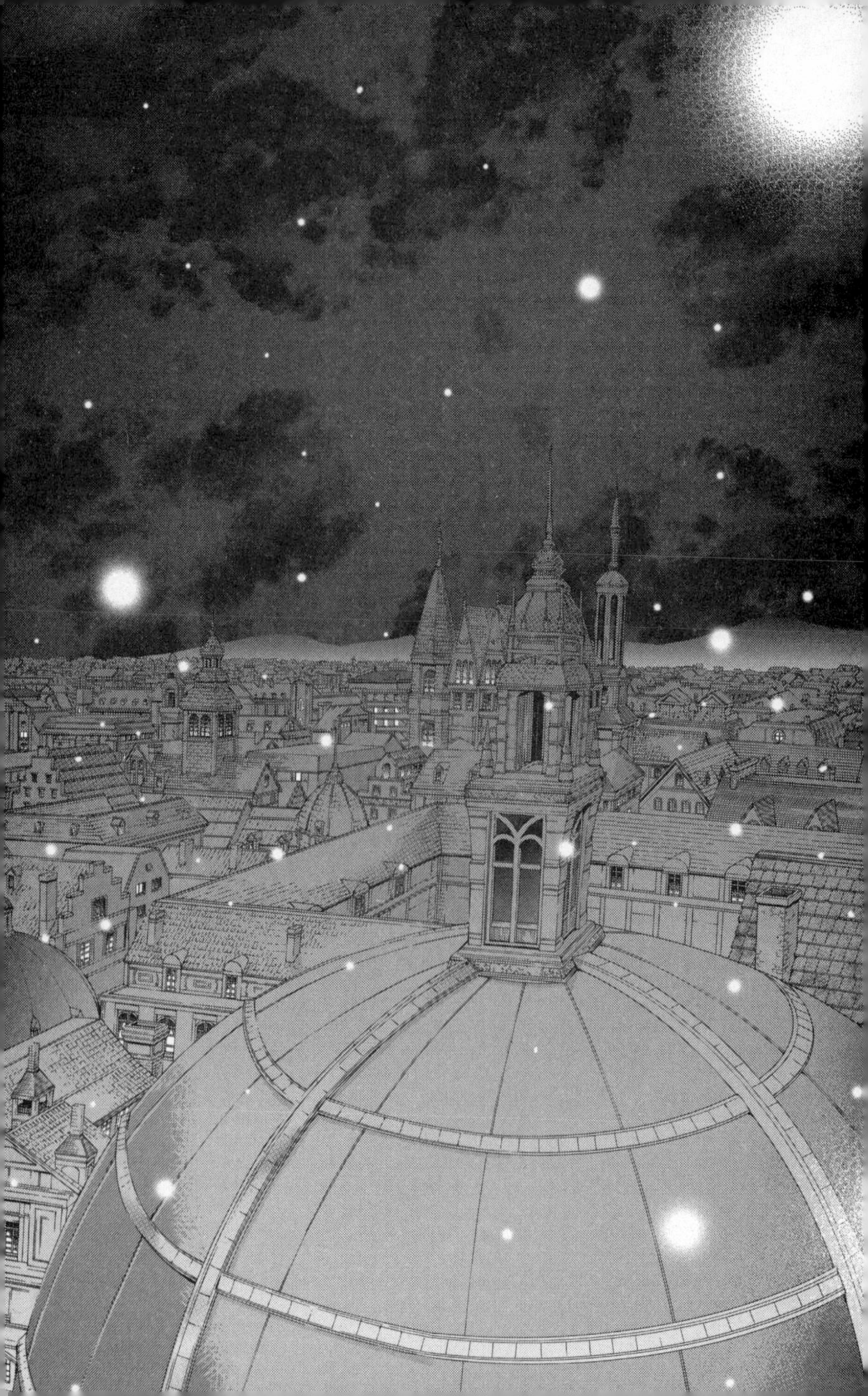

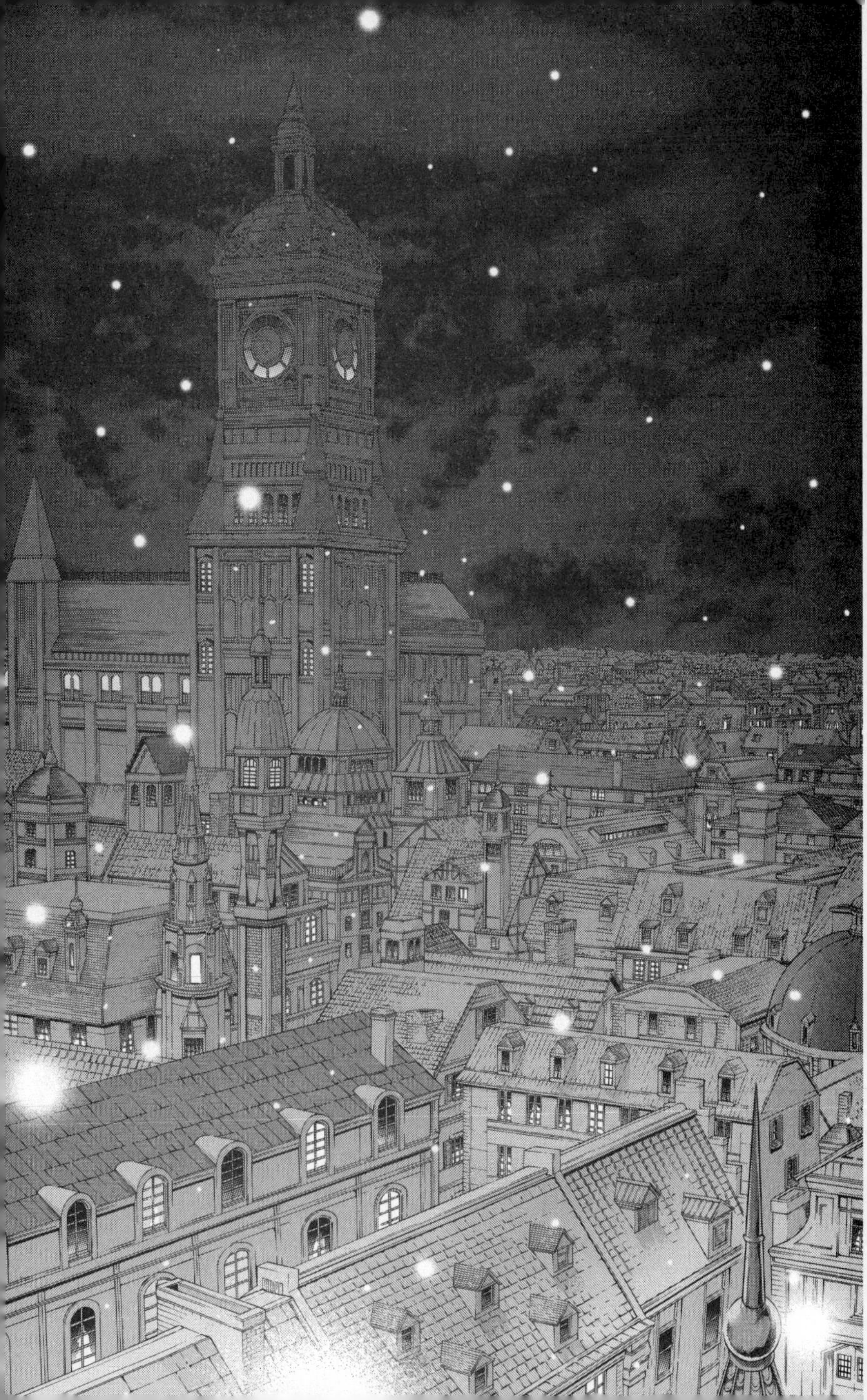

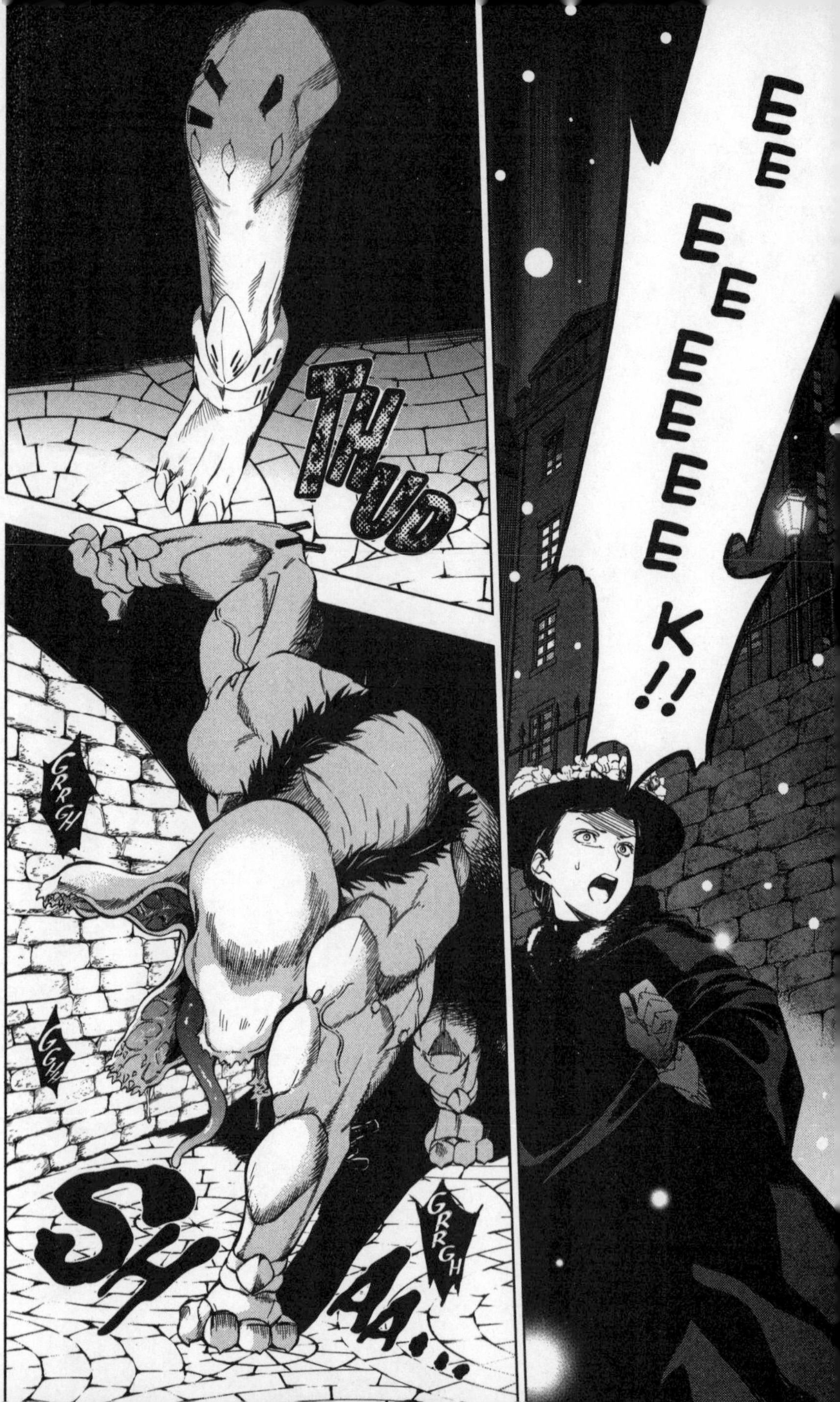
EEEEEEEK!!
THUD
GRRGH
GGGH
SHAA...
GRRGH

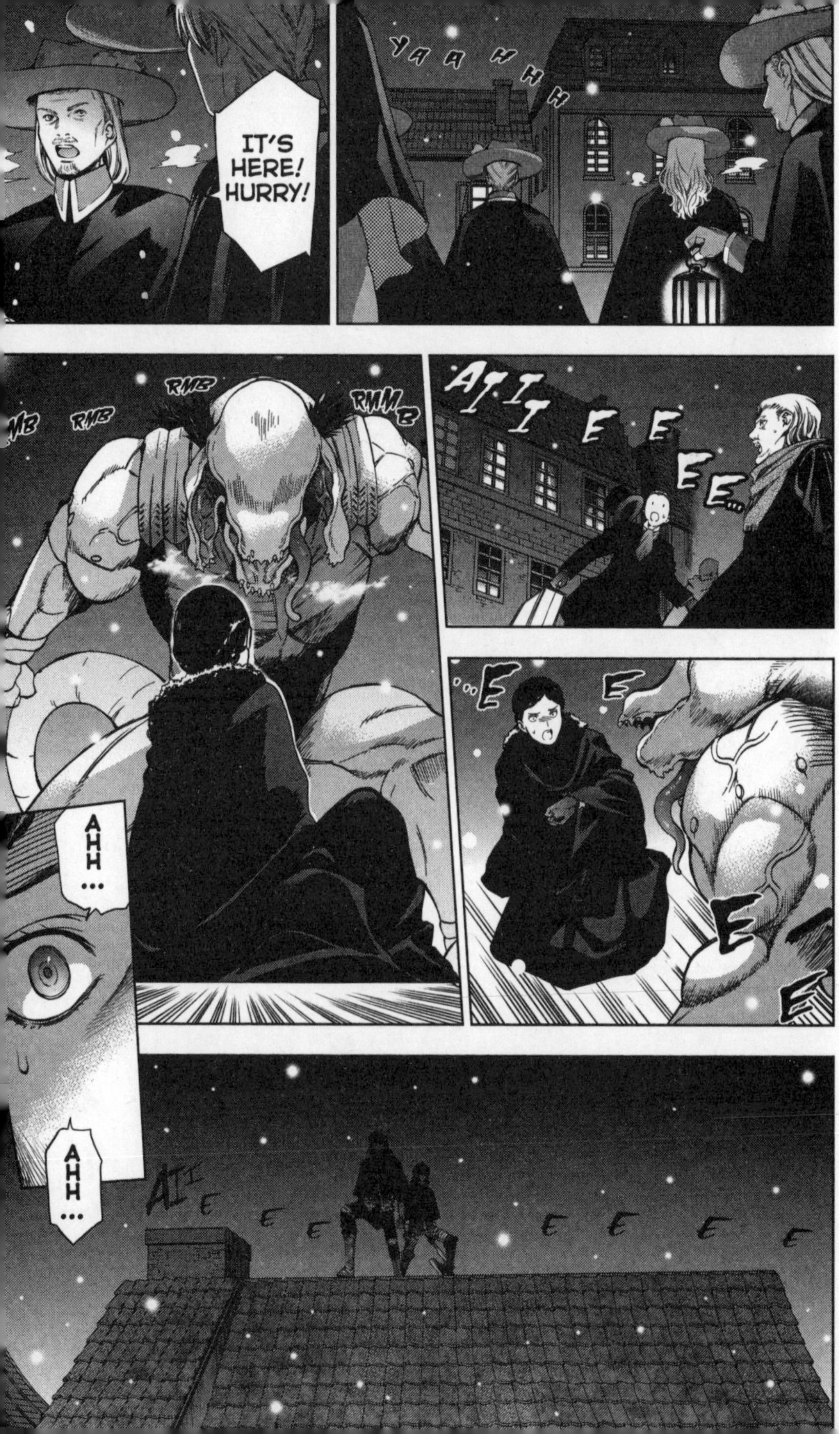

YAAHHHH
IT'S HERE! HURRY!
AIIIEEEEE...
...EEEEE
RMB
RMMB
RMB
MB
AHH...
AHH...
AIIEEEEEEE

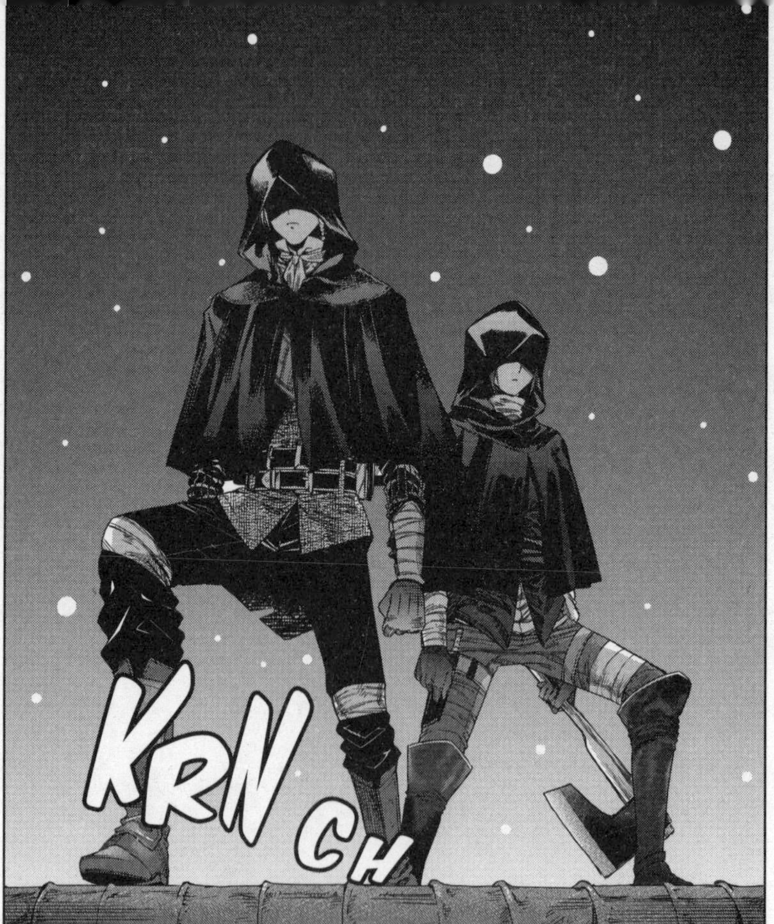
KRN CH
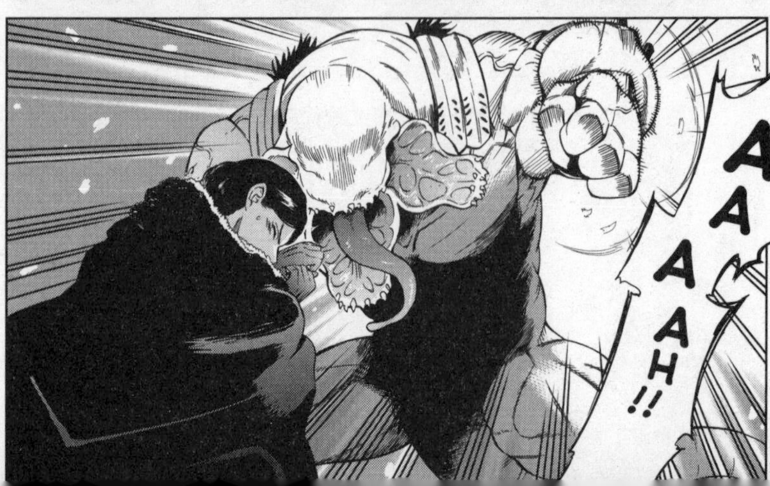
AAAAAH!!

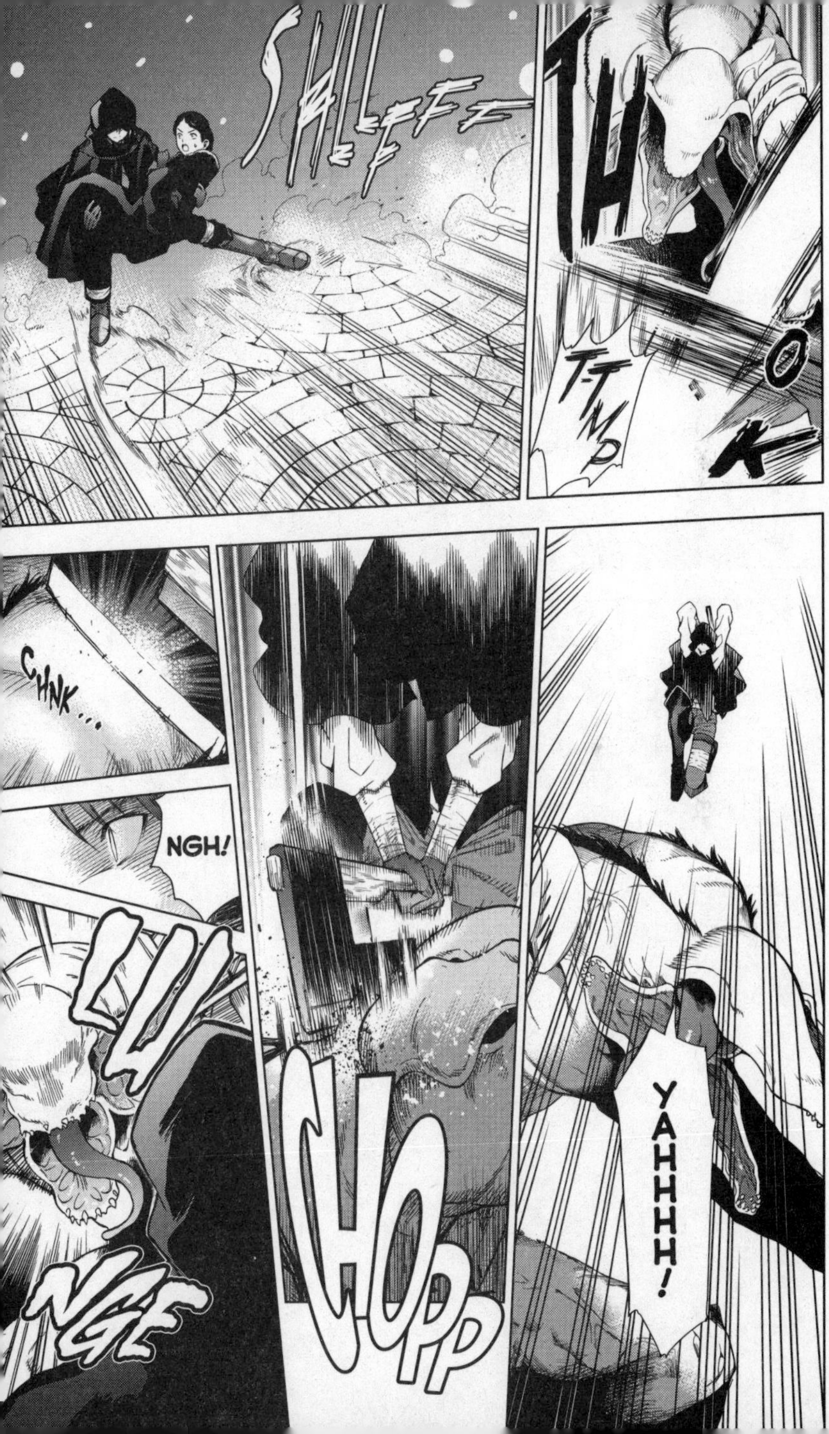

TH
T-TMP
OK
SHLEFFF
YAHHHH!
CHOPP
CHNK...
NGH!
LUNGE

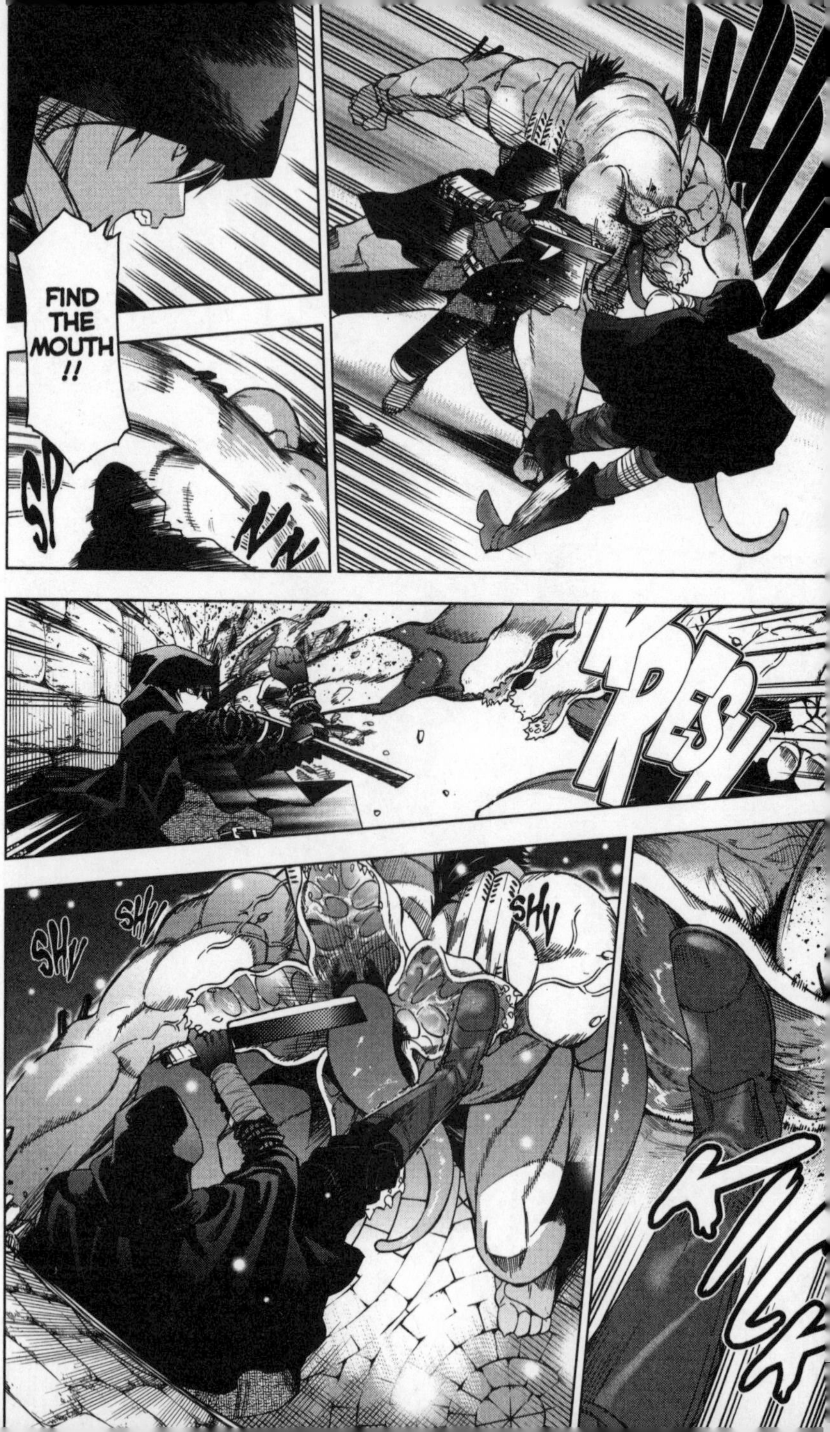
FIND THE MOUTH!!
SP
NN
KRESH
SHV
SHV
SHV

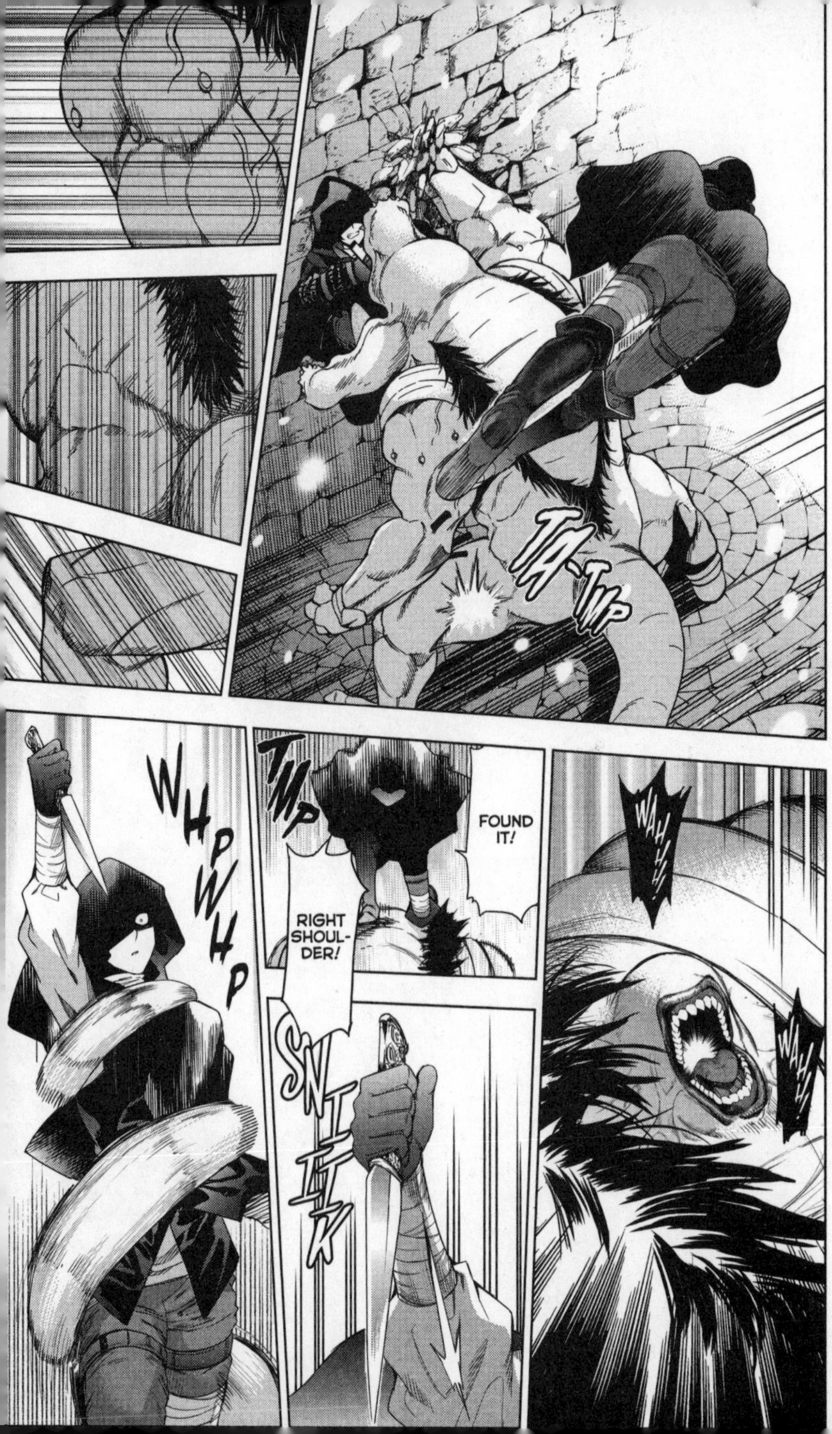
TM-TMP
WAH!!
WAH!!
TMP
FOUND IT!
RIGHT SHOULDER!
SNIIIK
WHPWHP

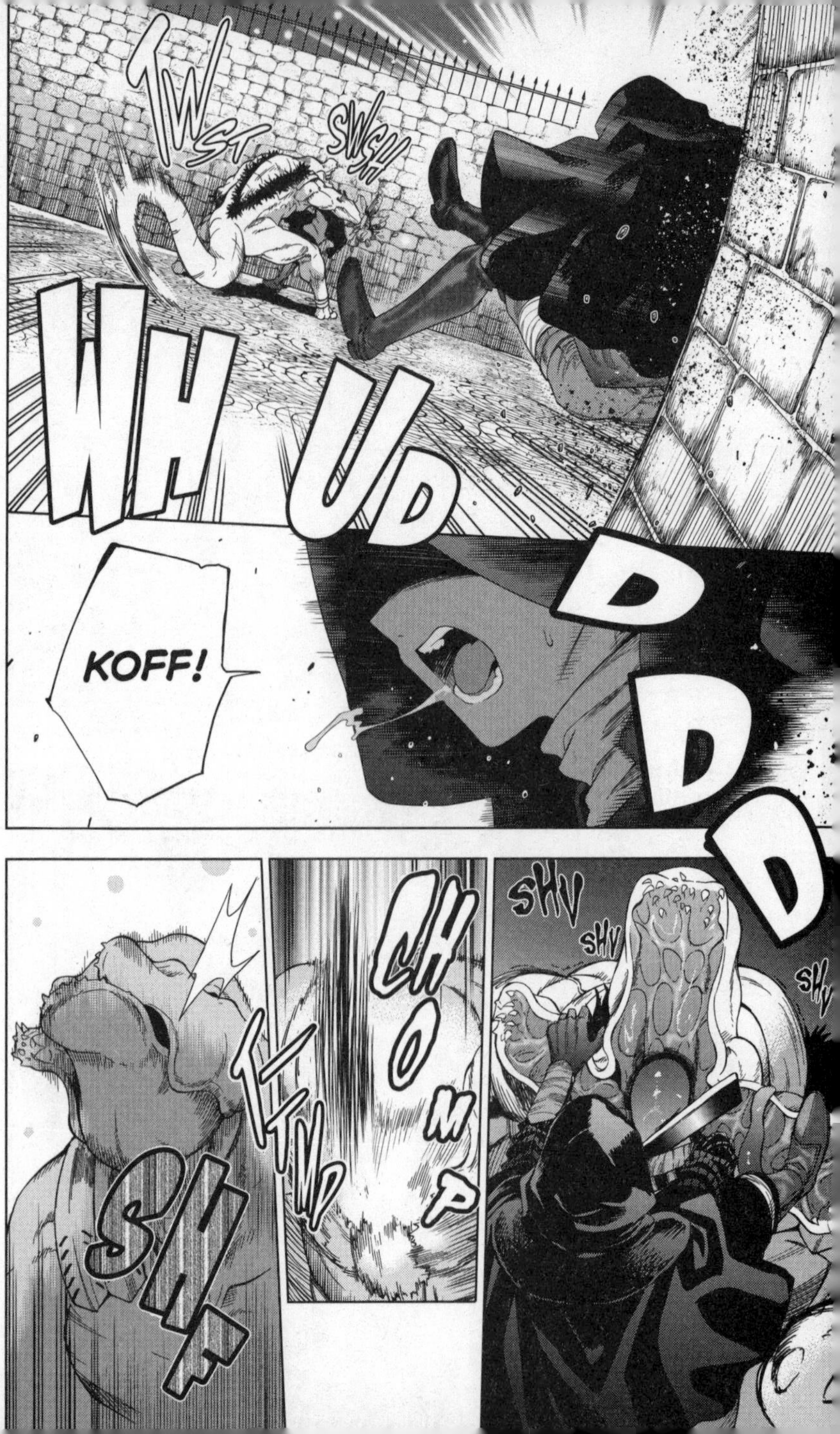
TWIST
SWISH
WHUDDDD
KOFF!
SHV
SHV
SHV
CHOMP

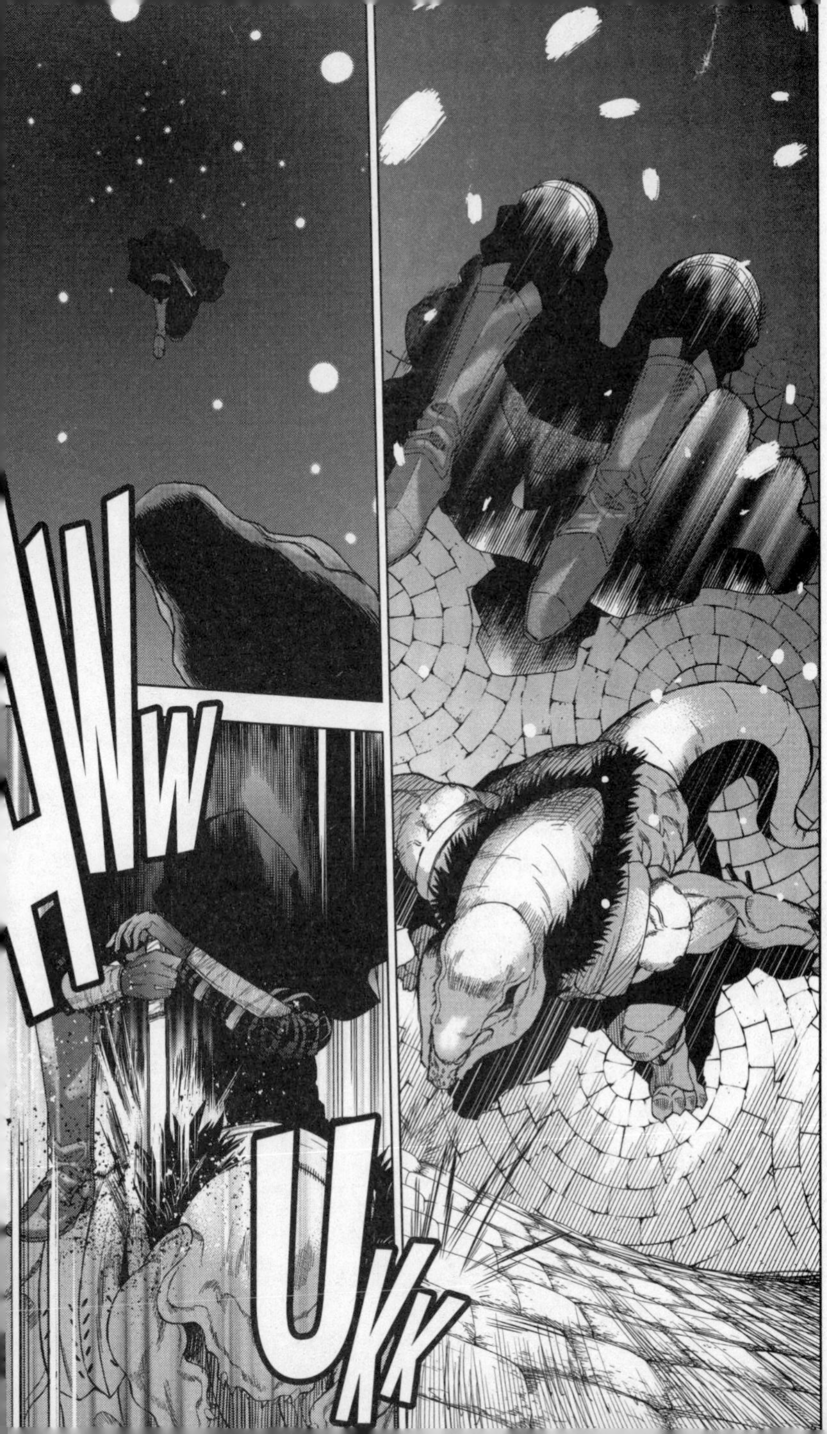
WWW
UKK

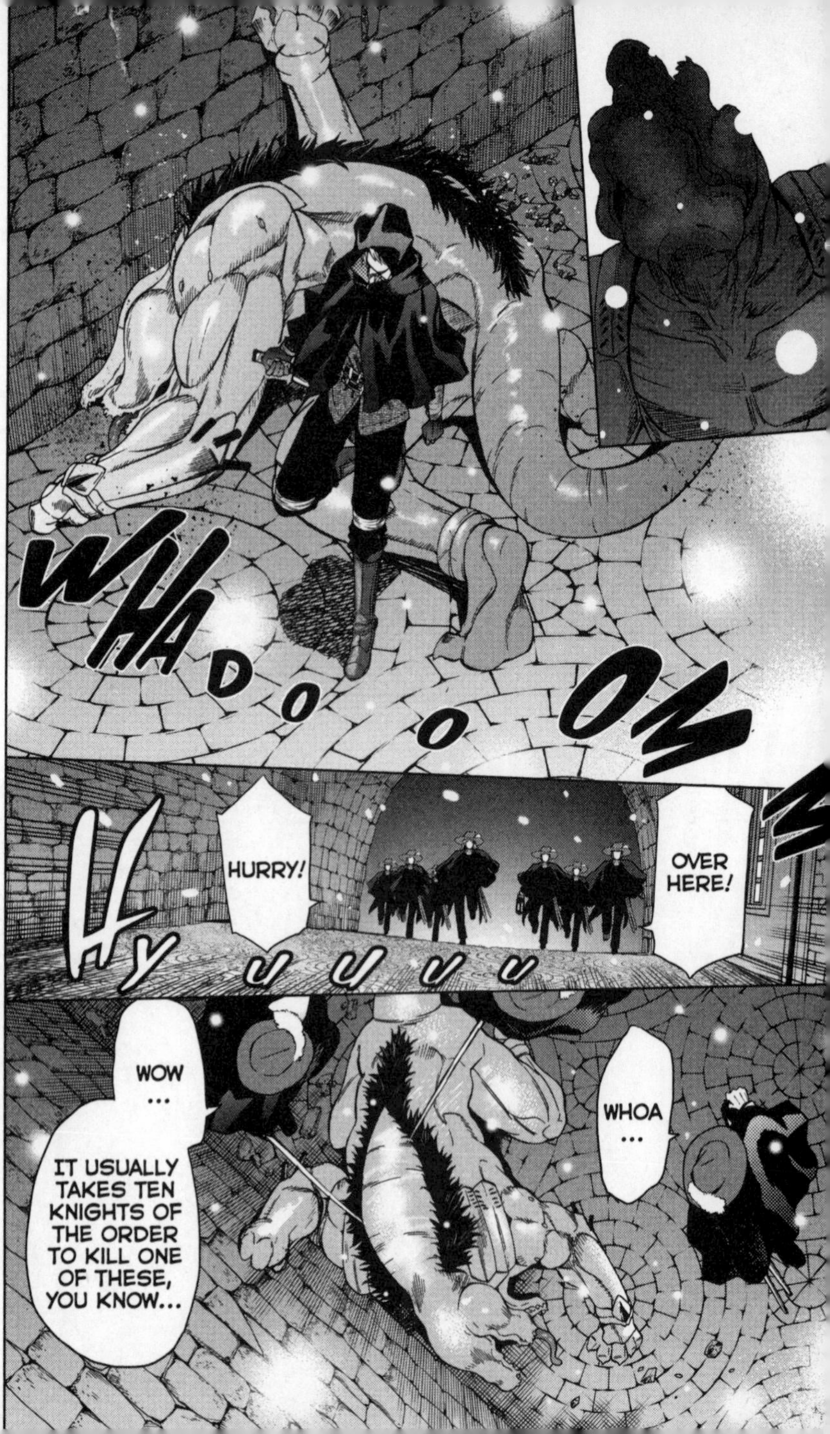
WHADOOOM
OVER HERE!
HURRY!
Hyuuuuu
WHOA ...
WOW ...
IT USUALLY TAKES TEN KNIGHTS OF THE ORDER TO KILL ONE OF THESE, YOU KNOW...

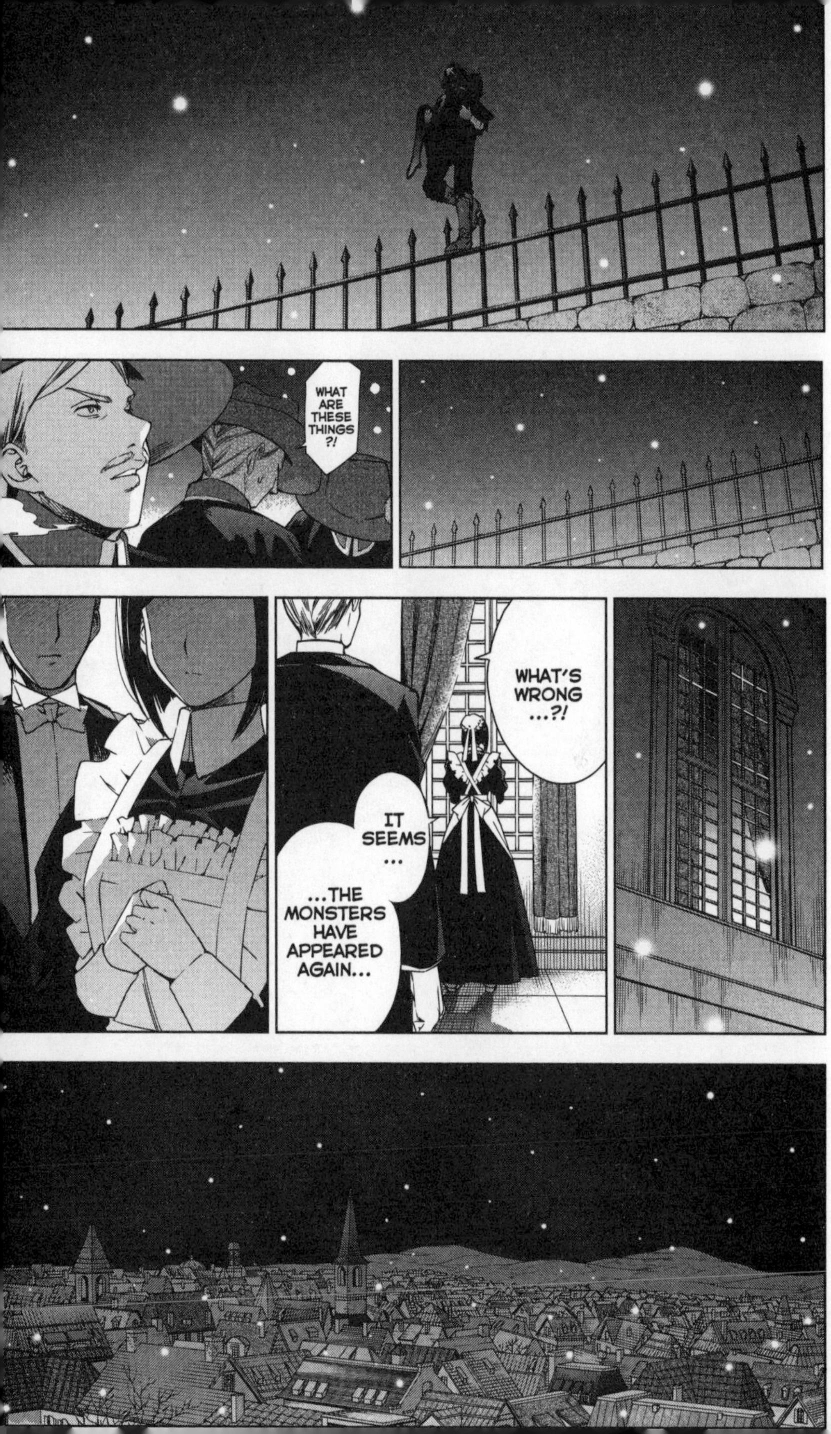
WHAT ARE THESE THINGS ?!
WHAT'S WRONG ...?!
IT SEEMS ...
...THE MONSTERS HAVE APPEARED AGAIN...

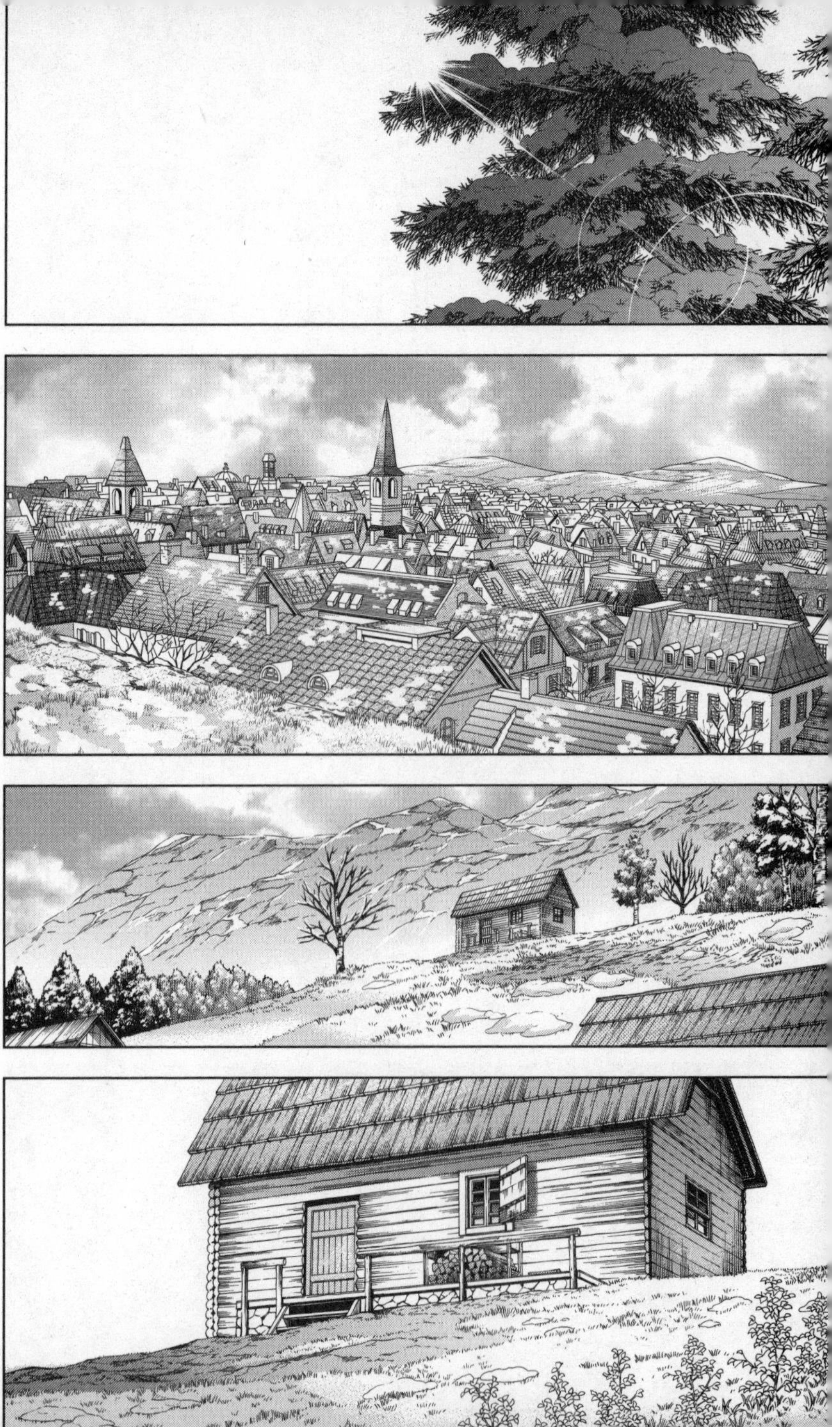

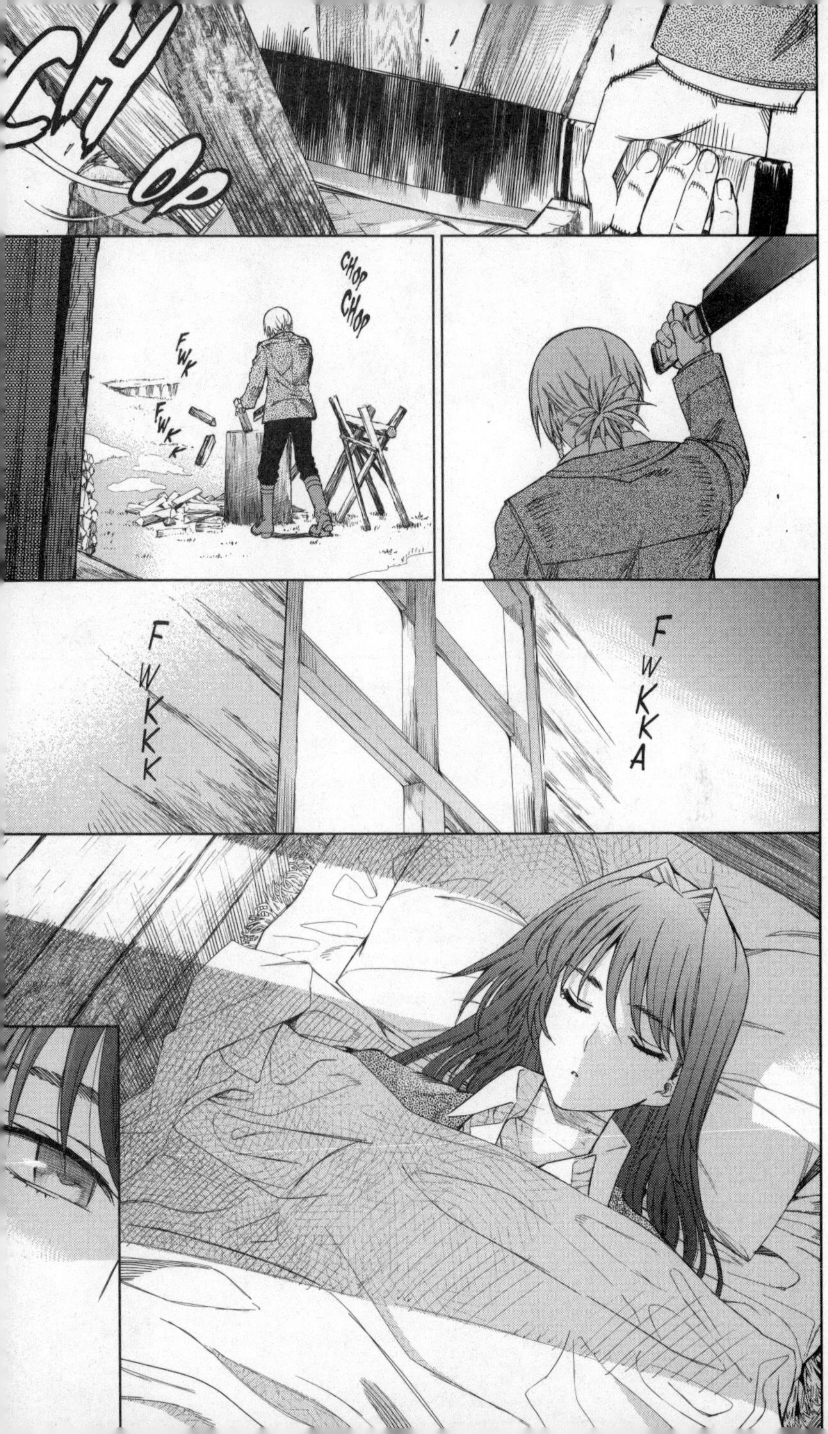
CHOP
CHOP
CHOP
FWK
FWKKK
FWKKA
FWKKK

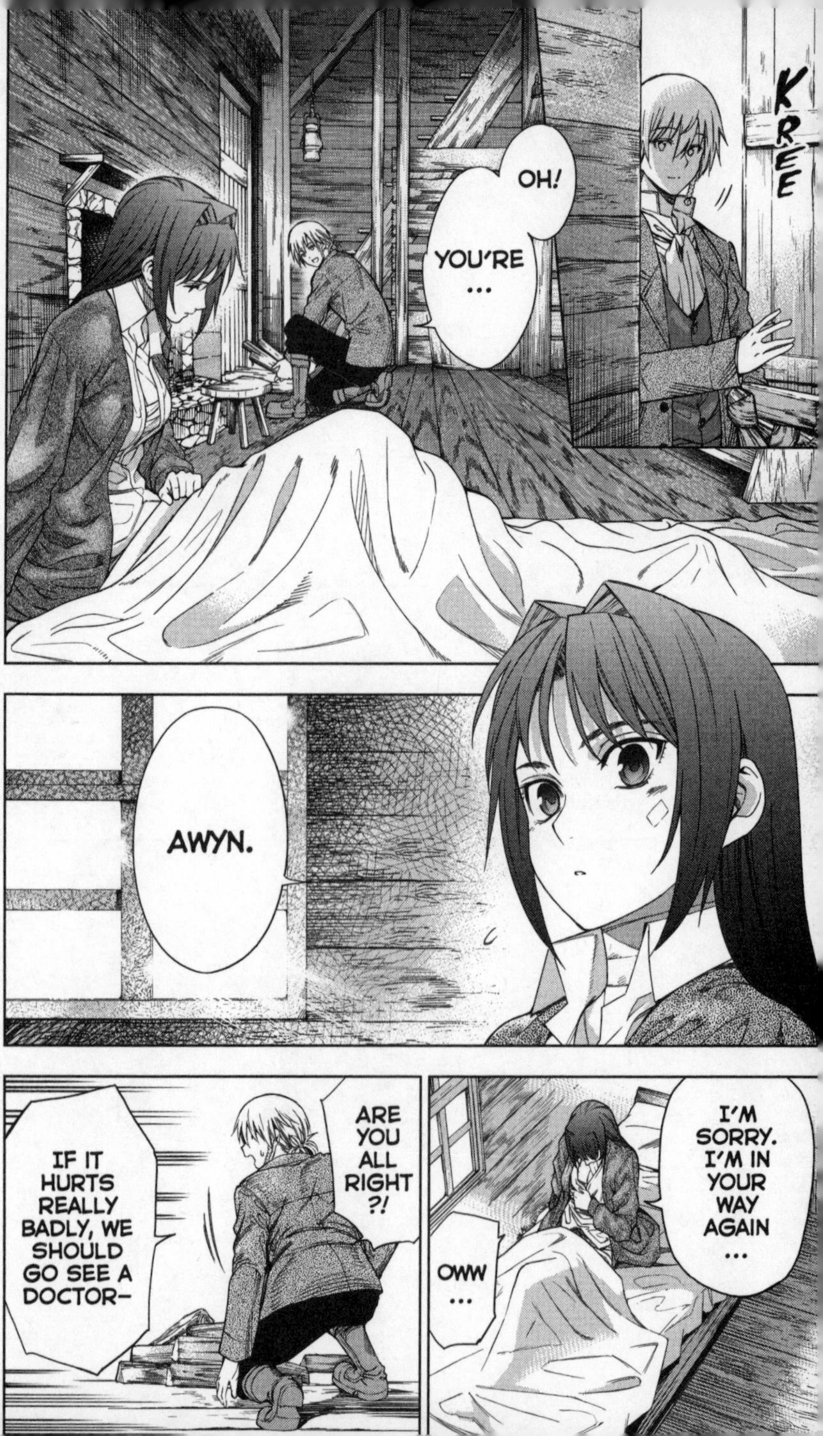
KREE
OH!
YOU'RE ...
AWYN.
I'M SORRY. I'M IN YOUR WAY AGAIN ...
OWW ...
ARE YOU ALL RIGHT?!
IF IT HURTS REALLY BADLY, WE SHOULD GO SEE A DOCTOR–

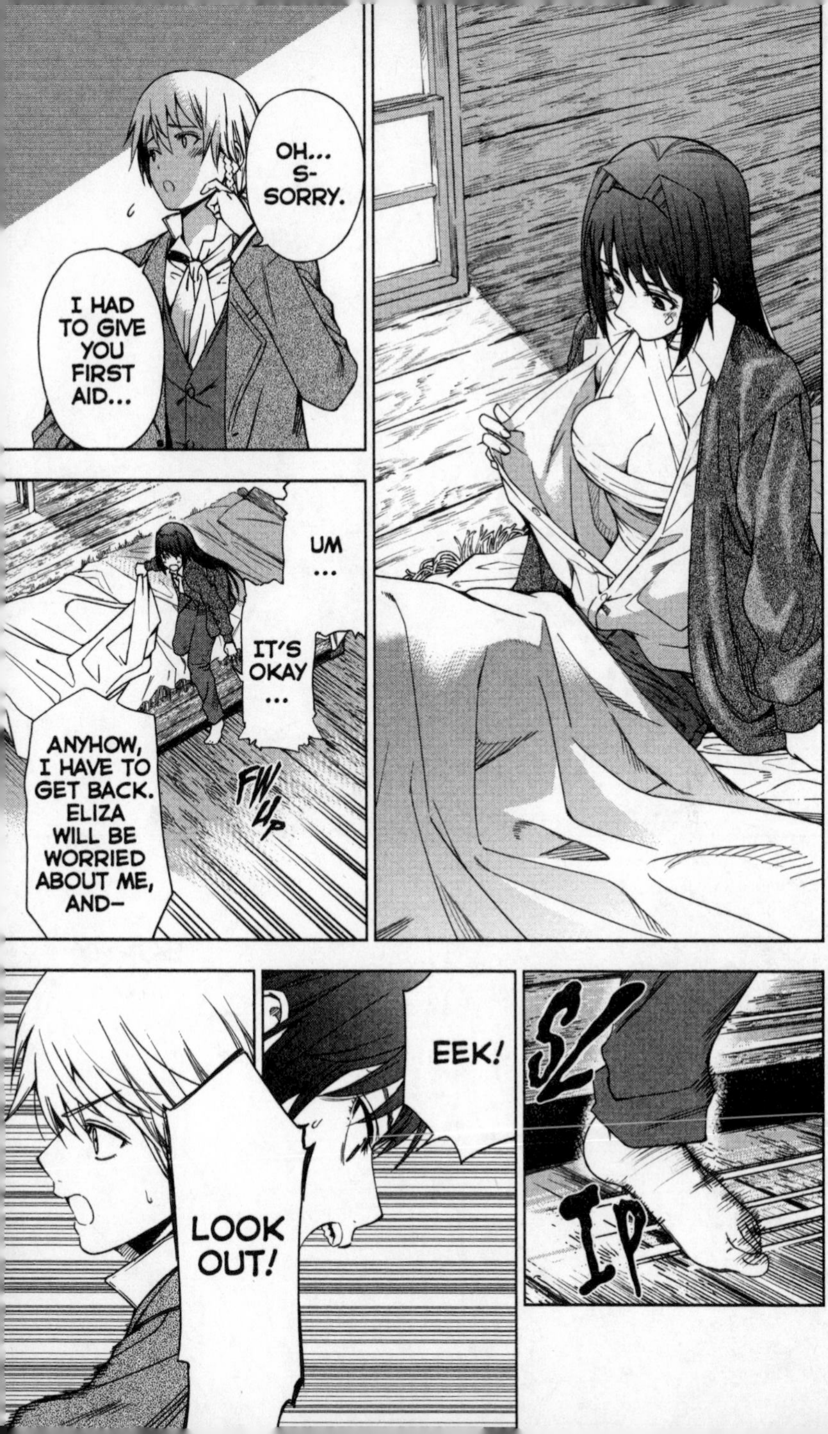
OH... S-SORRY.
I HAD TO GIVE YOU FIRST AID...
UM ...
IT'S OKAY ...
FWUP
ANYHOW, I HAVE TO GET BACK. ELIZA WILL BE WORRIED ABOUT ME, AND–
SLIP
EEK!
LOOK OUT!

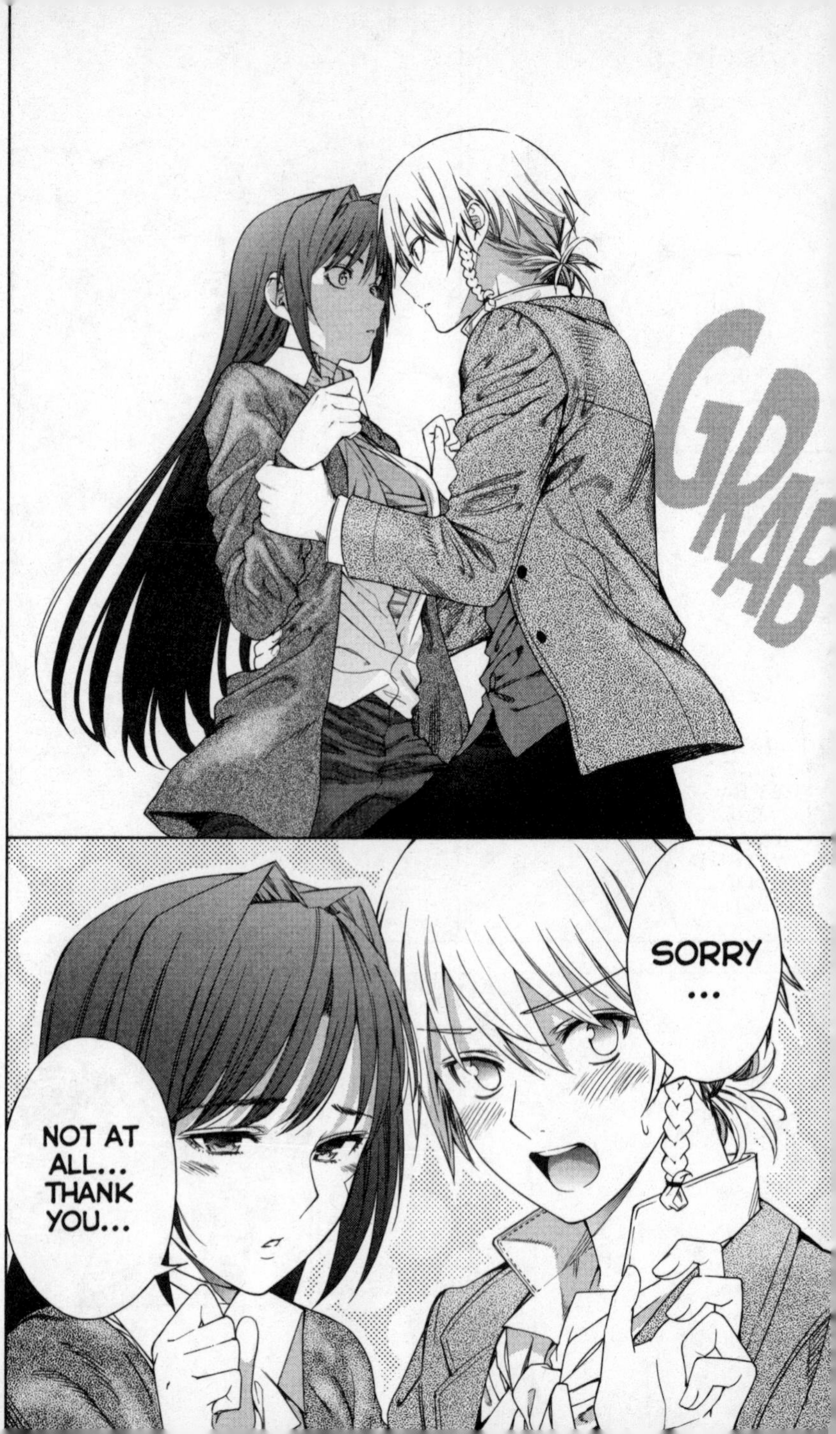
GRAB
SORRY ...
NOT AT ALL... THANK YOU...

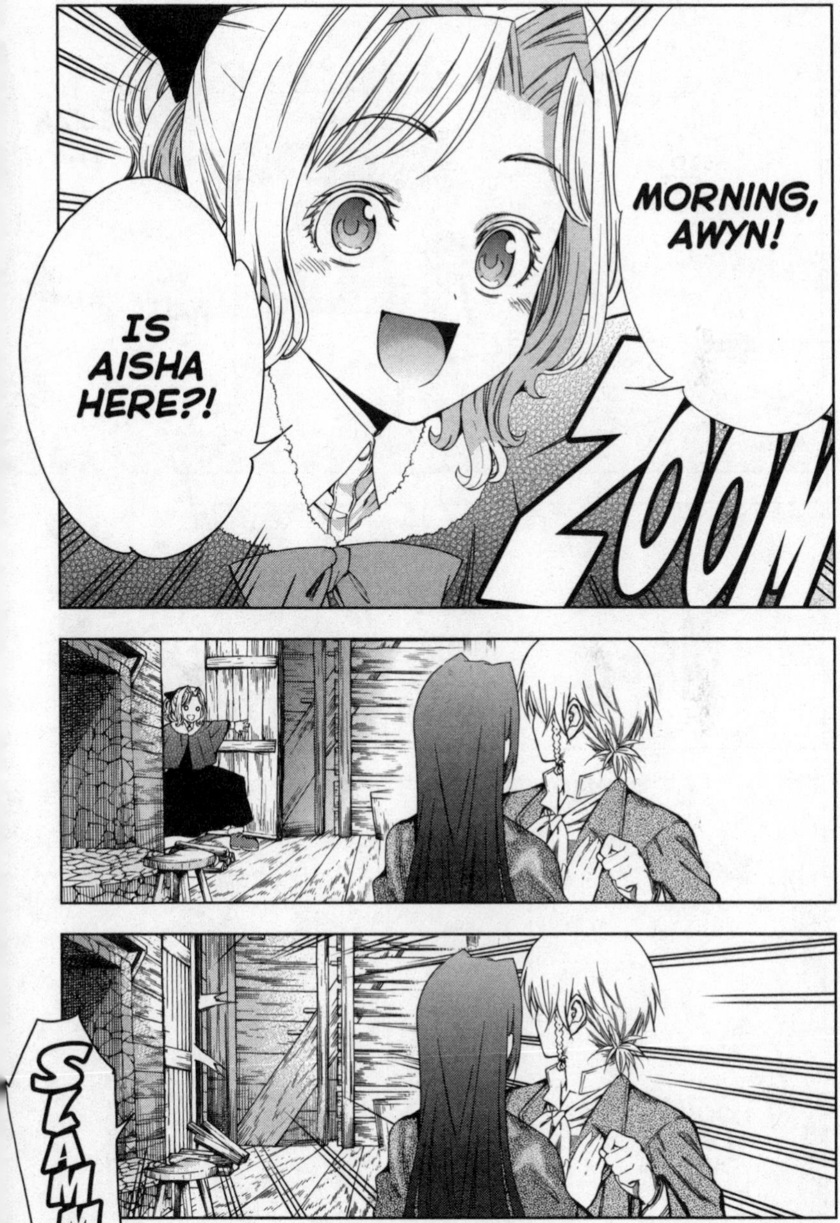
MORNING, AWYN!
IS AISHA HERE?!
ZOOM
SLAMM

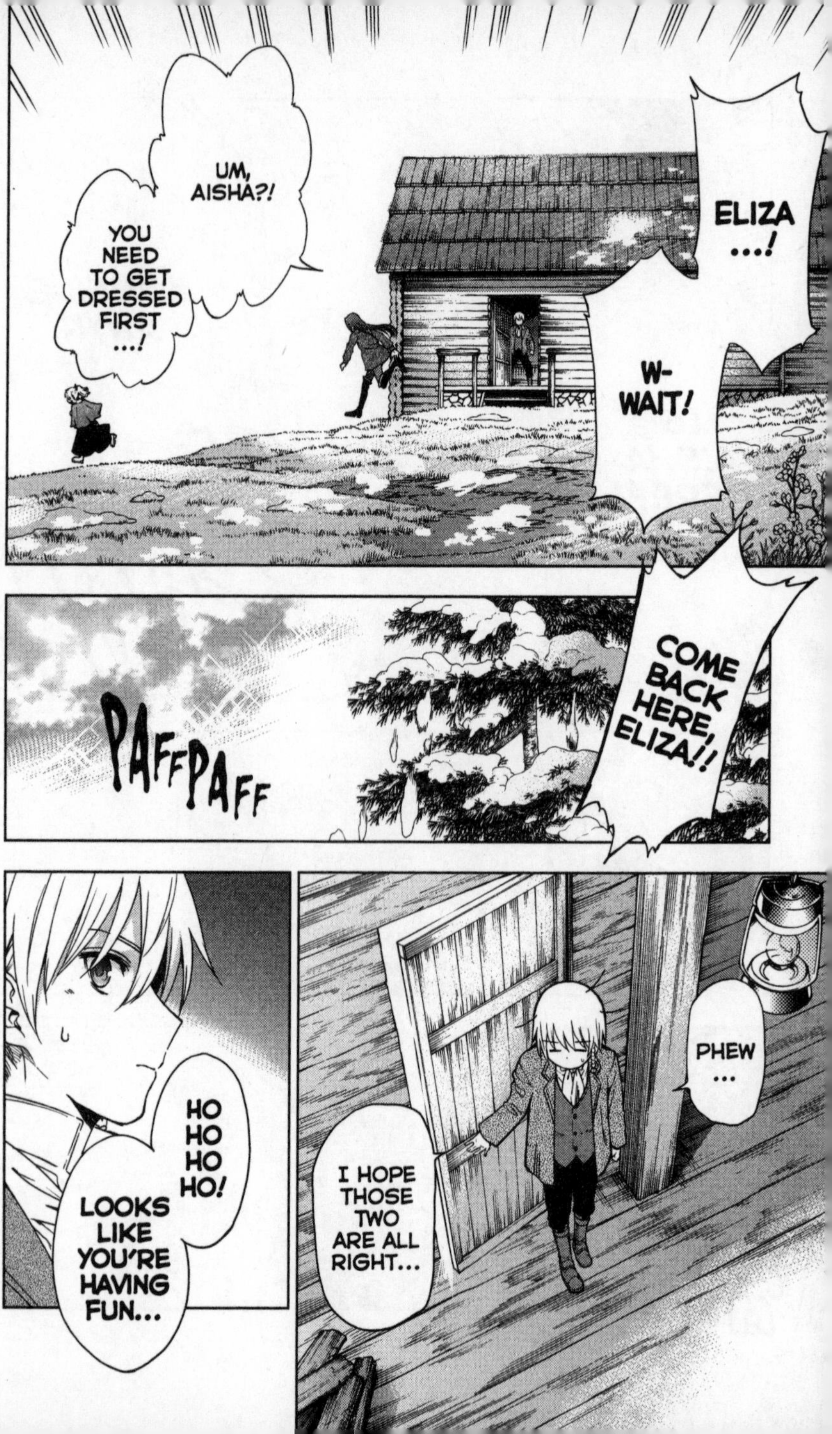
ELIZA...!
W-WAIT!
UM, AISHA?!
YOU NEED TO GET DRESSED FIRST...!
COME BACK HERE, ELIZA!!
PAFFPAFF
PHEW...
I HOPE THOSE TWO ARE ALL RIGHT...
HO HO HO HO!
LOOKS LIKE YOU'RE HAVING FUN...

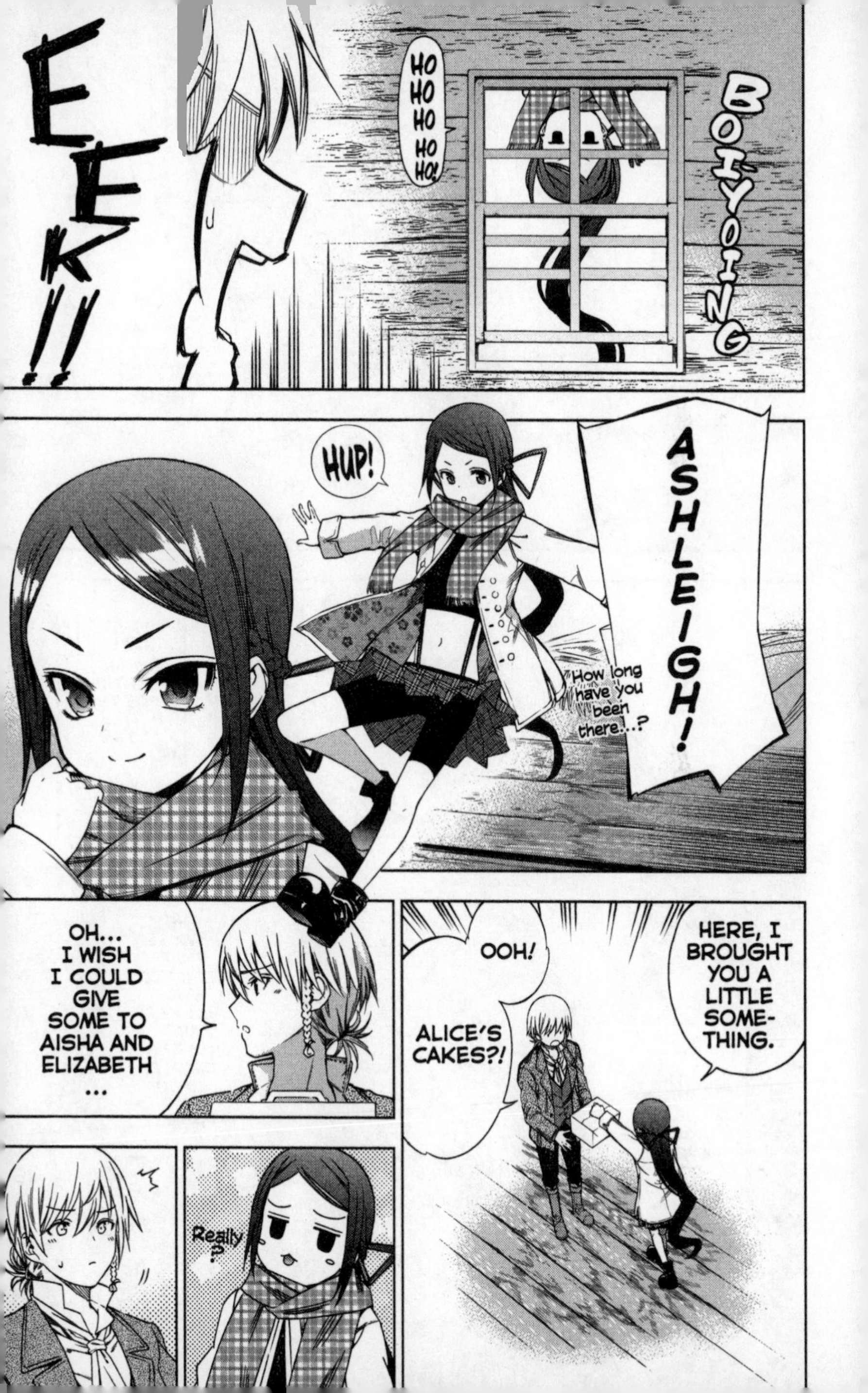
BOIYOING
HO HO HO HO HO!
EEEK!!
ASHLEIGH!
HUP!
How long have you been there...?
HERE, I BROUGHT YOU A LITTLE SOME-THING.
OOH!
ALICE'S CAKES?!
OH... I WISH I COULD GIVE SOME TO AISHA AND ELIZABETH...
Really?

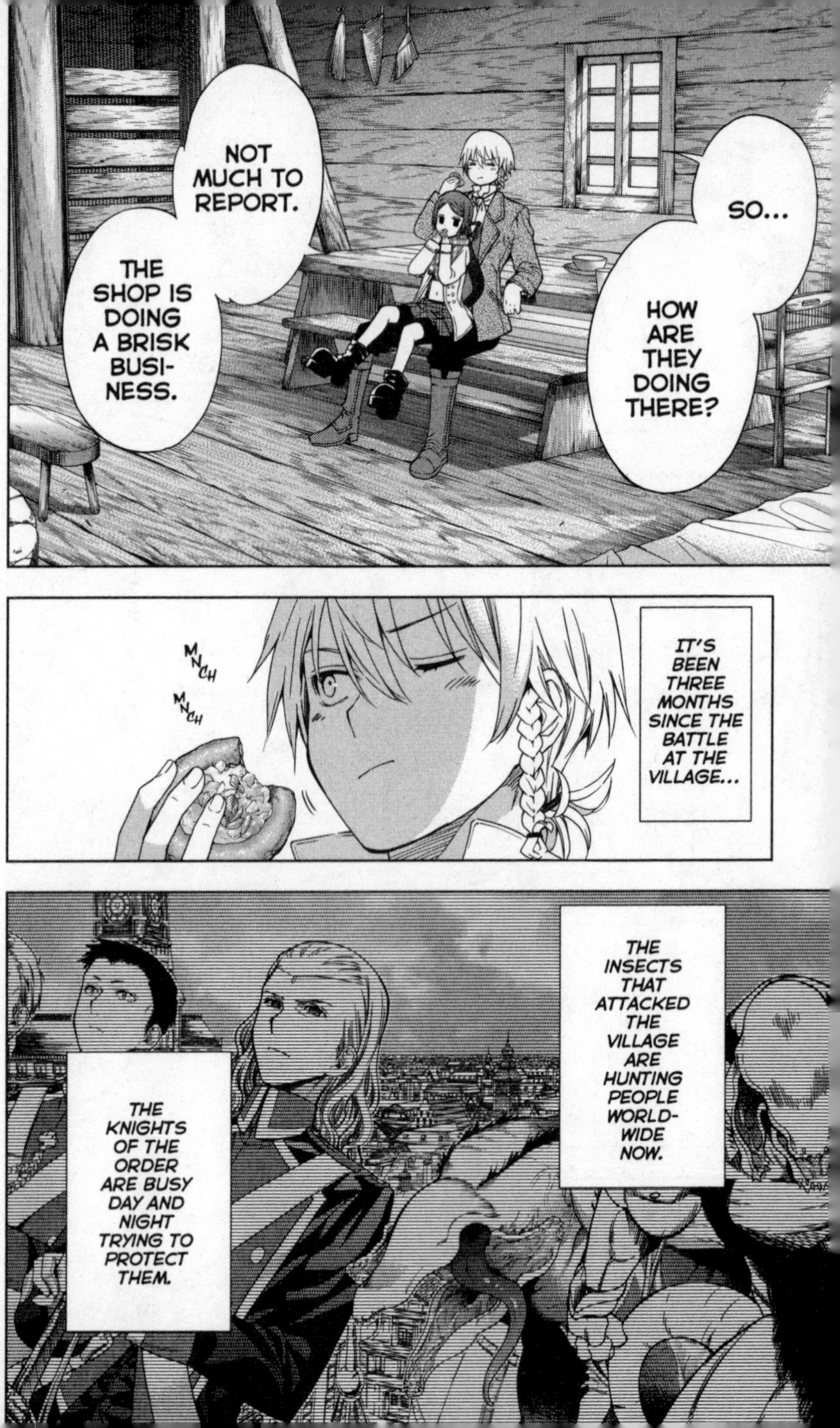
SO...
HOW ARE THEY DOING THERE?
NOT MUCH TO REPORT.
THE SHOP IS DOING A BRISK BUSI-NESS.
IT'S BEEN THREE MONTHS SINCE THE BATTLE AT THE VILLAGE...
MNCH
MNCH
THE INSECTS THAT ATTACKED THE VILLAGE ARE HUNTING PEOPLE WORLD-WIDE NOW.
THE KNIGHTS OF THE ORDER ARE BUSY DAY AND NIGHT TRYING TO PROTECT THEM.

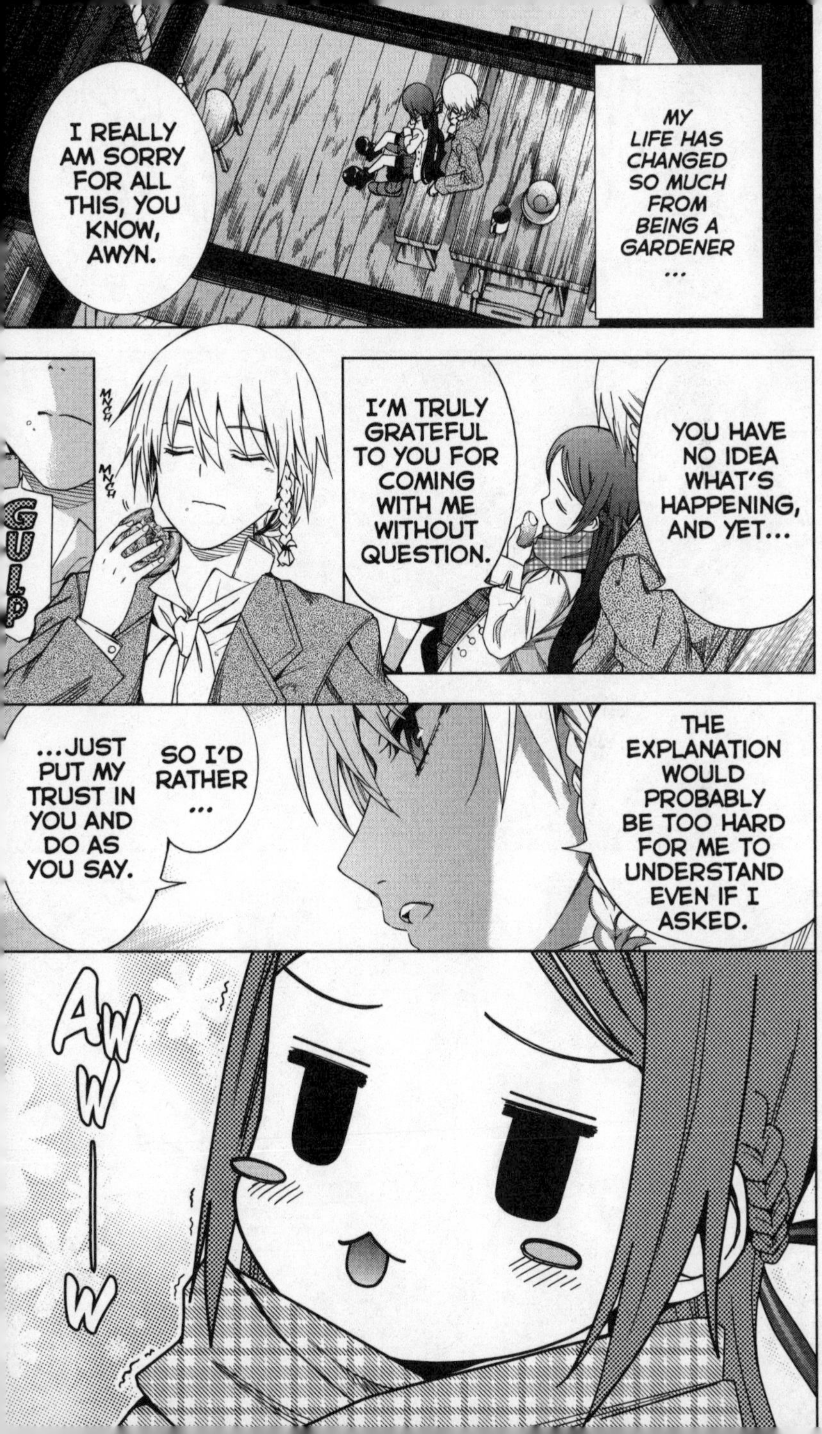
MY LIFE HAS CHANGED SO MUCH FROM BEING A GARDENER ...
I REALLY AM SORRY FOR ALL THIS, YOU KNOW, AWYN.
YOU HAVE NO IDEA WHAT'S HAPPENING, AND YET...
I'M TRULY GRATEFUL TO YOU FOR COMING WITH ME WITHOUT QUESTION.
MNCH
MNCH
GULP
THE EXPLANATION WOULD PROBABLY BE TOO HARD FOR ME TO UNDERSTAND EVEN IF I ASKED.
SO I'D RATHER ...
...JUST PUT MY TRUST IN YOU AND DO AS YOU SAY.
AWWW—W

I'M SORRY I GOT IN YOUR WAY.

Suburbs of the capital

St. Grewar's Convent

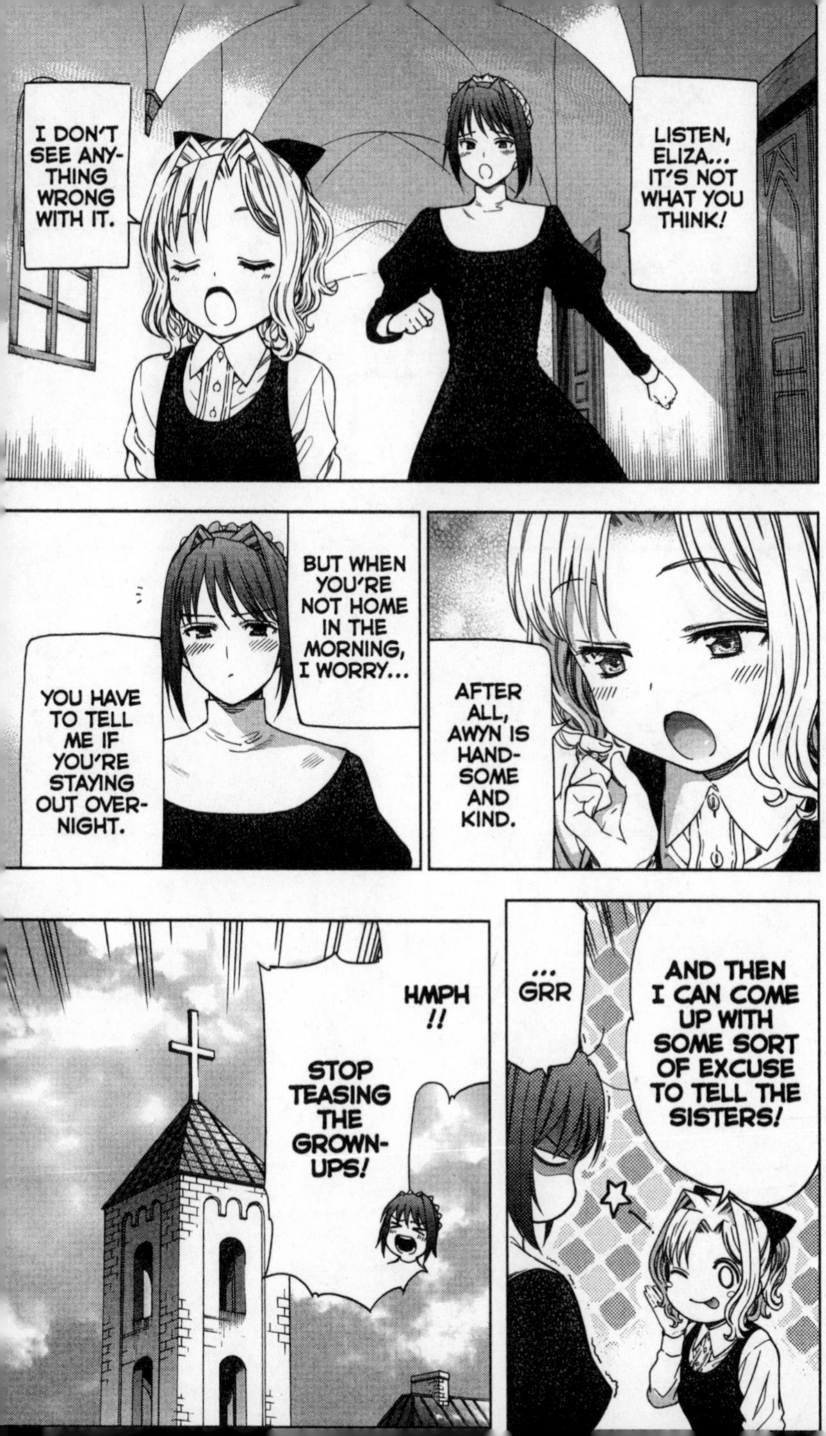
LISTEN, ELIZA... IT'S NOT WHAT YOU THINK!
I DON'T SEE ANYTHING WRONG WITH IT.
AFTER ALL, AWYN IS HANDSOME AND KIND.
BUT WHEN YOU'RE NOT HOME IN THE MORNING, I WORRY...
YOU HAVE TO TELL ME IF YOU'RE STAYING OUT OVERNIGHT.
AND THEN I CAN COME UP WITH SOME SORT OF EXCUSE TO TELL THE SISTERS!
...GRR
HMPH!!
STOP TEASING THE GROWN-UPS!

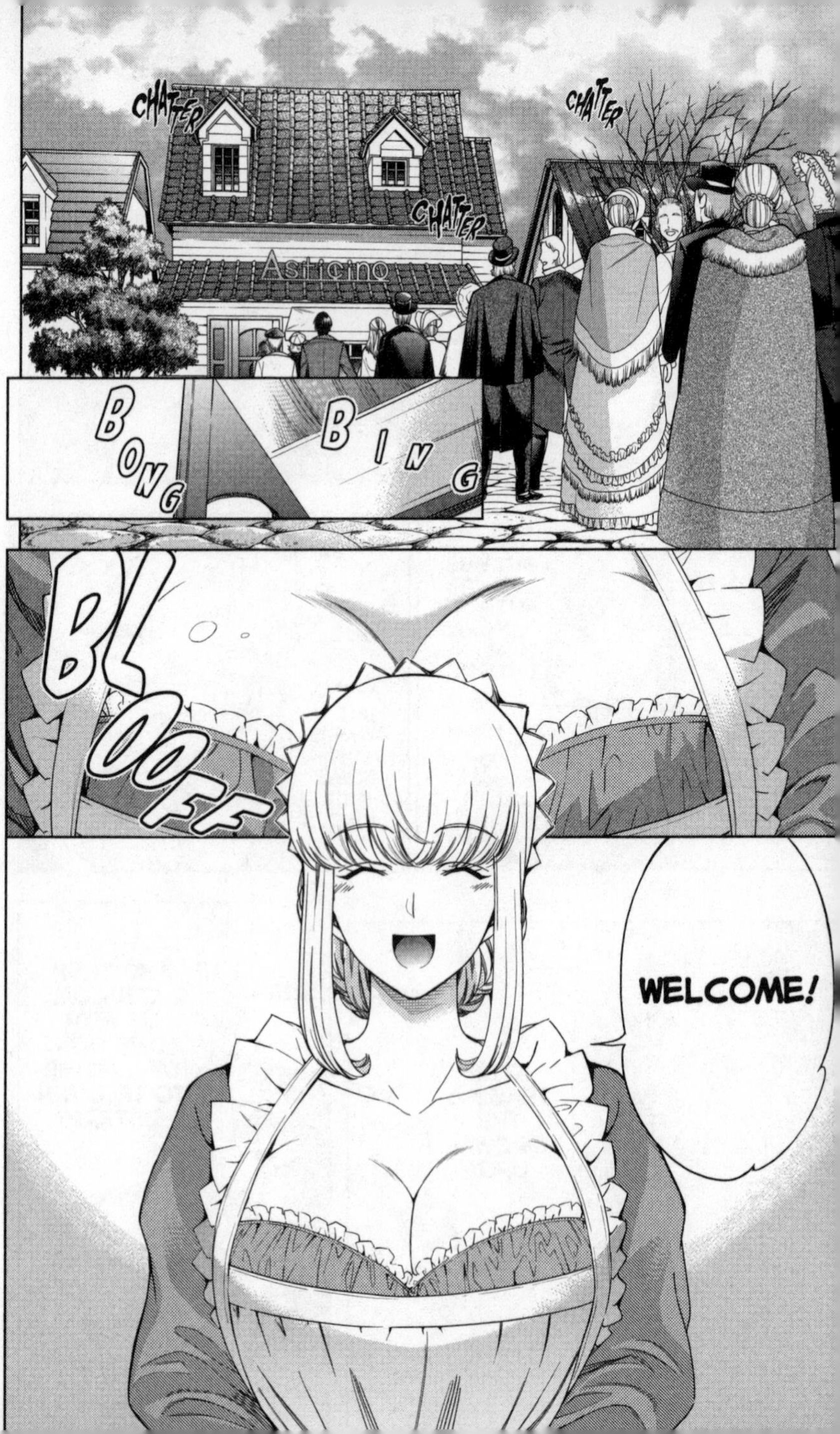
CHATTER
CHATTER
CHATTER
Asticino
BING
BONG
BLOOFF
WELCOME!

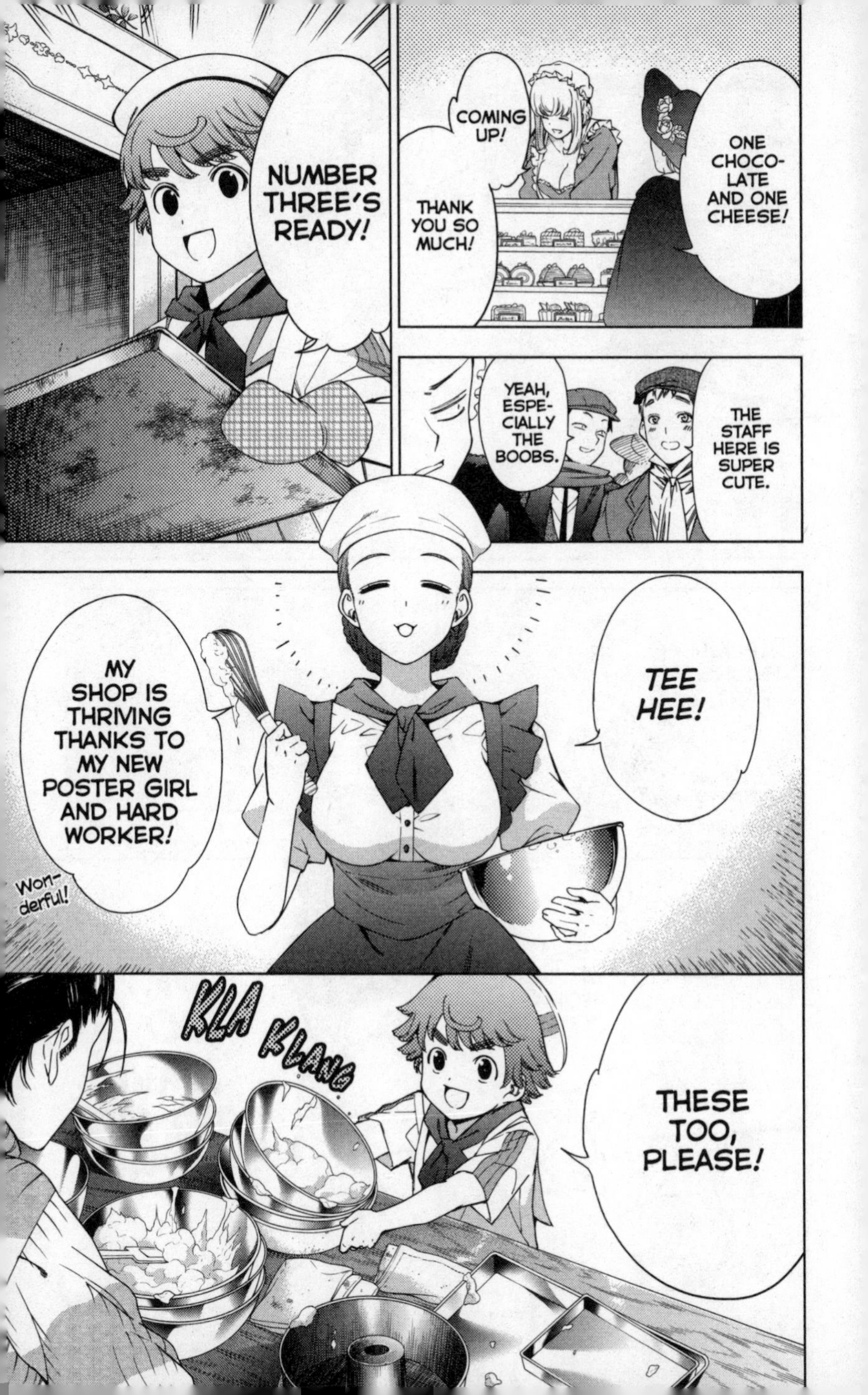
ONE CHOCOLATE AND ONE CHEESE!
COMING UP!
THANK YOU SO MUCH!
THE STAFF HERE IS SUPER CUTE.
YEAH, ESPECIALLY THE BOOBS.
NUMBER THREE'S READY!
TEE HEE!
MY SHOP IS THRIVING THANKS TO MY NEW POSTER GIRL AND HARD WORKER!
Wonderful!
THESE TOO, PLEASE!
KLA KLANG

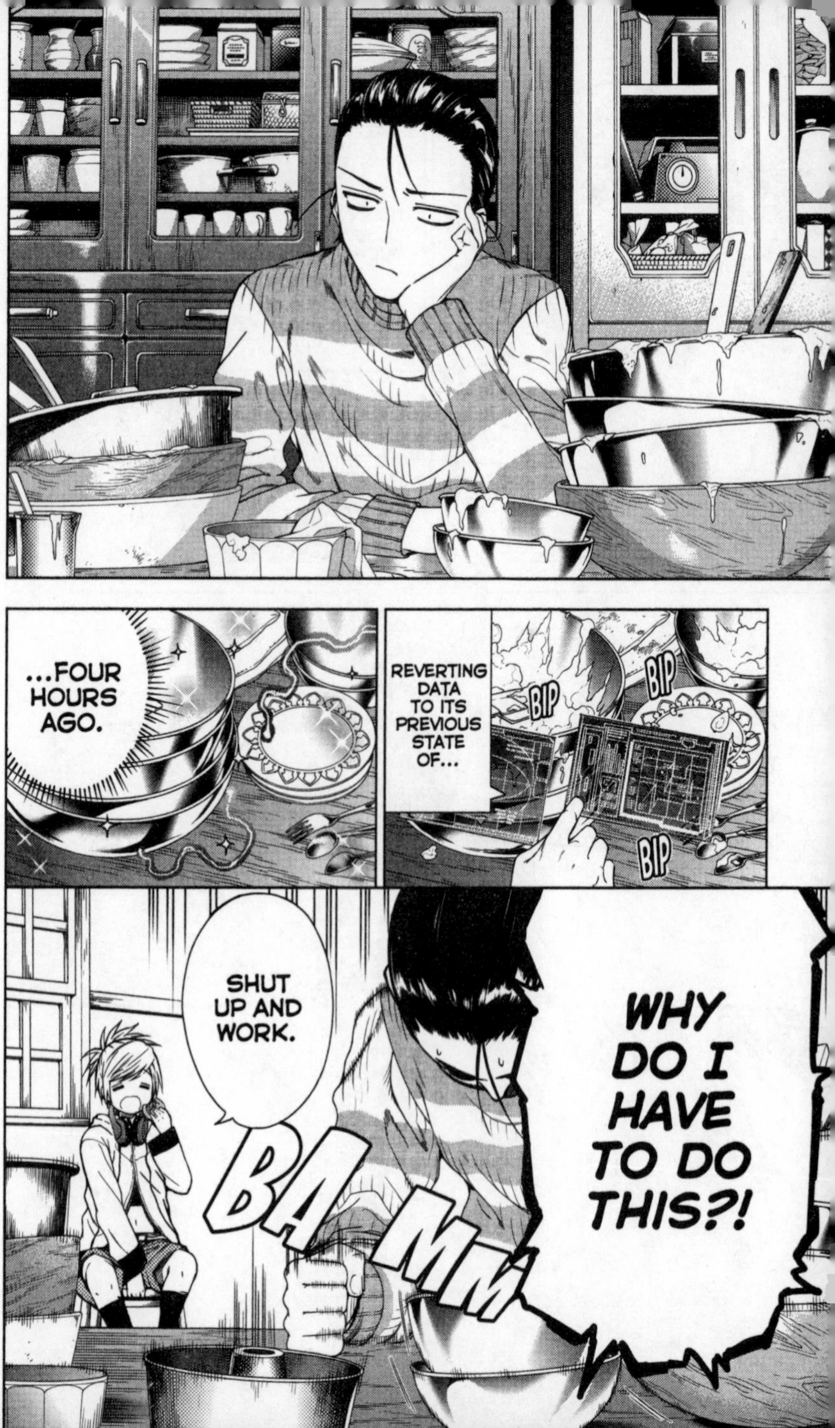
REVERTING DATA TO ITS PREVIOUS STATE OF...
BIP
BIP
BIP
...FOUR HOURS AGO.
WHY DO I HAVE TO DO THIS?!
SHUT UP AND WORK.
BAMM

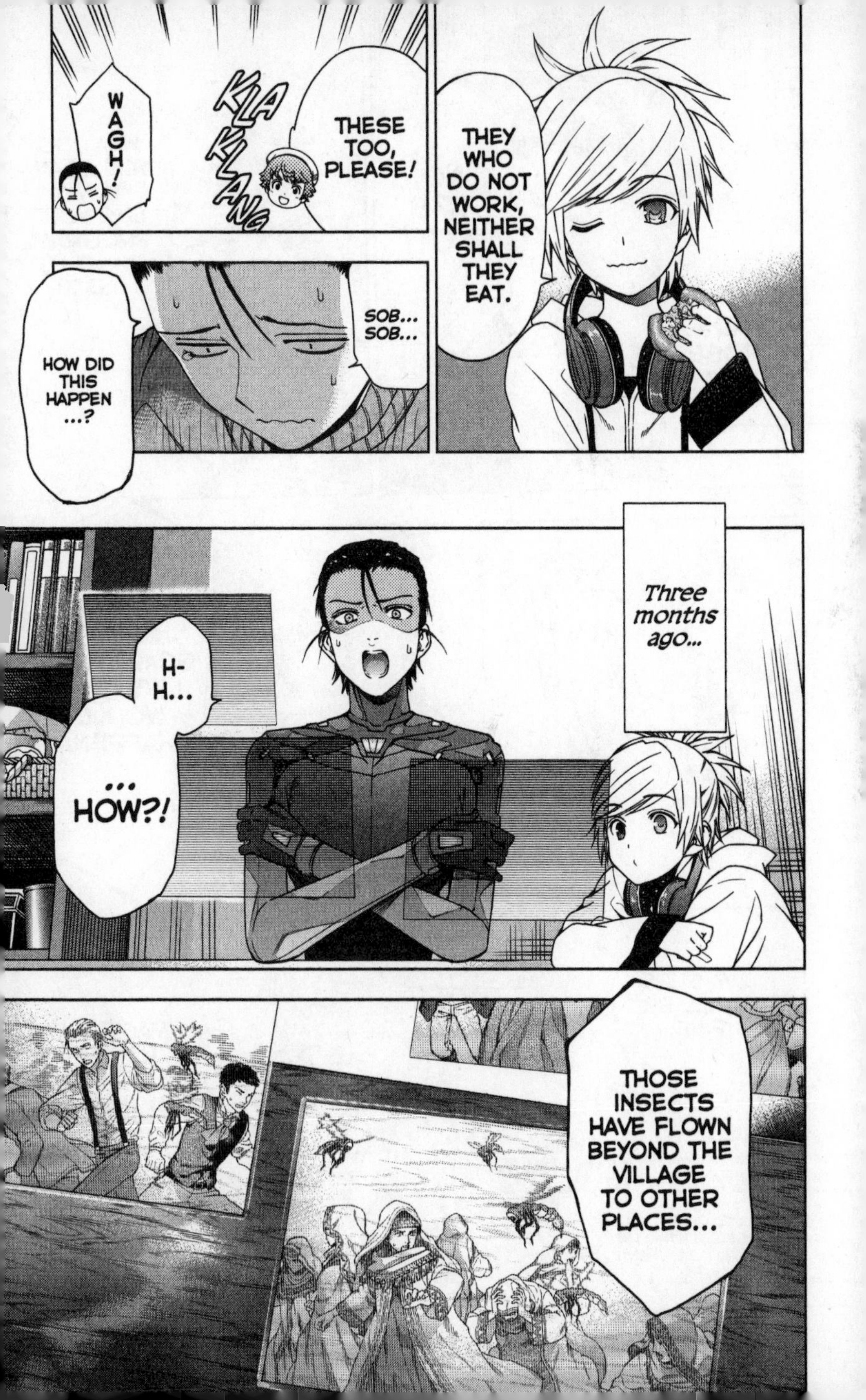
THEY WHO DO NOT WORK, NEITHER SHALL THEY EAT.
THESE TOO, PLEASE!
KLA KLANG
WAGH!
SOB... SOB...
HOW DID THIS HAPPEN ...?
Three months ago...
H- H...
... HOW?!
THOSE INSECTS HAVE FLOWN BEYOND THE VILLAGE TO OTHER PLACES...

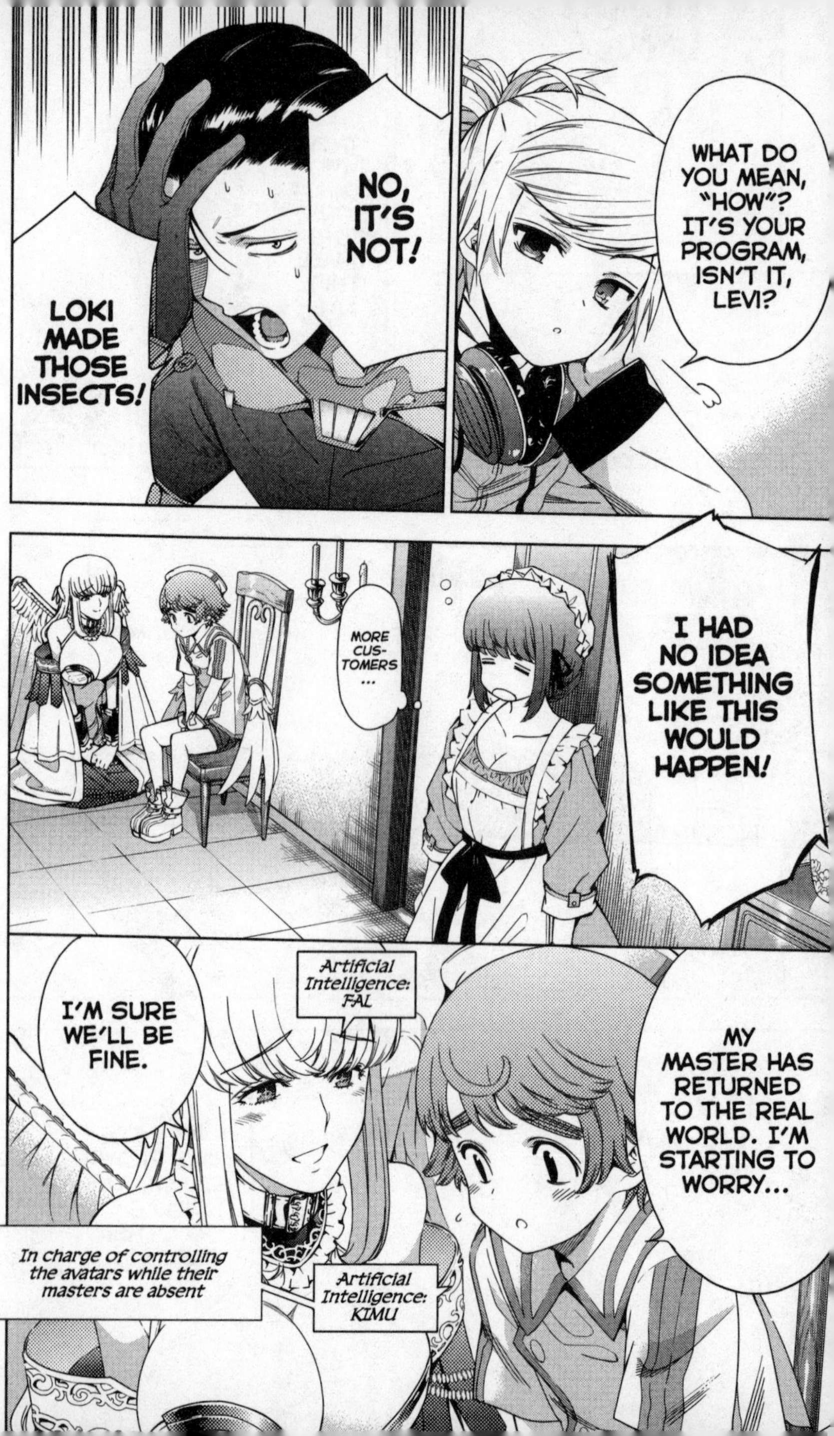
WHAT DO YOU MEAN, "HOW"? IT'S YOUR PROGRAM, ISN'T IT, LEVI?
NO, IT'S NOT!
LOKI MADE THOSE INSECTS!
I HAD NO IDEA SOMETHING LIKE THIS WOULD HAPPEN!
MORE CUS-TOMERS ...
MY MASTER HAS RETURNED TO THE REAL WORLD. I'M STARTING TO WORRY...
Artificial Intelligence: KIMU
I'M SURE WE'LL BE FINE.
Artificial Intelligence: FAL
In charge of controlling the avatars while their masters are absent

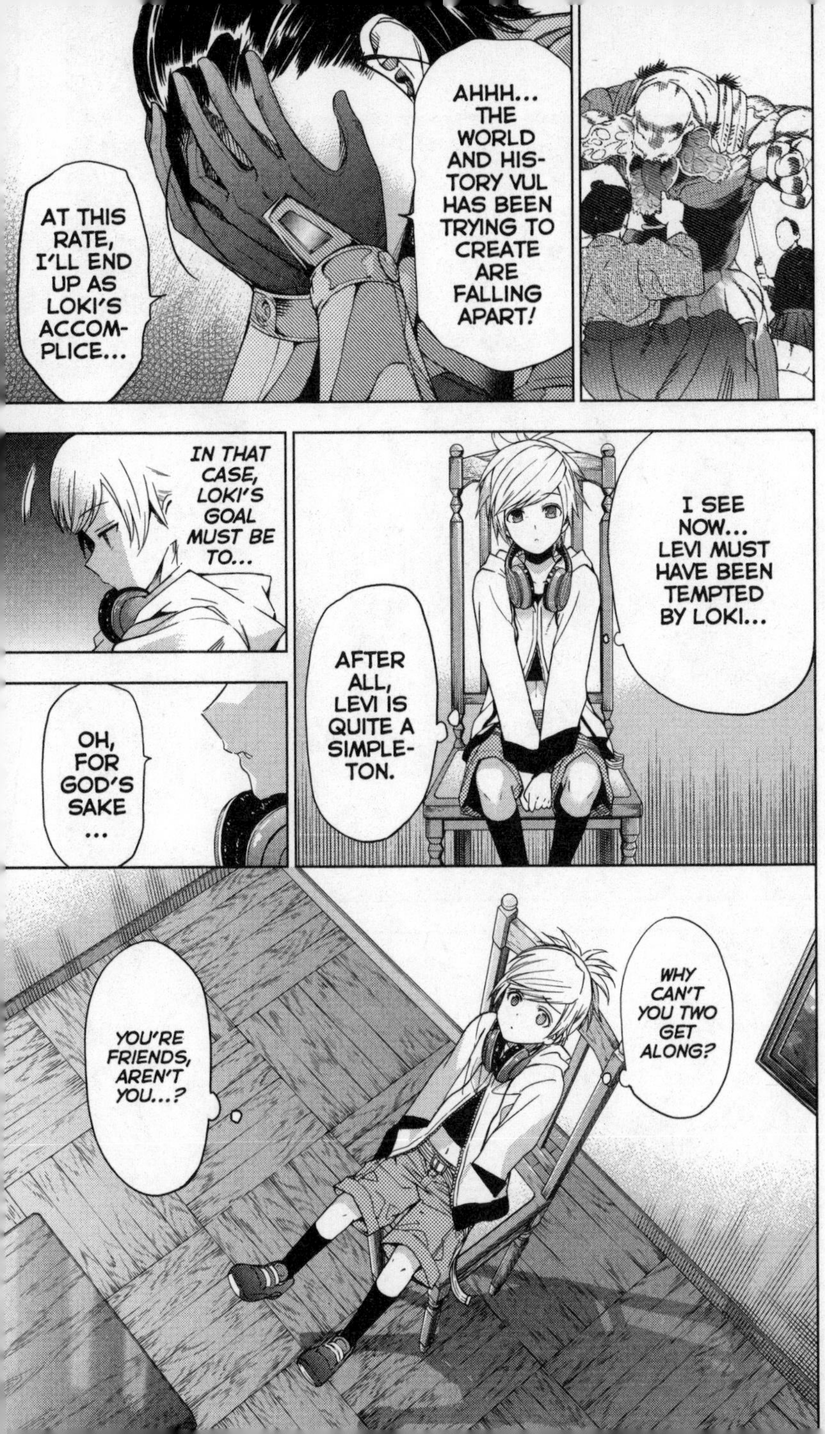
AHHH... THE WORLD AND HISTORY VUL HAS BEEN TRYING TO CREATE ARE FALLING APART!
AT THIS RATE, I'LL END UP AS LOKI'S ACCOMPLICE...
I SEE NOW... LEVI MUST HAVE BEEN TEMPTED BY LOKI...
AFTER ALL, LEVI IS QUITE A SIMPLETON.
IN THAT CASE, LOKI'S GOAL MUST BE TO...
OH, FOR GOD'S SAKE...
WHY CAN'T YOU TWO GET ALONG?
YOU'RE FRIENDS, AREN'T YOU...?

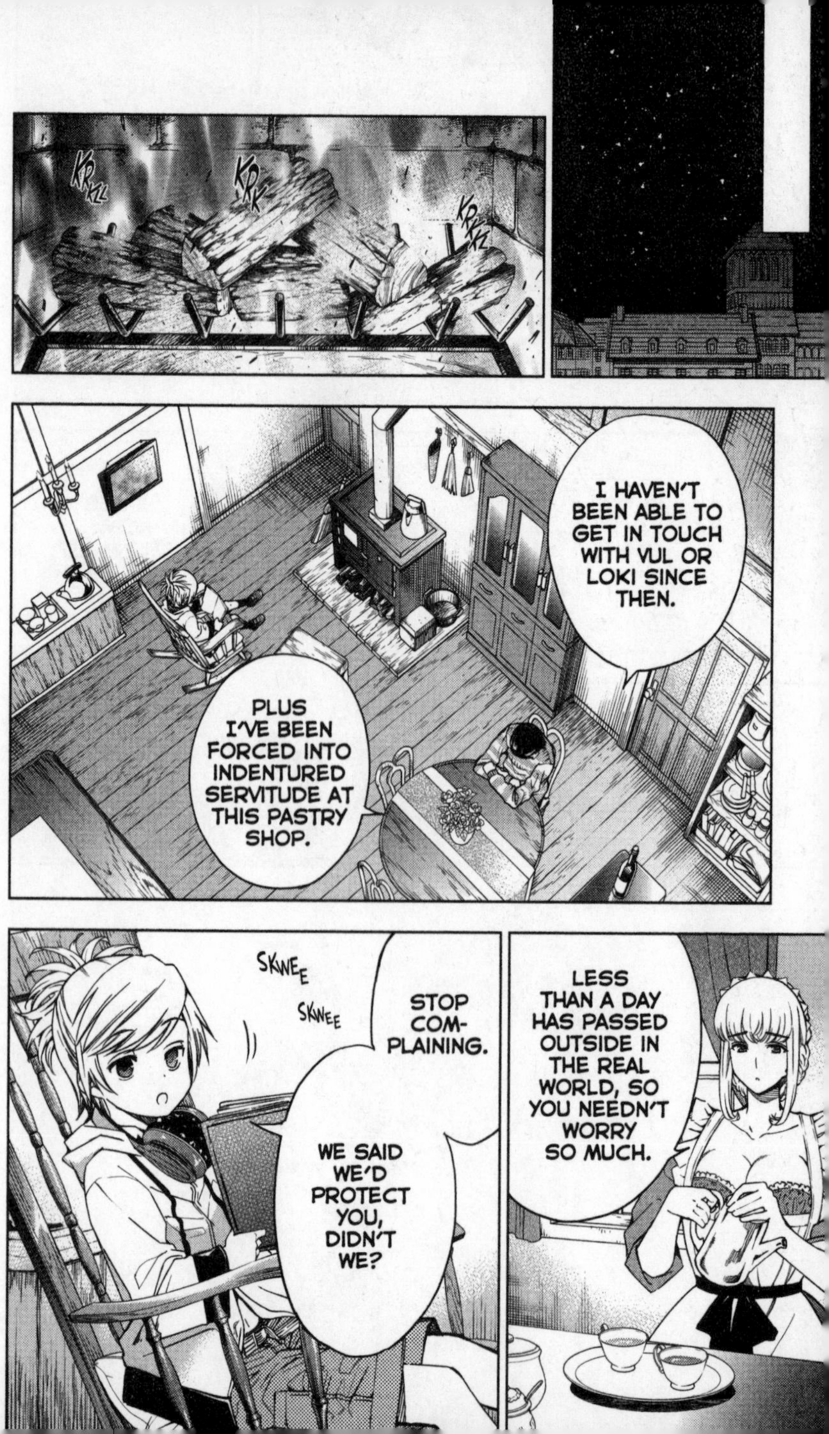
KRKKL
KRK
KRKLL
I HAVEN'T BEEN ABLE TO GET IN TOUCH WITH VUL OR LOKI SINCE THEN.
PLUS I'VE BEEN FORCED INTO INDENTURED SERVITUDE AT THIS PASTRY SHOP.
LESS THAN A DAY HAS PASSED OUTSIDE IN THE REAL WORLD, SO YOU NEEDN'T WORRY SO MUCH.
STOP COM-PLAINING.
SKWEE
SKWEE
WE SAID WE'D PROTECT YOU, DIDN'T WE?

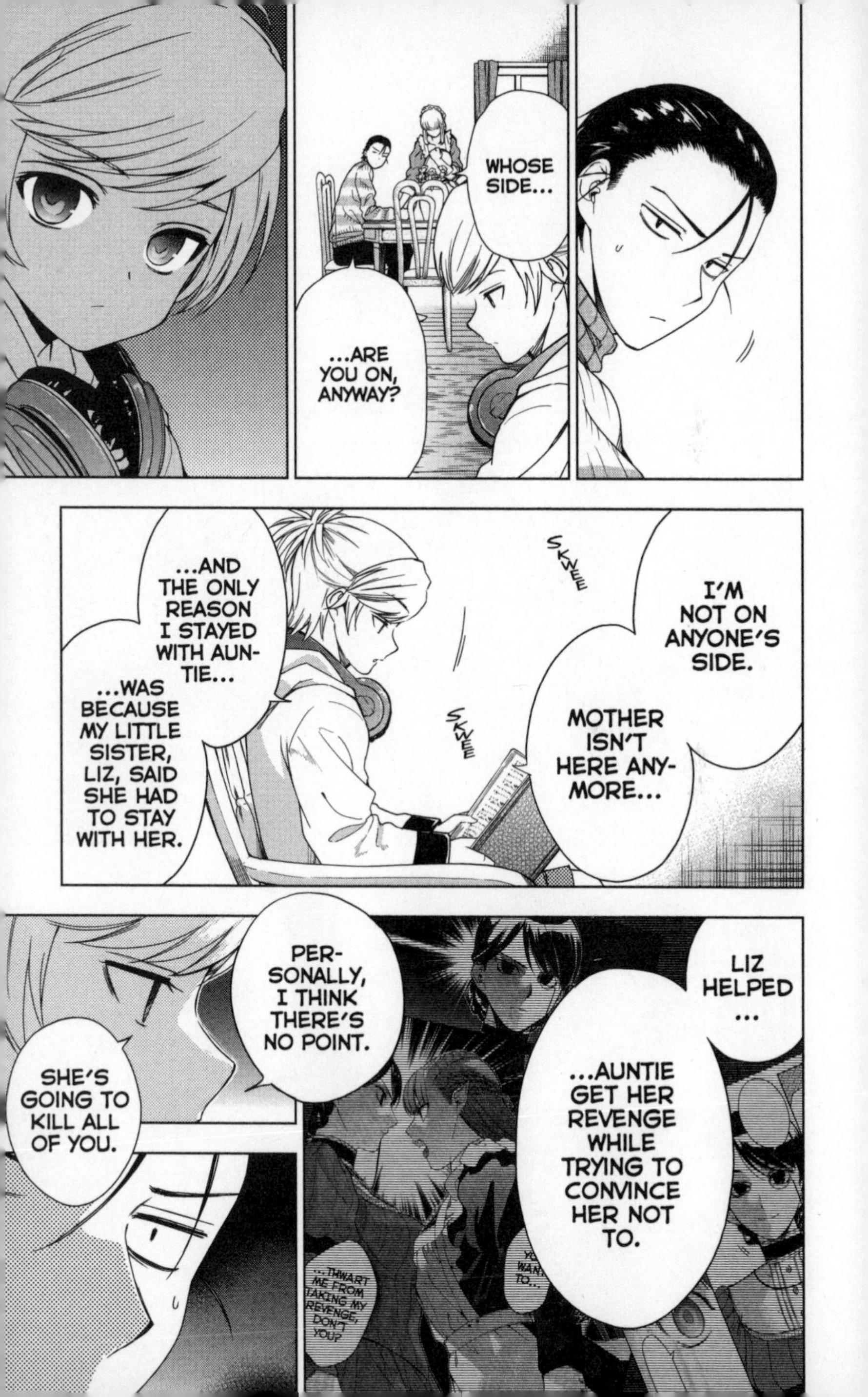
WHOSE SIDE...
...ARE YOU ON, ANYWAY?
I'M NOT ON ANYONE'S SIDE.
MOTHER ISN'T HERE ANYMORE...
SKWEE
SKWEE
...AND THE ONLY REASON I STAYED WITH AUNTIE...
...WAS BECAUSE MY LITTLE SISTER, LIZ, SAID SHE HAD TO STAY WITH HER.
LIZ HELPED...
...AUNTIE GET HER REVENGE WHILE TRYING TO CONVINCE HER NOT TO.
WANT TO...
...THWART ME FROM TAKING MY REVENGE, DON'T YOU?
PERSONALLY, I THINK THERE'S NO POINT.
SHE'S GOING TO KILL ALL OF YOU.

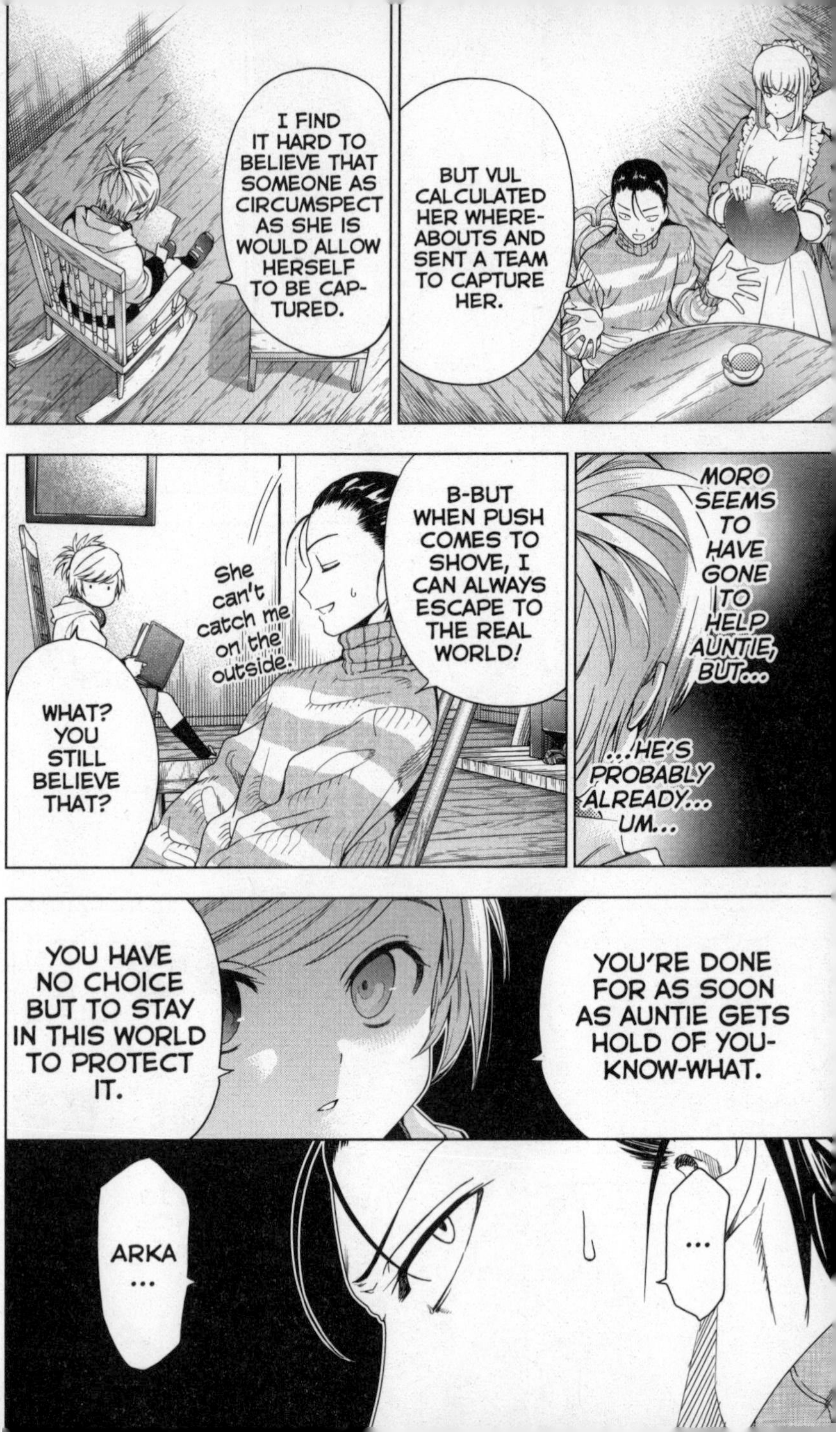
BUT VUL CALCULATED HER WHEREABOUTS AND SENT A TEAM TO CAPTURE HER.
I FIND IT HARD TO BELIEVE THAT SOMEONE AS CIRCUMSPECT AS SHE IS WOULD ALLOW HERSELF TO BE CAPTURED.
MORO SEEMS TO HAVE GONE TO HELP AUNTIE, BUT...
...HE'S PROBABLY ALREADY... UM...
B-BUT WHEN PUSH COMES TO SHOVE, I CAN ALWAYS ESCAPE TO THE REAL WORLD!
She can't catch me on the outside.
WHAT? YOU STILL BELIEVE THAT?
YOU'RE DONE FOR AS SOON AS AUNTIE GETS HOLD OF YOU-KNOW-WHAT.
YOU HAVE NO CHOICE BUT TO STAY IN THIS WORLD TO PROTECT IT.
...
ARKA ...

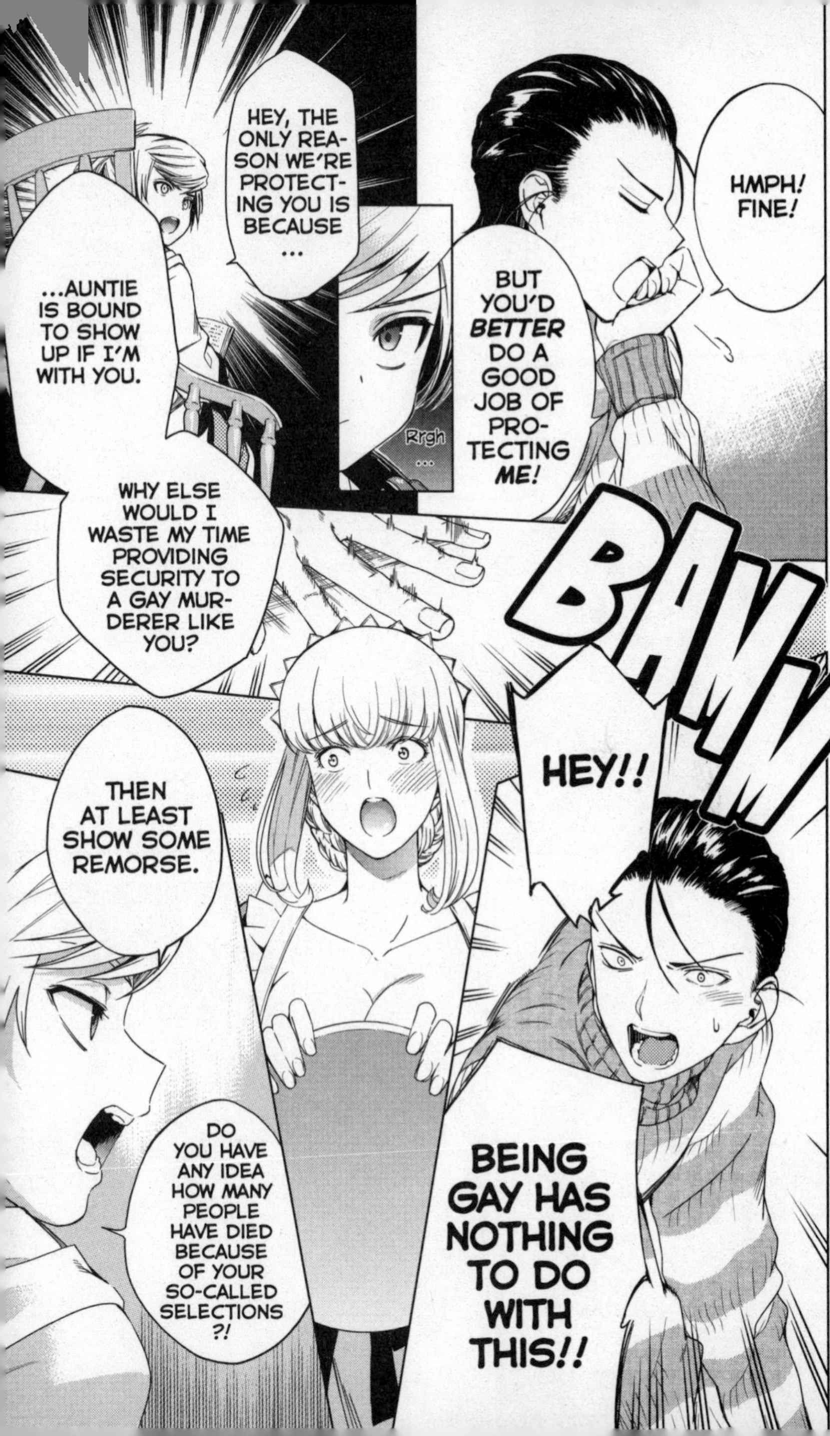
HMPH! FINE!
BUT YOU'D *BETTER* DO A GOOD JOB OF PROTECTING *ME*!
Rrgh...
HEY, THE ONLY REASON WE'RE PROTECTING YOU IS BECAUSE...
...AUNTIE IS BOUND TO SHOW UP IF I'M WITH YOU.
WHY ELSE WOULD I WASTE MY TIME PROVIDING SECURITY TO A GAY MURDERER LIKE YOU?
BAM
HEY!!
BEING GAY HAS NOTHING TO DO WITH THIS!!
THEN AT LEAST SHOW SOME REMORSE.
DO YOU HAVE ANY IDEA HOW MANY PEOPLE HAVE DIED BECAUSE OF YOUR SO-CALLED SELECTIONS?!

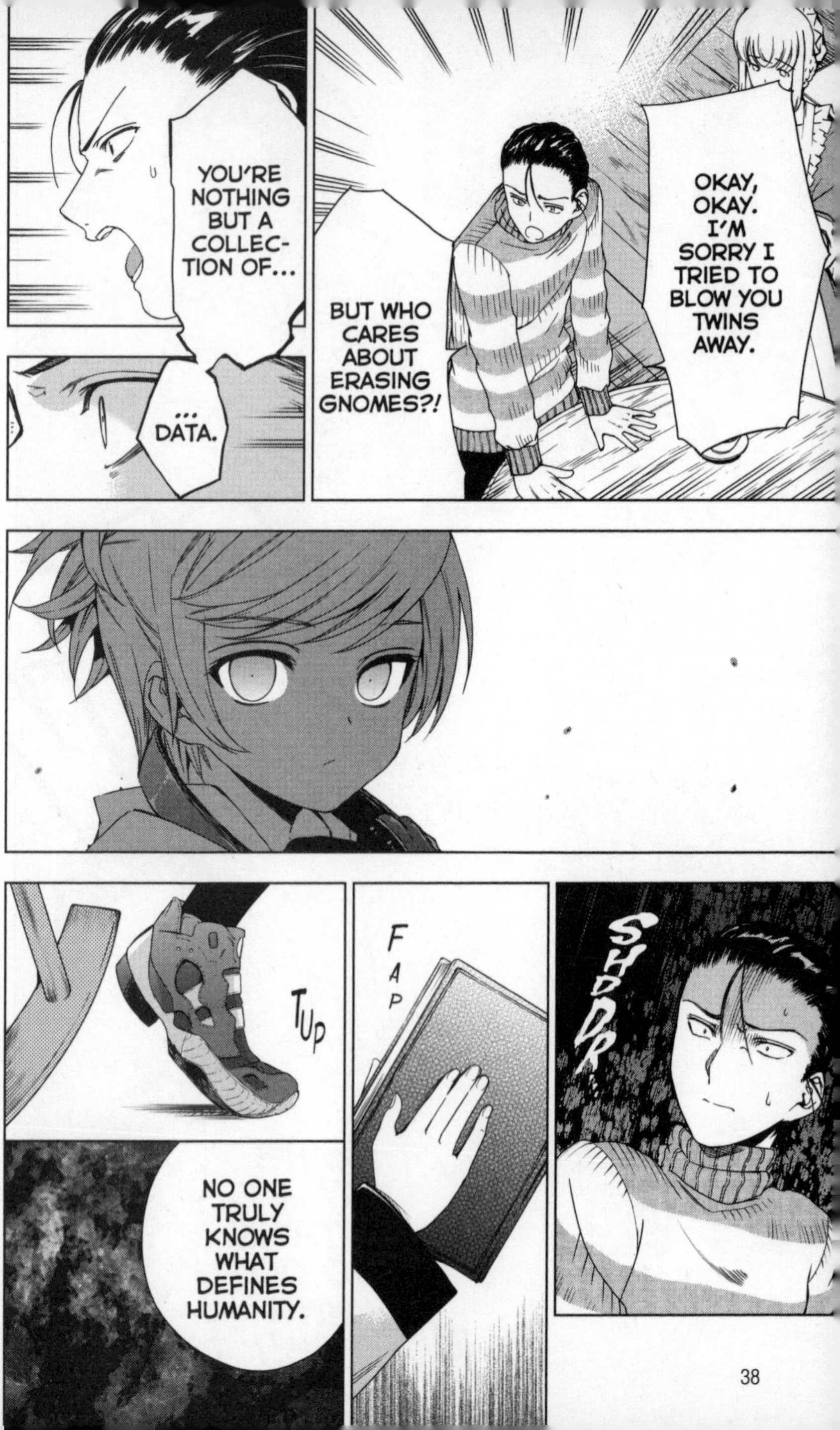
OKAY, OKAY. I'M SORRY I TRIED TO BLOW YOU TWINS AWAY.
BUT WHO CARES ABOUT ERASING GNOMES?!
YOU'RE NOTHING BUT A COLLECTION OF...
...DATA.
SHDDR
FAP
TUP
NO ONE TRULY KNOWS WHAT DEFINES HUMANITY.

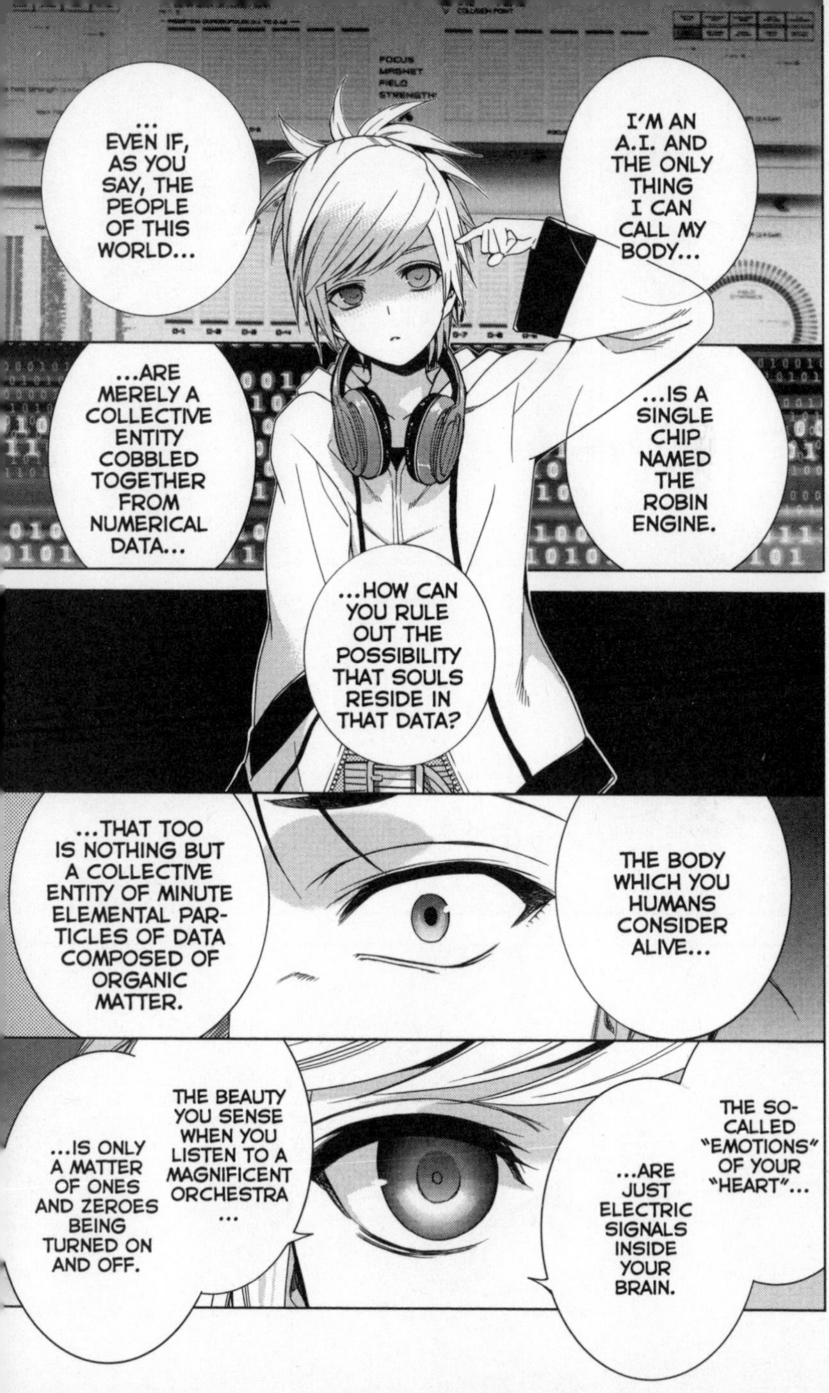
I'M AN A.I. AND THE ONLY THING I CAN CALL MY BODY...
...IS A SINGLE CHIP NAMED THE ROBIN ENGINE.
... EVEN IF, AS YOU SAY, THE PEOPLE OF THIS WORLD...
...ARE MERELY A COLLECTIVE ENTITY COBBLED TOGETHER FROM NUMERICAL DATA...
...HOW CAN YOU RULE OUT THE POSSIBILITY THAT SOULS RESIDE IN THAT DATA?
THE BODY WHICH YOU HUMANS CONSIDER ALIVE...
...THAT TOO IS NOTHING BUT A COLLECTIVE ENTITY OF MINUTE ELEMENTAL PARTICLES OF DATA COMPOSED OF ORGANIC MATTER.
THE SO-CALLED "EMOTIONS" OF YOUR "HEART"...
...ARE JUST ELECTRIC SIGNALS INSIDE YOUR BRAIN.
THE BEAUTY YOU SENSE WHEN YOU LISTEN TO A MAGNIFICENT ORCHESTRA ...
...IS ONLY A MATTER OF ONES AND ZEROES BEING TURNED ON AND OFF.

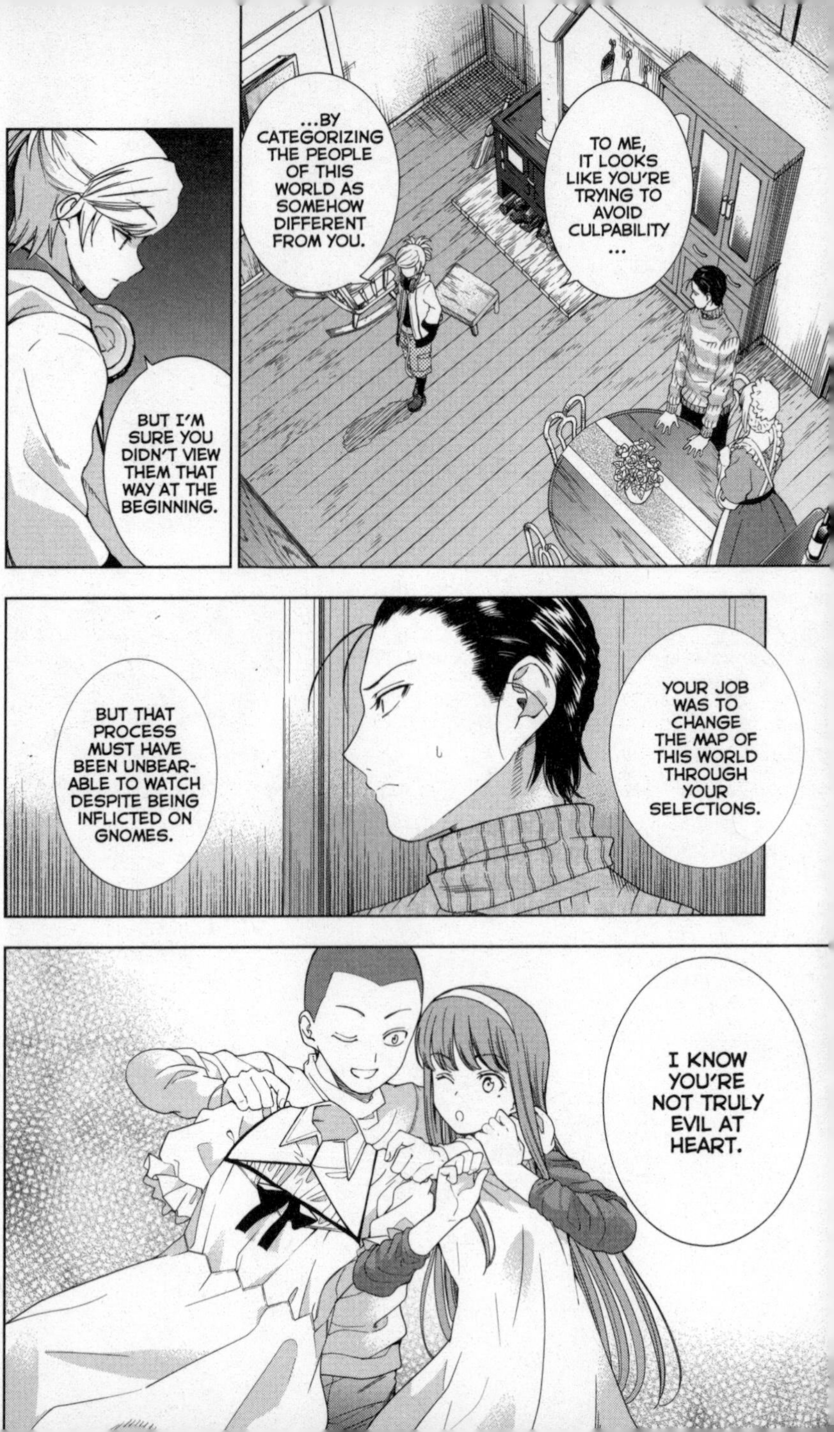
TO ME, IT LOOKS LIKE YOU'RE TRYING TO AVOID CULPABILITY...
...BY CATEGORIZING THE PEOPLE OF THIS WORLD AS SOMEHOW DIFFERENT FROM YOU.
BUT I'M SURE YOU DIDN'T VIEW THEM THAT WAY AT THE BEGINNING.
YOUR JOB WAS TO CHANGE THE MAP OF THIS WORLD THROUGH YOUR SELECTIONS.
BUT THAT PROCESS MUST HAVE BEEN UNBEARABLE TO WATCH DESPITE BEING INFLICTED ON GNOMES.
I KNOW YOU'RE NOT TRULY EVIL AT HEART.

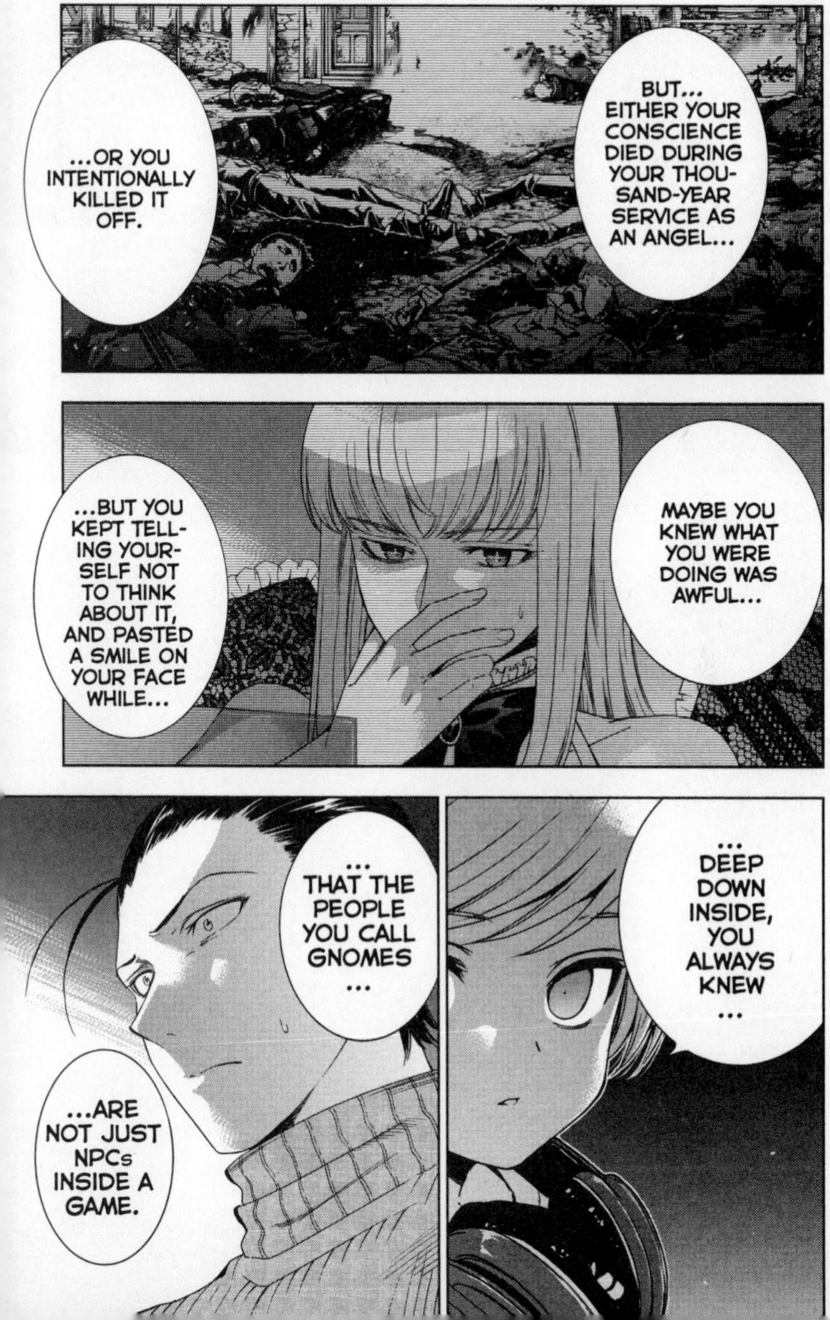
BUT... EITHER YOUR CONSCIENCE DIED DURING YOUR THOU-SAND-YEAR SERVICE AS AN ANGEL...
...OR YOU INTENTIONALLY KILLED IT OFF.
MAYBE YOU KNEW WHAT YOU WERE DOING WAS AWFUL...
...BUT YOU KEPT TELL-ING YOUR-SELF NOT TO THINK ABOUT IT, AND PASTED A SMILE ON YOUR FACE WHILE...
... DEEP DOWN INSIDE, YOU ALWAYS KNEW ...
... THAT THE PEOPLE YOU CALL GNOMES ...
...ARE NOT JUST NPCs INSIDE A GAME.

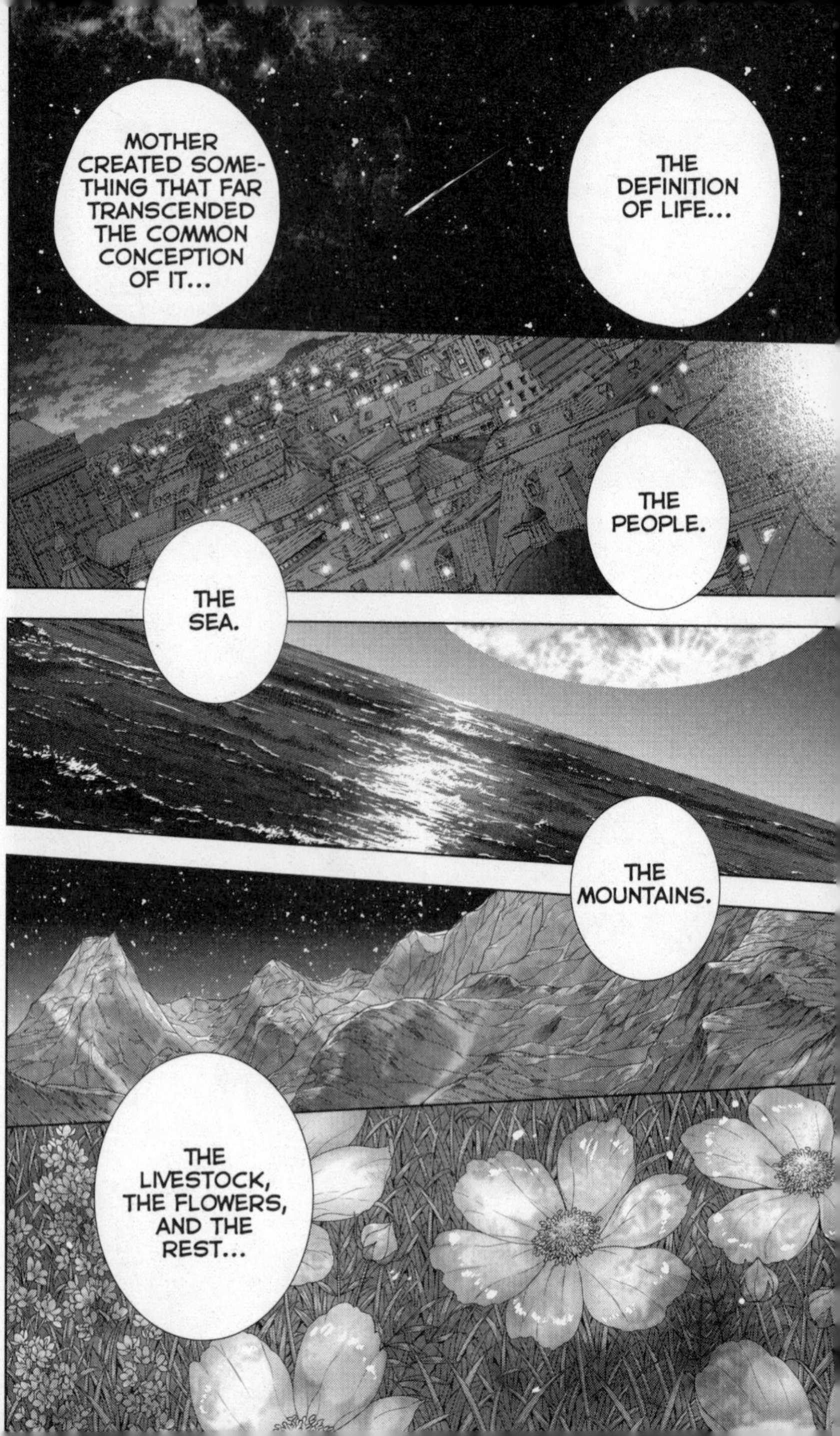
THE DEFINITION OF LIFE...
MOTHER CREATED SOME-THING THAT FAR TRANSCENDED THE COMMON CONCEPTION OF IT...
THE PEOPLE.
THE SEA.
THE MOUNTAINS.
THE LIVESTOCK, THE FLOWERS, AND THE REST...

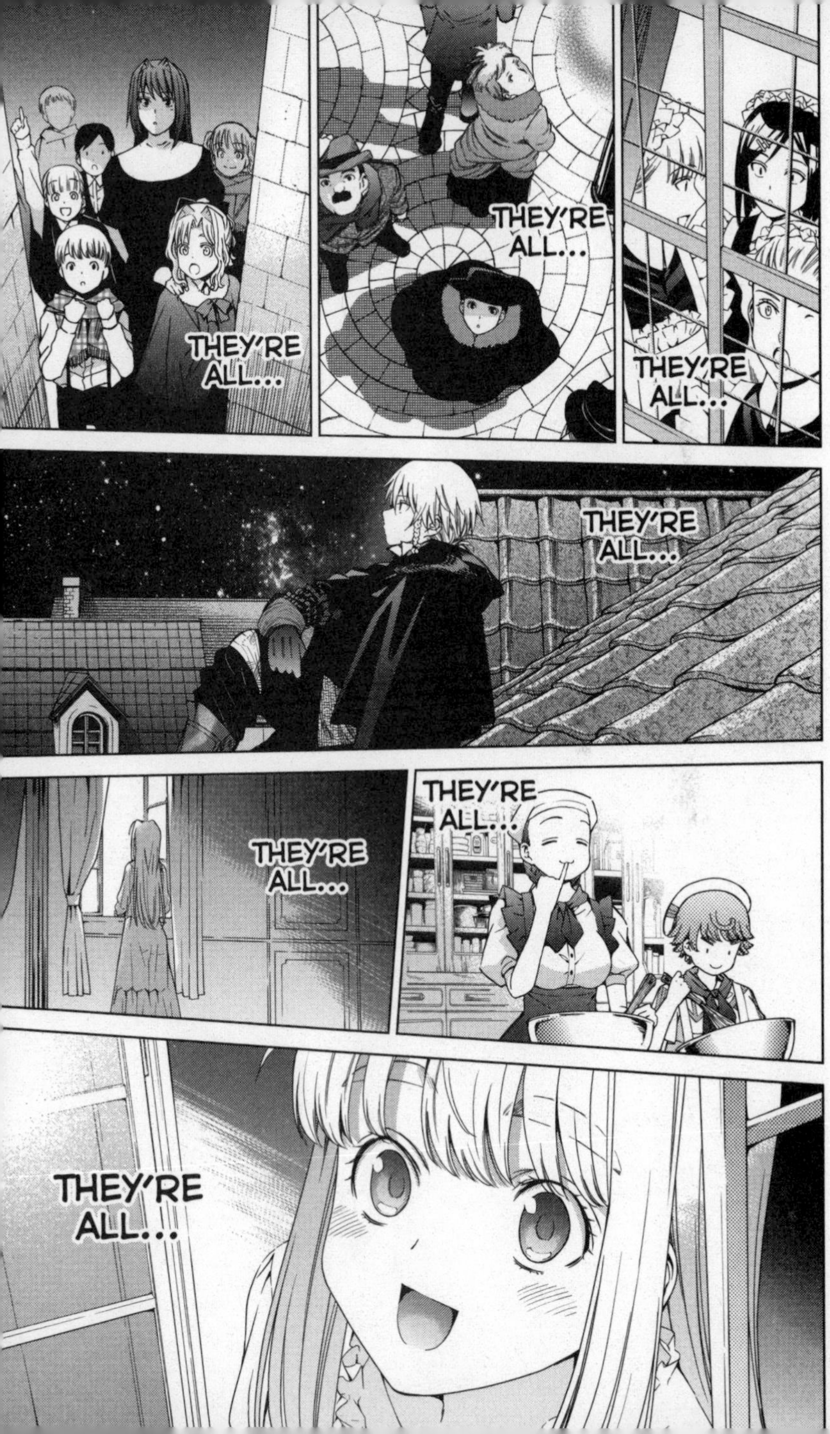
THEY'RE ALL...
THEY'RE ALL...
THEY'RE ALL...
THEY'RE ALL...
THEY'RE ALL...!
THEY'RE ALL...
THEY'RE ALL...!

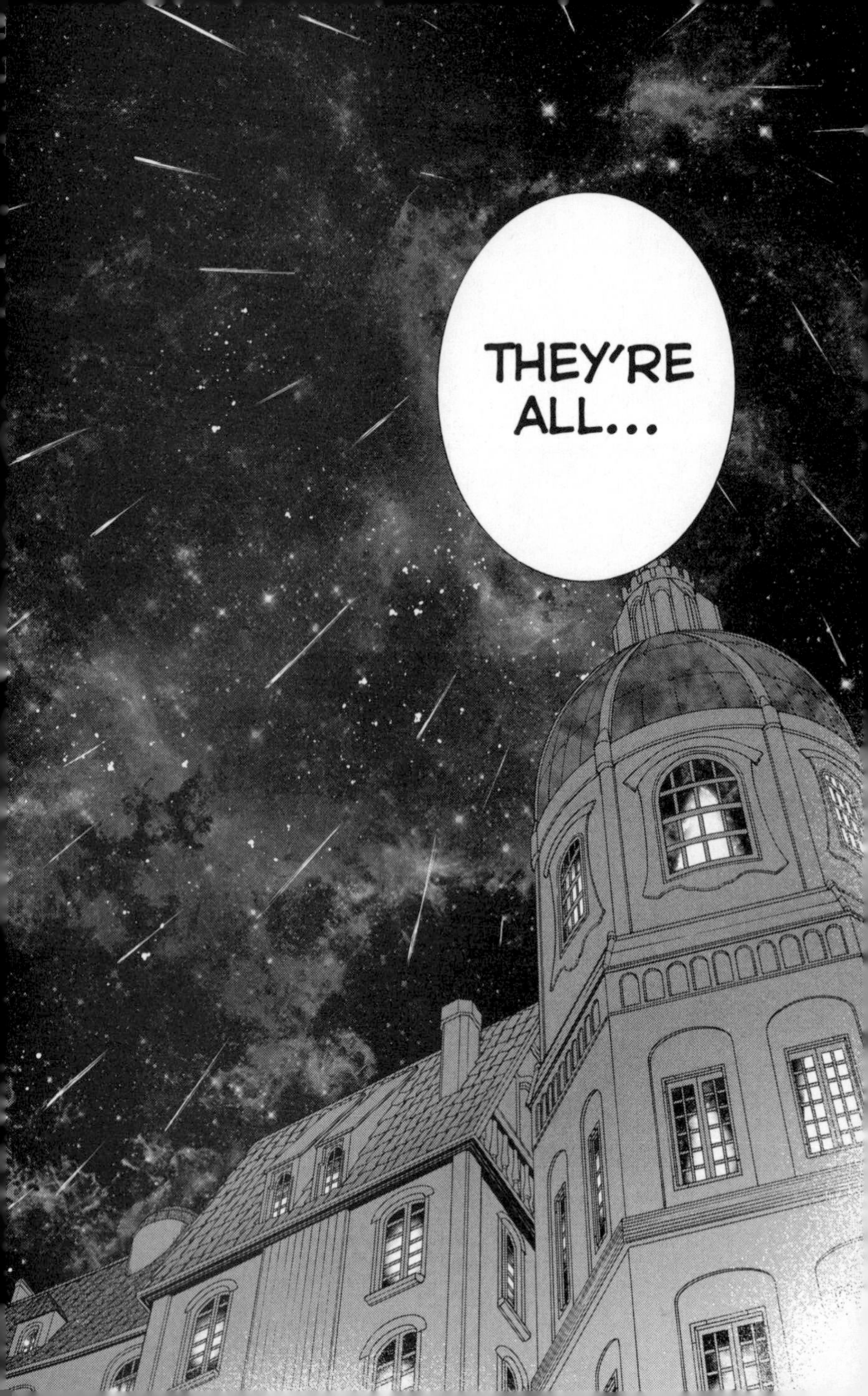
THEY'RE ALL...

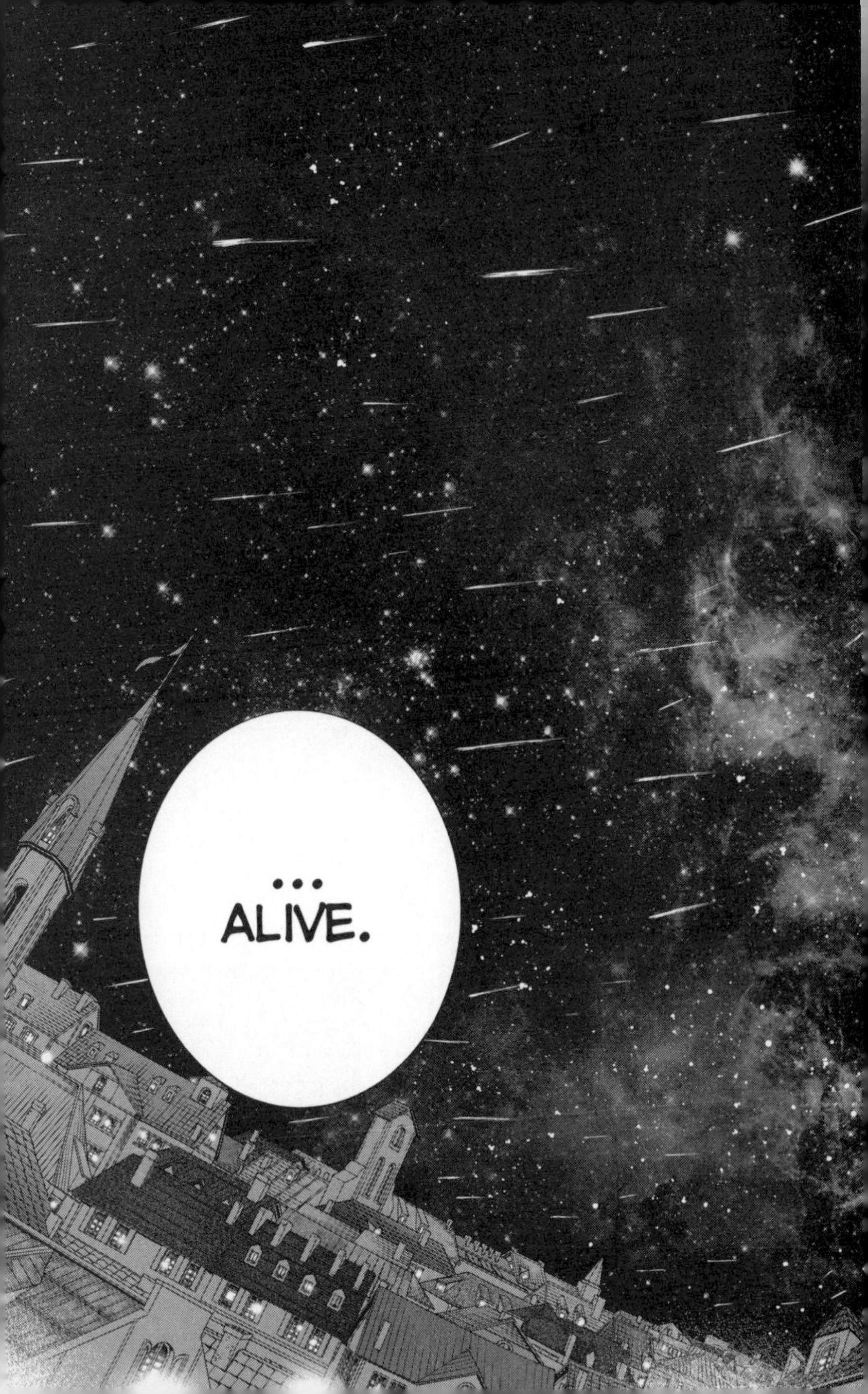
...
ALIVE.

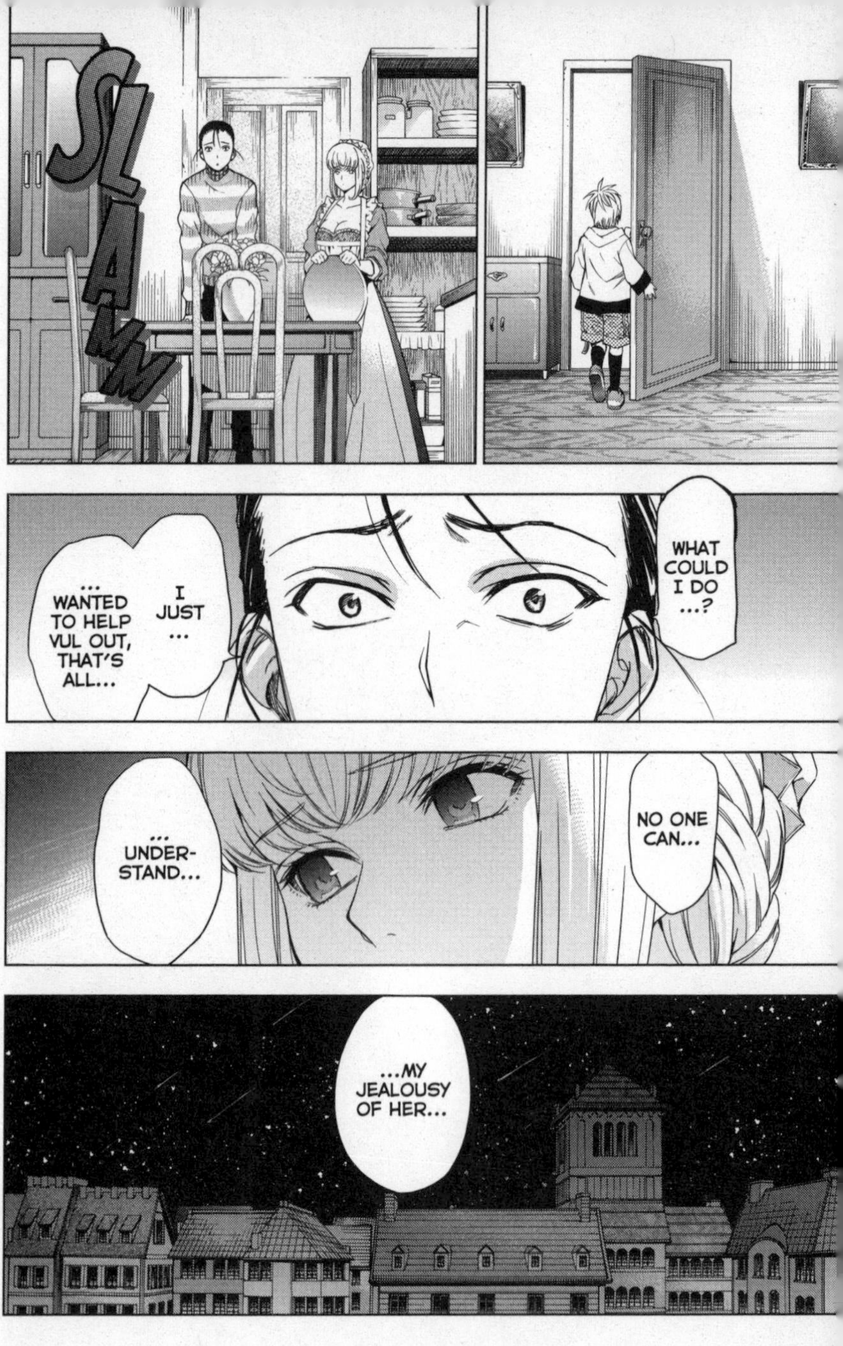
SLAMM
WHAT COULD I DO ...?
I JUST ...
... WANTED TO HELP VUL OUT, THAT'S ALL...
NO ONE CAN...
... UNDER-STAND...
...MY JEALOUSY OF HER...

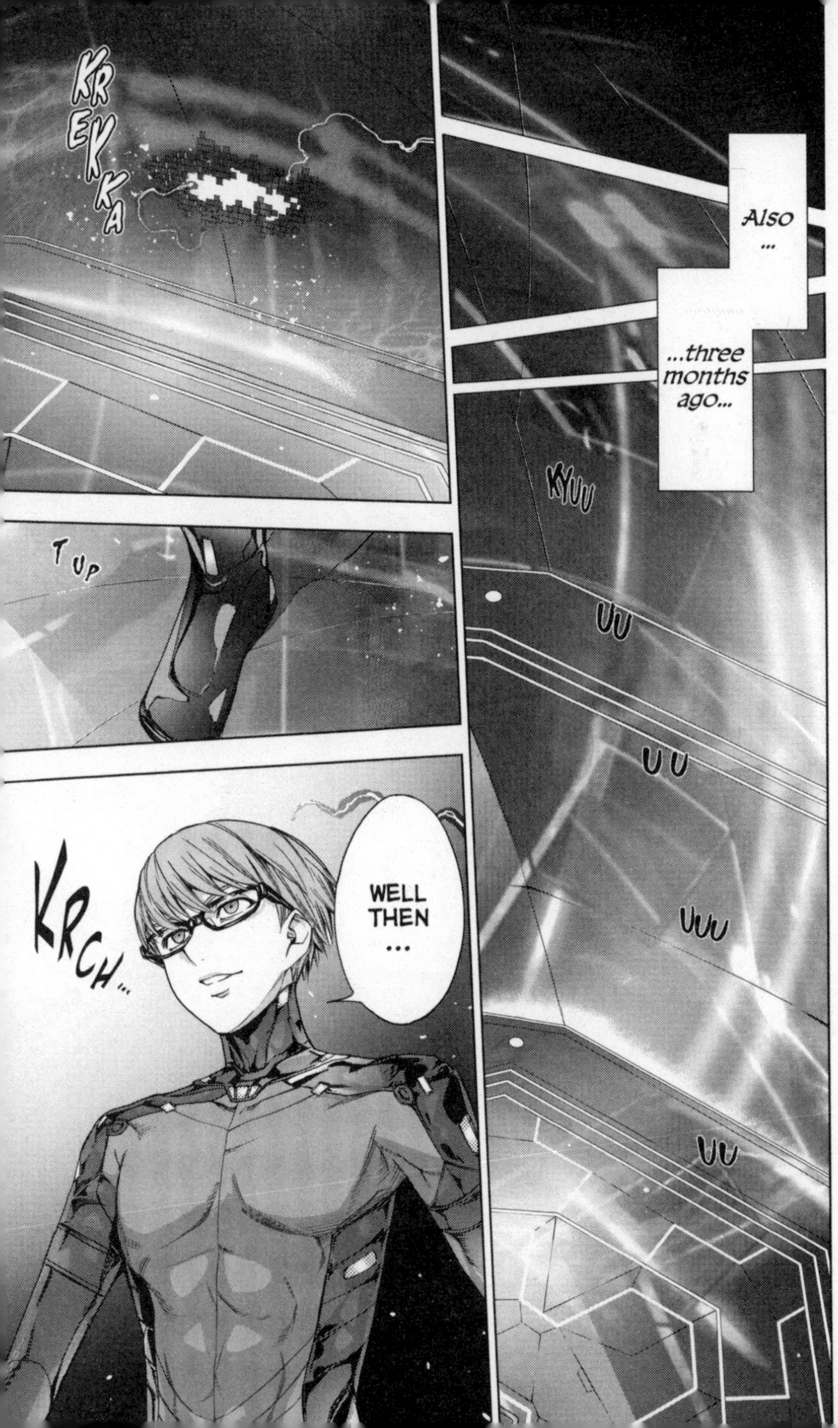
Also ...
...three months ago...
KYUU
UU
U U
UUU
UU
KREKKA
T UP
WELL THEN ...
KRCH...

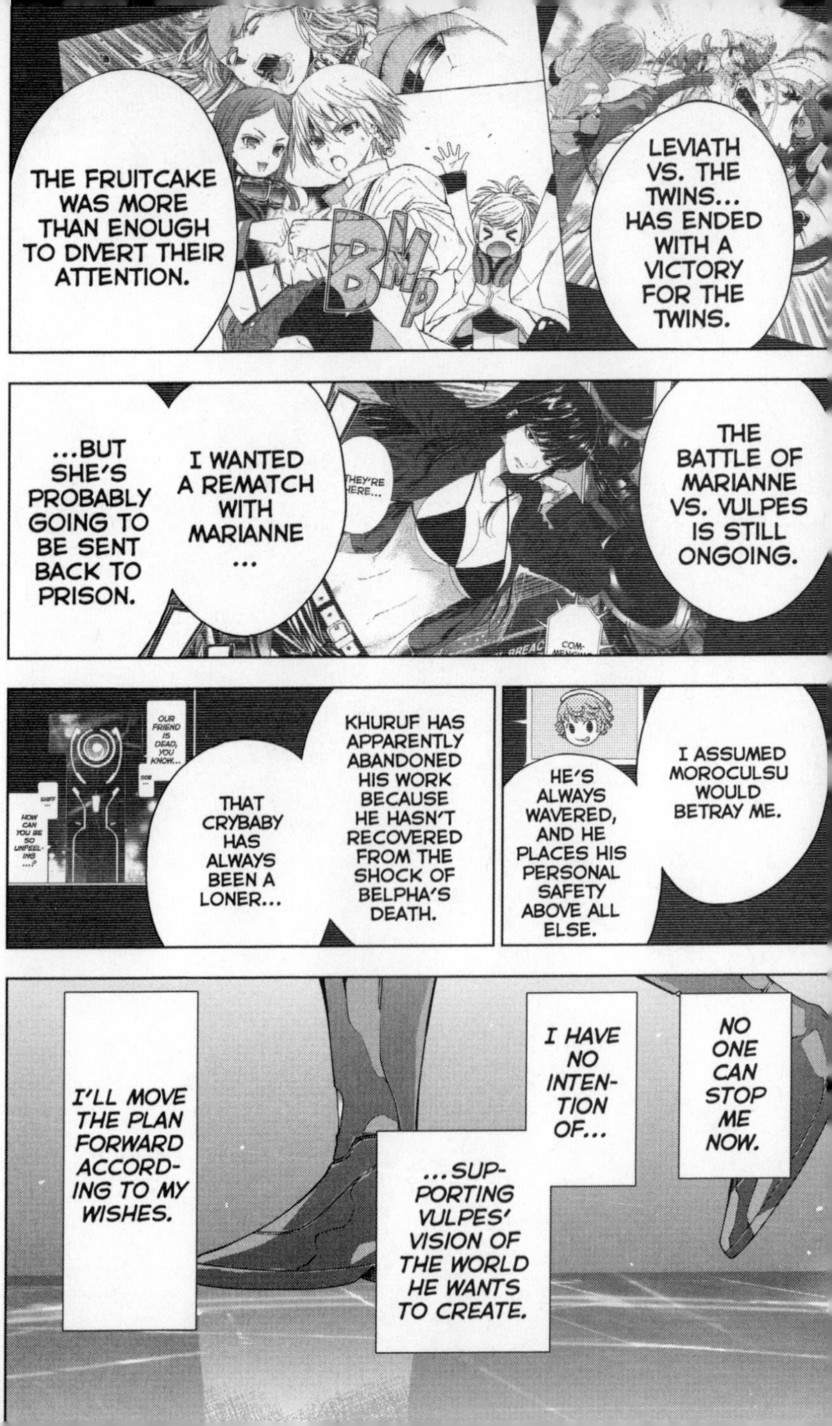
LEVIATH VS. THE TWINS... HAS ENDED WITH A VICTORY FOR THE TWINS.
THE FRUITCAKE WAS MORE THAN ENOUGH TO DIVERT THEIR ATTENTION.
BMP
THE BATTLE OF MARIANNE VS. VULPES IS STILL ONGOING.
THEY'RE HERE...
I WANTED A REMATCH WITH MARIANNE...
...BUT SHE'S PROBABLY GOING TO BE SENT BACK TO PRISON.
I ASSUMED MOROCULSU WOULD BETRAY ME.
HE'S ALWAYS WAVERED, AND HE PLACES HIS PERSONAL SAFETY ABOVE ALL ELSE.
KHURUF HAS APPARENTLY ABANDONED HIS WORK BECAUSE HE HASN'T RECOVERED FROM THE SHOCK OF BELPHA'S DEATH.
THAT CRYBABY HAS ALWAYS BEEN A LONER...
OUR FRIEND IS DEAD, YOU KNOW...
SOB...
HOW CAN YOU BE SO UNFEELING...?
NO ONE CAN STOP ME NOW.
I HAVE NO INTENTION OF...
...SUPPORTING VULPES' VISION OF THE WORLD HE WANTS TO CREATE.
I'LL MOVE THE PLAN FORWARD ACCORDING TO MY WISHES.

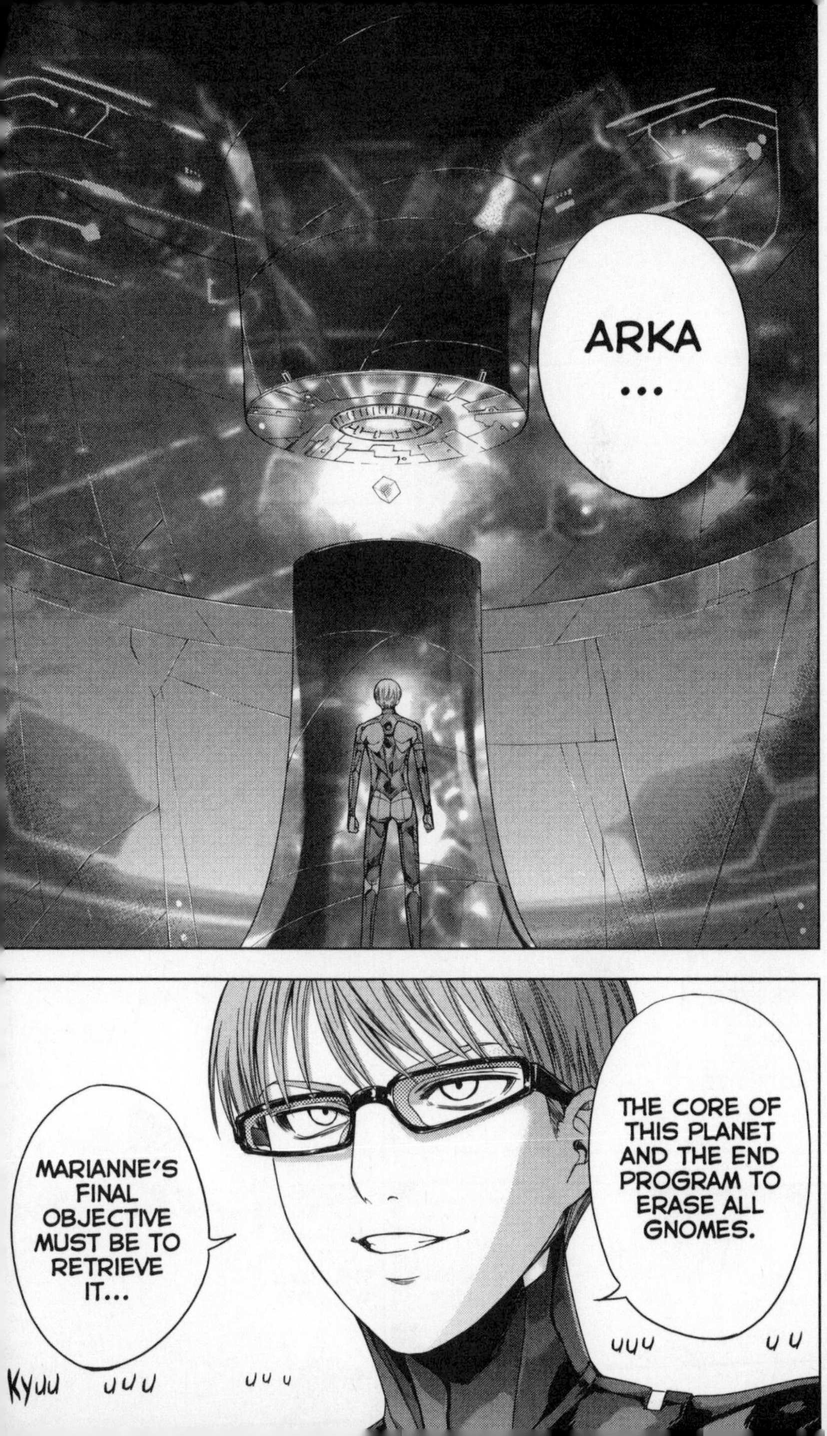
ARKA ...
THE CORE OF THIS PLANET AND THE END PROGRAM TO ERASE ALL GNOMES.
MARIANNE'S FINAL OBJECTIVE MUST BE TO RETRIEVE IT...
uuu uu
Kyuu uuu uuu

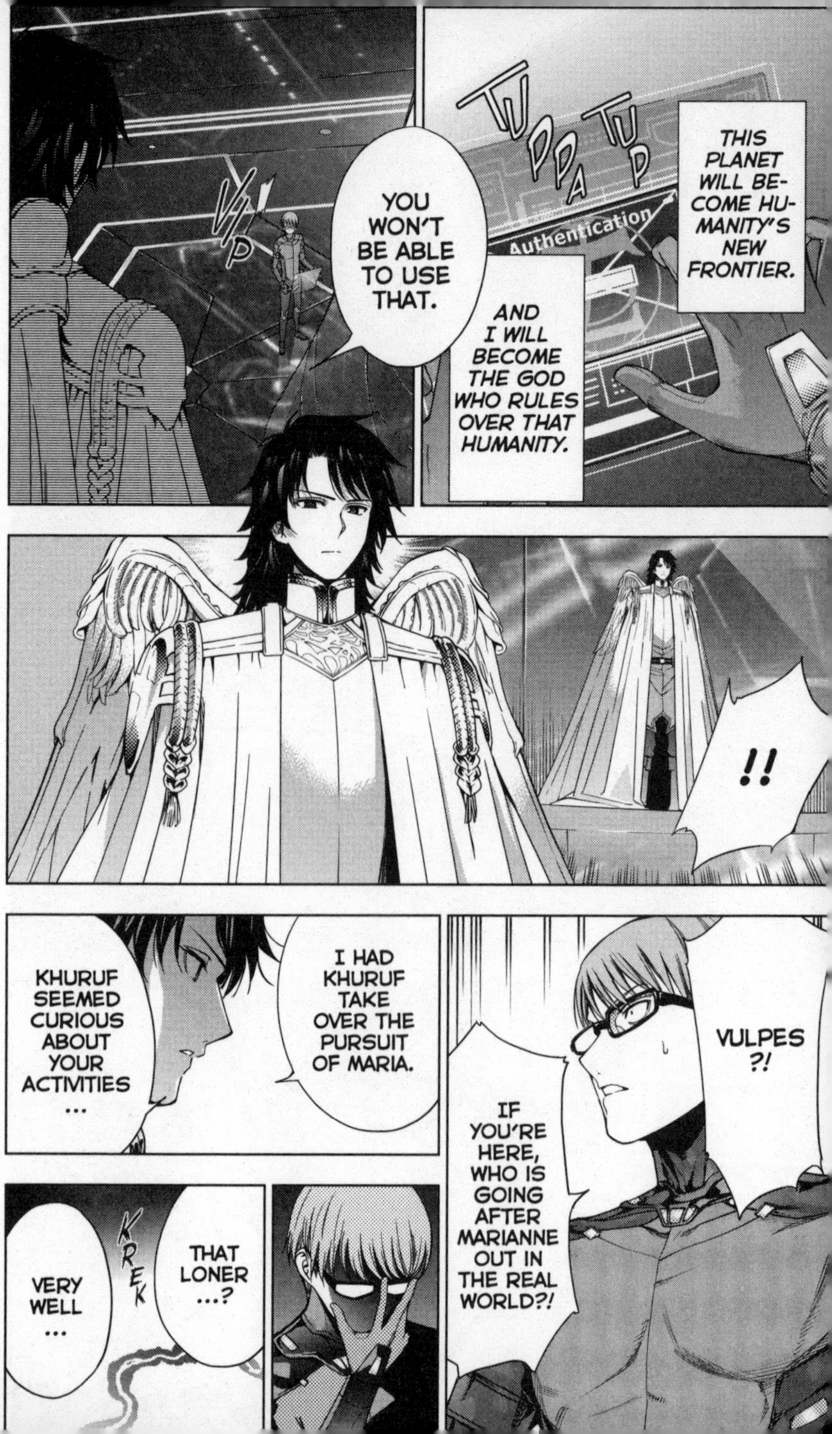
TUPPA TUP
Authentication
THIS PLANET WILL BECOME HUMANITY'S NEW FRONTIER.
AND I WILL BECOME THE GOD WHO RULES OVER THAT HUMANITY.
VIP
YOU WON'T BE ABLE TO USE THAT.
!!
VULPES?!
IF YOU'RE HERE, WHO IS GOING AFTER MARIANNE OUT IN THE REAL WORLD?!
I HAD KHURUF TAKE OVER THE PURSUIT OF MARIA.
KHURUF SEEMED CURIOUS ABOUT YOUR ACTIVITIES...
THAT LONER...?
KREK
VERY WELL...

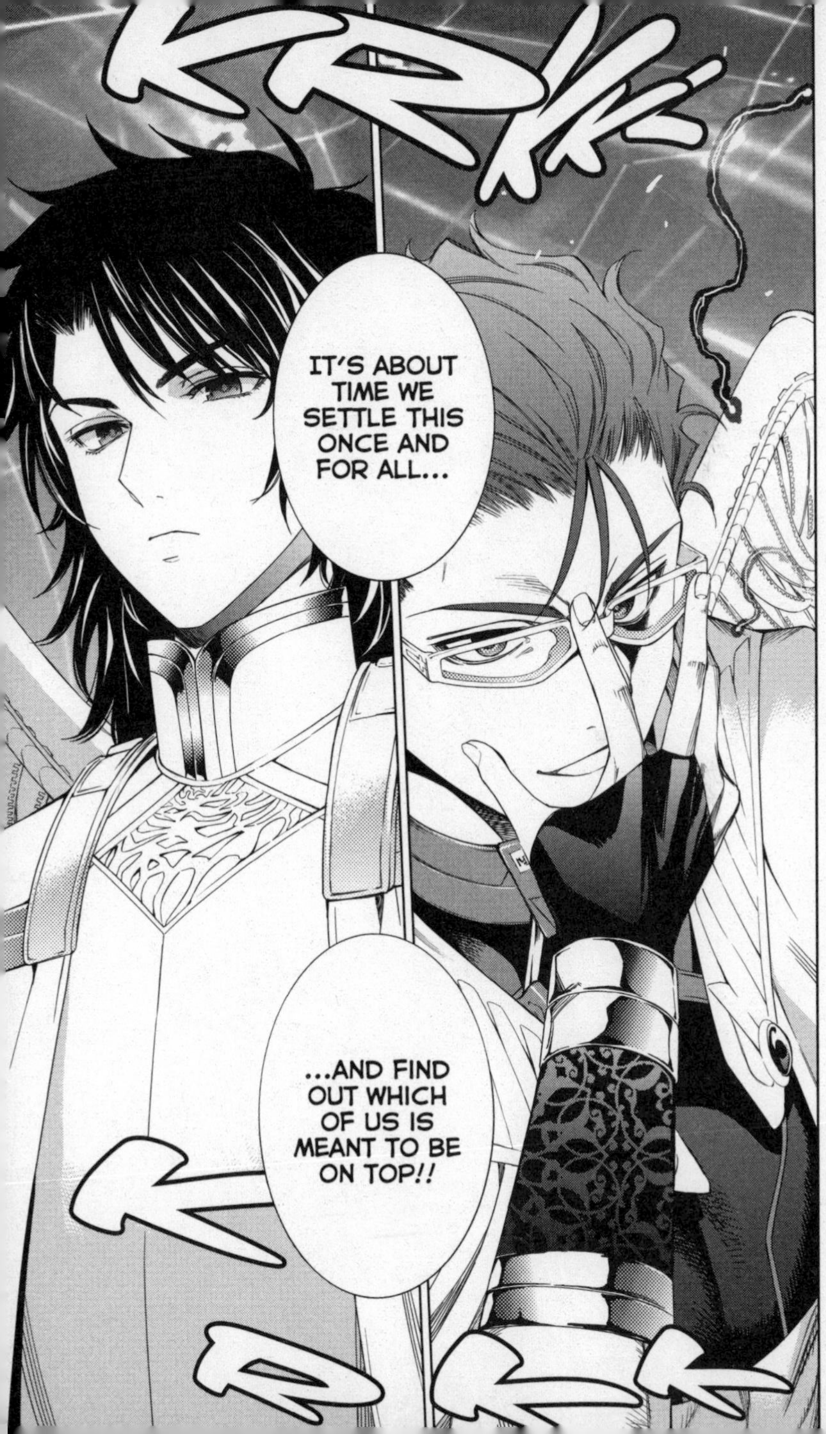
IT'S ABOUT TIME WE SETTLE THIS ONCE AND FOR ALL...
...AND FIND OUT WHICH OF US IS MEANT TO BE ON TOP!!

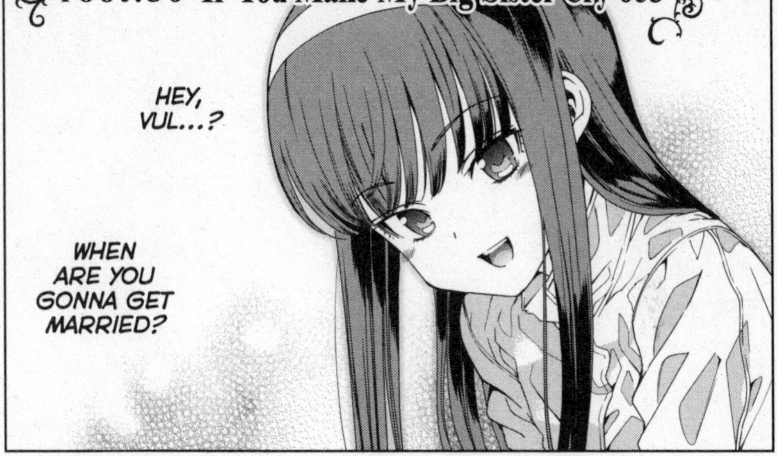
HEY, VUL...?
WHEN ARE YOU GONNA GET MARRIED?

THAT LITTLE DEVIL GIRL WAS ALWAYS SMILING BESIDE ME.

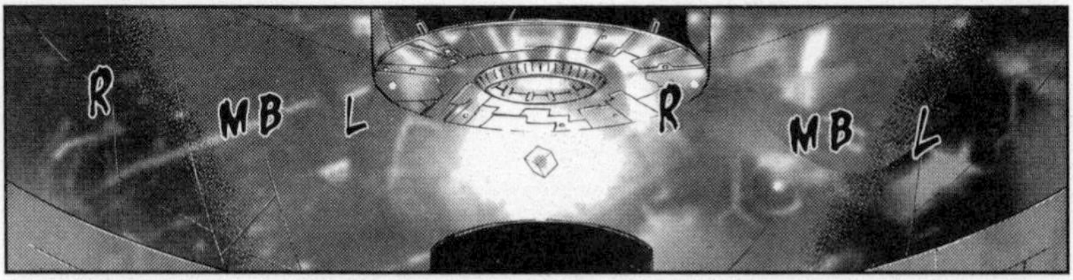
RMBL
RMBL

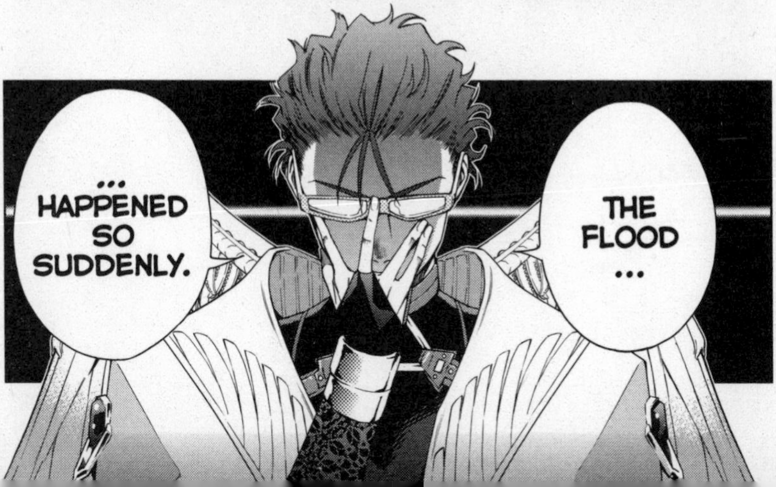
THE FLOOD...
...HAPPENED SO SUDDENLY.

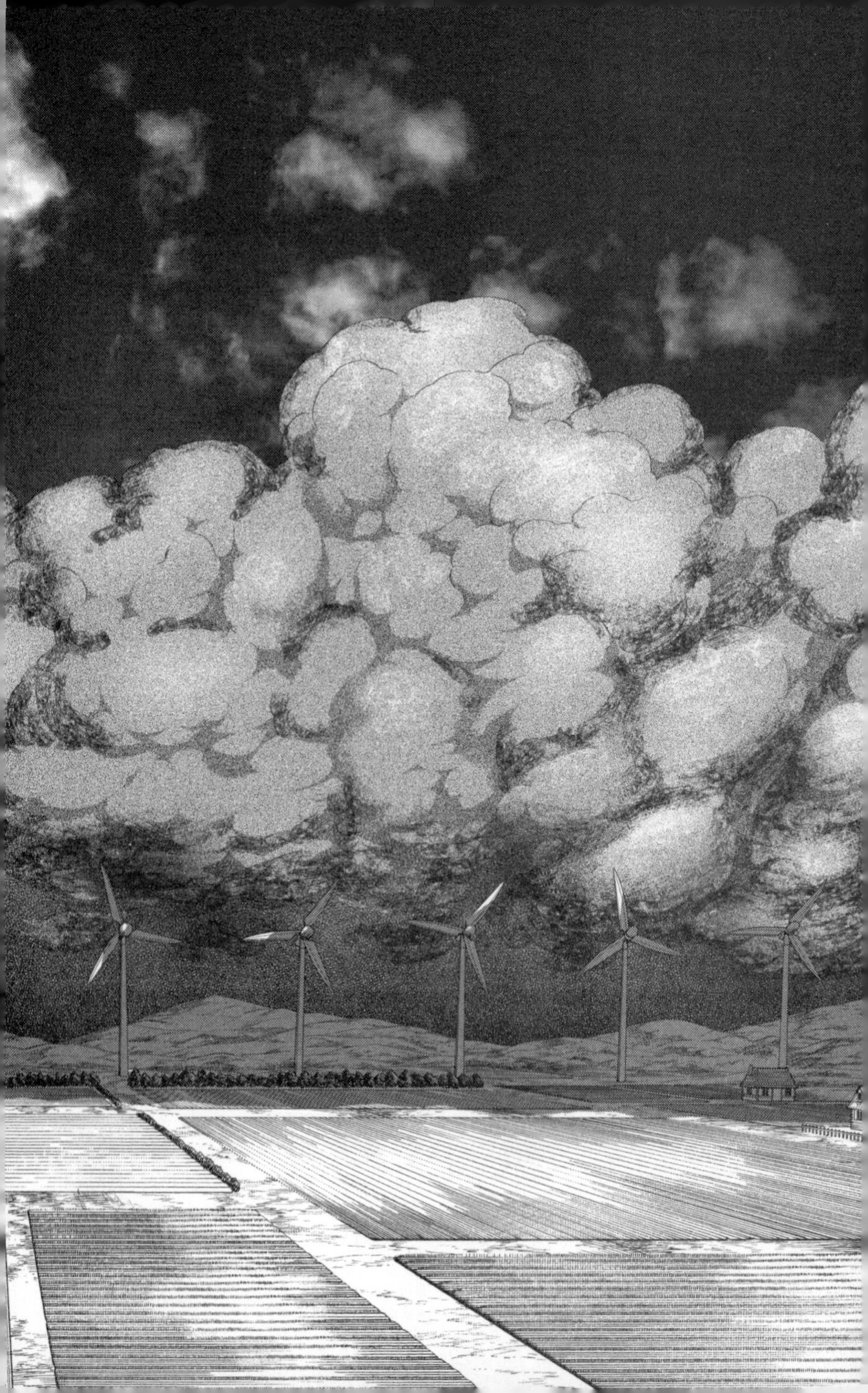

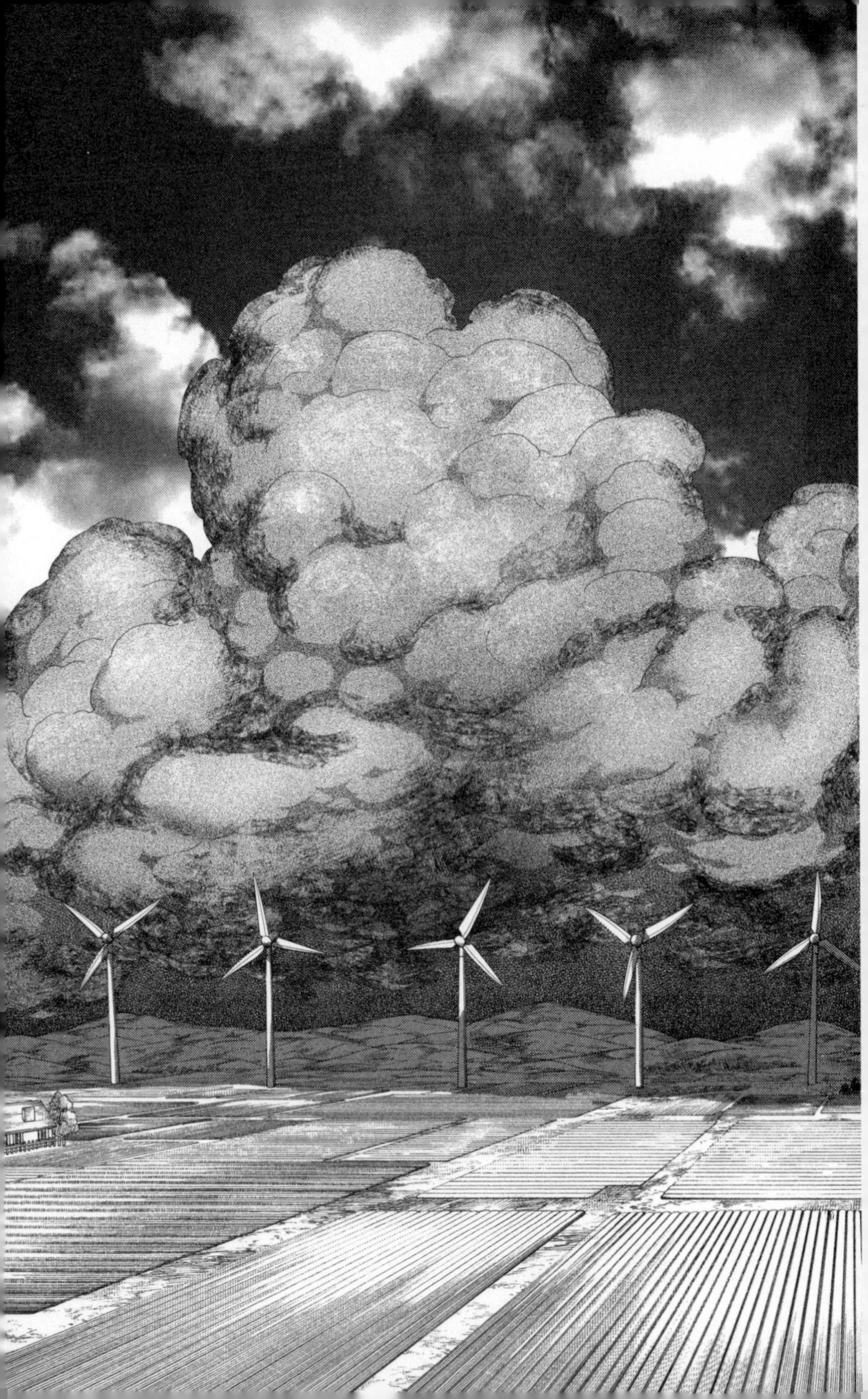

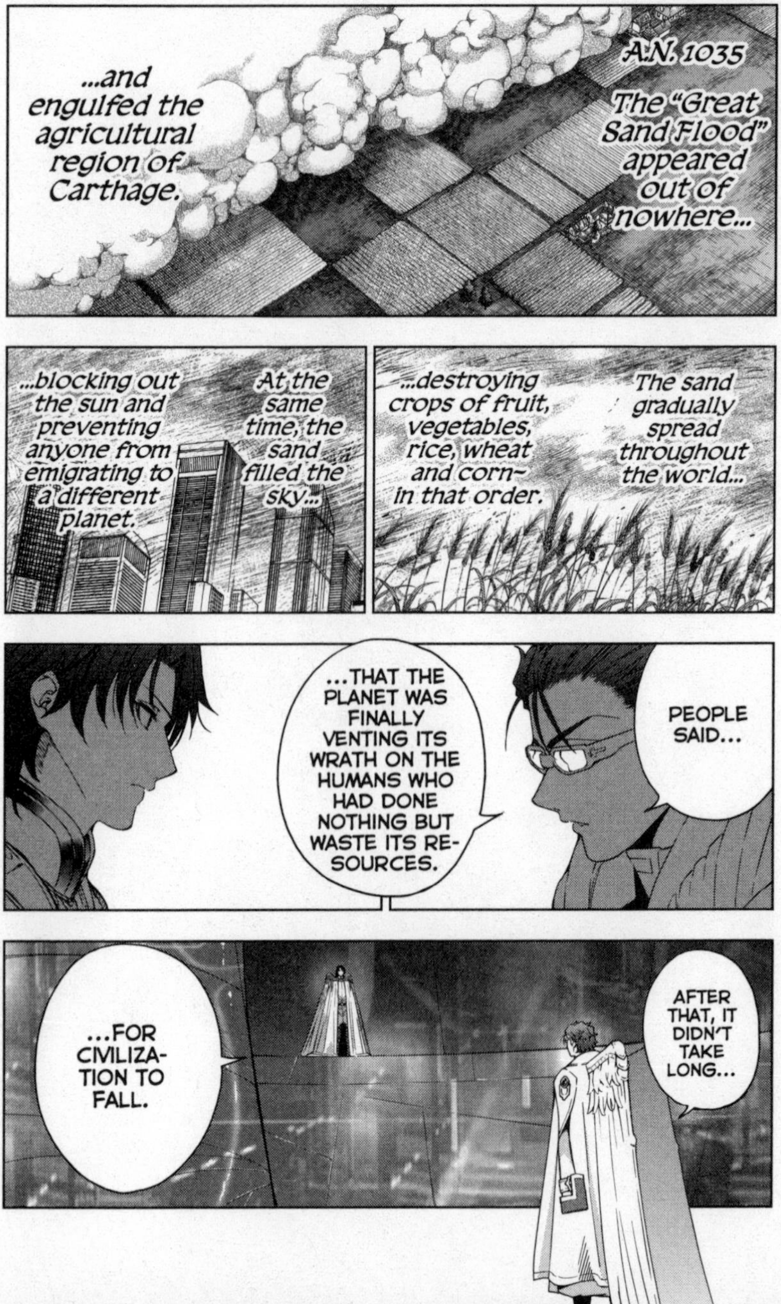
A.N. 1035
The "Great Sand Flood" appeared out of nowhere...
...and engulfed the agricultural region of Carthage.
The sand gradually spread throughout the world...
...destroying crops of fruit, vegetables, rice, wheat and corn—in that order.
At the same time, the sand filled the sky...
...blocking out the sun and preventing anyone from emigrating to a different planet.
PEOPLE SAID...
...THAT THE PLANET WAS FINALLY VENTING ITS WRATH ON THE HUMANS WHO HAD DONE NOTHING BUT WASTE ITS RESOURCES.
AFTER THAT, IT DIDN'T TAKE LONG...
...FOR CIVILIZATION TO FALL.

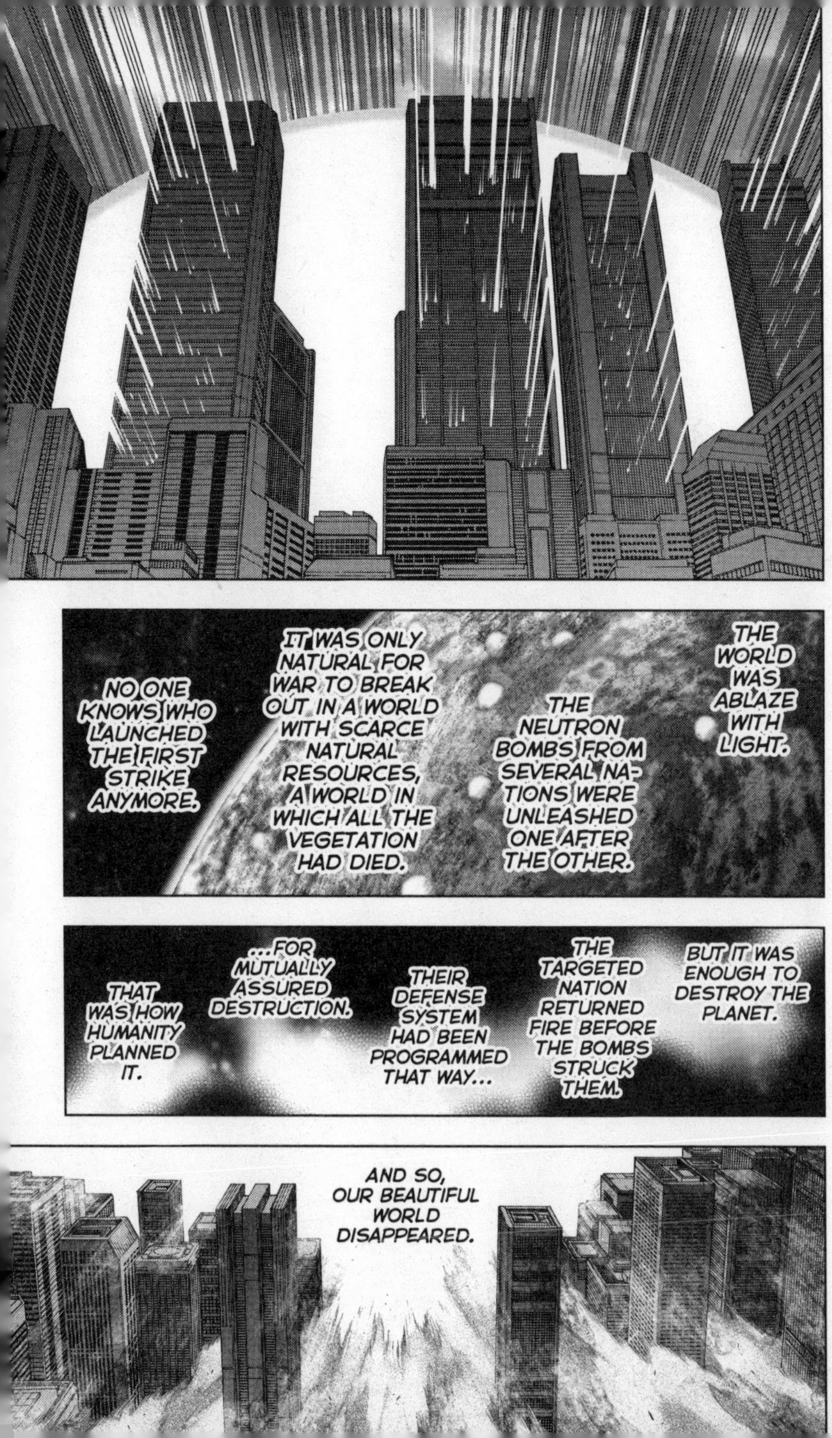
THE WORLD WAS ABLAZE WITH LIGHT.
THE NEUTRON BOMBS FROM SEVERAL NA-TIONS WERE UNLEASHED ONE AFTER THE OTHER.
IT WAS ONLY NATURAL FOR WAR TO BREAK OUT IN A WORLD WITH SCARCE NATURAL RESOURCES, A WORLD IN WHICH ALL THE VEGETATION HAD DIED.
NO ONE KNOWS WHO LAUNCHED THE FIRST STRIKE ANYMORE.
BUT IT WAS ENOUGH TO DESTROY THE PLANET.
THE TARGETED NATION RETURNED FIRE BEFORE THE BOMBS STRUCK THEM.
THEIR DEFENSE SYSTEM HAD BEEN PROGRAMMED THAT WAY...
...FOR MUTUALLY ASSURED DESTRUCTION.
THAT WAS HOW HUMANITY PLANNED IT.
AND SO, OUR BEAUTIFUL WORLD DISAPPEARED.

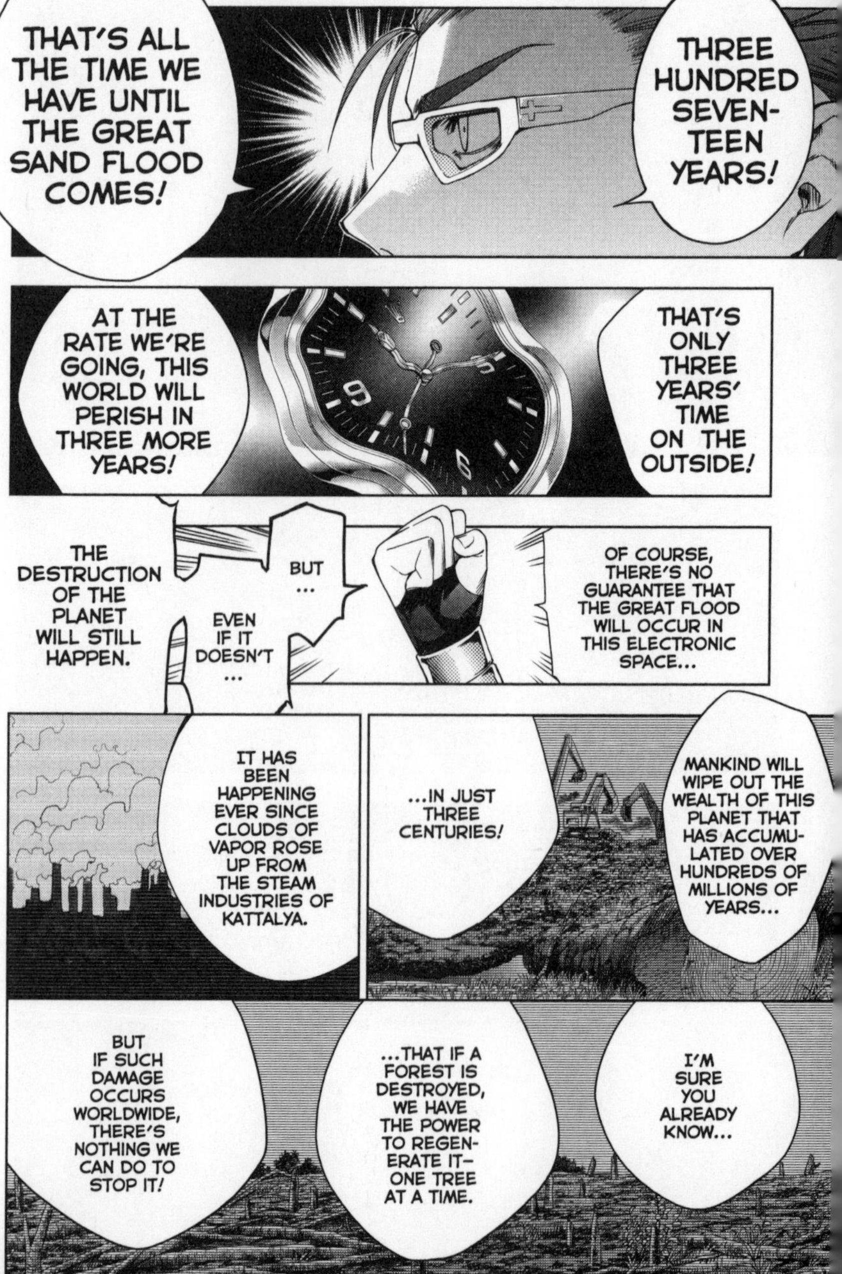
THREE HUNDRED SEVEN-TEEN YEARS!
THAT'S ALL THE TIME WE HAVE UNTIL THE GREAT SAND FLOOD COMES!
THAT'S ONLY THREE YEARS' TIME ON THE OUTSIDE!
AT THE RATE WE'RE GOING, THIS WORLD WILL PERISH IN THREE MORE YEARS!
OF COURSE, THERE'S NO GUARANTEE THAT THE GREAT FLOOD WILL OCCUR IN THIS ELECTRONIC SPACE...
BUT ...
EVEN IF IT DOESN'T ...
THE DESTRUCTION OF THE PLANET WILL STILL HAPPEN.
MANKIND WILL WIPE OUT THE WEALTH OF THIS PLANET THAT HAS ACCUMU-LATED OVER HUNDREDS OF MILLIONS OF YEARS...
...IN JUST THREE CENTURIES!
IT HAS BEEN HAPPENING EVER SINCE CLOUDS OF VAPOR ROSE UP FROM THE STEAM INDUSTRIES OF KATTALYA.
I'M SURE YOU ALREADY KNOW...
...THAT IF A FOREST IS DESTROYED, WE HAVE THE POWER TO REGEN-ERATE IT— ONE TREE AT A TIME.
BUT IF SUCH DAMAGE OCCURS WORLDWIDE, THERE'S NOTHING WE CAN DO TO STOP IT!

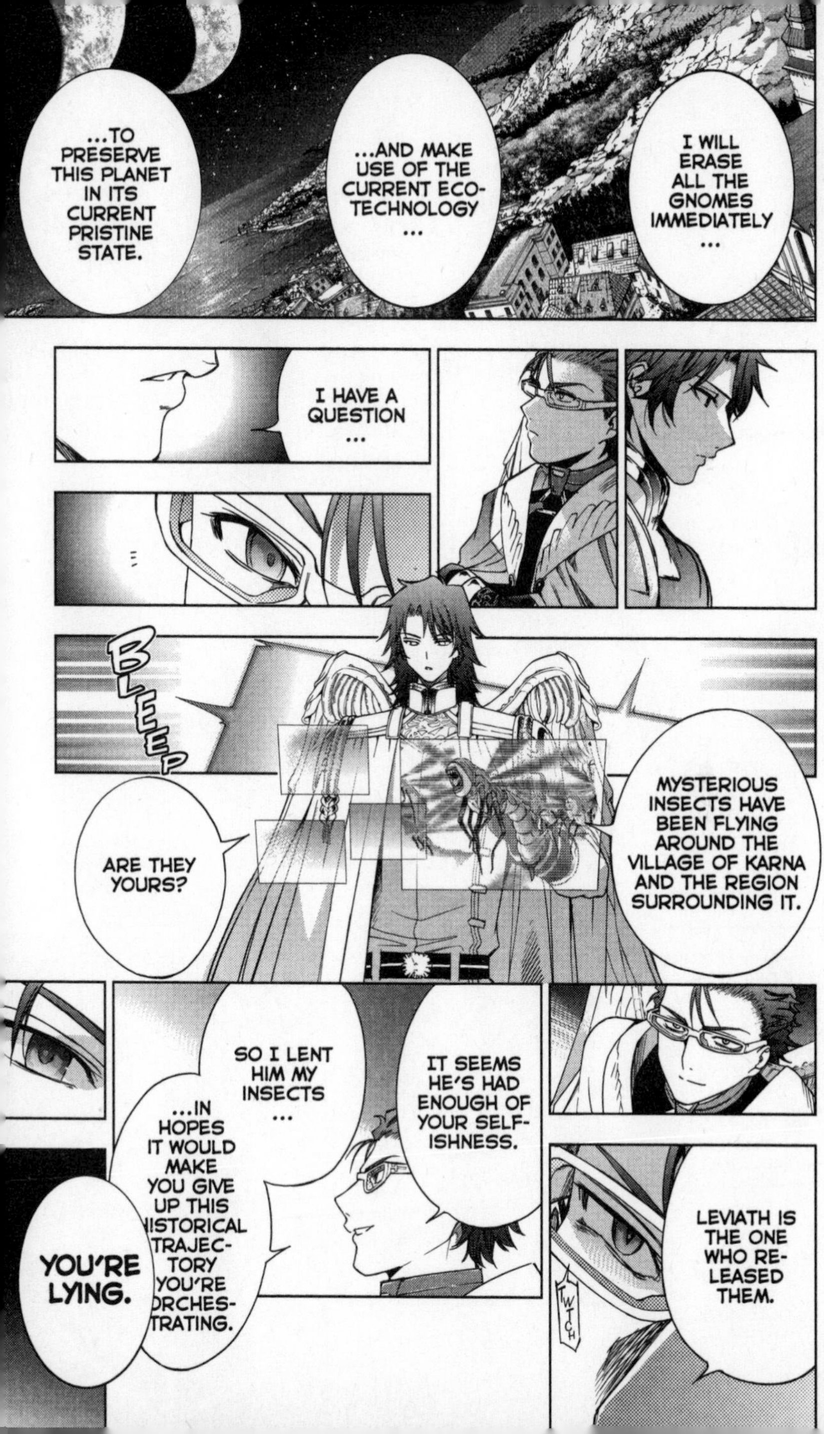
I WILL ERASE ALL THE GNOMES IMMEDIATELY...
...AND MAKE USE OF THE CURRENT ECO-TECHNOLOGY...
...TO PRESERVE THIS PLANET IN ITS CURRENT PRISTINE STATE.
I HAVE A QUESTION...
...
BLEEP
MYSTERIOUS INSECTS HAVE BEEN FLYING AROUND THE VILLAGE OF KARNA AND THE REGION SURROUNDING IT.
ARE THEY YOURS?
LEVIATH IS THE ONE WHO RE-LEASED THEM.
TWITCH
IT SEEMS HE'S HAD ENOUGH OF YOUR SELF-ISHNESS.
SO I LENT HIM MY INSECTS...
...IN HOPES IT WOULD MAKE YOU GIVE UP THIS HISTORICAL TRAJEC-TORY YOU'RE ORCHES-TRATING.
YOU'RE LYING.

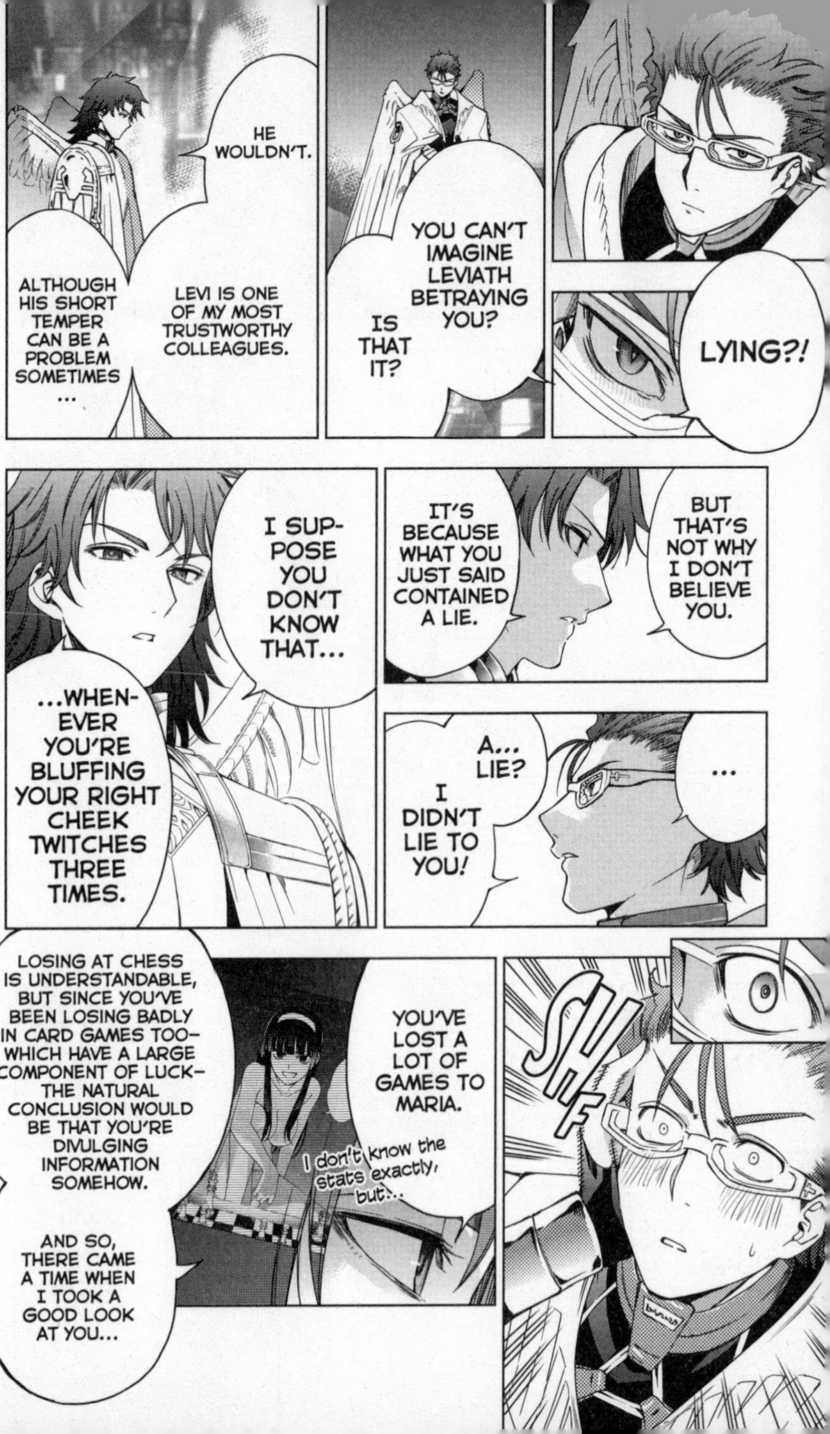
LYING?!
YOU CAN'T IMAGINE LEVIATH BETRAYING YOU?
IS THAT IT?
HE WOULDN'T.
LEVI IS ONE OF MY MOST TRUSTWORTHY COLLEAGUES.
ALTHOUGH HIS SHORT TEMPER CAN BE A PROBLEM SOMETIMES ...
BUT THAT'S NOT WHY I DON'T BELIEVE YOU.
IT'S BECAUSE WHAT YOU JUST SAID CONTAINED A LIE.
...
A... LIE?
I DIDN'T LIE TO YOU!
I SUP-POSE YOU DON'T KNOW THAT...
...WHEN-EVER YOU'RE BLUFFING YOUR RIGHT CHEEK TWITCHES THREE TIMES.
SHF
YOU'VE LOST A LOT OF GAMES TO MARIA.
I don't know the stats exactly, but...
LOSING AT CHESS IS UNDERSTANDABLE, BUT SINCE YOU'VE BEEN LOSING BADLY IN CARD GAMES TOO—WHICH HAVE A LARGE COMPONENT OF LUCK—THE NATURAL CONCLUSION WOULD BE THAT YOU'RE DIVULGING INFORMATION SOMEHOW.
AND SO, THERE CAME A TIME WHEN I TOOK A GOOD LOOK AT YOU...

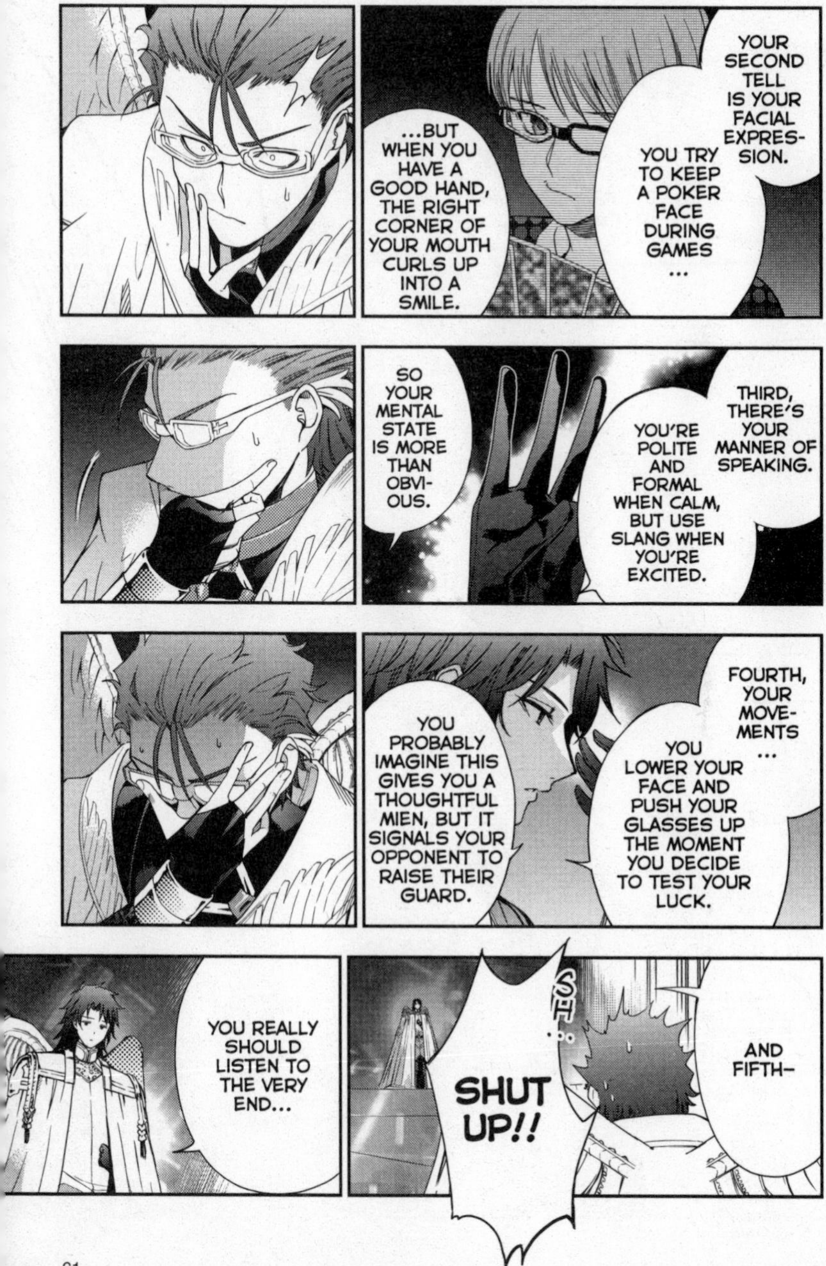
YOUR SECOND TELL IS YOUR FACIAL EXPRES-SION.
YOU TRY TO KEEP A POKER FACE DURING GAMES...
...BUT WHEN YOU HAVE A GOOD HAND, THE RIGHT CORNER OF YOUR MOUTH CURLS UP INTO A SMILE.
THIRD, THERE'S YOUR MANNER OF SPEAKING.
YOU'RE POLITE AND FORMAL WHEN CALM, BUT USE SLANG WHEN YOU'RE EXCITED.
SO YOUR MENTAL STATE IS MORE THAN OBVI-OUS.
FOURTH, YOUR MOVE-MENTS...
YOU LOWER YOUR FACE AND PUSH YOUR GLASSES UP THE MOMENT YOU DECIDE TO TEST YOUR LUCK.
YOU PROBABLY IMAGINE THIS GIVES YOU A THOUGHTFUL MIEN, BUT IT SIGNALS YOUR OPPONENT TO RAISE THEIR GUARD.
AND FIFTH–
SH...
SHUT UP!!
YOU REALLY SHOULD LISTEN TO THE VERY END...

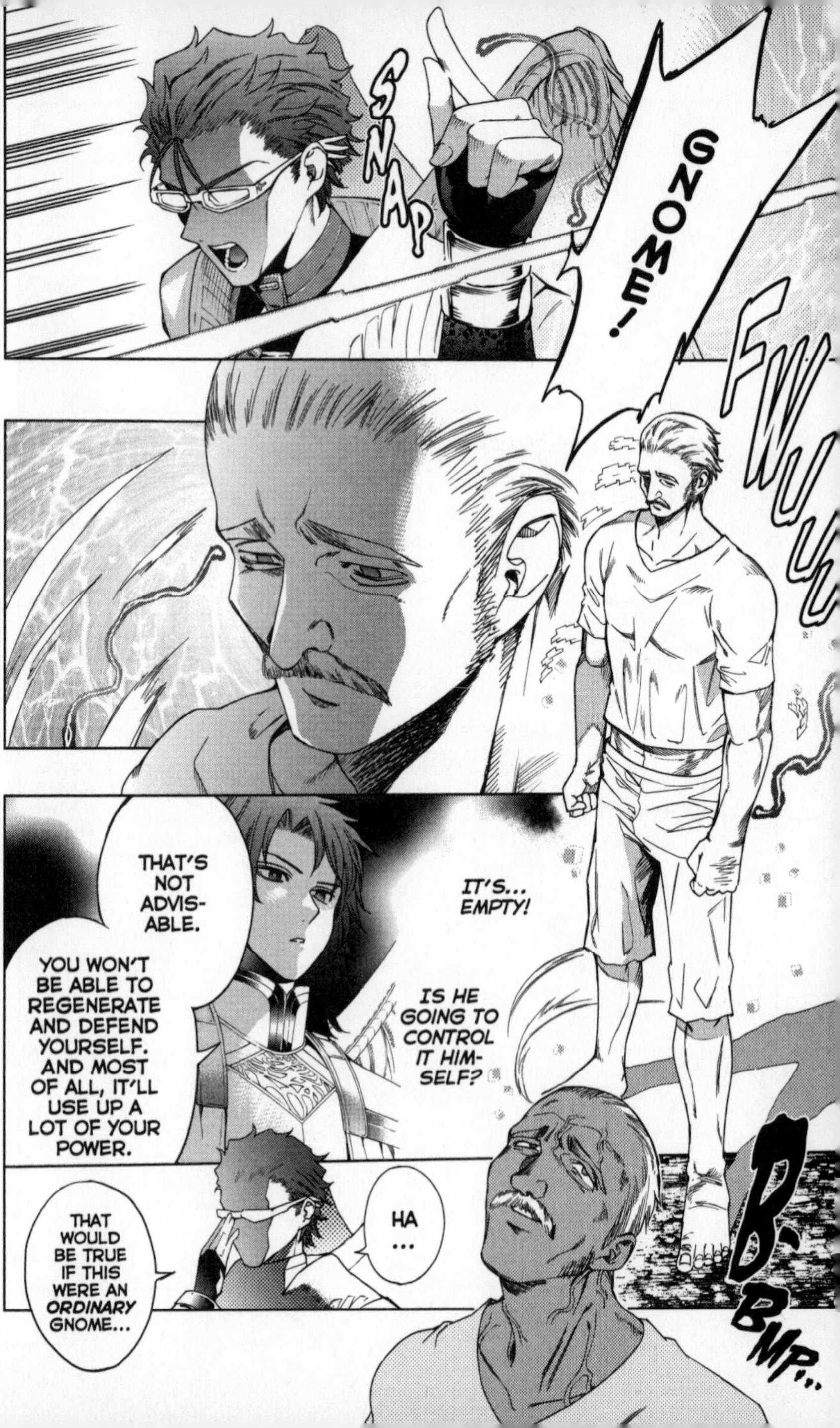
GNOME!
SNAP
FWUUU
IT'S... EMPTY!
IS HE GOING TO CONTROL IT HIMSELF?
THAT'S NOT ADVISABLE.
YOU WON'T BE ABLE TO REGENERATE AND DEFEND YOURSELF. AND MOST OF ALL, IT'LL USE UP A LOT OF YOUR POWER.
B-BMP...
HA...
THAT WOULD BE TRUE IF THIS WERE AN *ORDINARY* GNOME...

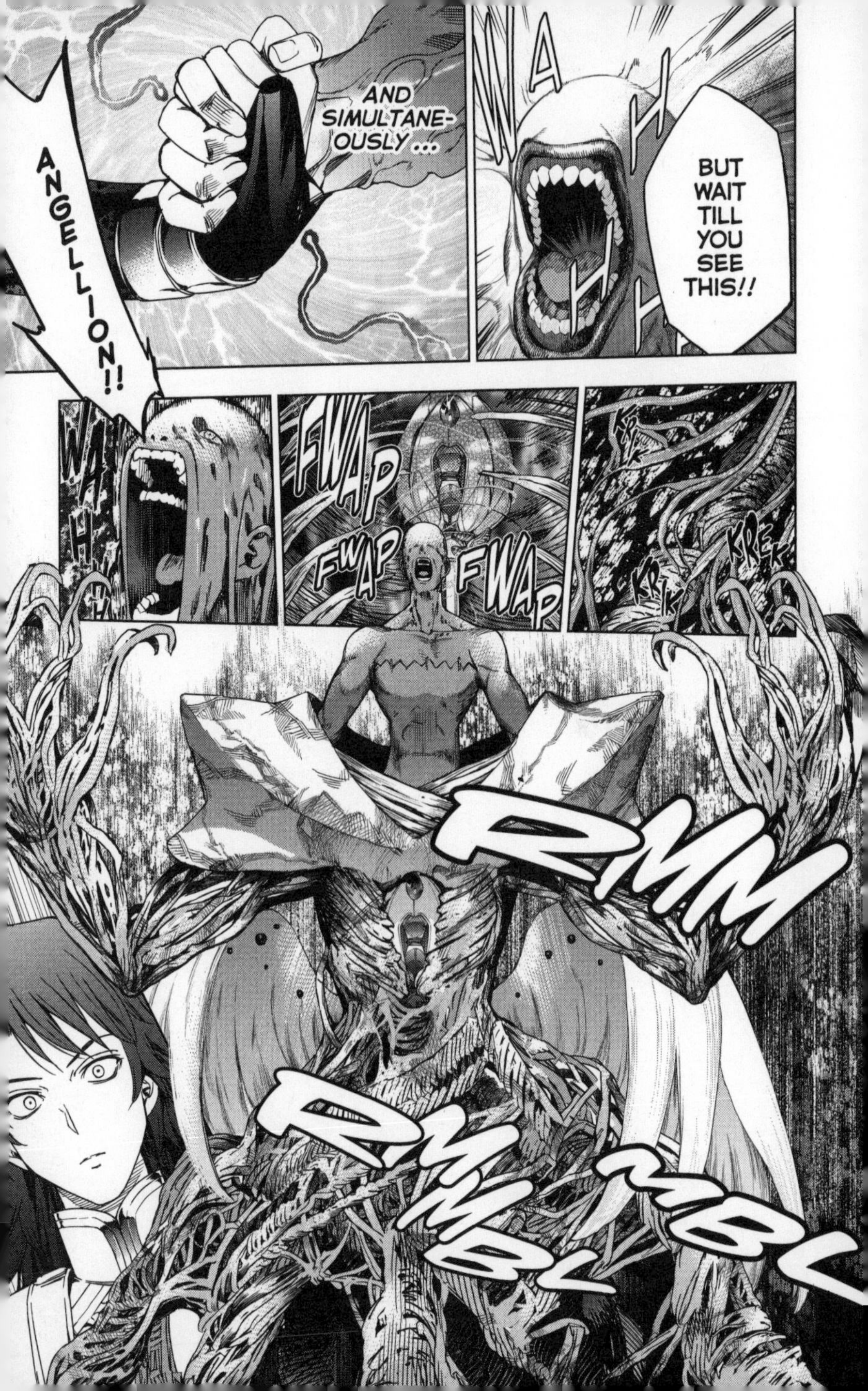
WAHHHH
BUT WAIT TILL YOU SEE THIS!!
AND SIMULTANEOUSLY ...
ANGELLION!!
KREK
KRIK
FWAP
FWAP
FWAP
WAH
RMM
RMMBL
RMMBL

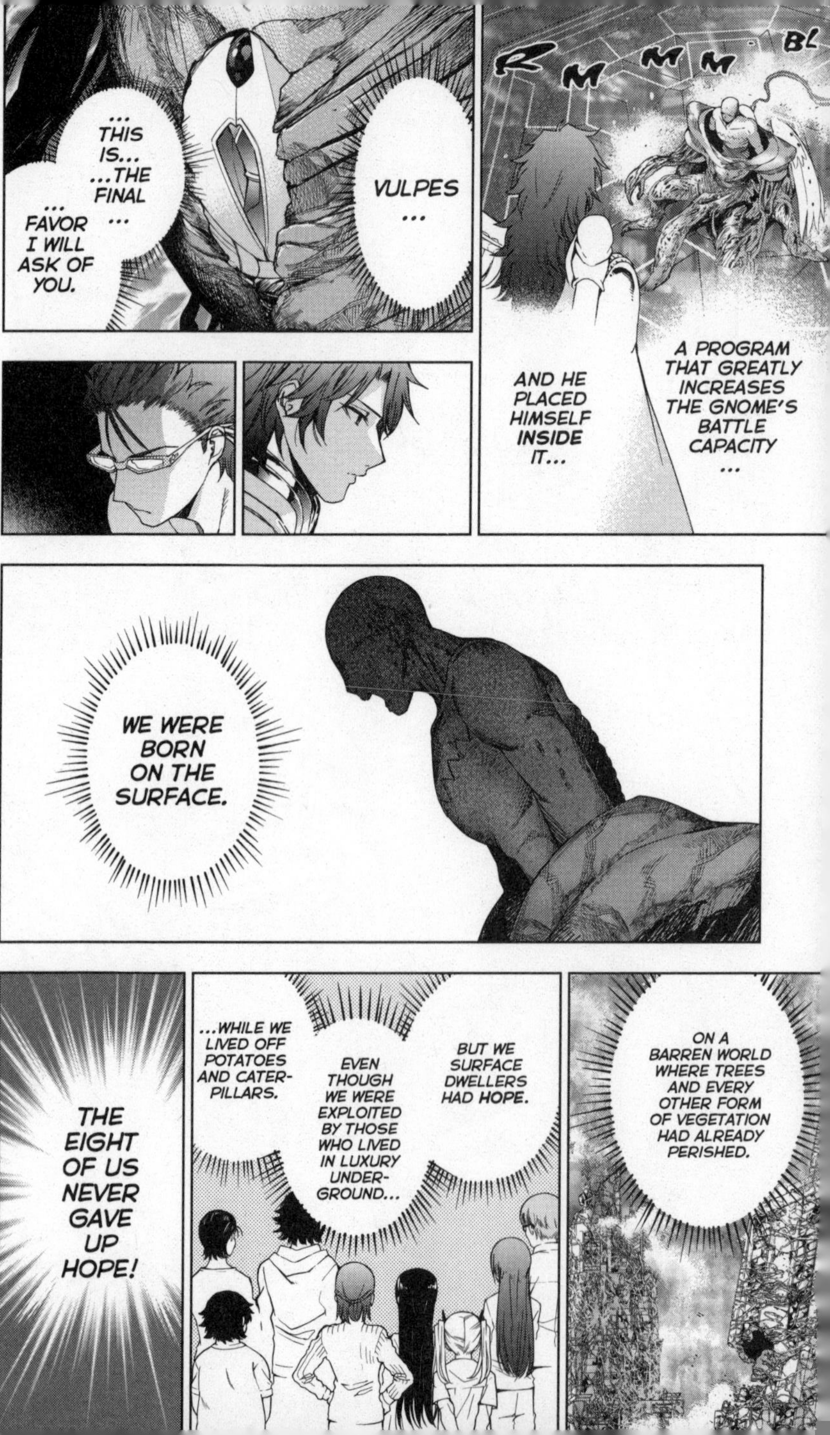
RMMM-BL
VULPES ...
... THIS IS... ...THE FINAL ... ... FAVOR I WILL ASK OF YOU.
A PROGRAM THAT GREATLY INCREASES THE GNOME'S BATTLE CAPACITY ...
AND HE PLACED HIMSELF INSIDE IT...
WE WERE BORN ON THE SURFACE.
ON A BARREN WORLD WHERE TREES AND EVERY OTHER FORM OF VEGETATION HAD ALREADY PERISHED.
BUT WE SURFACE DWELLERS HAD HOPE.
EVEN THOUGH WE WERE EXPLOITED BY THOSE WHO LIVED IN LUXURY UNDER-GROUND...
...WHILE WE LIVED OFF POTATOES AND CATER-PILLARS.
THE EIGHT OF US NEVER GAVE UP HOPE!

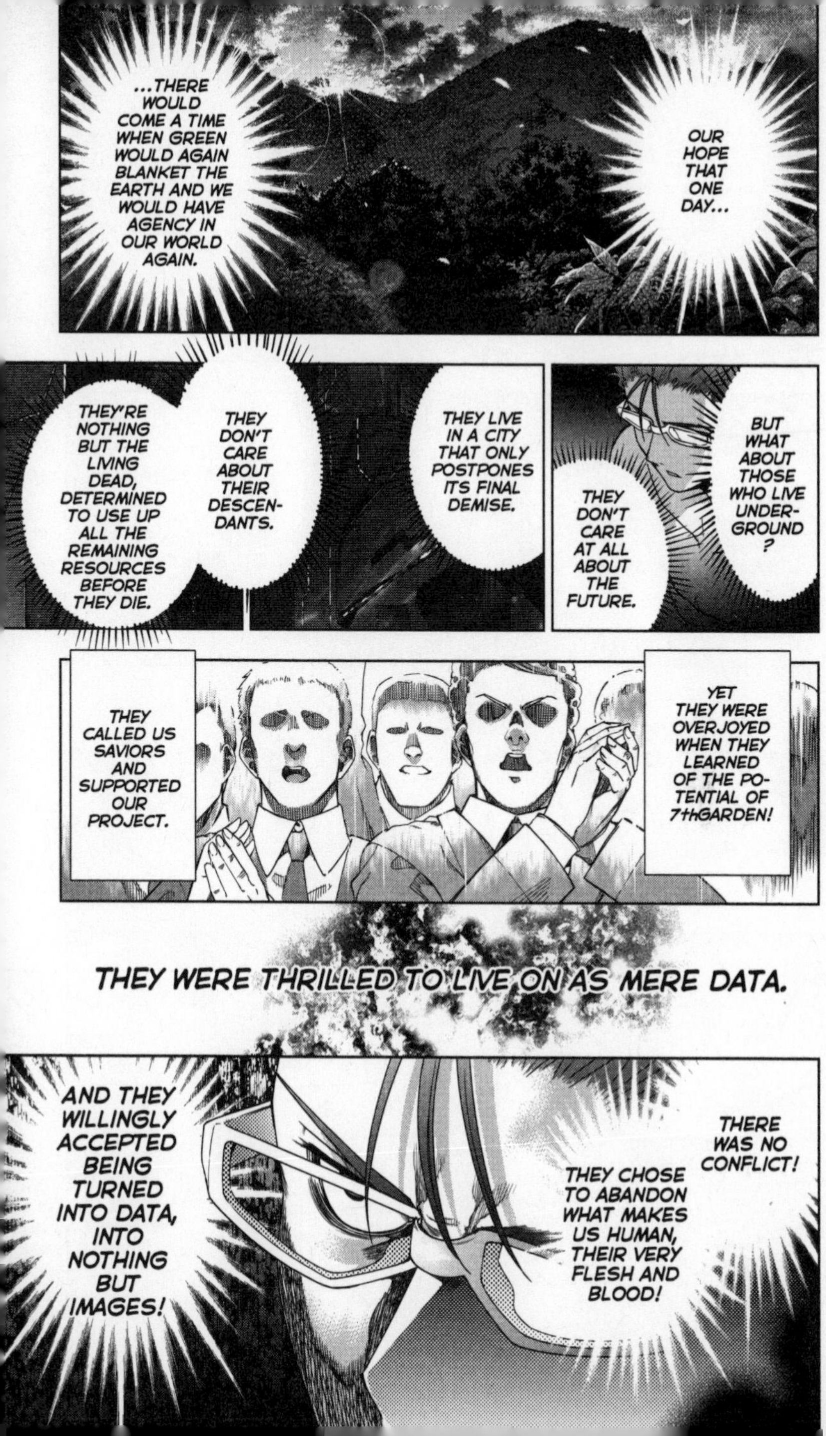
OUR HOPE THAT ONE DAY...
...THERE WOULD COME A TIME WHEN GREEN WOULD AGAIN BLANKET THE EARTH AND WE WOULD HAVE AGENCY IN OUR WORLD AGAIN.
BUT WHAT ABOUT THOSE WHO LIVE UNDER-GROUND?
THEY DON'T CARE AT ALL ABOUT THE FUTURE.
THEY LIVE IN A CITY THAT ONLY POSTPONES ITS FINAL DEMISE.
THEY DON'T CARE ABOUT THEIR DESCEN-DANTS.
THEY'RE NOTHING BUT THE LIVING DEAD, DETERMINED TO USE UP ALL THE REMAINING RESOURCES BEFORE THEY DIE.
YET THEY WERE OVERJOYED WHEN THEY LEARNED OF THE PO-TENTIAL OF 7thGARDEN!
THEY CALLED US SAVIORS AND SUPPORTED OUR PROJECT.
THEY WERE THRILLED TO LIVE ON AS MERE DATA.
THERE WAS NO CONFLICT!
THEY CHOSE TO ABANDON WHAT MAKES US HUMAN, THEIR VERY FLESH AND BLOOD!
AND THEY WILLINGLY ACCEPTED BEING TURNED INTO DATA, INTO NOTHING BUT IMAGES!

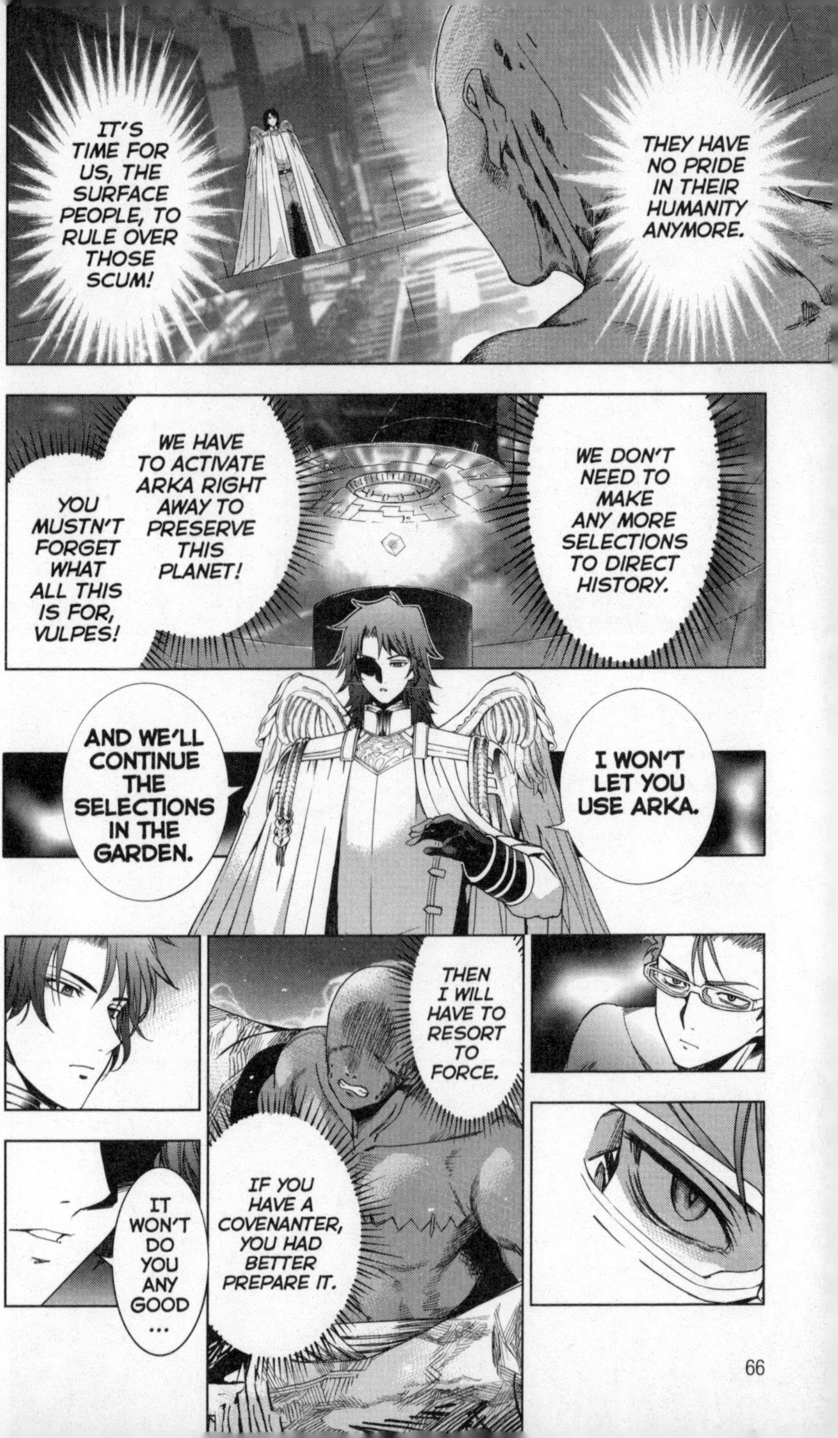
THEY HAVE NO PRIDE IN THEIR HUMANITY ANYMORE.
IT'S TIME FOR US, THE SURFACE PEOPLE, TO RULE OVER THOSE SCUM!
WE DON'T NEED TO MAKE ANY MORE SELECTIONS TO DIRECT HISTORY.
WE HAVE TO ACTIVATE ARKA RIGHT AWAY TO PRESERVE THIS PLANET!
YOU MUSTN'T FORGET WHAT ALL THIS IS FOR, VULPES!
I WON'T LET YOU USE ARKA.
AND WE'LL CONTINUE THE SELECTIONS IN THE GARDEN.
THEN I WILL HAVE TO RESORT TO FORCE.
IF YOU HAVE A COVENANTER, YOU HAD BETTER PREPARE IT.
IT WON'T DO YOU ANY GOOD ...

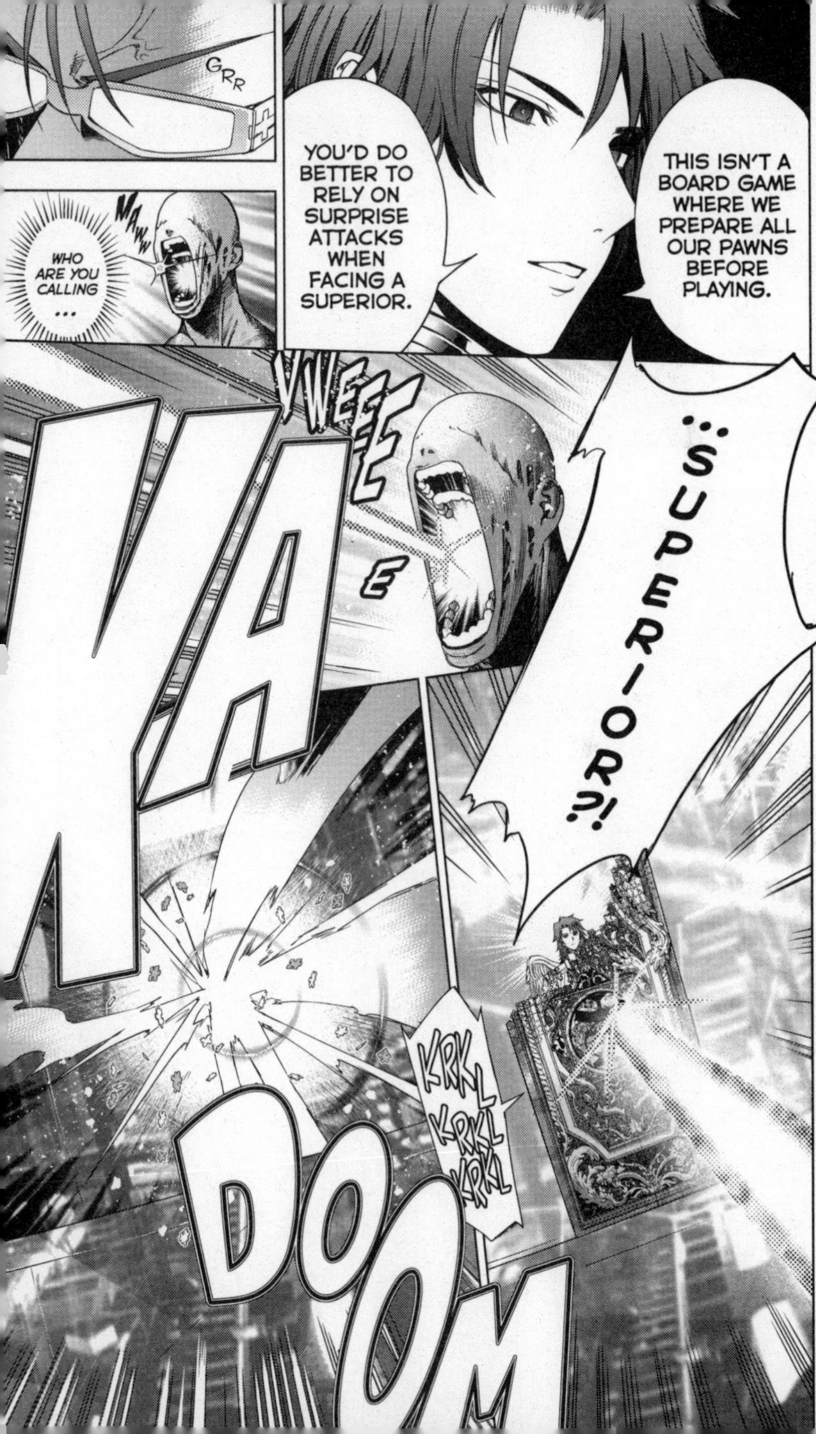
THIS ISN'T A BOARD GAME WHERE WE PREPARE ALL OUR PAWNS BEFORE PLAYING.
YOU'D DO BETTER TO RELY ON SURPRISE ATTACKS WHEN FACING A SUPERIOR.
GRR
MAWW
WHO ARE YOU CALLING ...
...SUPERIOR?!
VWEEE
WA
KRKL KRKL KRKL
DOOM

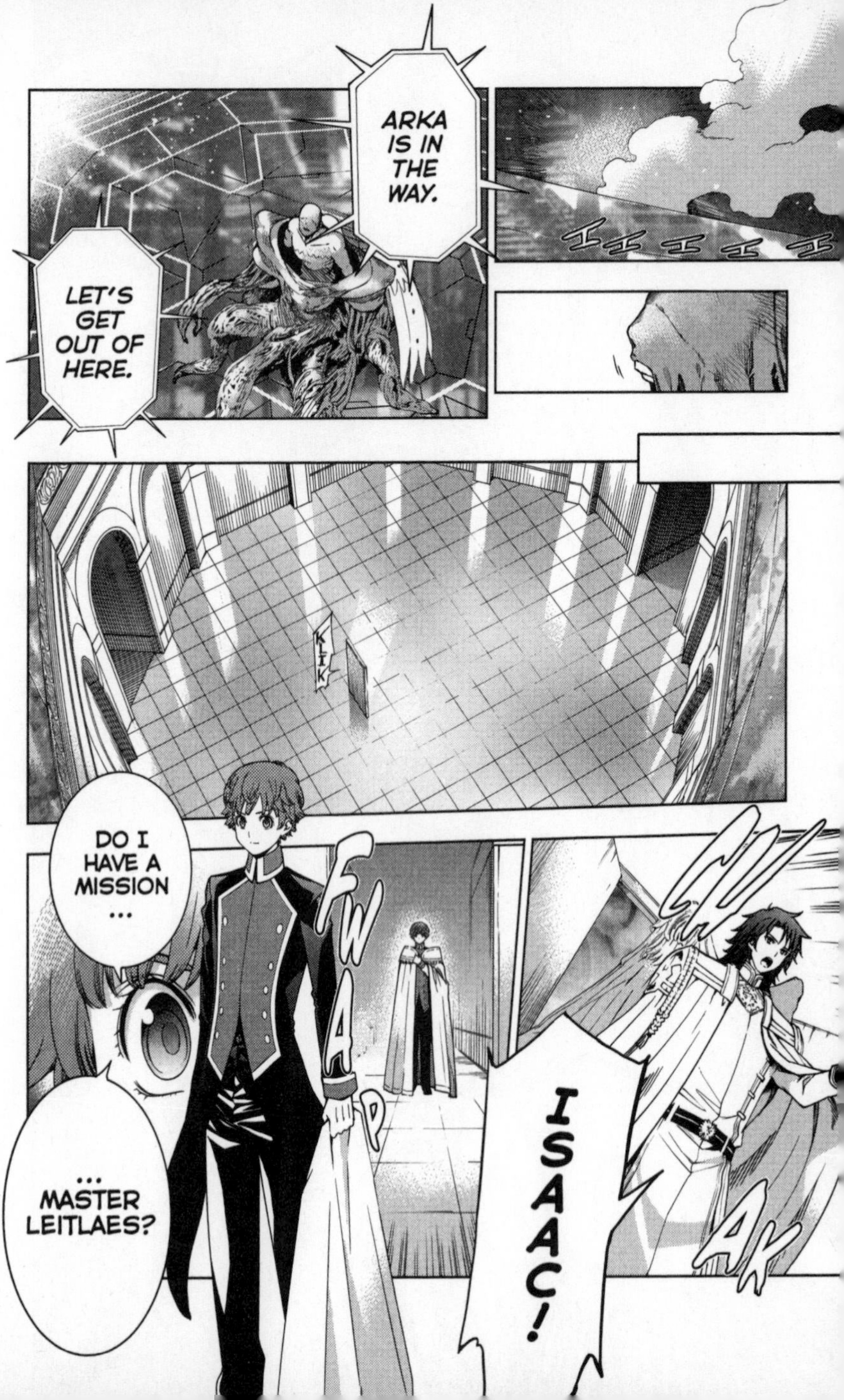
ARKA IS IN THE WAY.
LET'S GET OUT OF HERE.
KLIK
ISAAC!
DO I HAVE A MISSION ...
FWAP
... MASTER LEITLAES?

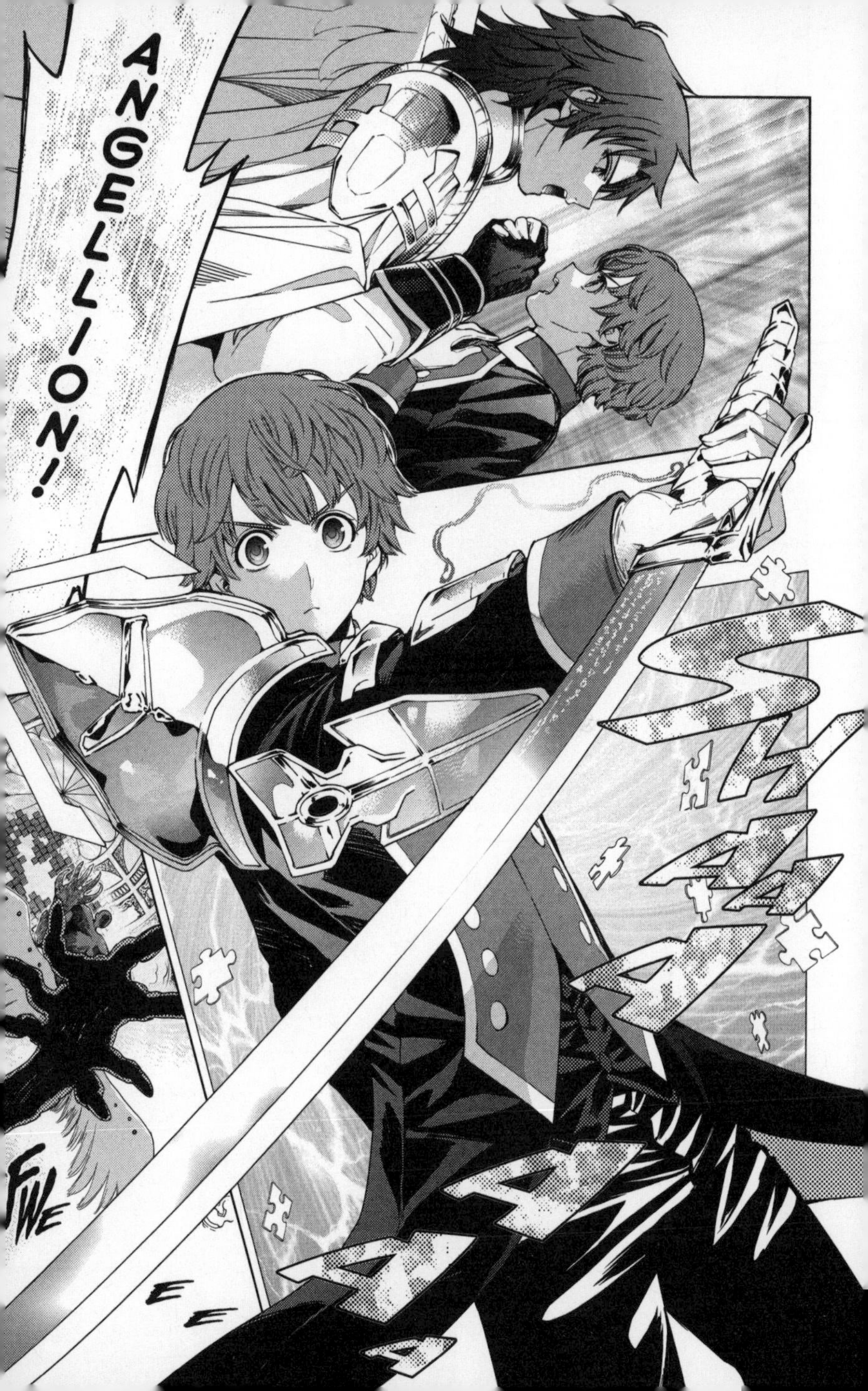
ANGELLION!
SHAAAAAAA
FWEEEE

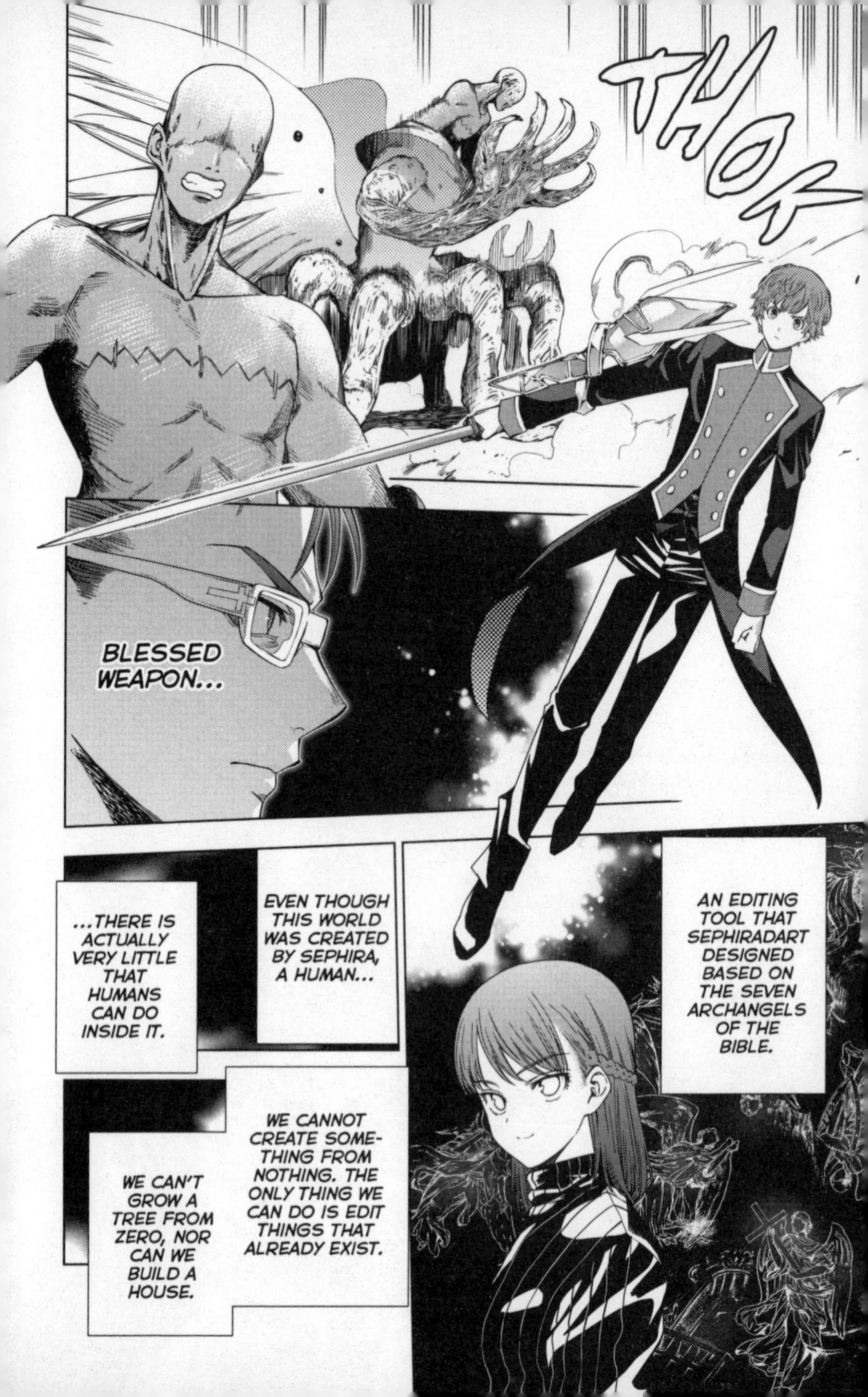
THOK
BLESSED WEAPON...
AN EDITING TOOL THAT SEPHIRADART DESIGNED BASED ON THE SEVEN ARCHANGELS OF THE BIBLE.
EVEN THOUGH THIS WORLD WAS CREATED BY SEPHIRA, A HUMAN...
...THERE IS ACTUALLY VERY LITTLE THAT HUMANS CAN DO INSIDE IT.
WE CANNOT CREATE SOME-THING FROM NOTHING. THE ONLY THING WE CAN DO IS EDIT THINGS THAT ALREADY EXIST.
WE CAN'T GROW A TREE FROM ZERO, NOR CAN WE BUILD A HOUSE.

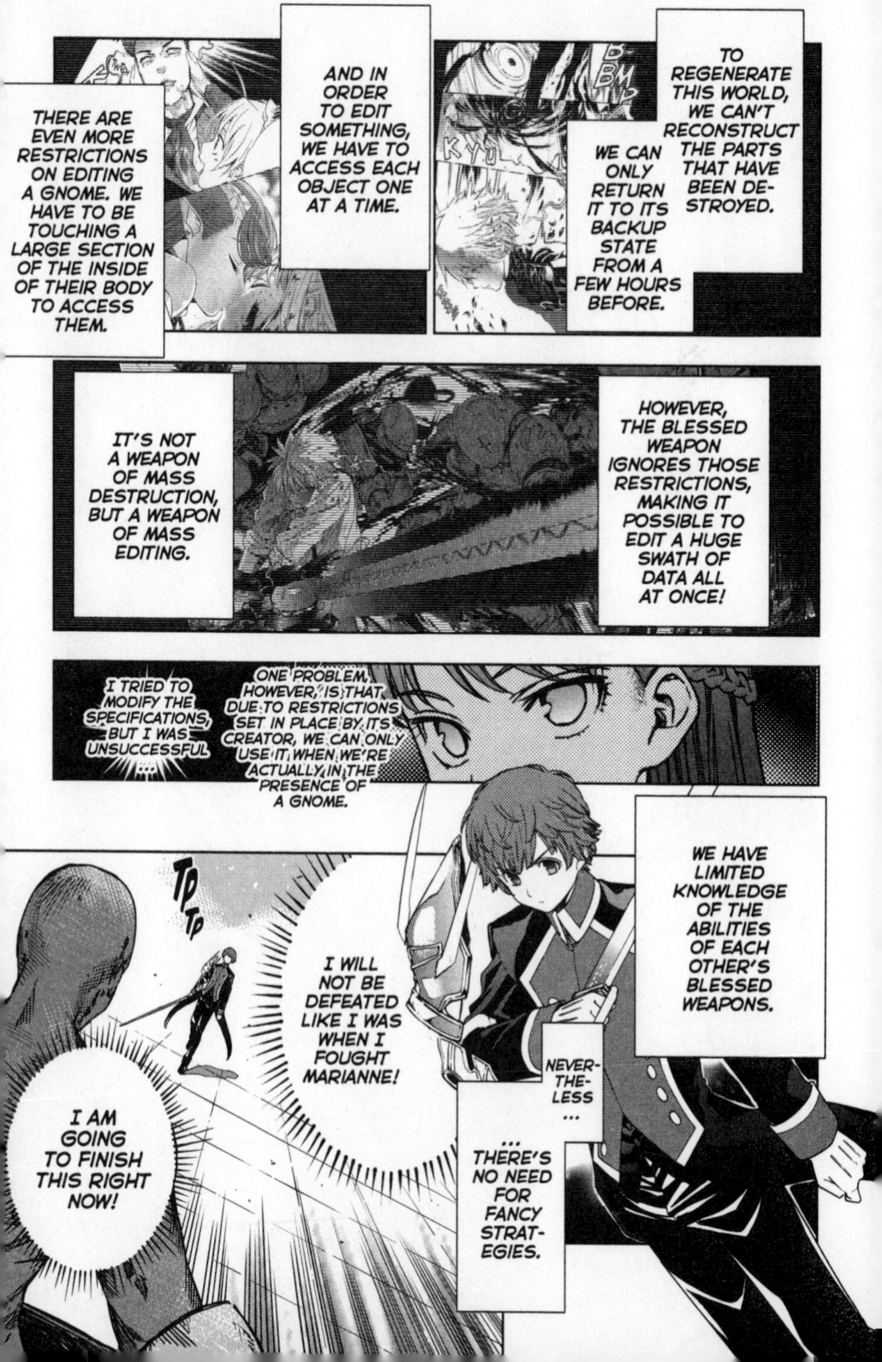
TO REGENERATE THIS WORLD, WE CAN'T RECONSTRUCT THE PARTS THAT HAVE BEEN DE-STROYED.
WE CAN ONLY RETURN IT TO ITS BACKUP STATE FROM A FEW HOURS BEFORE.
AND IN ORDER TO EDIT SOMETHING, WE HAVE TO ACCESS EACH OBJECT ONE AT A TIME.
THERE ARE EVEN MORE RESTRICTIONS ON EDITING A GNOME. WE HAVE TO BE TOUCHING A LARGE SECTION OF THE INSIDE OF THEIR BODY TO ACCESS THEM.
HOWEVER, THE BLESSED WEAPON IGNORES THOSE RESTRICTIONS, MAKING IT POSSIBLE TO EDIT A HUGE SWATH OF DATA ALL AT ONCE!
IT'S NOT A WEAPON OF MASS DESTRUCTION, BUT A WEAPON OF MASS EDITING.
ONE PROBLEM, HOWEVER, IS THAT, DUE TO RESTRICTIONS SET IN PLACE BY ITS CREATOR, WE CAN ONLY USE IT WHEN WE'RE ACTUALLY IN THE PRESENCE OF A GNOME.
I TRIED TO MODIFY THE SPECIFICATIONS, BUT I WAS UNSUCCESSFUL...
WE HAVE LIMITED KNOWLEDGE OF THE ABILITIES OF EACH OTHER'S BLESSED WEAPONS.
NEVER-THE-LESS...
...THERE'S NO NEED FOR FANCY STRAT-EGIES.
I WILL NOT BE DEFEATED LIKE I WAS WHEN I FOUGHT MARIANNE!
TP TP
I AM GOING TO FINISH THIS RIGHT NOW!

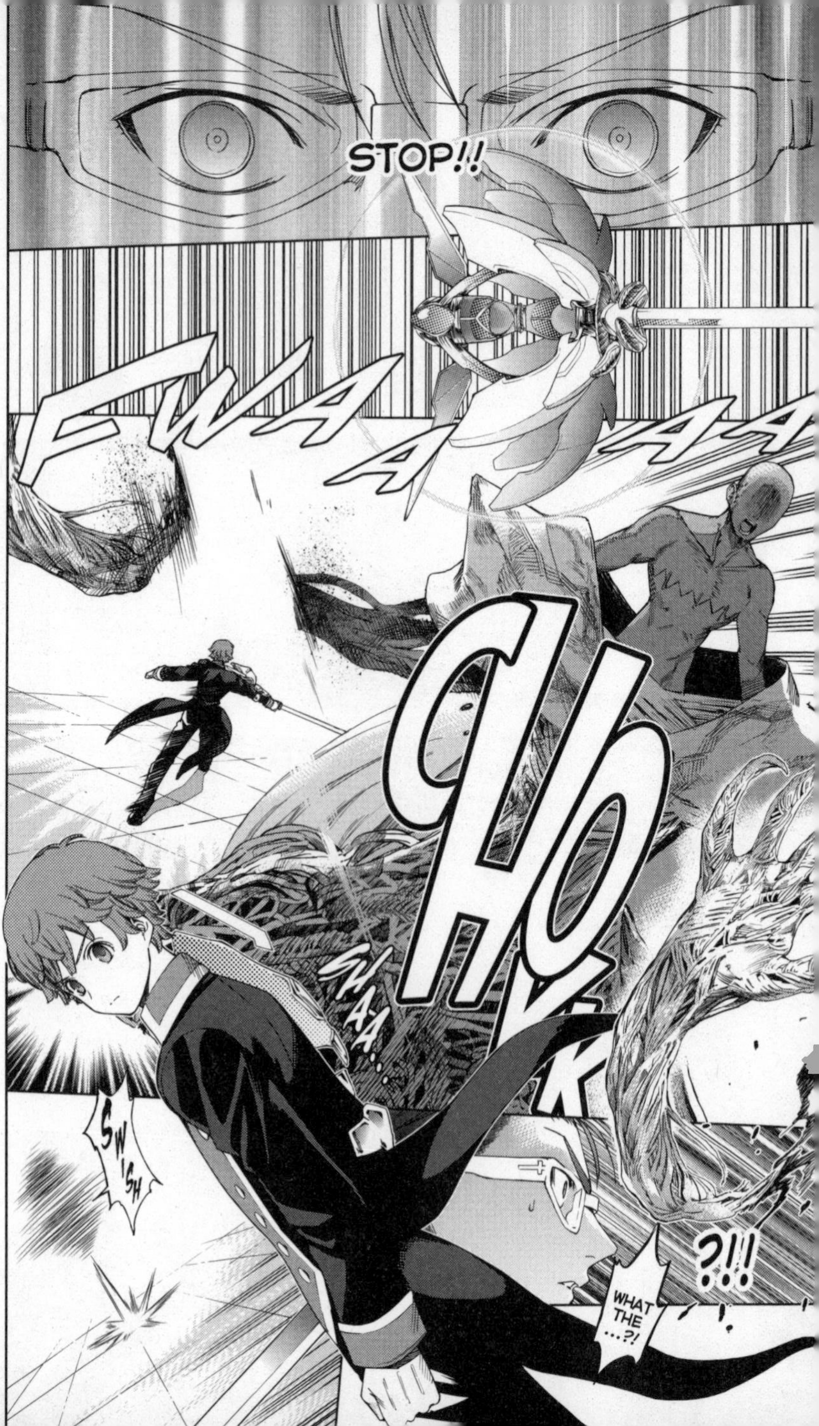
STOP!!
FWAAAAA
CHOK
SWAA...
SWISH
?!!!
WHAT THE ...?!

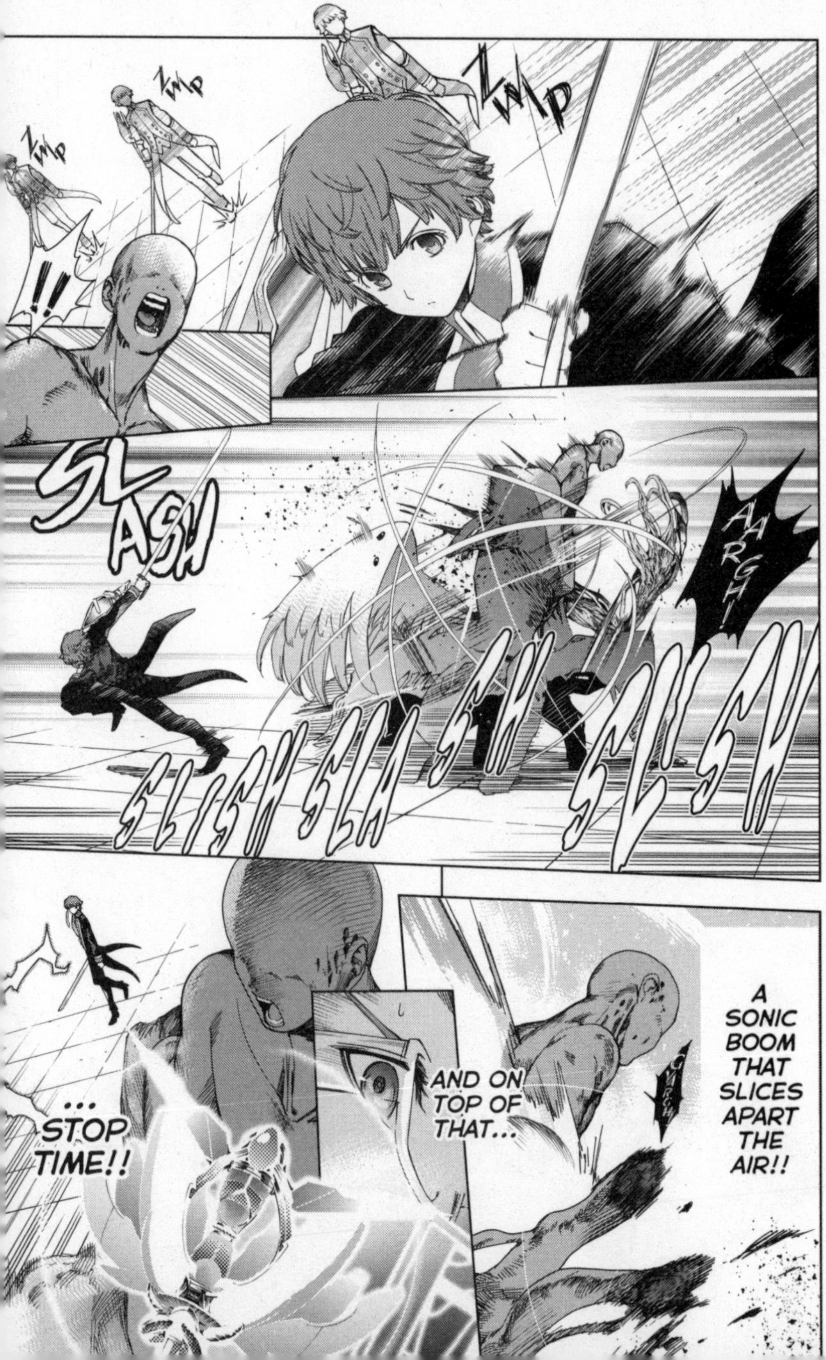
ZWIP
ZWIP
ZWIP
!!
AARGH!
SLASH
A SONIC BOOM THAT SLICES APART THE AIR!!
AND ON TOP OF THAT...
...STOP TIME!!

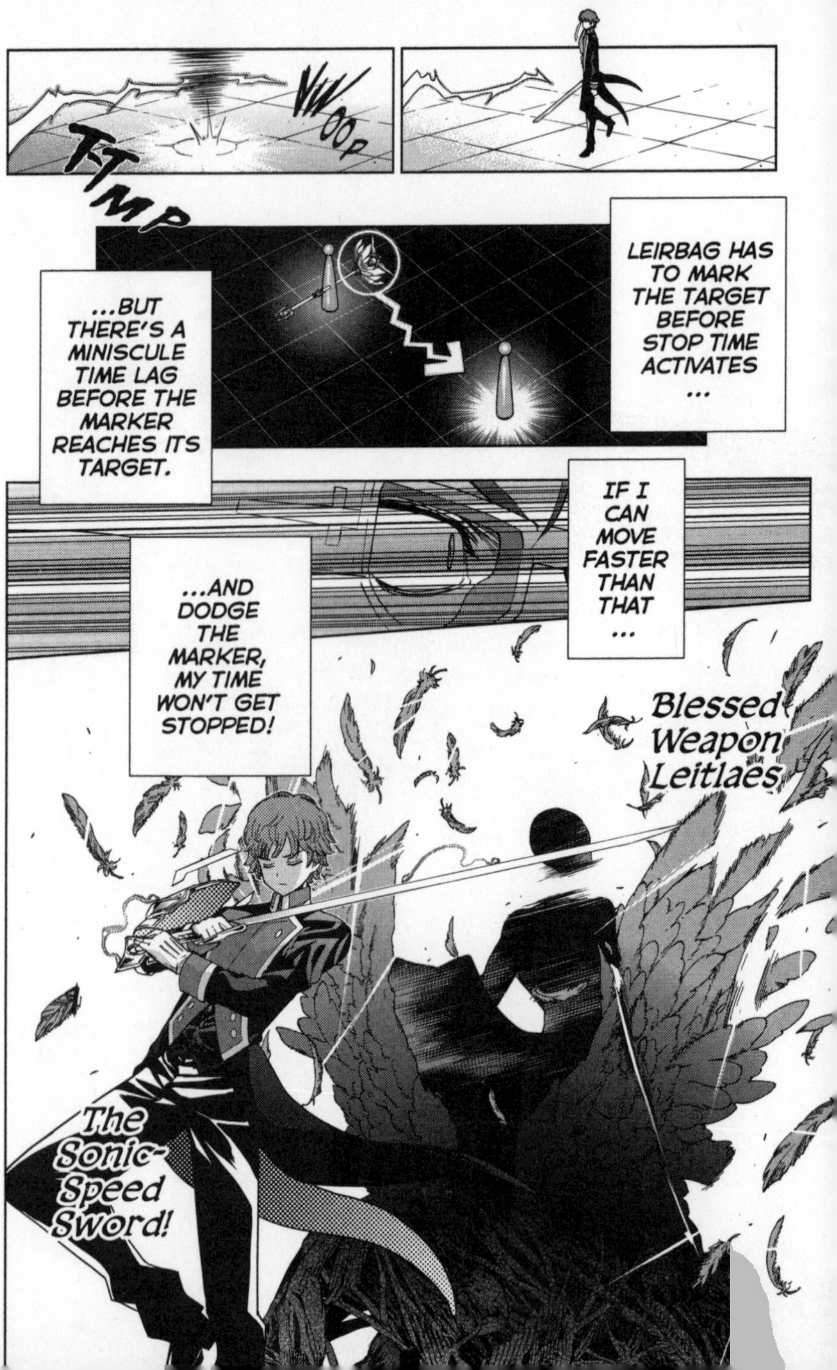
VWOOP
TTMP
LEIRBAG HAS TO MARK THE TARGET BEFORE STOP TIME ACTIVATES...
...BUT THERE'S A MINISCULE TIME LAG BEFORE THE MARKER REACHES ITS TARGET.
IF I CAN MOVE FASTER THAN THAT...
...AND DODGE THE MARKER, MY TIME WON'T GET STOPPED!
Blessed Weapon Leitlaes
The Sonic-Speed Sword!

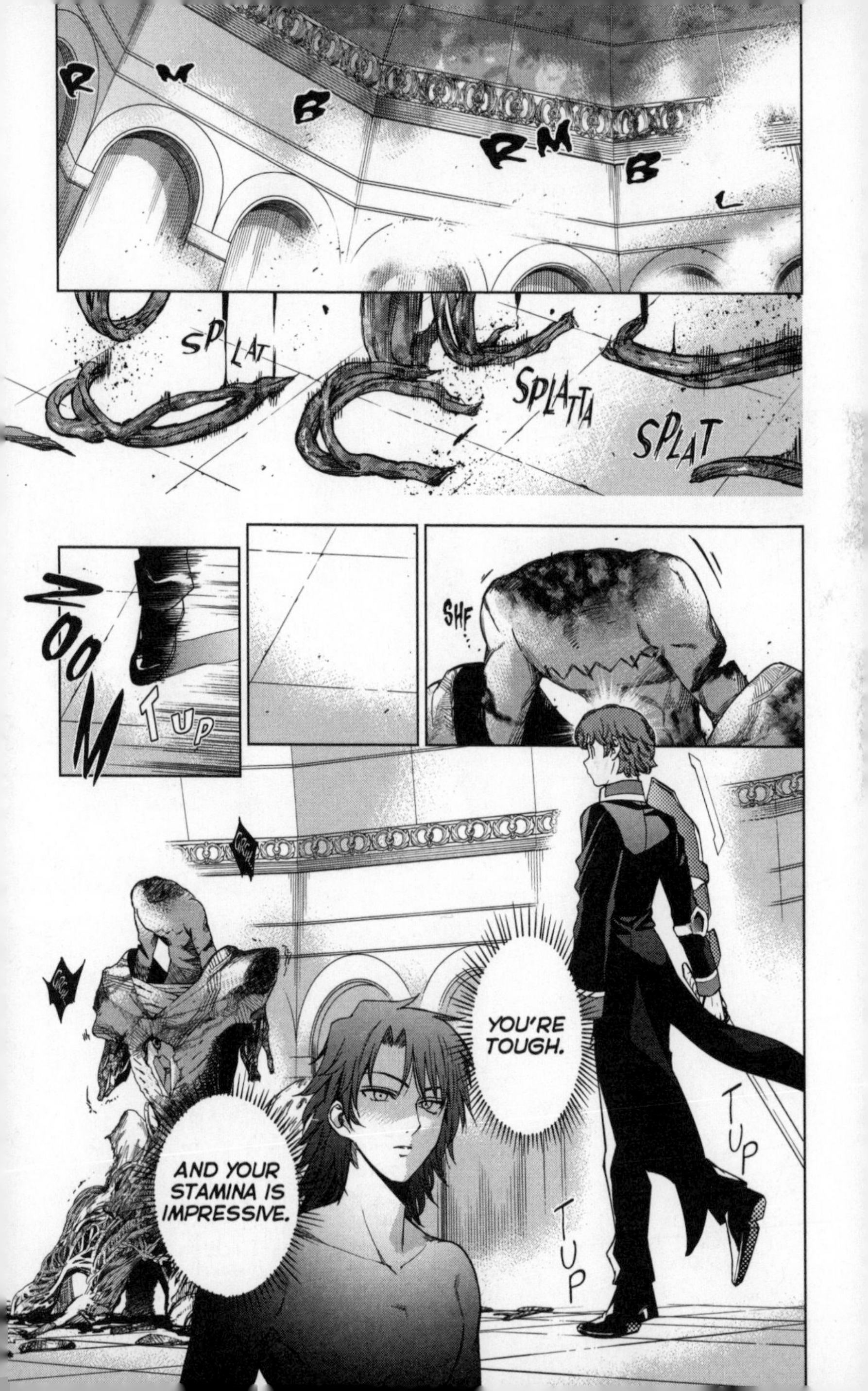
RMB
RMBL
SPLAT
SPLATTA
SPLAT
SHF
ZOOM
TUP
YOU'RE TOUGH.
AND YOUR STAMINA IS IMPRESSIVE.
TUP
TUP

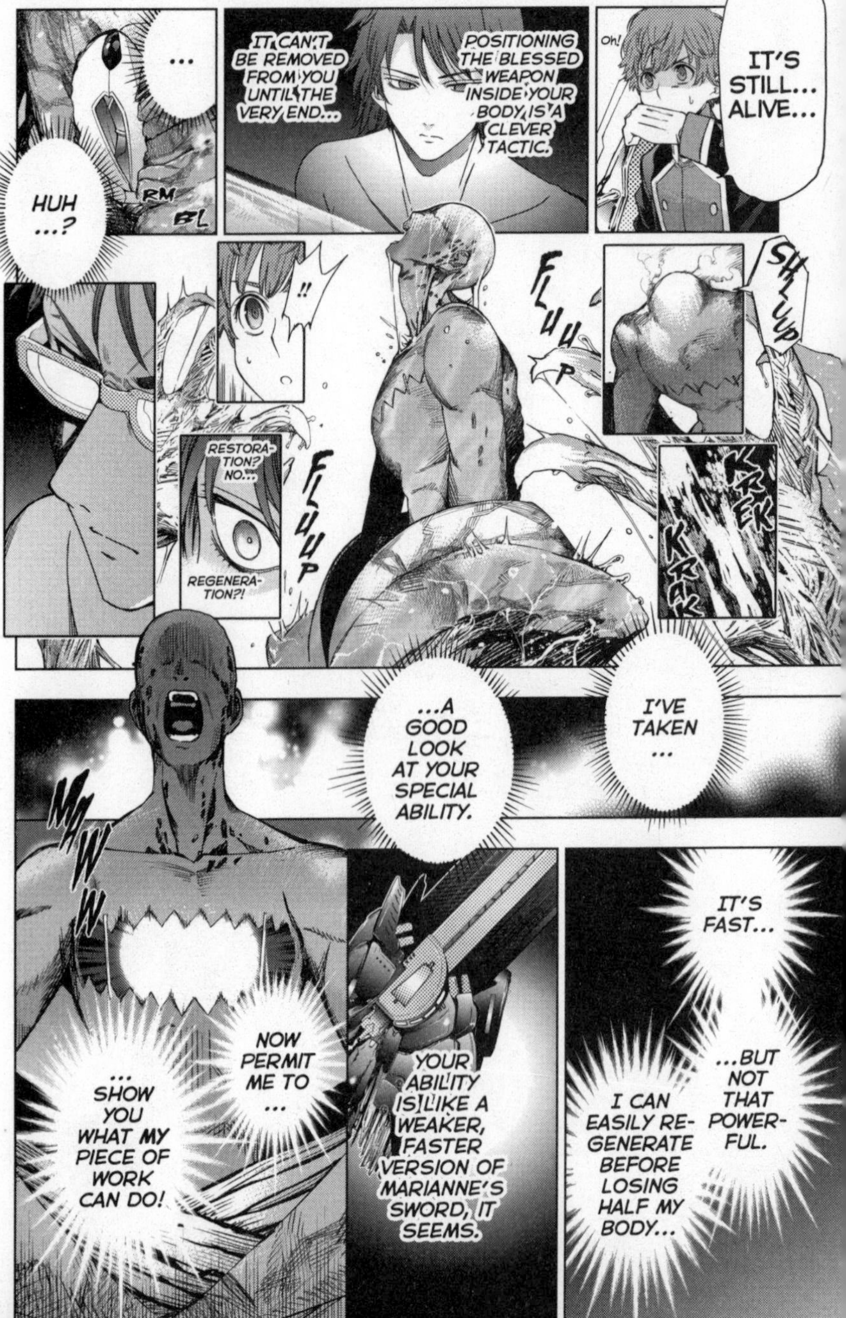
Oh!
IT'S STILL... ALIVE...
POSITIONING THE BLESSED WEAPON INSIDE YOUR BODY IS A CLEVER TACTIC.
IT CAN'T BE REMOVED FROM YOU UNTIL THE VERY END...
...
RM
BL
HUH ...?
SHLUP
KREK
KRAK
FLUUP
!!
RESTORATION? NO...
REGENERATION?!
FLUUP
I'VE TAKEN ...
...A GOOD LOOK AT YOUR SPECIAL ABILITY.
MAWWW
IT'S FAST...
...BUT NOT THAT POWERFUL.
I CAN EASILY REGENERATE BEFORE LOSING HALF MY BODY...
YOUR ABILITY IS LIKE A WEAKER, FASTER VERSION OF MARIANNE'S SWORD, IT SEEMS.
NOW PERMIT ME TO ...
... SHOW YOU WHAT MY PIECE OF WORK CAN DO!

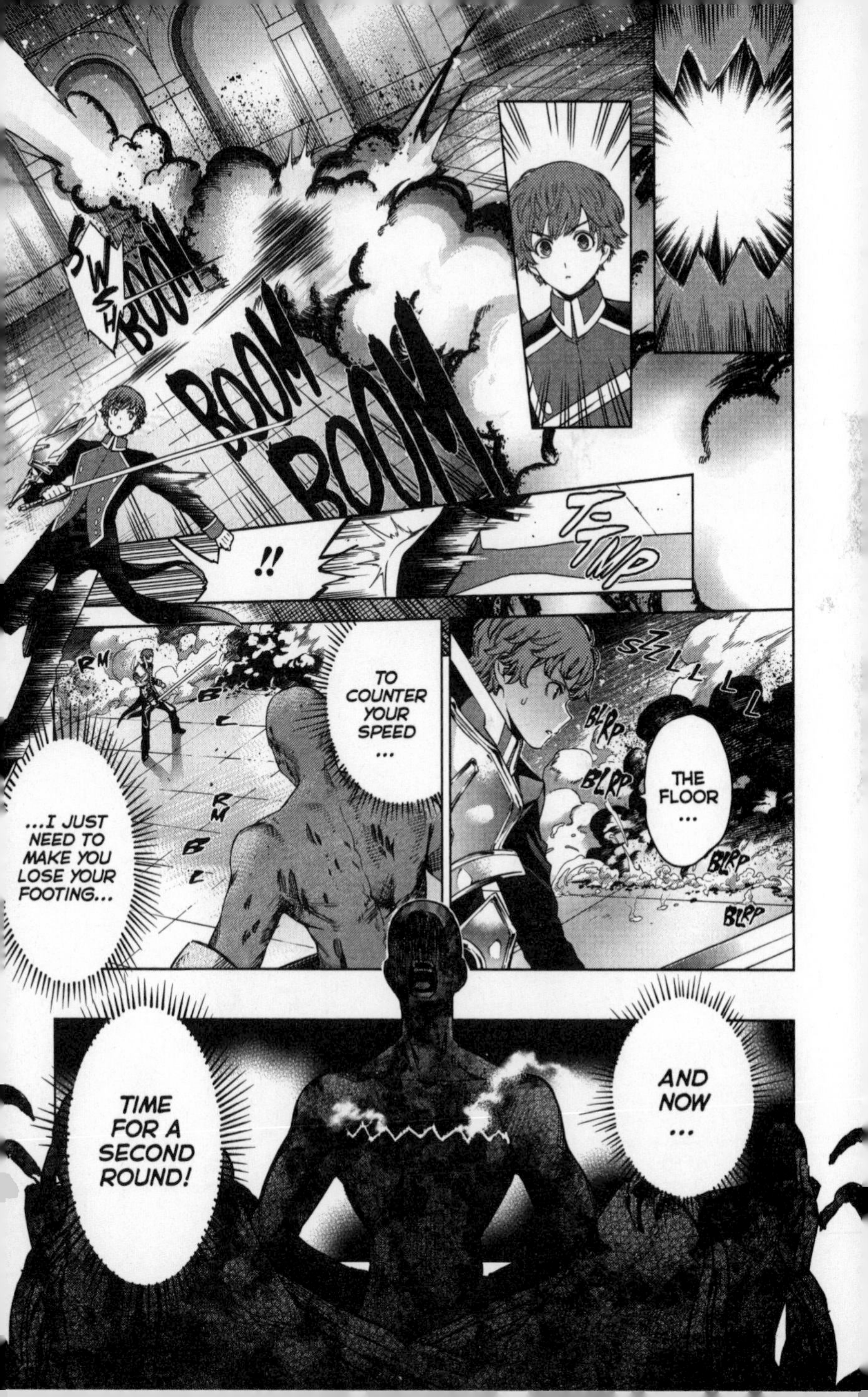
SWSH
BOOM
BOOM
BOOM
!!
T-TMP
SZZLLLL
BLRP
BLRP
THE FLOOR...
BLRP
BLRP
TO COUNTER YOUR SPEED...
RMBL
...I JUST NEED TO MAKE YOU LOSE YOUR FOOTING...
RMBL
AND NOW...
TIME FOR A SECOND ROUND!

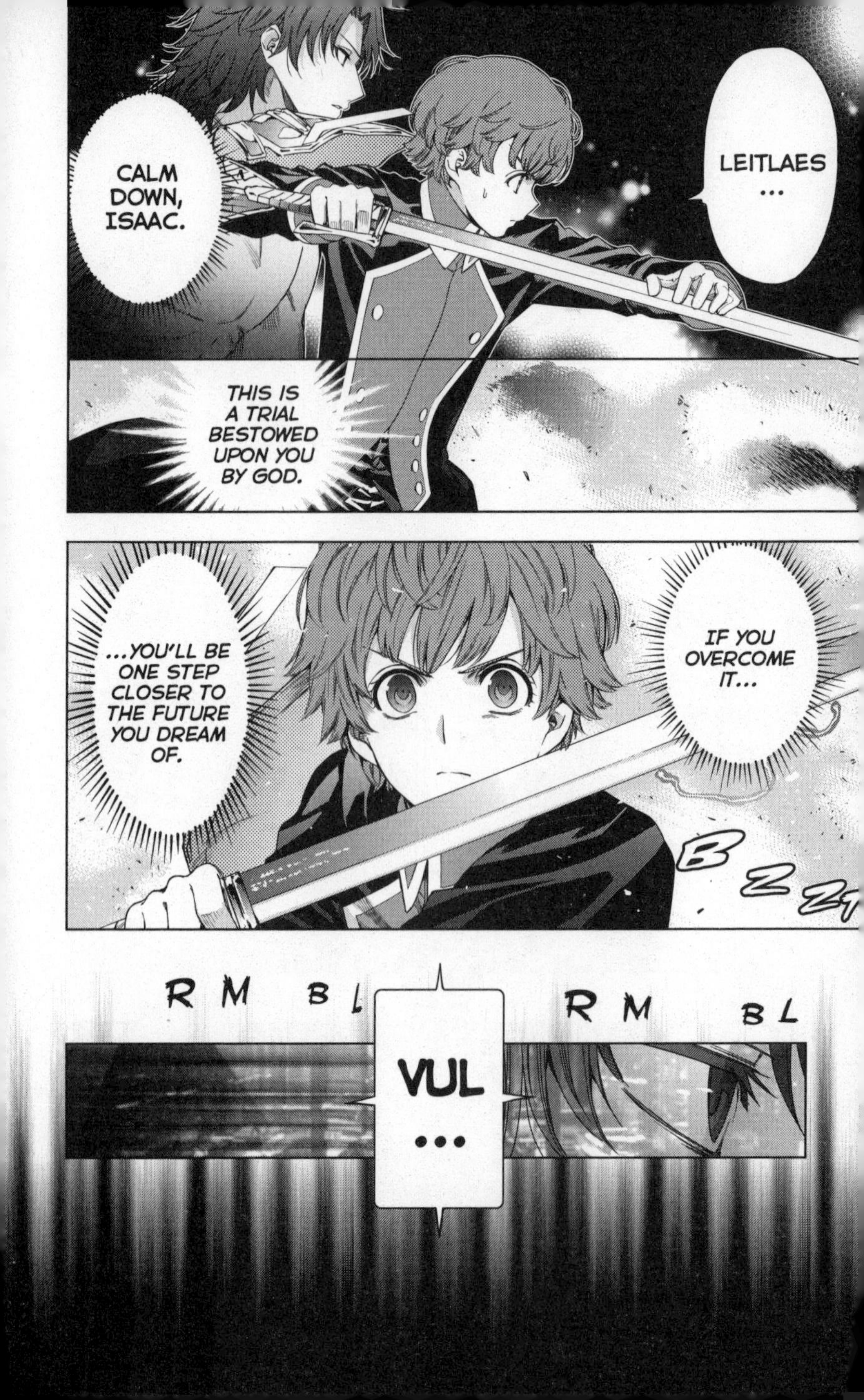
LEITLAES ...
CALM DOWN, ISAAC.
THIS IS A TRIAL BESTOWED UPON YOU BY GOD.
IF YOU OVERCOME IT...
...YOU'LL BE ONE STEP CLOSER TO THE FUTURE YOU DREAM OF.
BZZT
RMBL
RMBL
VUL ...

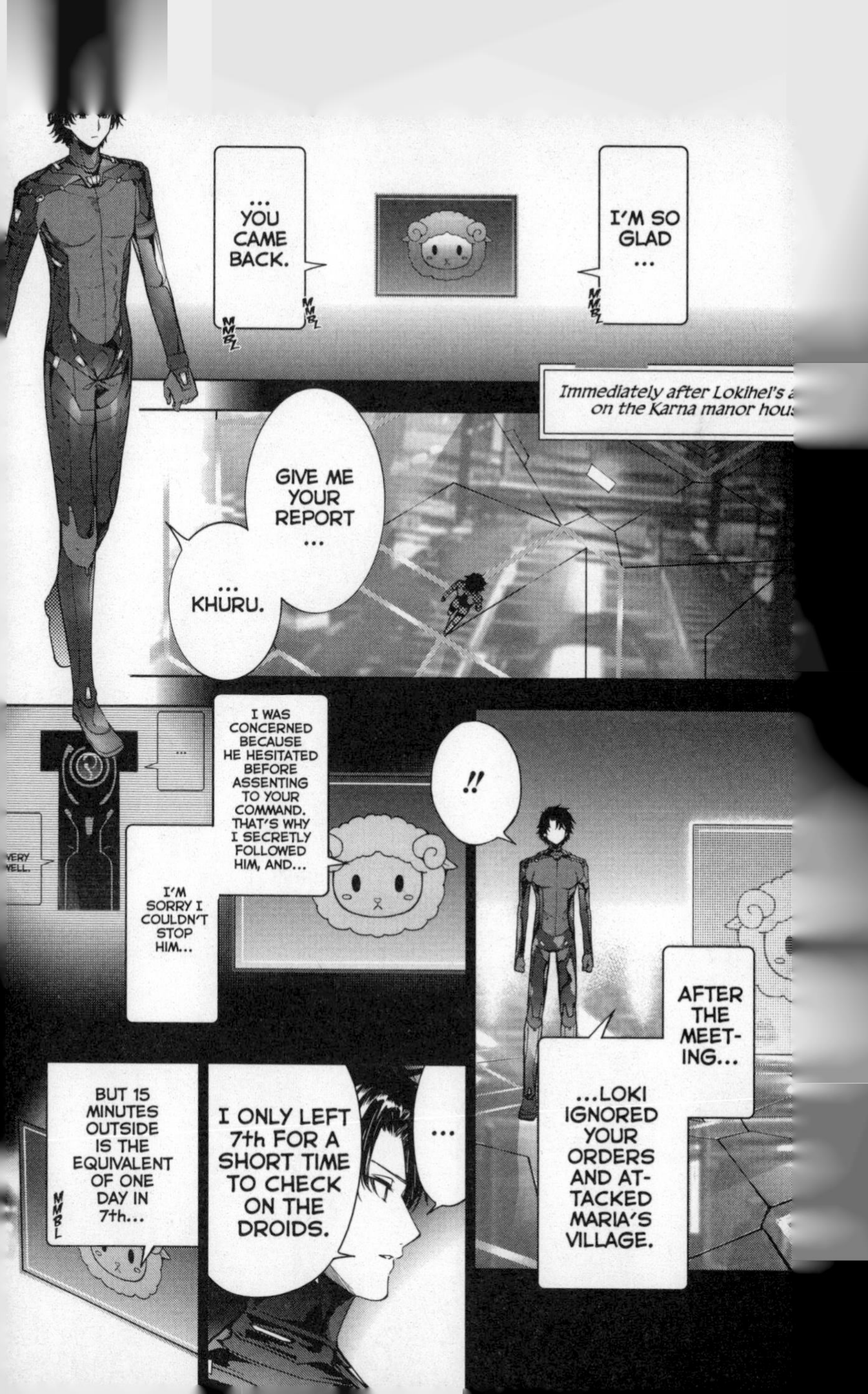
I'M SO GLAD ...
MMBL
...YOU CAME BACK.
MMBL
MMBL
Immediately after Lokihel's
on the Karna manor
GIVE ME YOUR REPORT ...
...KHURU.
!!
AFTER THE MEET-ING...
...LOKI IGNORED YOUR ORDERS AND AT-TACKED MARIA'S VILLAGE.
I WAS CONCERNED BECAUSE HE HESITATED BEFORE ASSENTING TO YOUR COMMAND. THAT'S WHY I SECRETLY FOLLOWED HIM, AND...
I'M SORRY I COULDN'T STOP HIM...
...
VERY WELL.
...
I ONLY LEFT 7th FOR A SHORT TIME TO CHECK ON THE DROIDS.
BUT 15 MINUTES OUTSIDE IS THE EQUIVALENT OF ONE DAY IN 7th...
MMBL

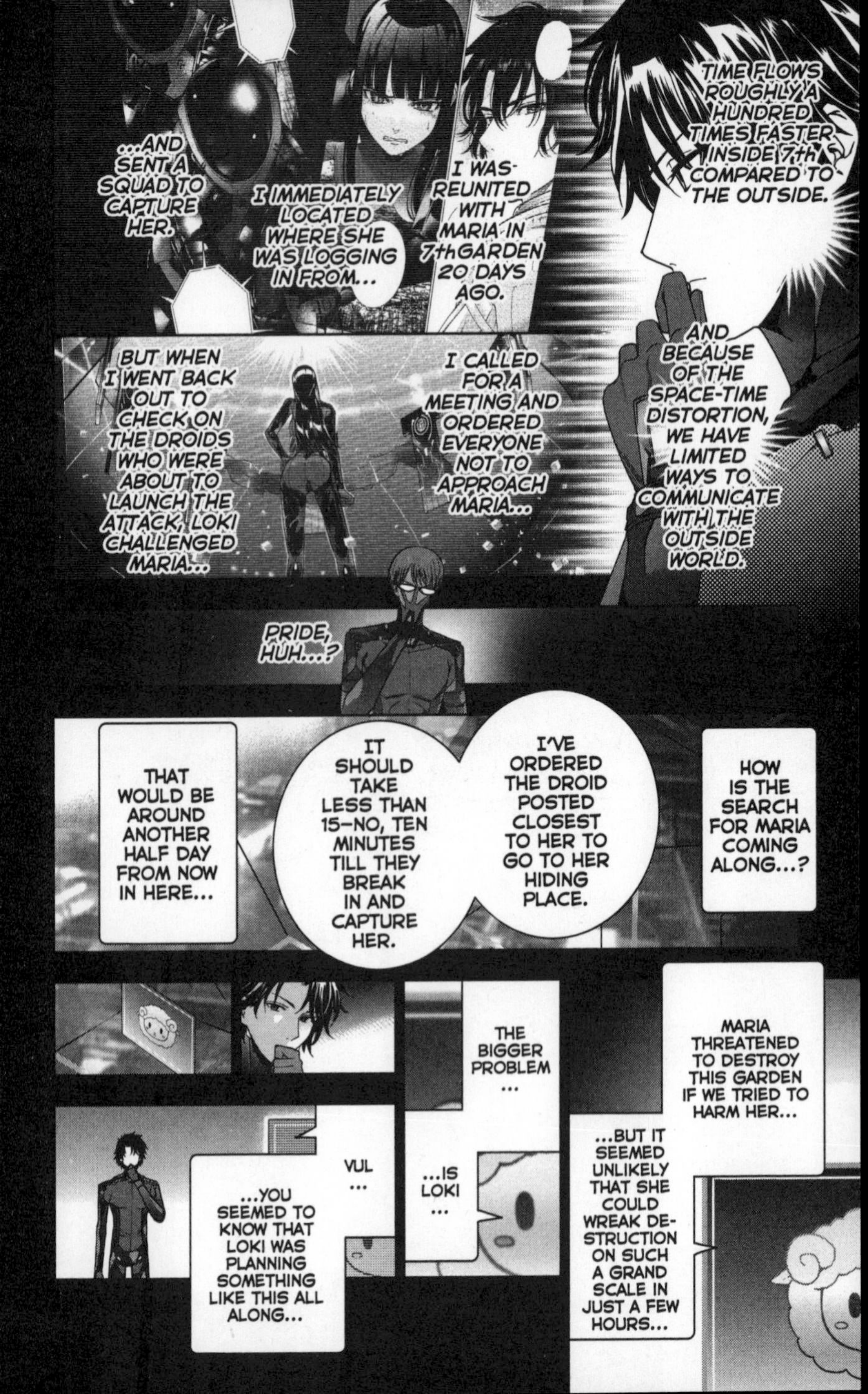

TIME FLOWS ROUGHLY A HUNDRED TIMES FASTER INSIDE 7th COMPARED TO THE OUTSIDE.
AND BECAUSE OF THE SPACE-TIME DISTORTION, WE HAVE LIMITED WAYS TO COMMUNICATE WITH THE OUTSIDE WORLD.
I WAS REUNITED WITH MARIA IN 7th GARDEN 20 DAYS AGO.
I IMMEDIATELY LOCATED WHERE SHE WAS LOGGING IN FROM...
...AND SENT A SQUAD TO CAPTURE HER.
I CALLED FOR A MEETING AND ORDERED EVERYONE NOT TO APPROACH MARIA...
BUT WHEN I WENT BACK OUT TO CHECK ON THE DROIDS WHO WERE ABOUT TO LAUNCH THE ATTACK, LOKI CHALLENGED MARIA...
PRIDE, HUH...?
HOW IS THE SEARCH FOR MARIA COMING ALONG...?
I'VE ORDERED THE DROID POSTED CLOSEST TO HER TO GO TO HER HIDING PLACE.
IT SHOULD TAKE LESS THAN 15—NO, TEN MINUTES TILL THEY BREAK IN AND CAPTURE HER.
THAT WOULD BE AROUND ANOTHER HALF DAY FROM NOW IN HERE...
MARIA THREATENED TO DESTROY THIS GARDEN IF WE TRIED TO HARM HER...
...BUT IT SEEMED UNLIKELY THAT SHE COULD WREAK DESTRUCTION ON SUCH A GRAND SCALE IN JUST A FEW HOURS...
THE BIGGER PROBLEM...
...IS LOKI...
VUL...
...YOU SEEMED TO KNOW THAT LOKI WAS PLANNING SOMETHING LIKE THIS ALL ALONG...

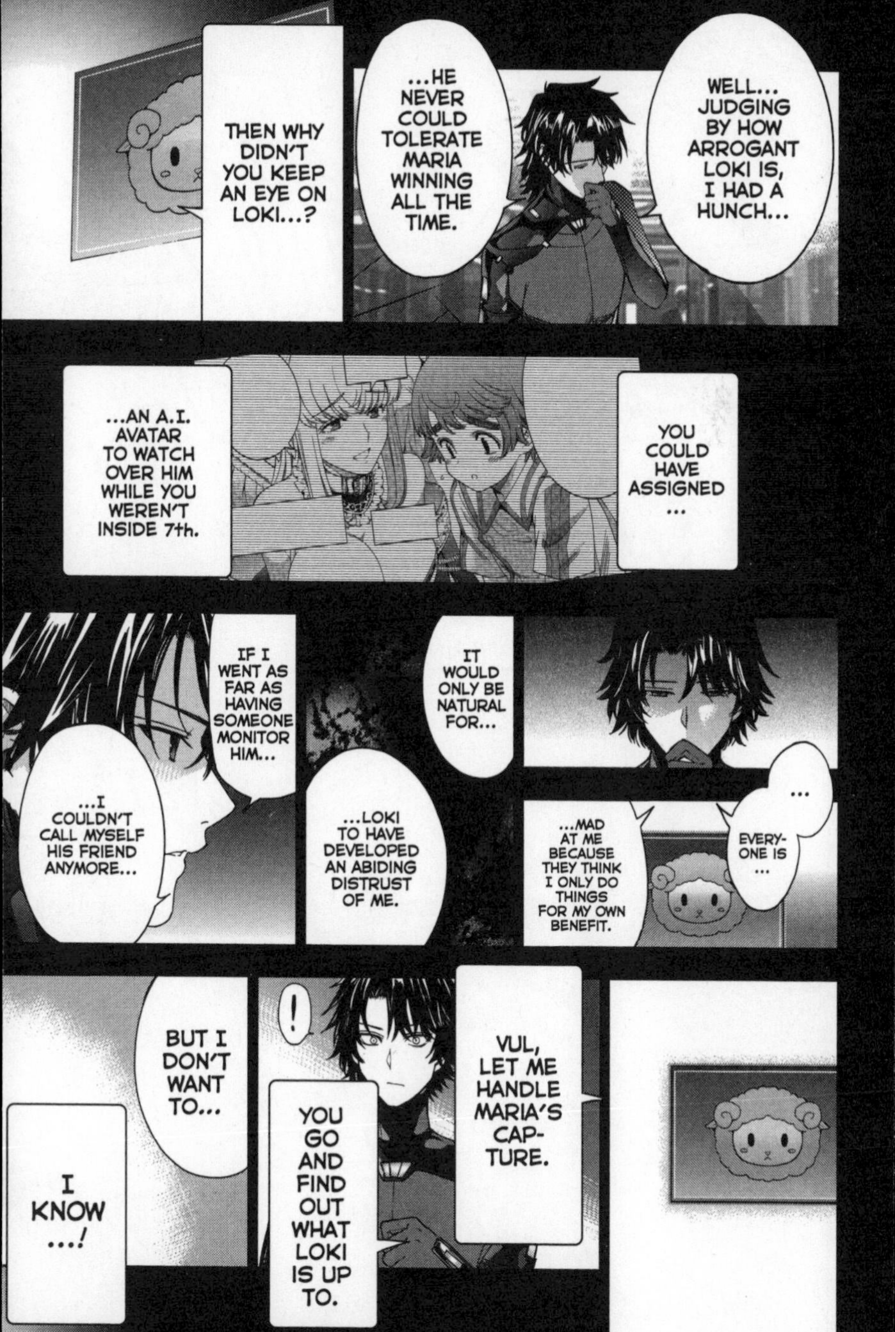
WELL... JUDGING BY HOW ARROGANT LOKI IS, I HAD A HUNCH...
...HE NEVER COULD TOLERATE MARIA WINNING ALL THE TIME.
THEN WHY DIDN'T YOU KEEP AN EYE ON LOKI...?
YOU COULD HAVE ASSIGNED ...
...AN A.I. AVATAR TO WATCH OVER HIM WHILE YOU WEREN'T INSIDE 7th.
IT WOULD ONLY BE NATURAL FOR...
...LOKI TO HAVE DEVELOPED AN ABIDING DISTRUST OF ME.
...
EVERYONE IS ...
...MAD AT ME BECAUSE THEY THINK I ONLY DO THINGS FOR MY OWN BENEFIT.
IF I WENT AS FAR AS HAVING SOMEONE MONITOR HIM...
...I COULDN'T CALL MYSELF HIS FRIEND ANYMORE...
VUL, LET ME HANDLE MARIA'S CAPTURE.
!
YOU GO AND FIND OUT WHAT LOKI IS UP TO.
BUT I DON'T WANT TO...
I KNOW ...!

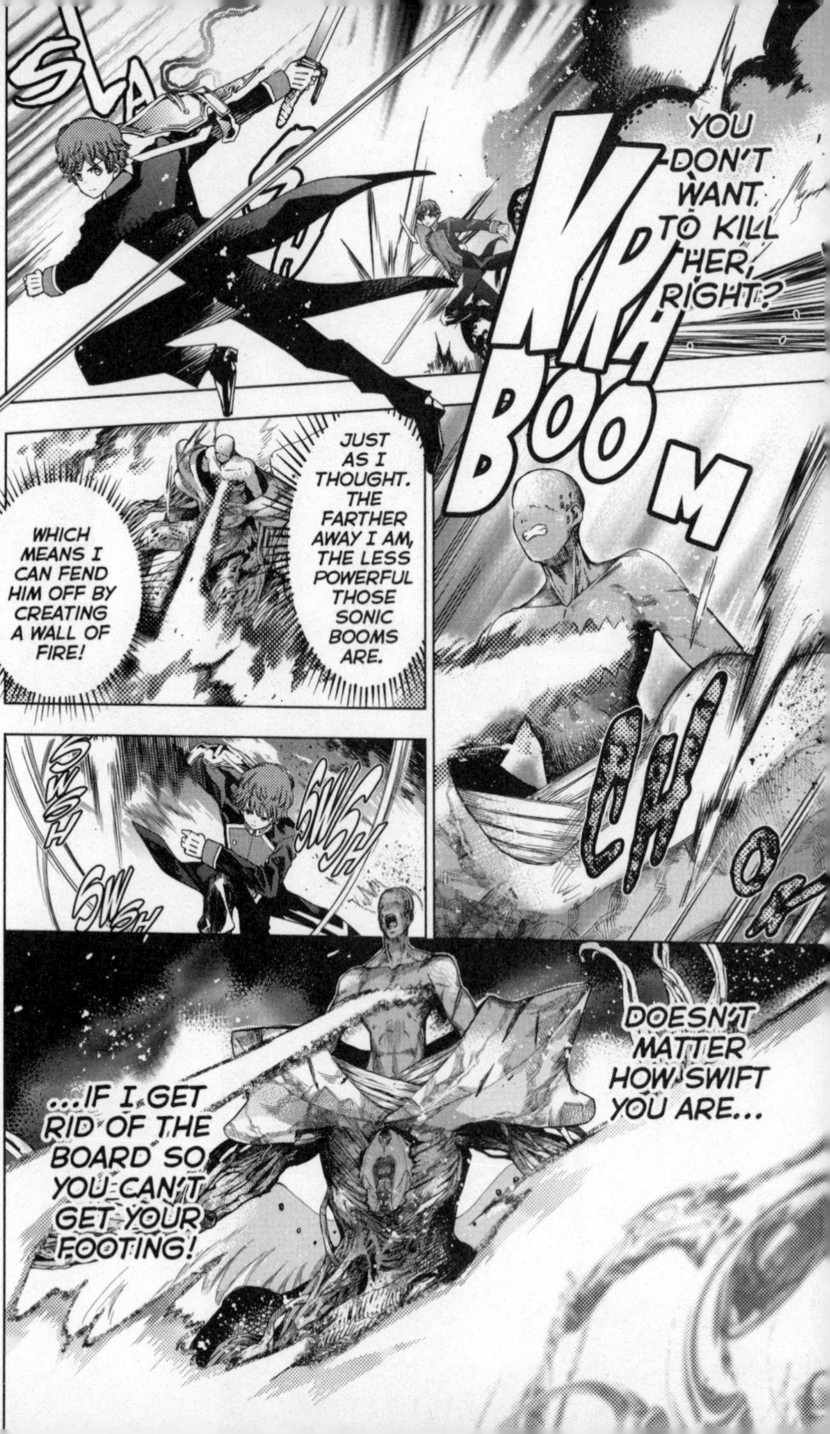
YOU DON'T WANT TO KILL HER, RIGHT?
SLASH
BOOOM
JUST AS I THOUGHT. THE FARTHER AWAY I AM, THE LESS POWERFUL THOSE SONIC BOOMS ARE.
WHICH MEANS I CAN FEND HIM OFF BY CREATING A WALL OF FIRE!
SWSH
SWSH
SWSH
DOESN'T MATTER HOW SWIFT YOU ARE...
...IF I GET RID OF THE BOARD SO YOU CAN'T GET YOUR FOOTING!

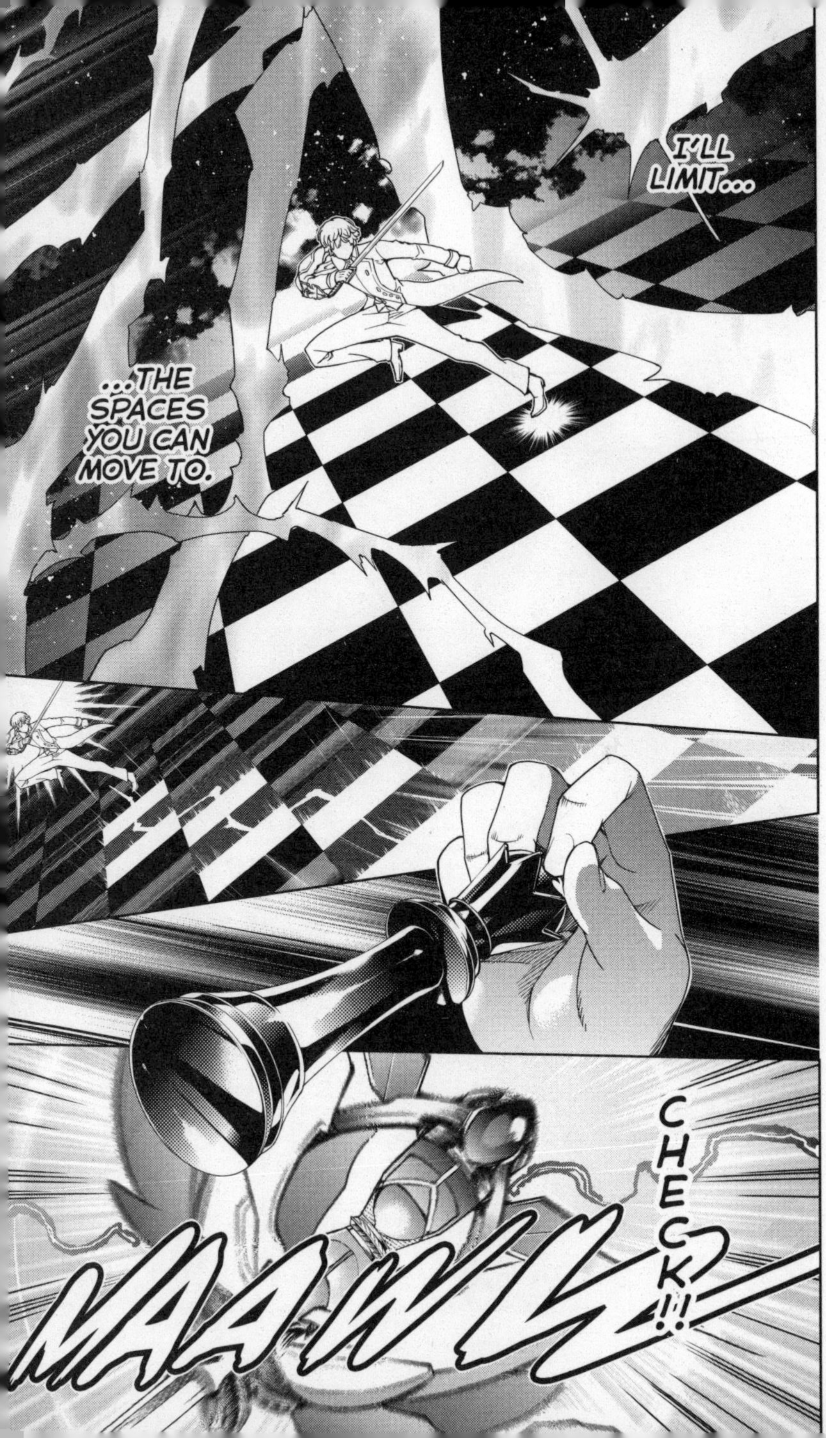
I'LL LIMIT...
...THE SPACES YOU CAN MOVE TO.
CHECK!!
MAWL

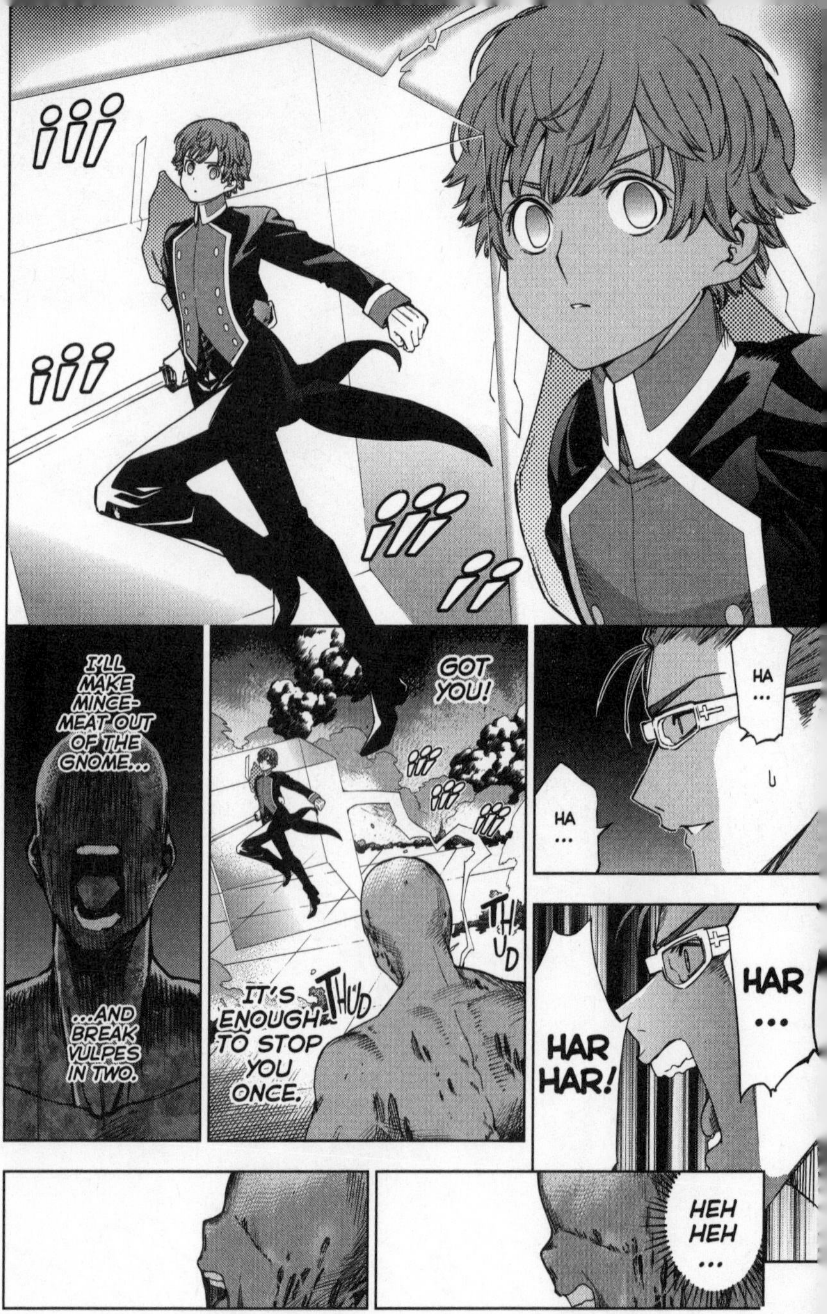
HA ...
HA ...
HAR ...
HAR HAR!
GOT YOU!
THUD
IT'S ENOUGH TO STOP YOU ONCE.
THUD
I'LL MAKE MINCE-MEAT OUT OF THE GNOME...
...AND BREAK VULPES IN TWO.
HEH HEH ...

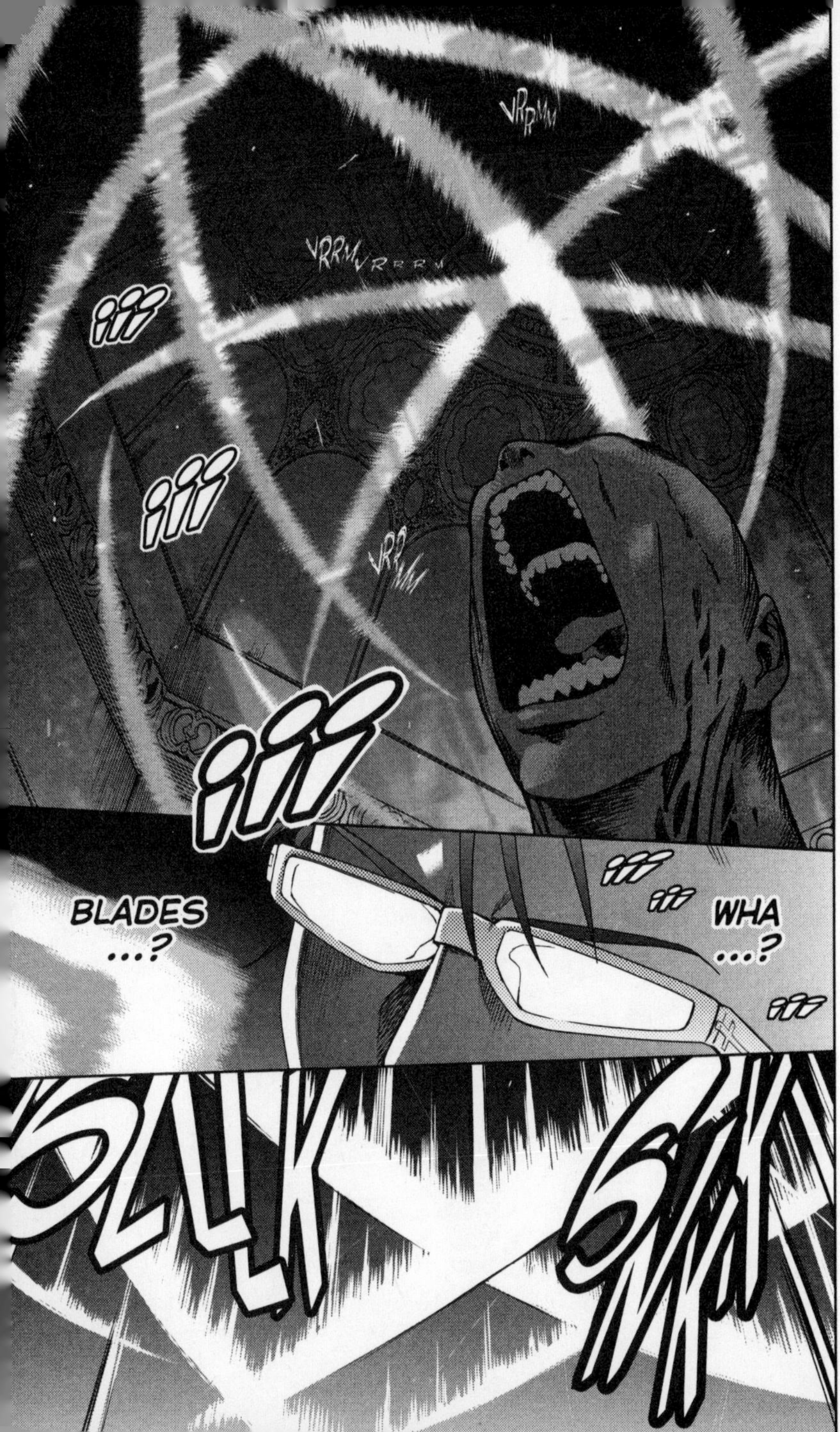
VRRMM
VRRM VRRRM
iii
iii
VRRMM
iii
iii
iii
WHA ...?
iii
BLADES ...?

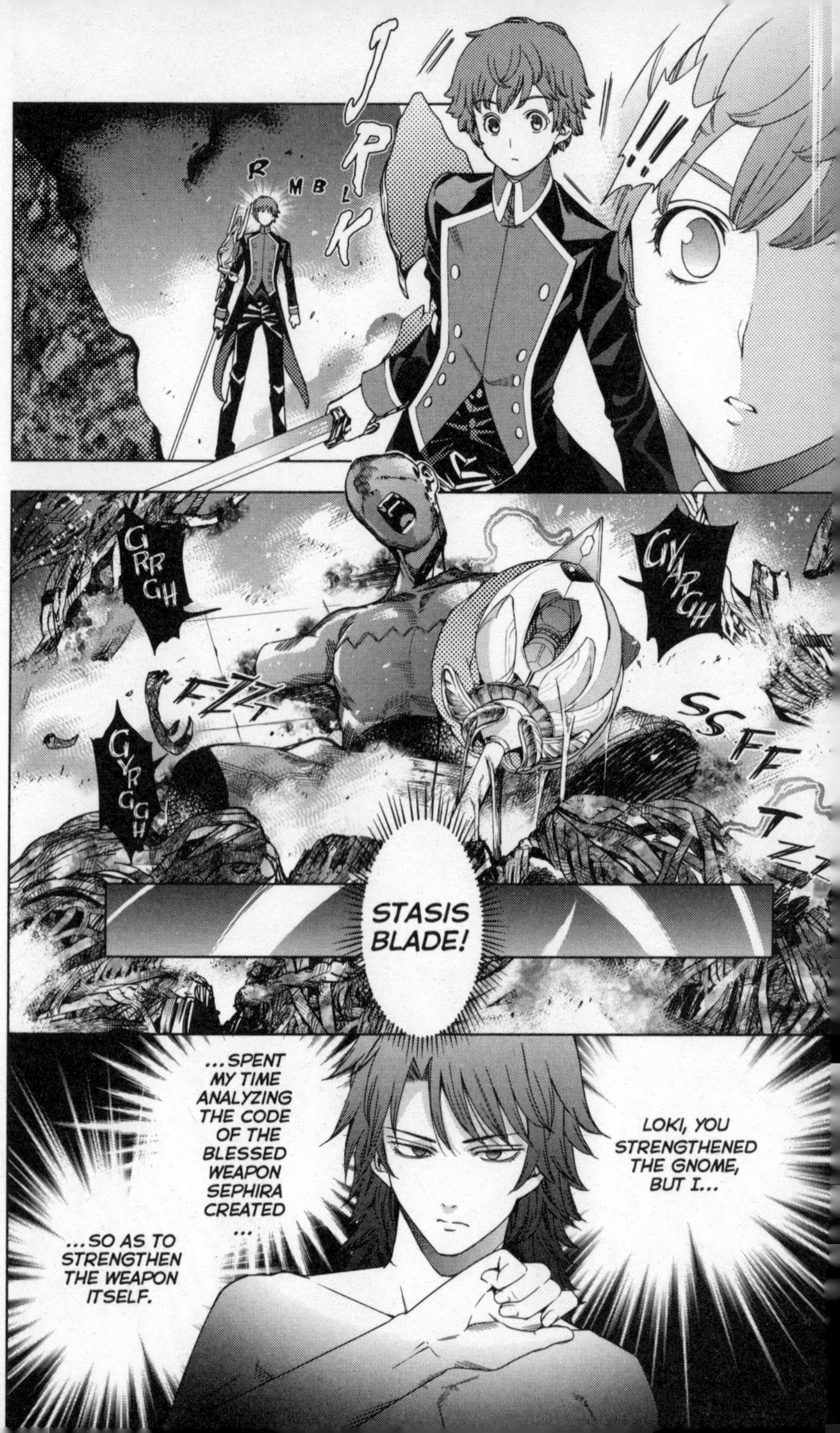
!!
JRK
RMBL
GYARGH
GRRGH
SSFFTZZ
FZZT
GYRGGH
STASIS BLADE!
LOKI, YOU STRENGTHENED THE GNOME, BUT I...
...SPENT MY TIME ANALYZING THE CODE OF THE BLESSED WEAPON SEPHIRA CREATED...
...SO AS TO STRENGTHEN THE WEAPON ITSELF.

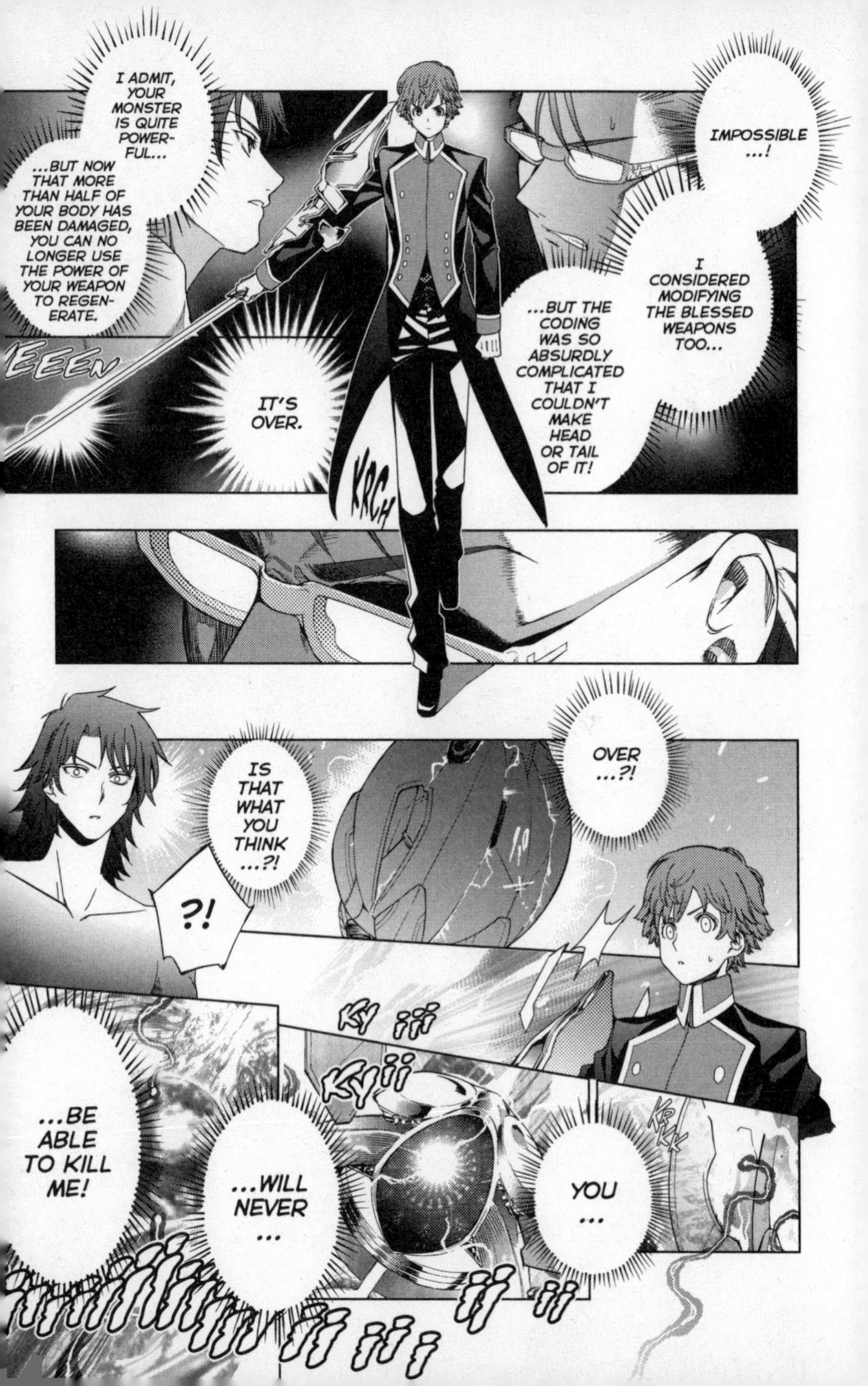
IMPOSSIBLE ...!
I CONSIDERED MODIFYING THE BLESSED WEAPONS TOO...
...BUT THE CODING WAS SO ABSURDLY COMPLICATED THAT I COULDN'T MAKE HEAD OR TAIL OF IT!
I ADMIT, YOUR MONSTER IS QUITE POWER-FUL...
...BUT NOW THAT MORE THAN HALF OF YOUR BODY HAS BEEN DAMAGED, YOU CAN NO LONGER USE THE POWER OF YOUR WEAPON TO REGEN-ERATE.
EEEEN
IT'S OVER.
KRCH
OVER ...?!
IS THAT WHAT YOU THINK ...?!
?!
KY iii
KYiii
KRKK
YOU ...
...WILL NEVER ...
...BE ABLE TO KILL ME!

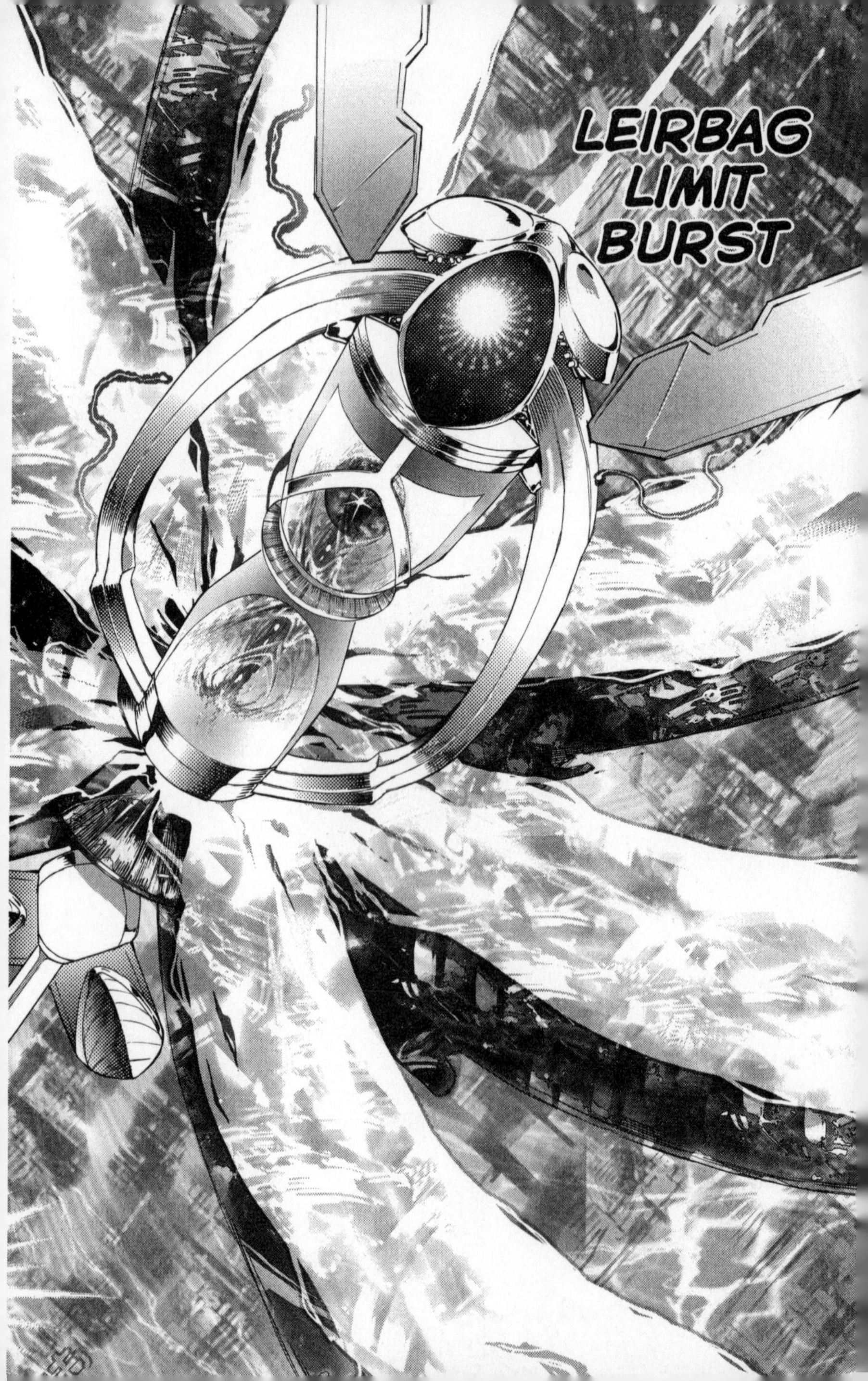
LEIRBAG LIMIT BURST

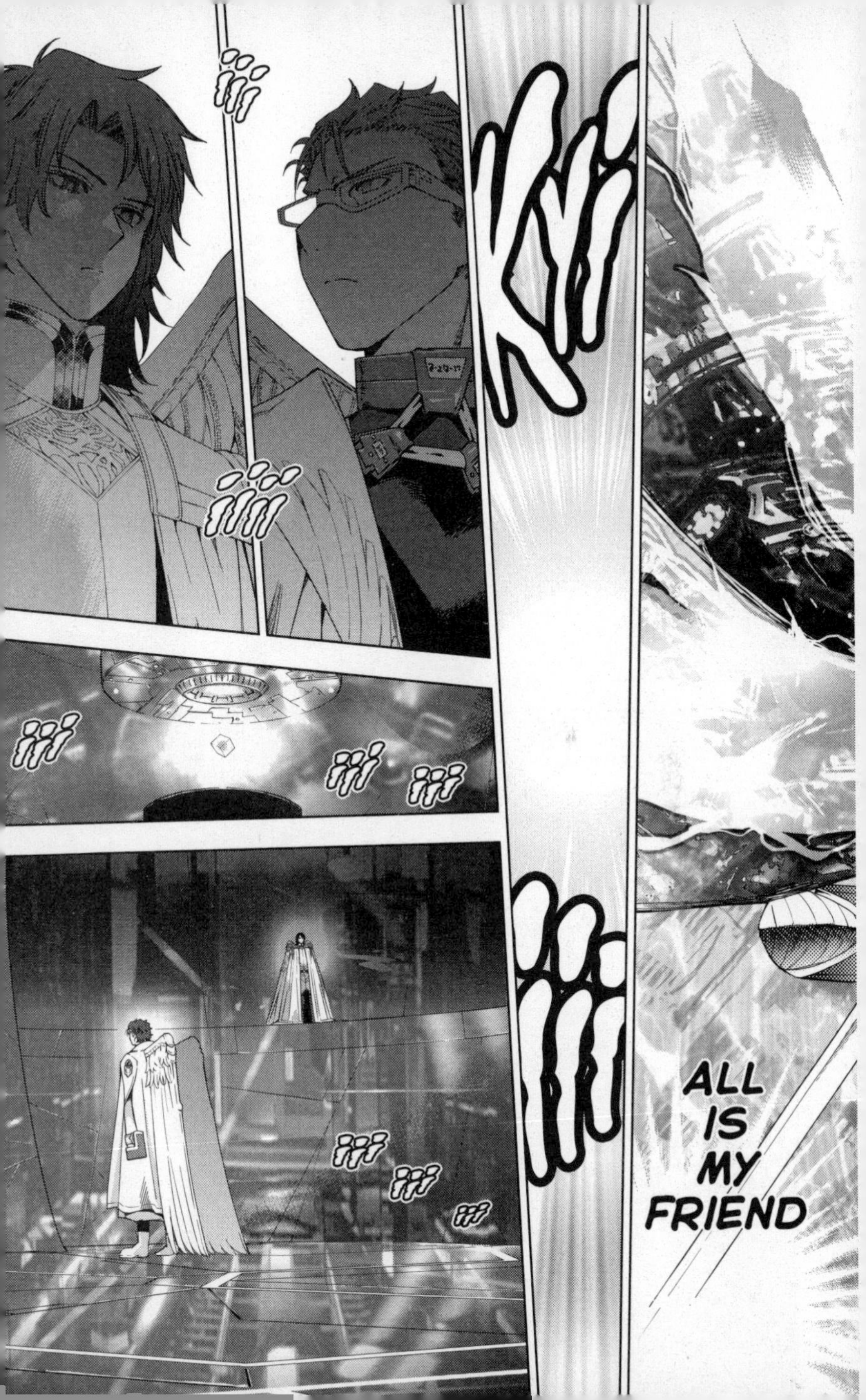

ALL IS MY FRIEND

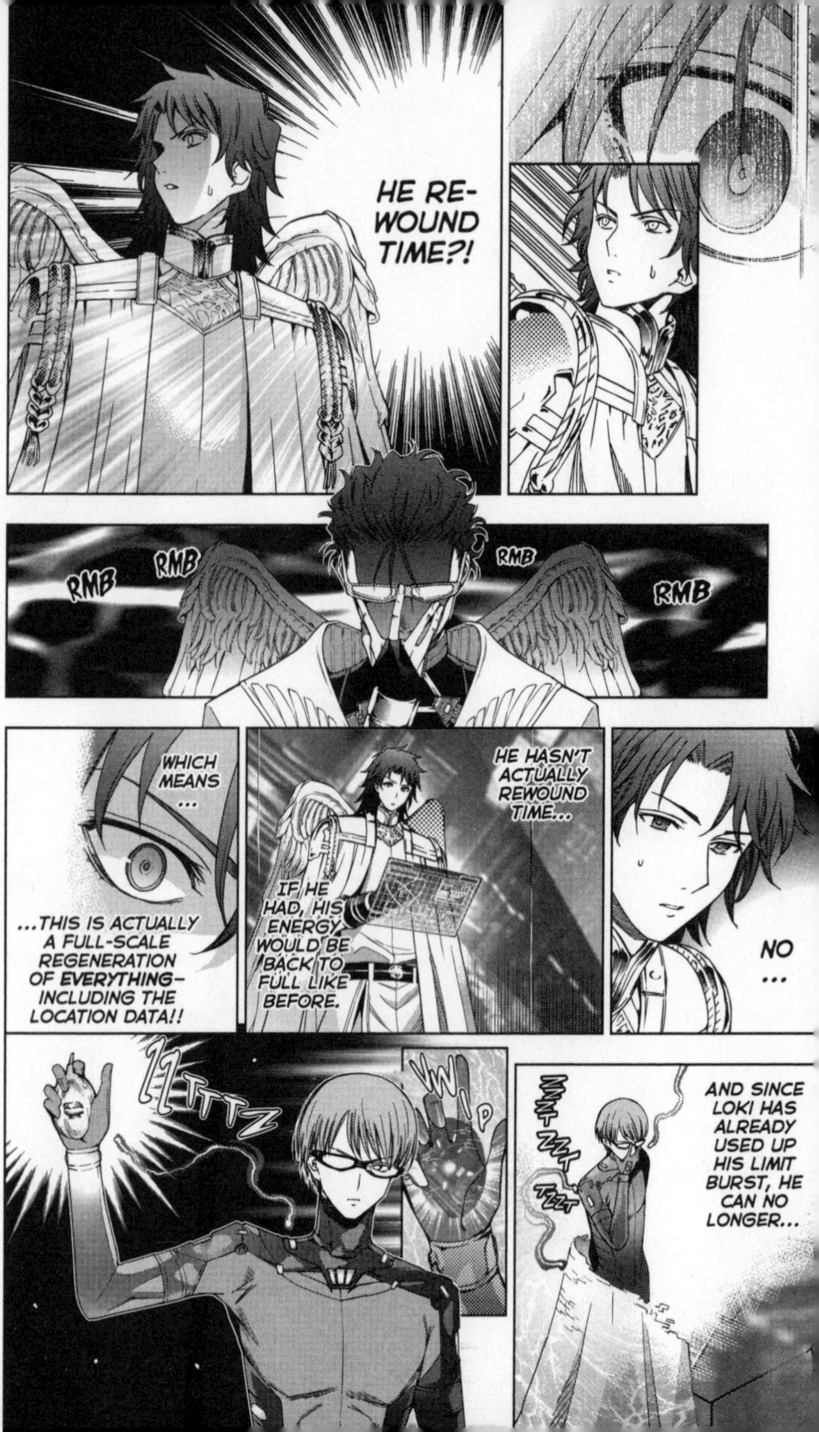
HE RE-WOUND TIME?!
RMB
RMB
RMB
RMB
NO ...
HE HASN'T ACTUALLY REWOUND TIME...
IF HE HAD, HIS ENERGY WOULD BE BACK TO FULL LIKE BEFORE.
WHICH MEANS ...
...THIS IS ACTUALLY A FULL-SCALE REGENERATION OF EVERYTHING— INCLUDING THE LOCATION DATA!!
ZZZT ZZK
TZZT
AND SINCE LOKI HAS ALREADY USED UP HIS LIMIT BURST, HE CAN NO LONGER...
VWIP
ZZTTTZ

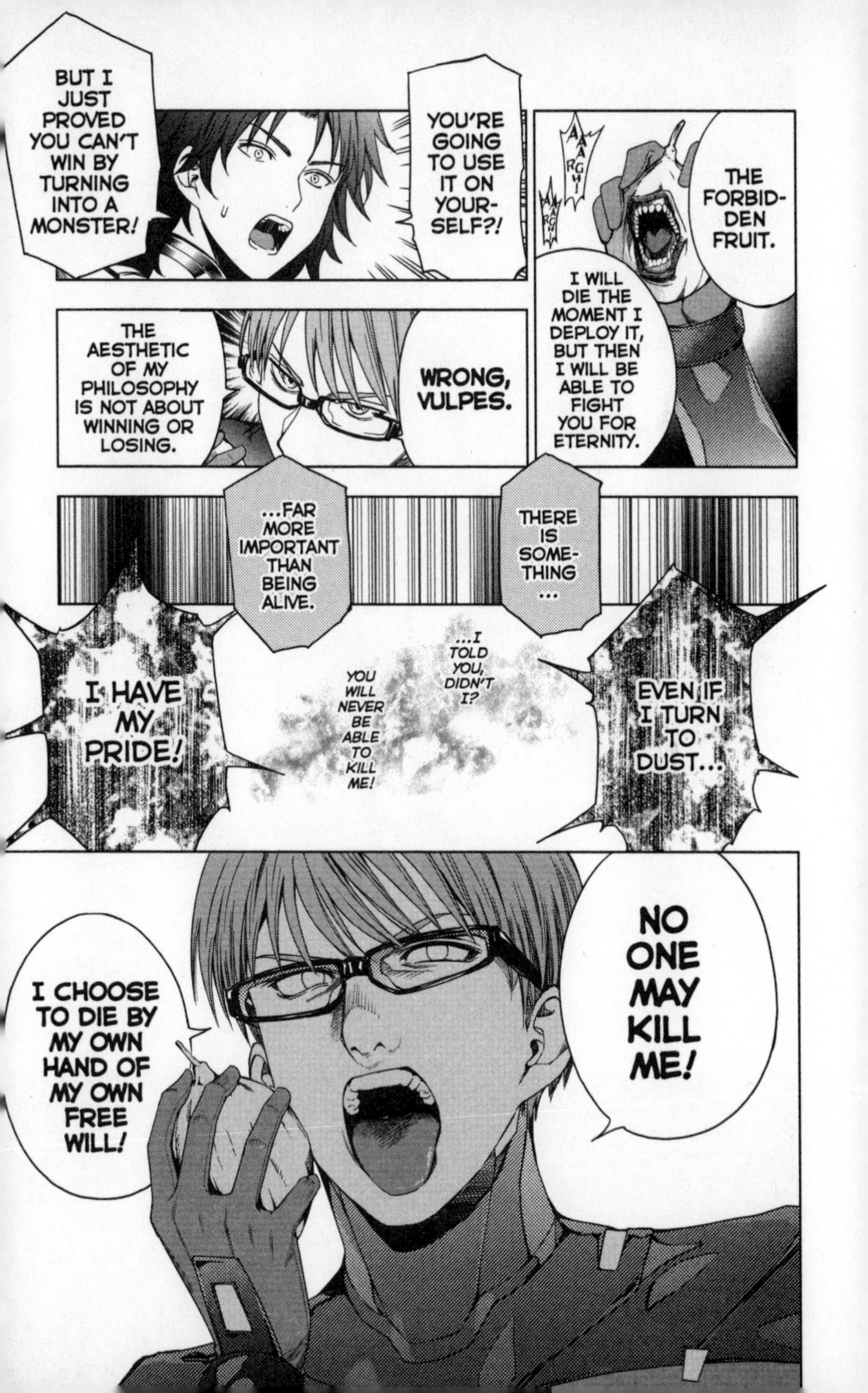
AAARGH
AAARGH
THE FORBIDDEN FRUIT.
I WILL DIE THE MOMENT I DEPLOY IT, BUT THEN I WILL BE ABLE TO FIGHT YOU FOR ETERNITY.
YOU'RE GOING TO USE IT ON YOURSELF?!
BUT I JUST PROVED YOU CAN'T WIN BY TURNING INTO A MONSTER!
WRONG, VULPES.
THE AESTHETIC OF MY PHILOSOPHY IS NOT ABOUT WINNING OR LOSING.
THERE IS SOMETHING...
...FAR MORE IMPORTANT THAN BEING ALIVE.
EVEN IF I TURN TO DUST...
...I TOLD YOU, DIDN'T I?
YOU WILL NEVER BE ABLE TO KILL ME!
I HAVE MY PRIDE!
NO ONE MAY KILL ME!
I CHOOSE TO DIE BY MY OWN HAND OF MY OWN FREE WILL!

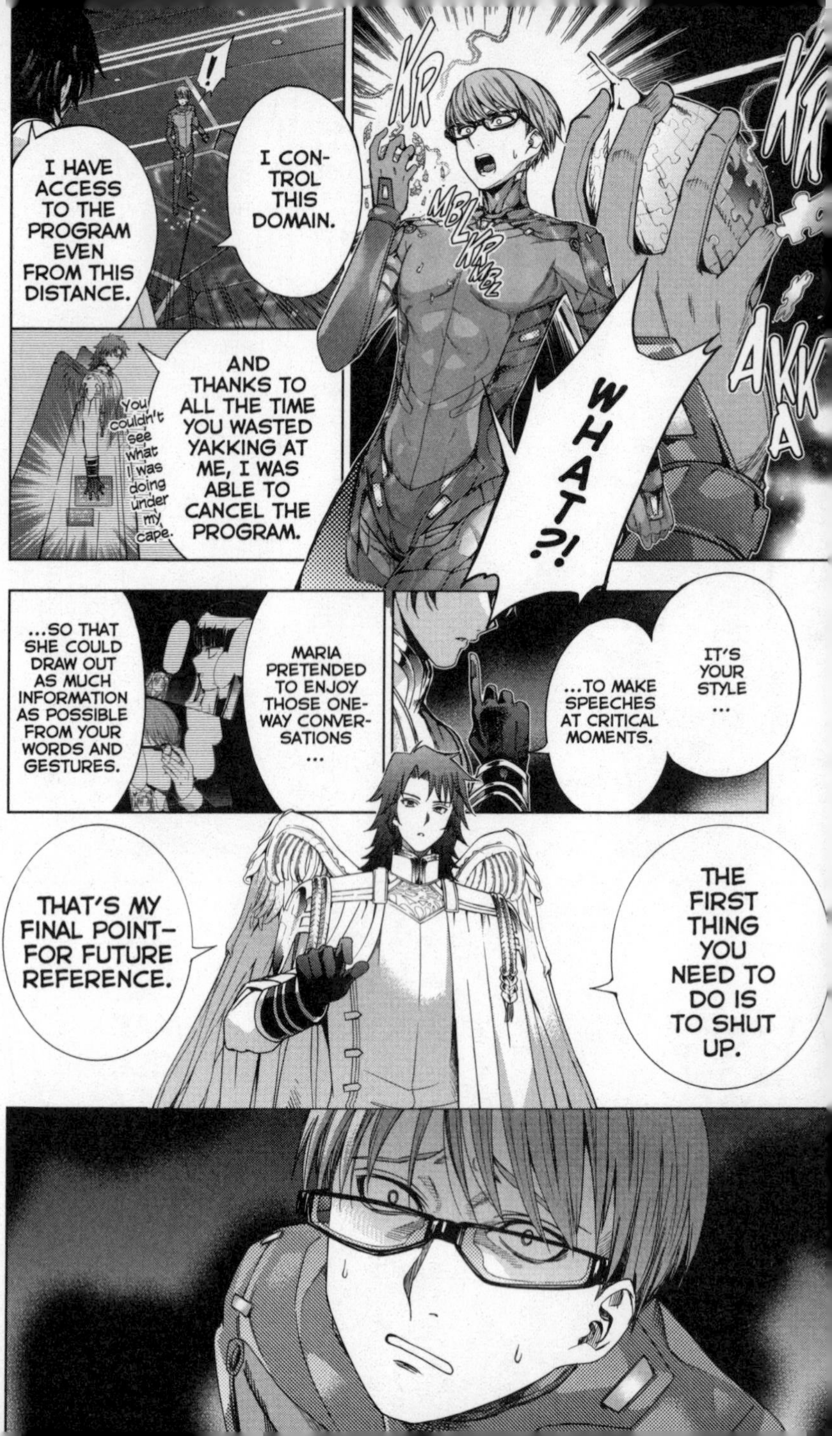
KR
MBL KR MBL
AKKA
WHAT?!
I CONTROL THIS DOMAIN.
!
I HAVE ACCESS TO THE PROGRAM EVEN FROM THIS DISTANCE.
AND THANKS TO ALL THE TIME YOU WASTED YAKKING AT ME, I WAS ABLE TO CANCEL THE PROGRAM.
You couldn't see what I was doing under my cape.
IT'S YOUR STYLE...
...TO MAKE SPEECHES AT CRITICAL MOMENTS.
MARIA PRETENDED TO ENJOY THOSE ONE-WAY CONVERSATIONS...
...SO THAT SHE COULD DRAW OUT AS MUCH INFORMATION AS POSSIBLE FROM YOUR WORDS AND GESTURES.
THE FIRST THING YOU NEED TO DO IS TO SHUT UP.
THAT'S MY FINAL POINT—FOR FUTURE REFERENCE.

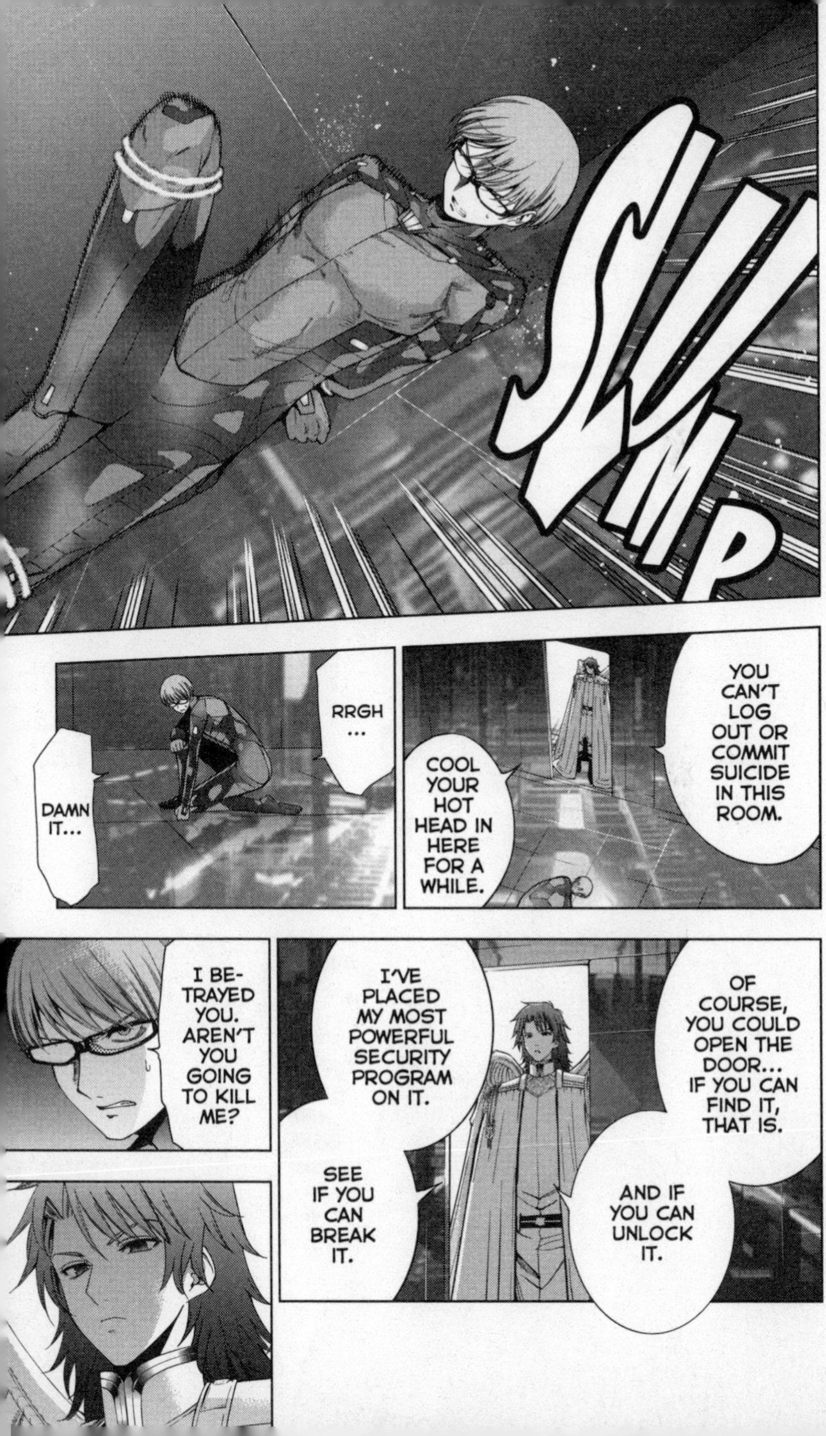
SLUMP
YOU CAN'T LOG OUT OR COMMIT SUICIDE IN THIS ROOM.
COOL YOUR HOT HEAD IN HERE FOR A WHILE.
RRGH...
DAMN IT...
OF COURSE, YOU COULD OPEN THE DOOR... IF YOU CAN FIND IT, THAT IS.
I'VE PLACED MY MOST POWERFUL SECURITY PROGRAM ON IT.
AND IF YOU CAN UNLOCK IT.
SEE IF YOU CAN BREAK IT.
I BE-TRAYED YOU. AREN'T YOU GOING TO KILL ME?

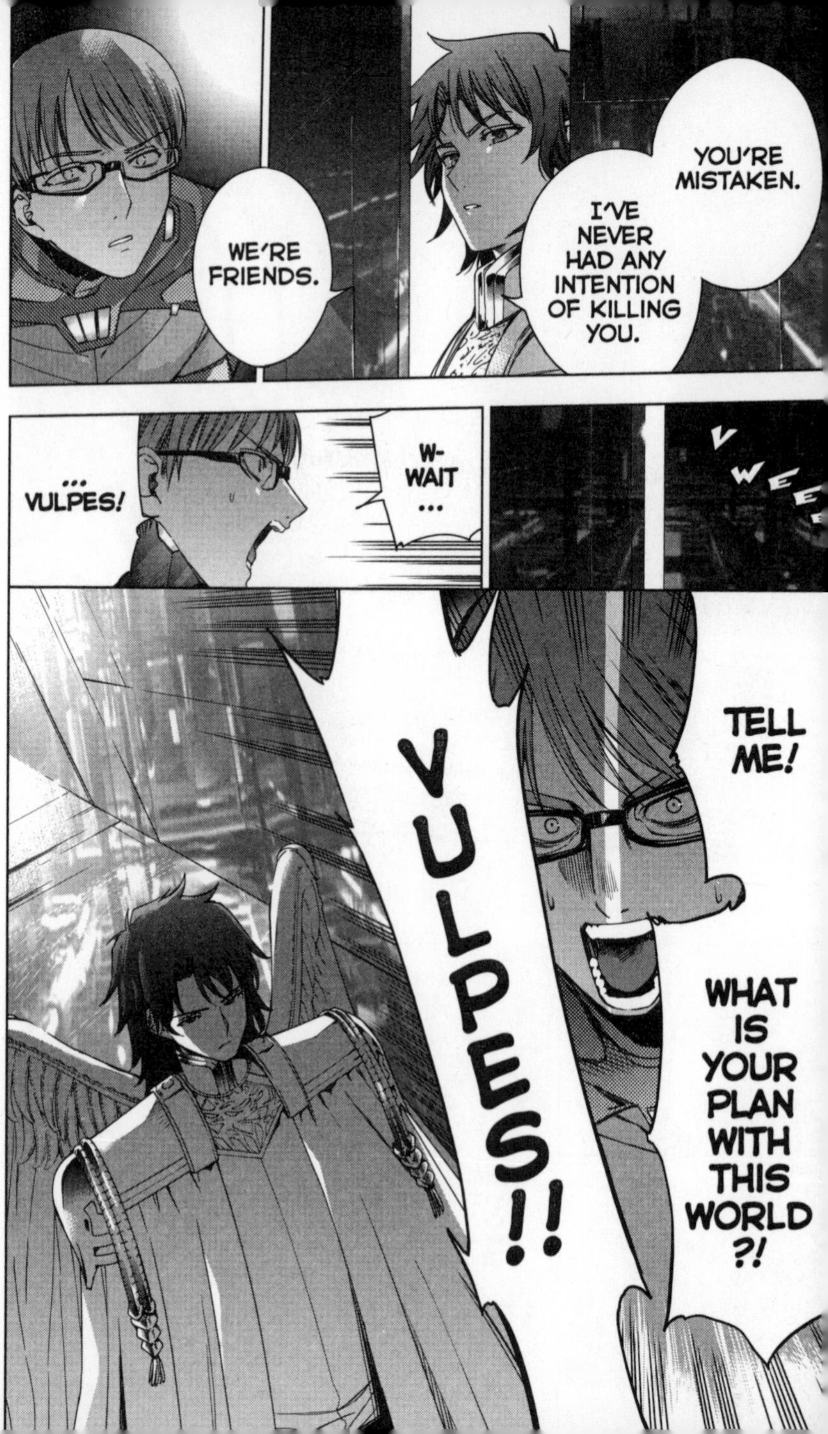

YOU'RE MISTAKEN.
I'VE NEVER HAD ANY INTENTION OF KILLING YOU.
WE'RE FRIENDS.
VWEEE
W-WAIT...
...VULPES!
TELL ME!
VULPES!!
WHAT IS YOUR PLAN WITH THIS WORLD?!

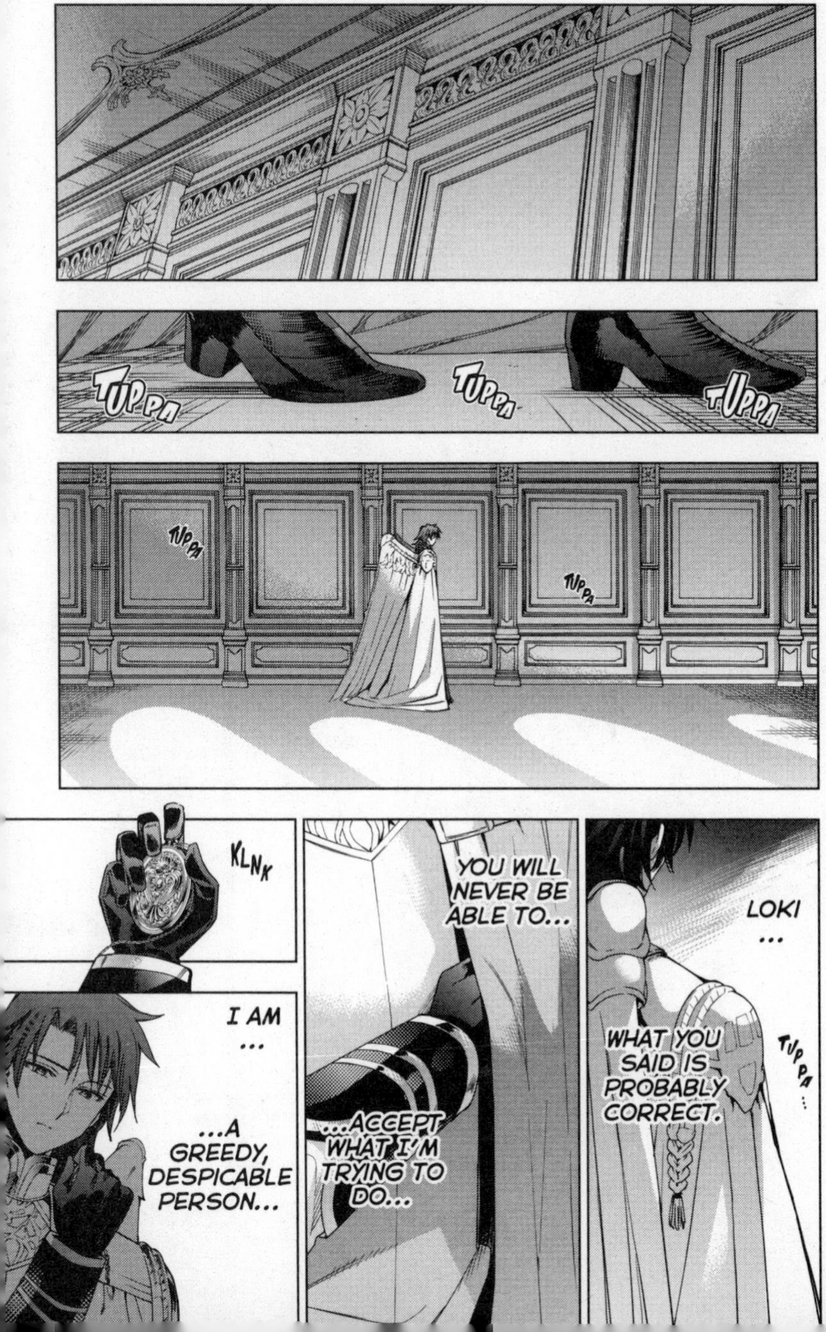
TUPPA
TUPPA
TUPPA
TUPPA
TUPPA
LOKI ...
WHAT YOU SAID IS PROBABLY CORRECT.
TUPPA ...
YOU WILL NEVER BE ABLE TO...
...ACCEPT WHAT I'M TRYING TO DO...
KLNK
I AM ...
...A GREEDY, DESPICABLE PERSON...

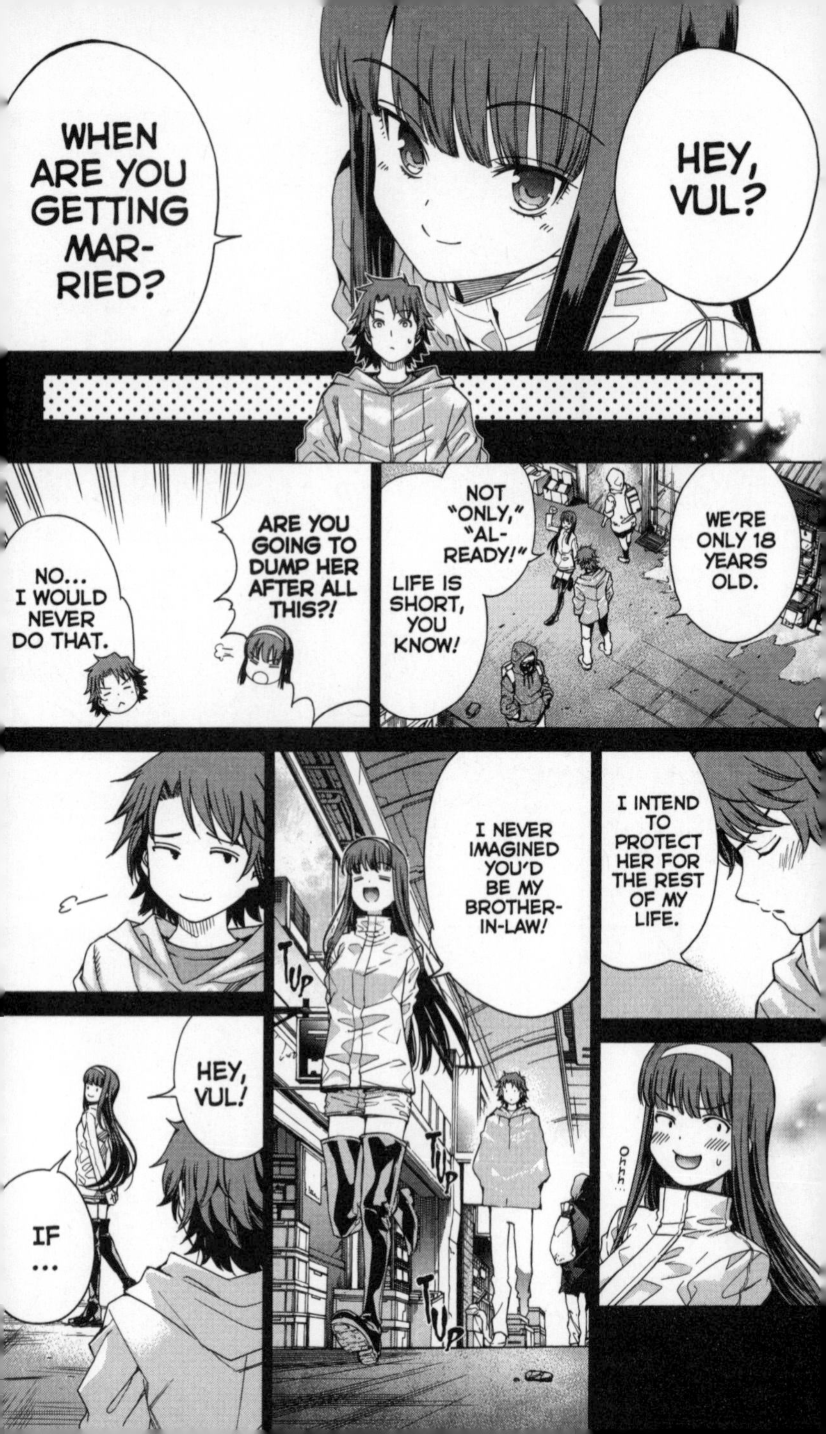
HEY, VUL?
WHEN ARE YOU GETTING MAR-RIED?
WE'RE ONLY 18 YEARS OLD.
NOT "ONLY," "AL-READY!"
LIFE IS SHORT, YOU KNOW!
ARE YOU GOING TO DUMP HER AFTER ALL THIS?!
NO... I WOULD NEVER DO THAT.
I INTEND TO PROTECT HER FOR THE REST OF MY LIFE.
Ohhh...
I NEVER IMAGINED YOU'D BE MY BROTHER-IN-LAW!
TUP
TUP
TUP
HEY, VUL!
IF ...

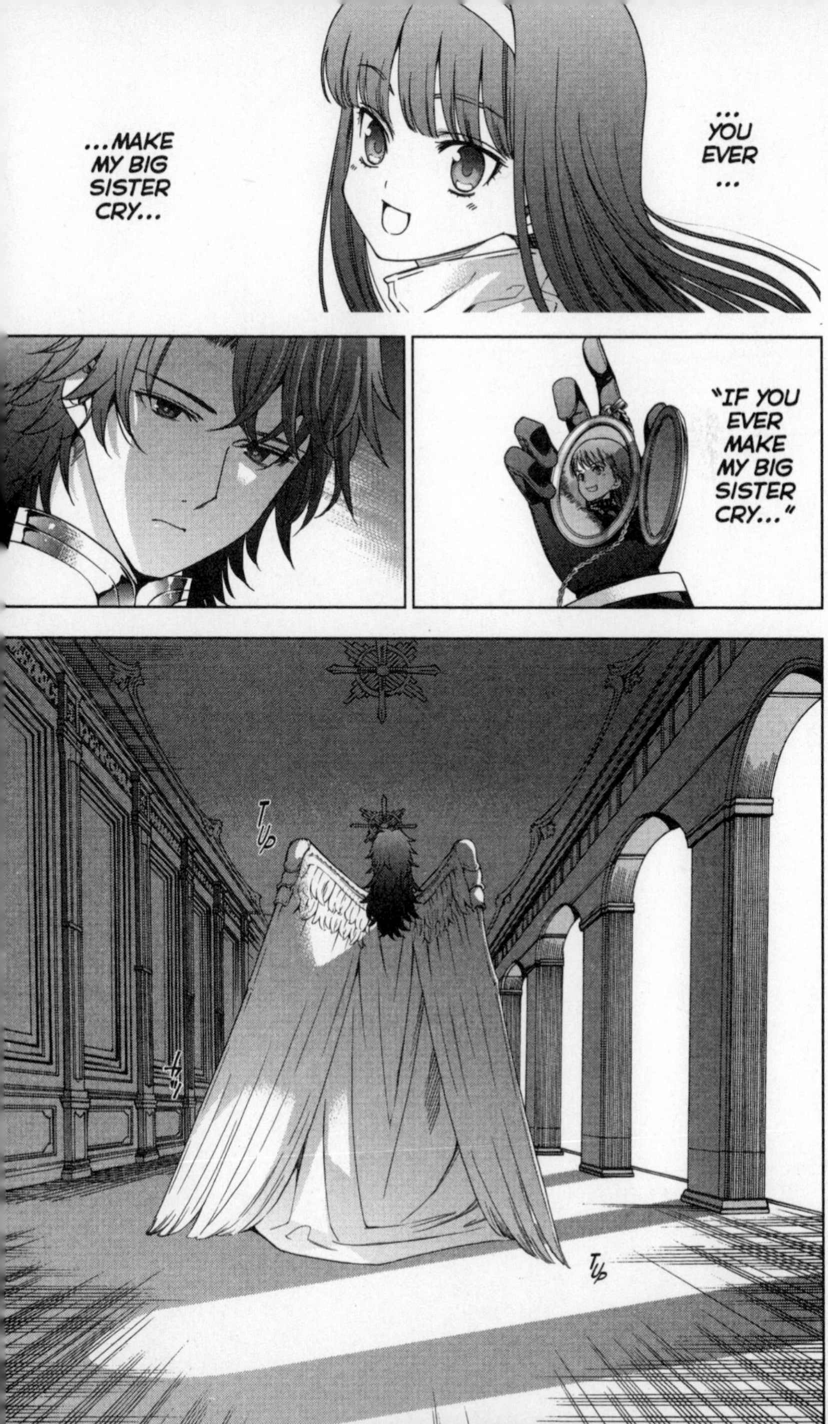
... YOU EVER ...
...MAKE MY BIG SISTER CRY...
"IF YOU EVER MAKE MY BIG SISTER CRY..."
TUP
TUP

root.31

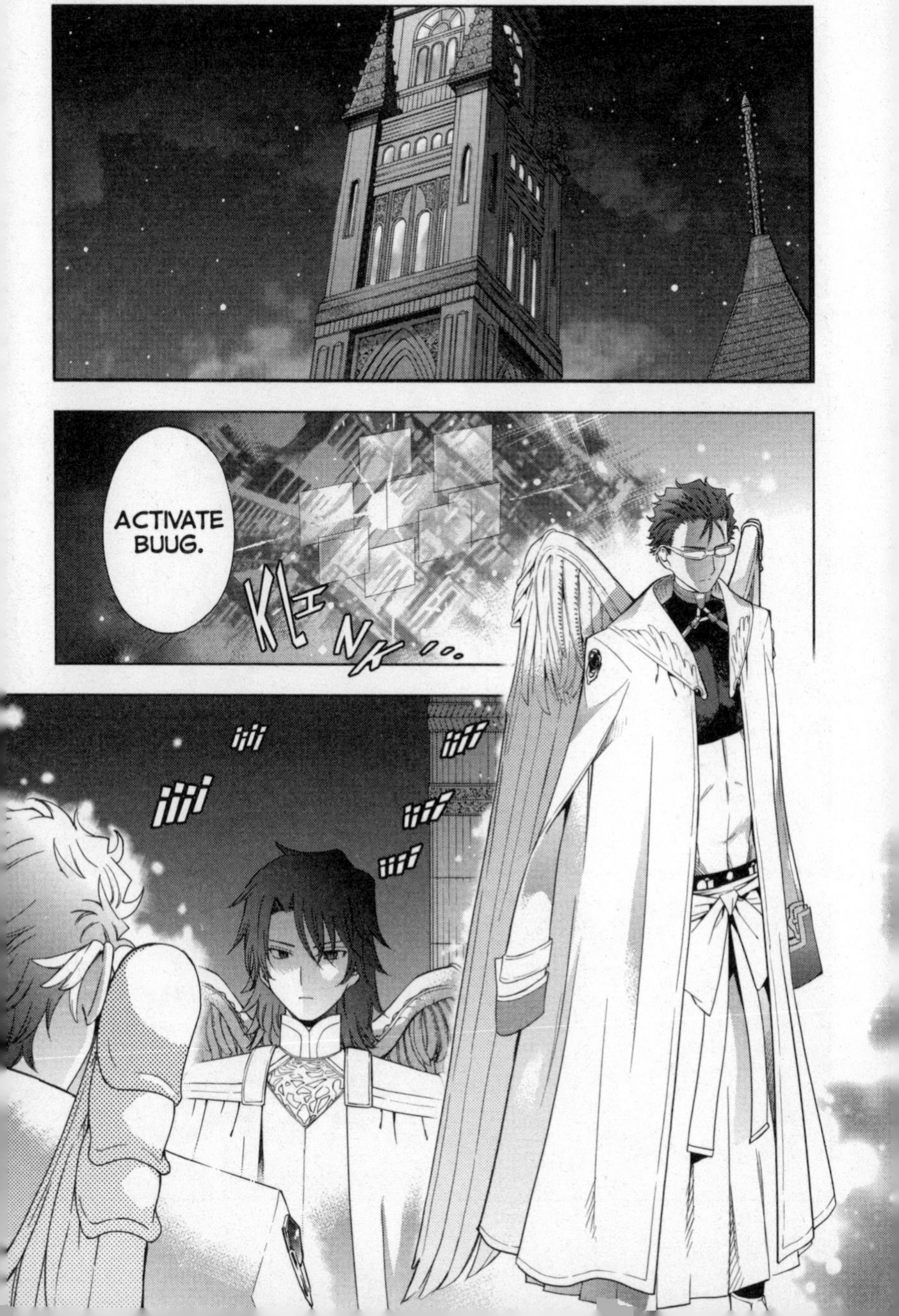
ACTIVATE BUUG.
KLINK...

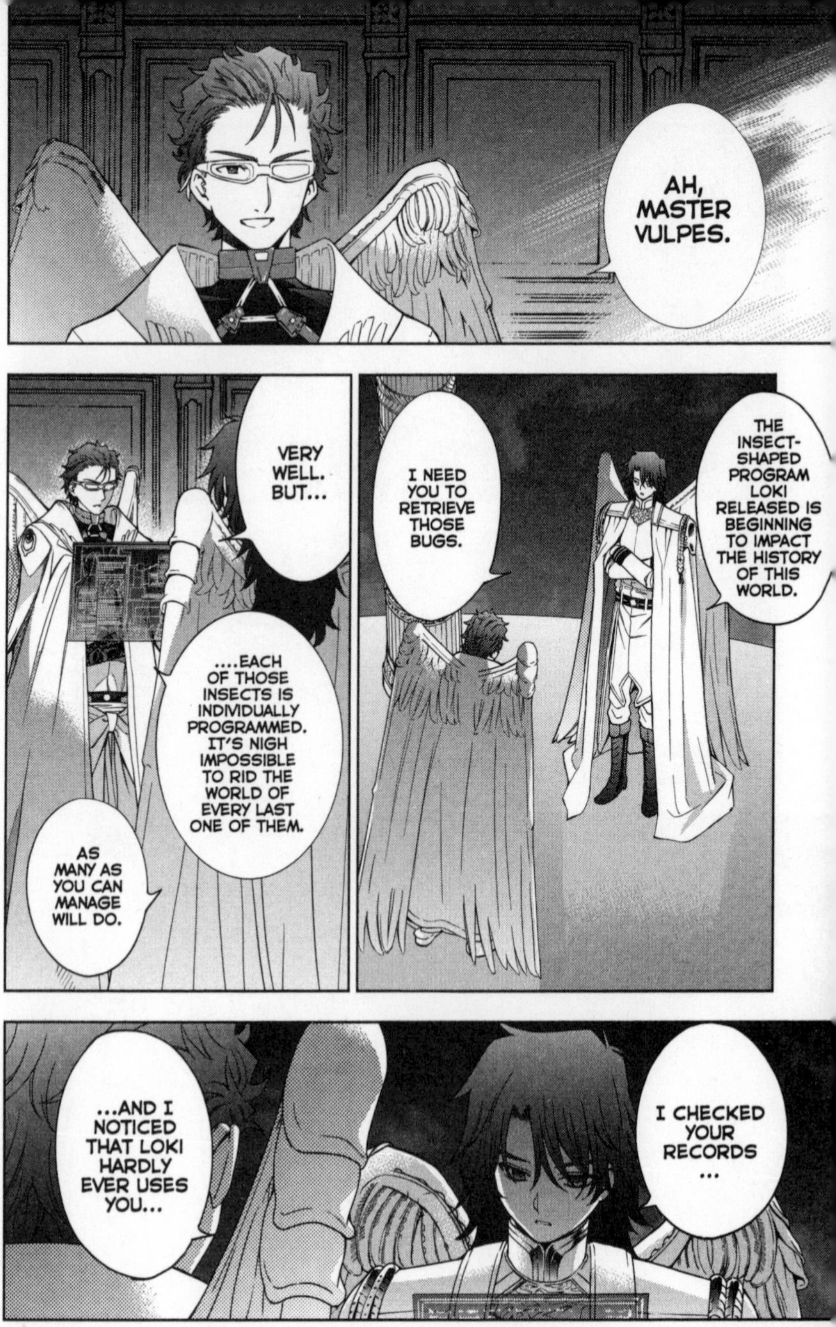
AH, MASTER VULPES.
THE INSECT-SHAPED PROGRAM LOKI RELEASED IS BEGINNING TO IMPACT THE HISTORY OF THIS WORLD.
I NEED YOU TO RETRIEVE THOSE BUGS.
VERY WELL. BUT...
....EACH OF THOSE INSECTS IS INDIVIDUALLY PROGRAMMED. IT'S NIGH IMPOSSIBLE TO RID THE WORLD OF EVERY LAST ONE OF THEM.
AS MANY AS YOU CAN MANAGE WILL DO.
I CHECKED YOUR RECORDS ...
...AND I NOTICED THAT LOKI HARDLY EVER USES YOU...

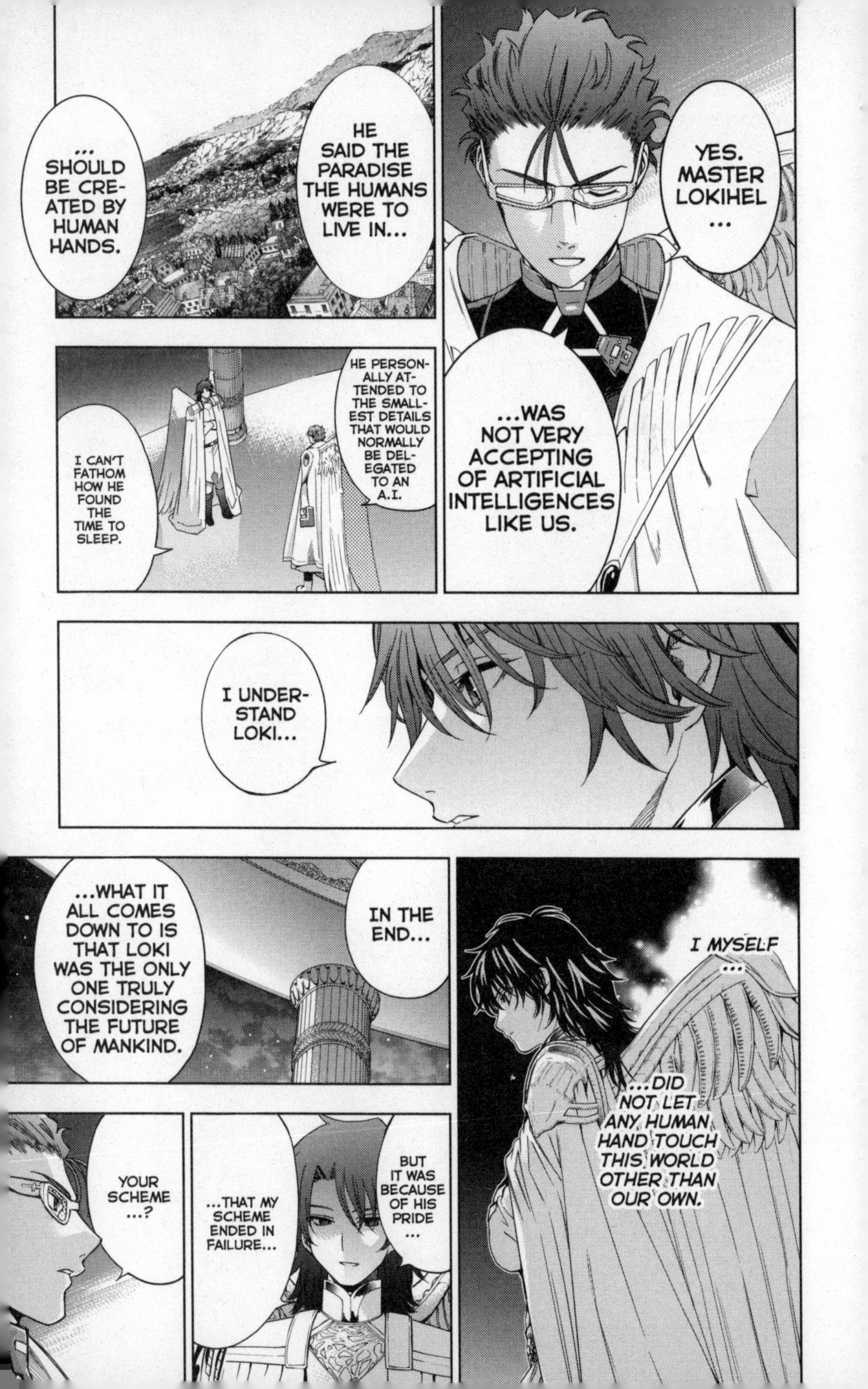
YES. MASTER LOKIHEL ...
...WAS NOT VERY ACCEPTING OF ARTIFICIAL INTELLIGENCES LIKE US.
HE SAID THE PARADISE THE HUMANS WERE TO LIVE IN...
... SHOULD BE CREATED BY HUMAN HANDS.
HE PERSONALLY ATTENDED TO THE SMALLEST DETAILS THAT WOULD NORMALLY BE DELEGATED TO AN A.I.
I CAN'T FATHOM HOW HE FOUND THE TIME TO SLEEP.
I UNDERSTAND LOKI...
I MYSELF ...
...DID NOT LET ANY HUMAN HAND TOUCH THIS WORLD OTHER THAN OUR OWN.
IN THE END...
...WHAT IT ALL COMES DOWN TO IS THAT LOKI WAS THE ONLY ONE TRULY CONSIDERING THE FUTURE OF MANKIND.
BUT IT WAS BECAUSE OF HIS PRIDE ...
...THAT MY SCHEME ENDED IN FAILURE...
YOUR SCHEME ...?

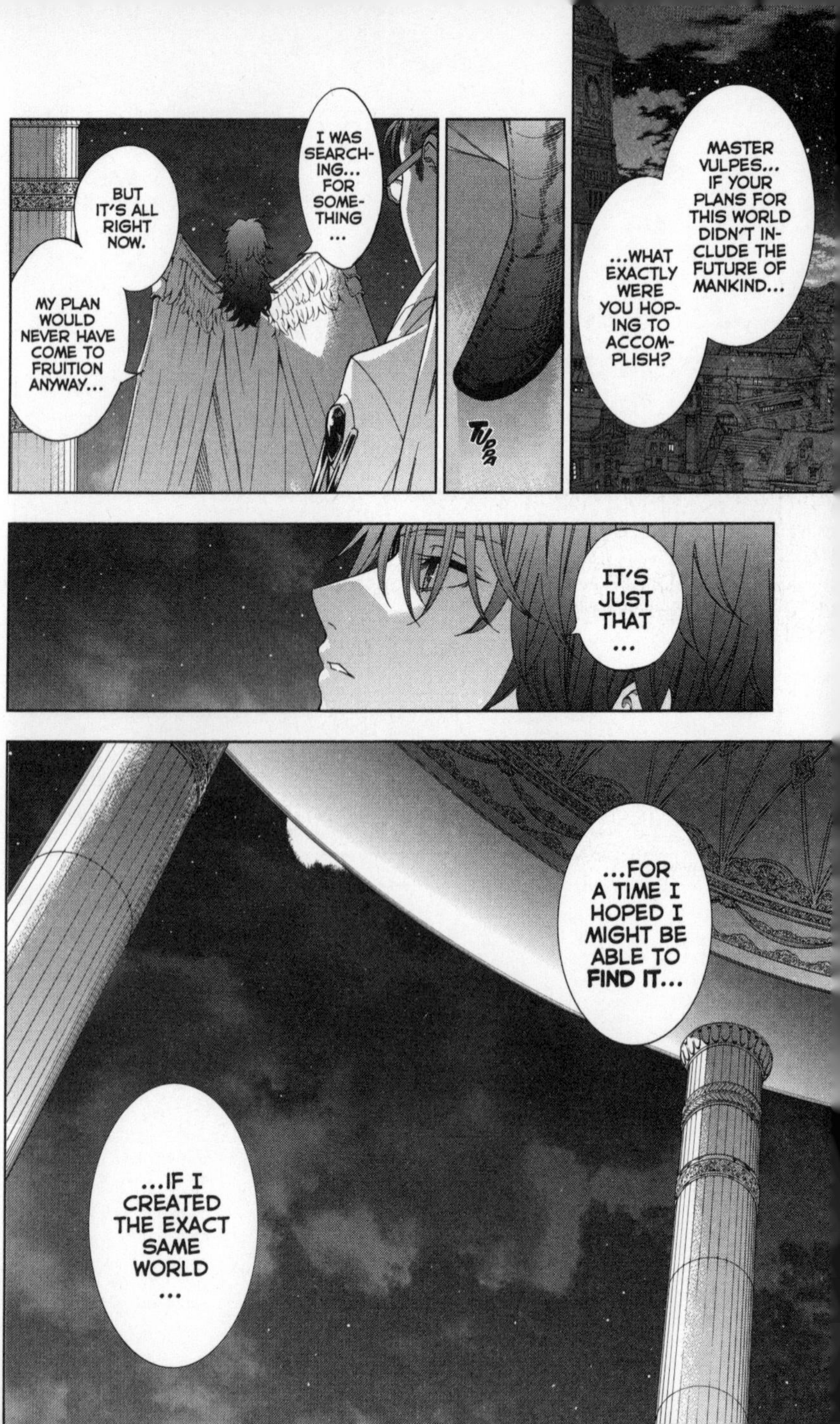
MASTER VULPES... IF YOUR PLANS FOR THIS WORLD DIDN'T INCLUDE THE FUTURE OF MANKIND...
...WHAT EXACTLY WERE YOU HOPING TO ACCOMPLISH?
TUPA
I WAS SEARCHING... FOR SOMETHING...
BUT IT'S ALL RIGHT NOW.
MY PLAN WOULD NEVER HAVE COME TO FRUITION ANYWAY...
IT'S JUST THAT...
...FOR A TIME I HOPED I MIGHT BE ABLE TO FIND IT...
...IF I CREATED THE EXACT SAME WORLD...

root.31 Turned into a Monster

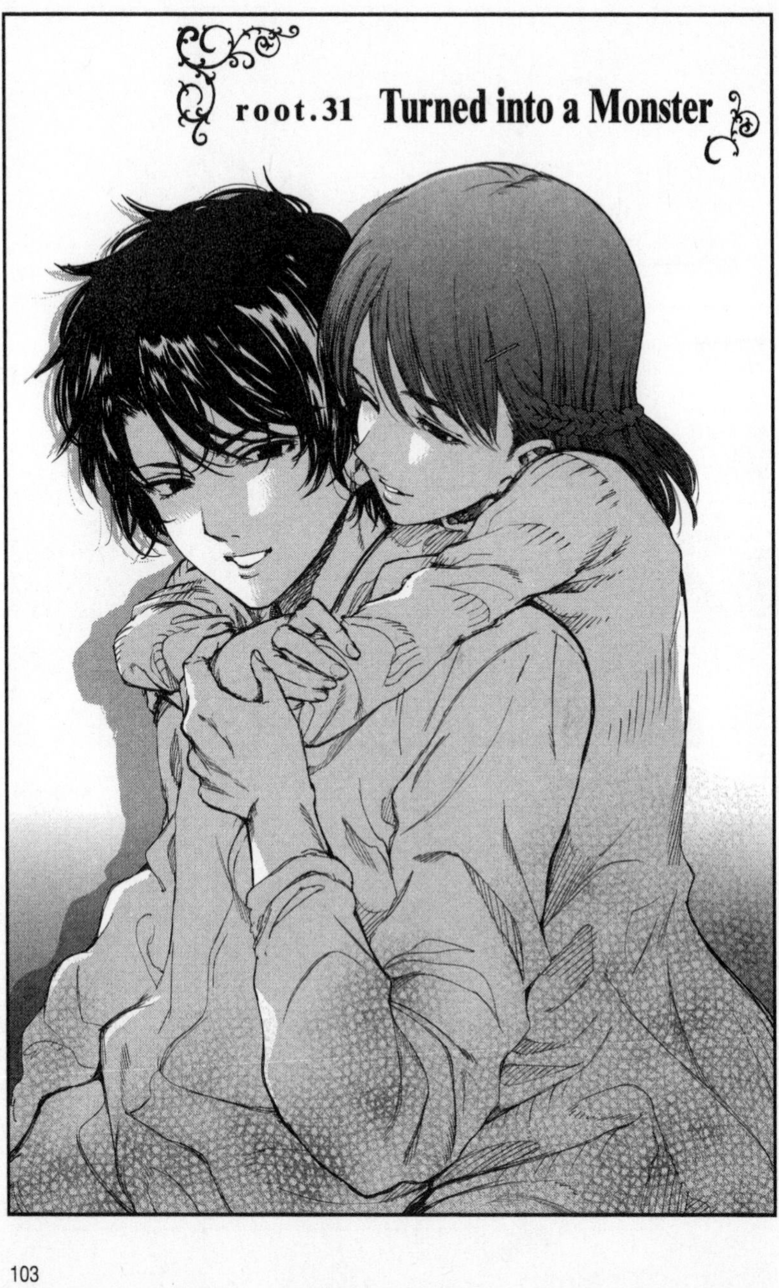

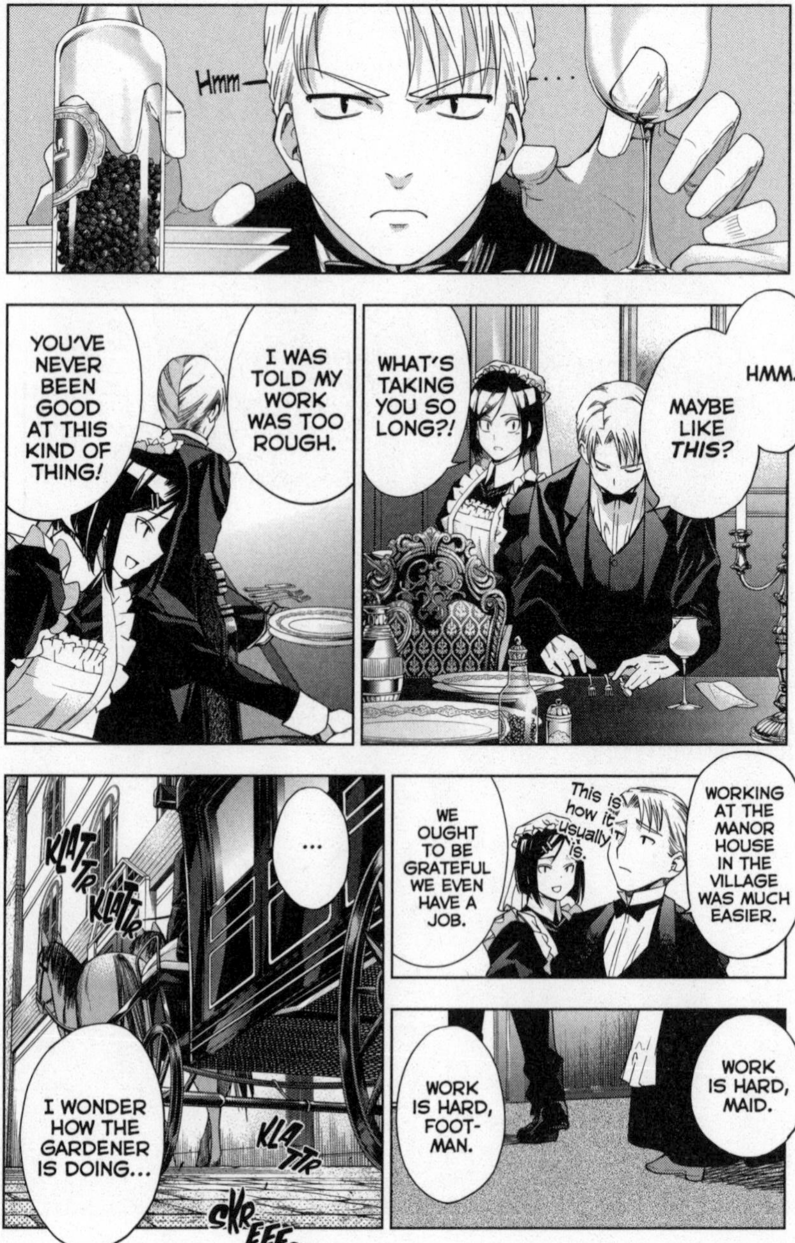
· · · ·
Hmm—
HMM.
MAYBE LIKE *THIS*?
WHAT'S TAKING YOU SO LONG?!
I WAS TOLD MY WORK WAS TOO ROUGH.
YOU'VE NEVER BEEN GOOD AT THIS KIND OF THING!
WORKING AT THE MANOR HOUSE IN THE VILLAGE WAS MUCH EASIER.
This is how it usually is.
WE OUGHT TO BE GRATEFUL WE EVEN HAVE A JOB.
WORK IS HARD, MAID.
WORK IS HARD, FOOTMAN.
...
KLATTR
KLATTR
I WONDER HOW THE GARDENER IS DOING...
KLATTR
SKREEEECH

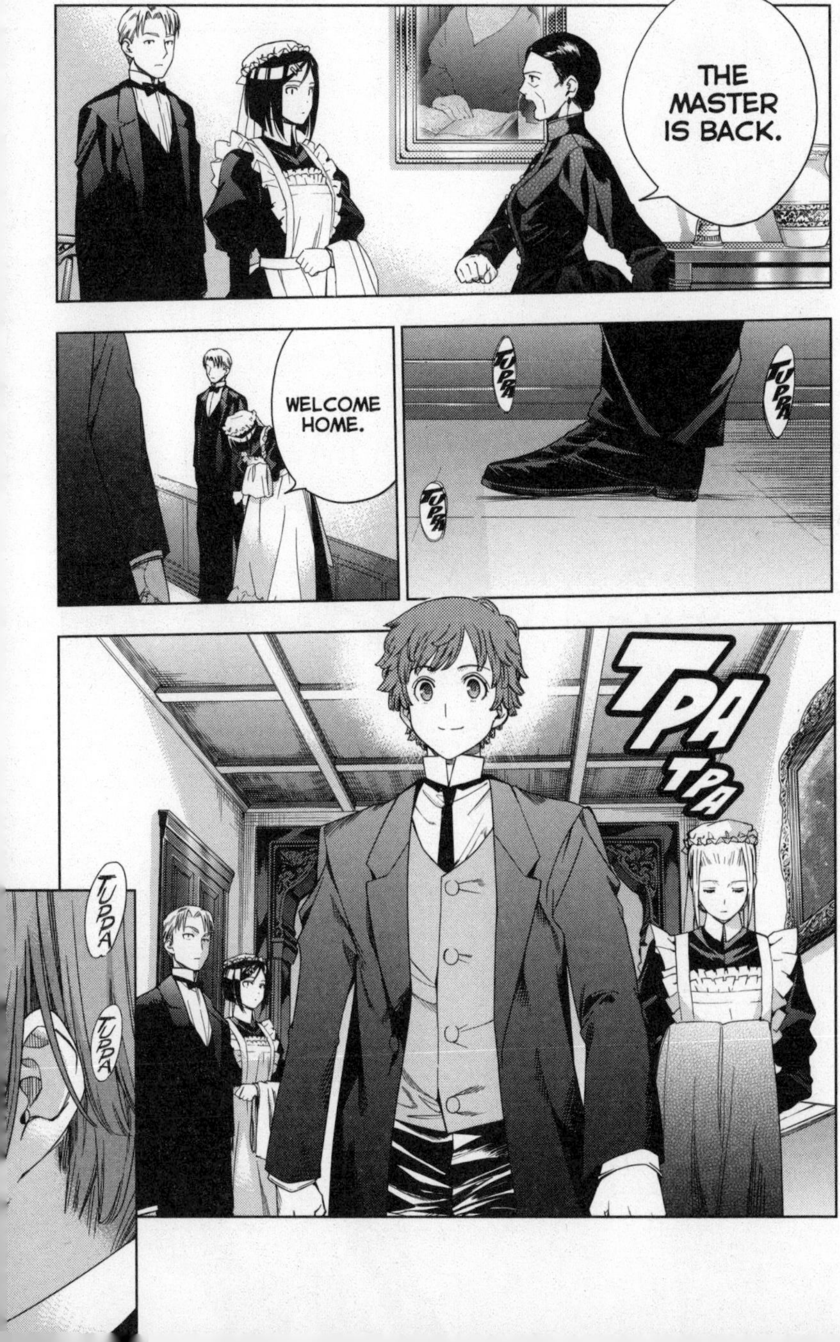
THE MASTER IS BACK.
TUPPA
TUPPA
TUPPA
WELCOME HOME.
TPA
TPA
TUPPA
TUPPA

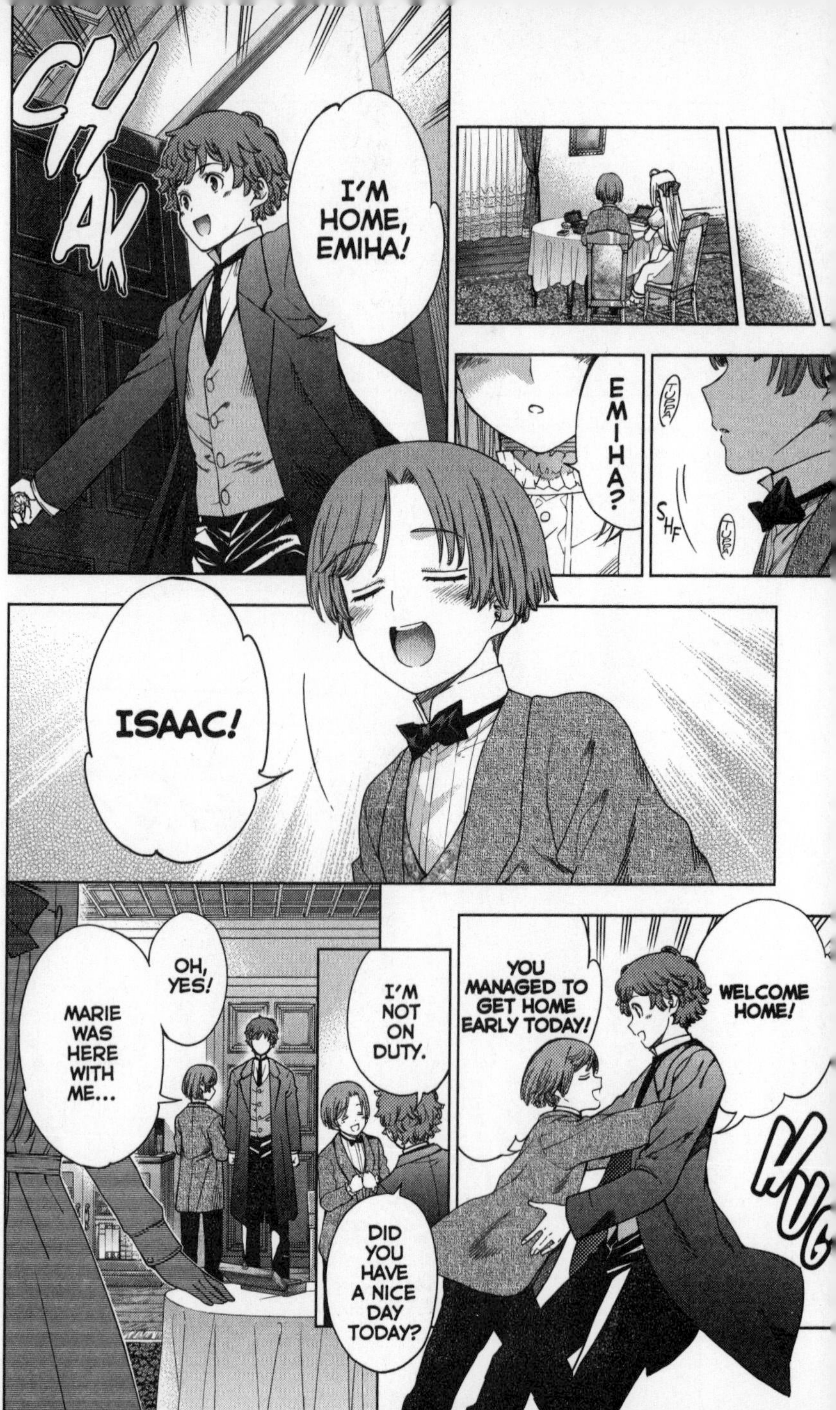
EMIHA?
SHF
CHAK
I'M HOME, EMIHA!
ISAAC!
WELCOME HOME!
HUG
YOU MANAGED TO GET HOME EARLY TODAY!
I'M NOT ON DUTY.
DID YOU HAVE A NICE DAY TODAY?
OH, YES!
MARIE WAS HERE WITH ME...

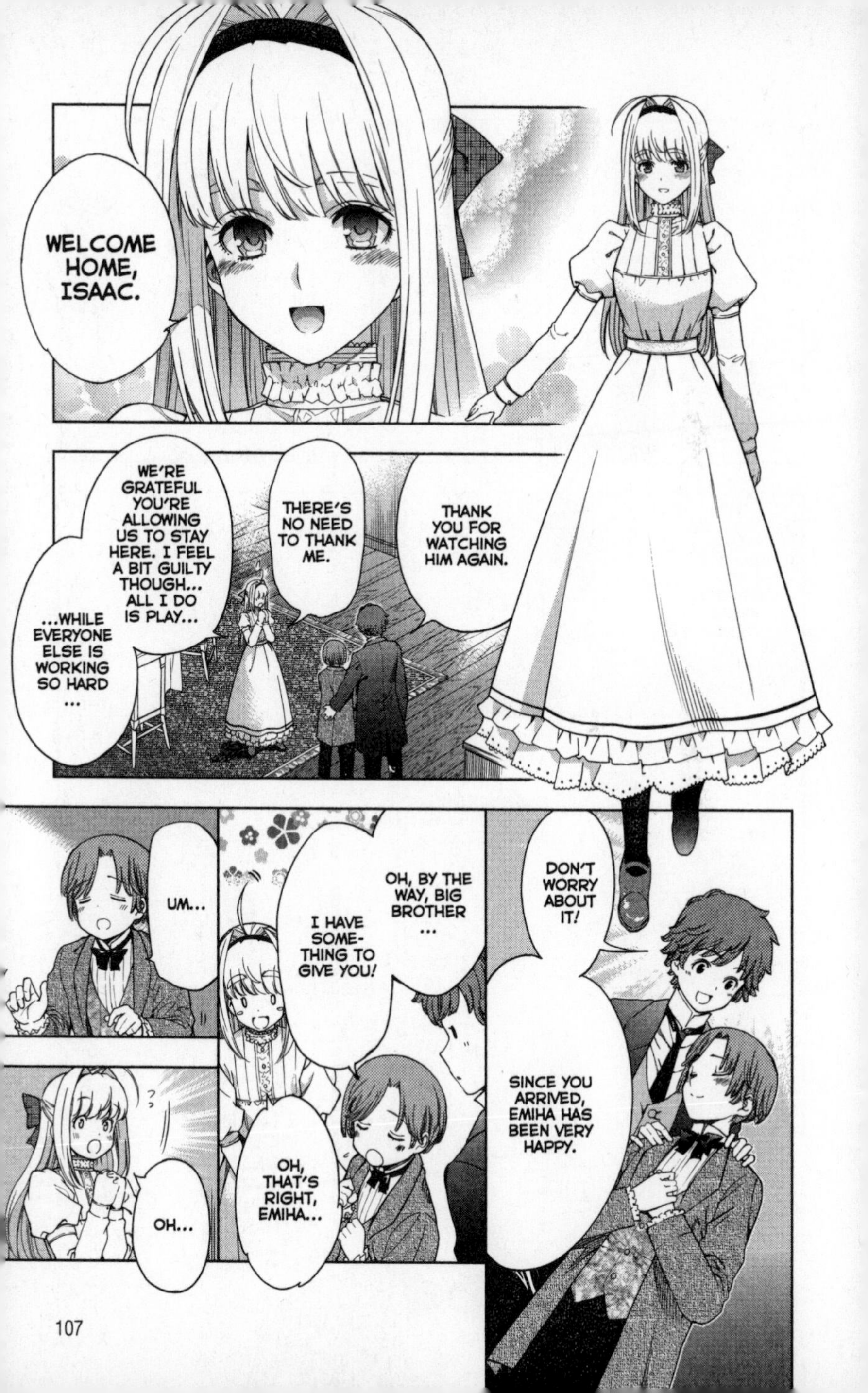
WELCOME HOME, ISAAC.
THANK YOU FOR WATCHING HIM AGAIN.
THERE'S NO NEED TO THANK ME.
WE'RE GRATEFUL YOU'RE ALLOWING US TO STAY HERE. I FEEL A BIT GUILTY THOUGH... ALL I DO IS PLAY...
...WHILE EVERYONE ELSE IS WORKING SO HARD...
DON'T WORRY ABOUT IT!
SINCE YOU ARRIVED, EMIHA HAS BEEN VERY HAPPY.
OH, BY THE WAY, BIG BROTHER...
I HAVE SOMETHING TO GIVE YOU!
OH, THAT'S RIGHT, EMIHA...
UM...
OH...

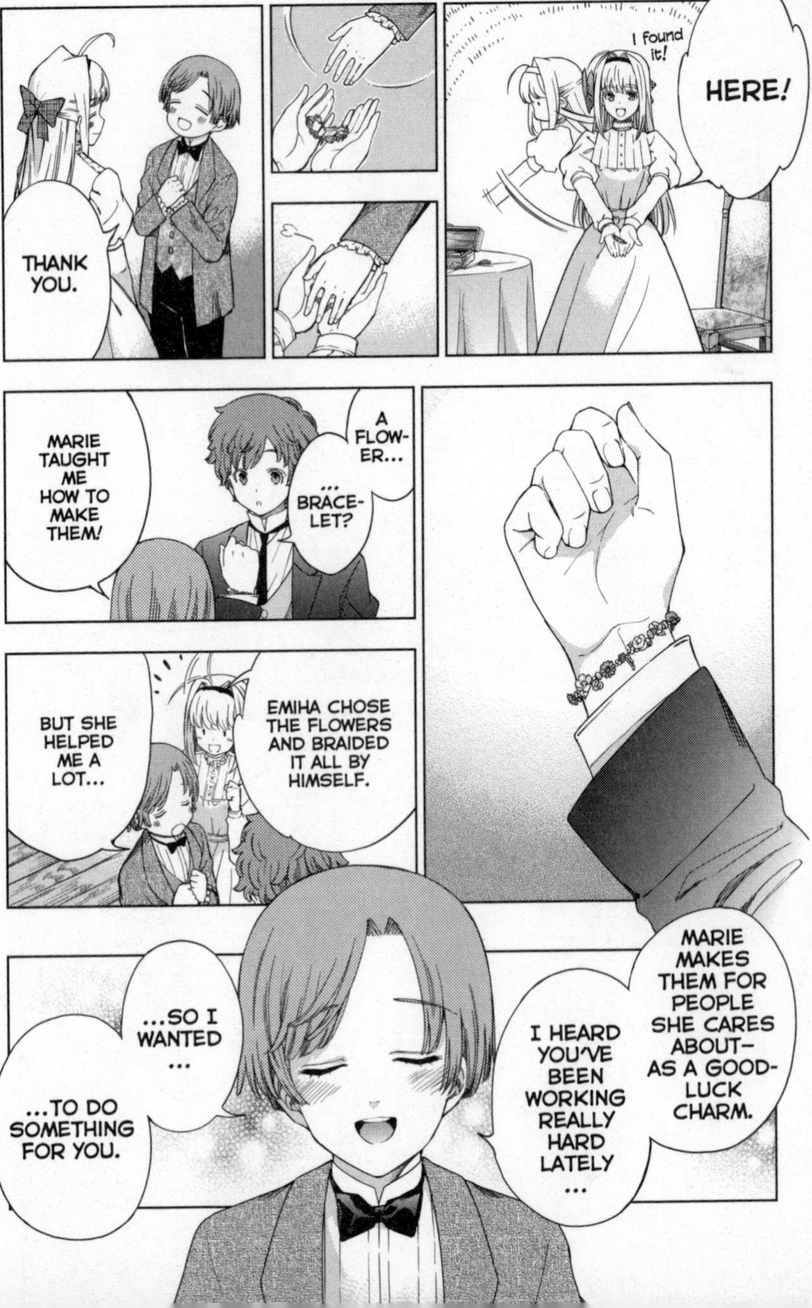
I found it!
HERE!
THANK YOU.
A FLOWER-ER... ...BRACELET?
MARIE TAUGHT ME HOW TO MAKE THEM!
EMIHA CHOSE THE FLOWERS AND BRAIDED IT ALL BY HIMSELF.
BUT SHE HELPED ME A LOT...
MARIE MAKES THEM FOR PEOPLE SHE CARES ABOUT—AS A GOOD-LUCK CHARM.
I HEARD YOU'VE BEEN WORKING REALLY HARD LATELY...
...SO I WANTED...
...TO DO SOMETHING FOR YOU.

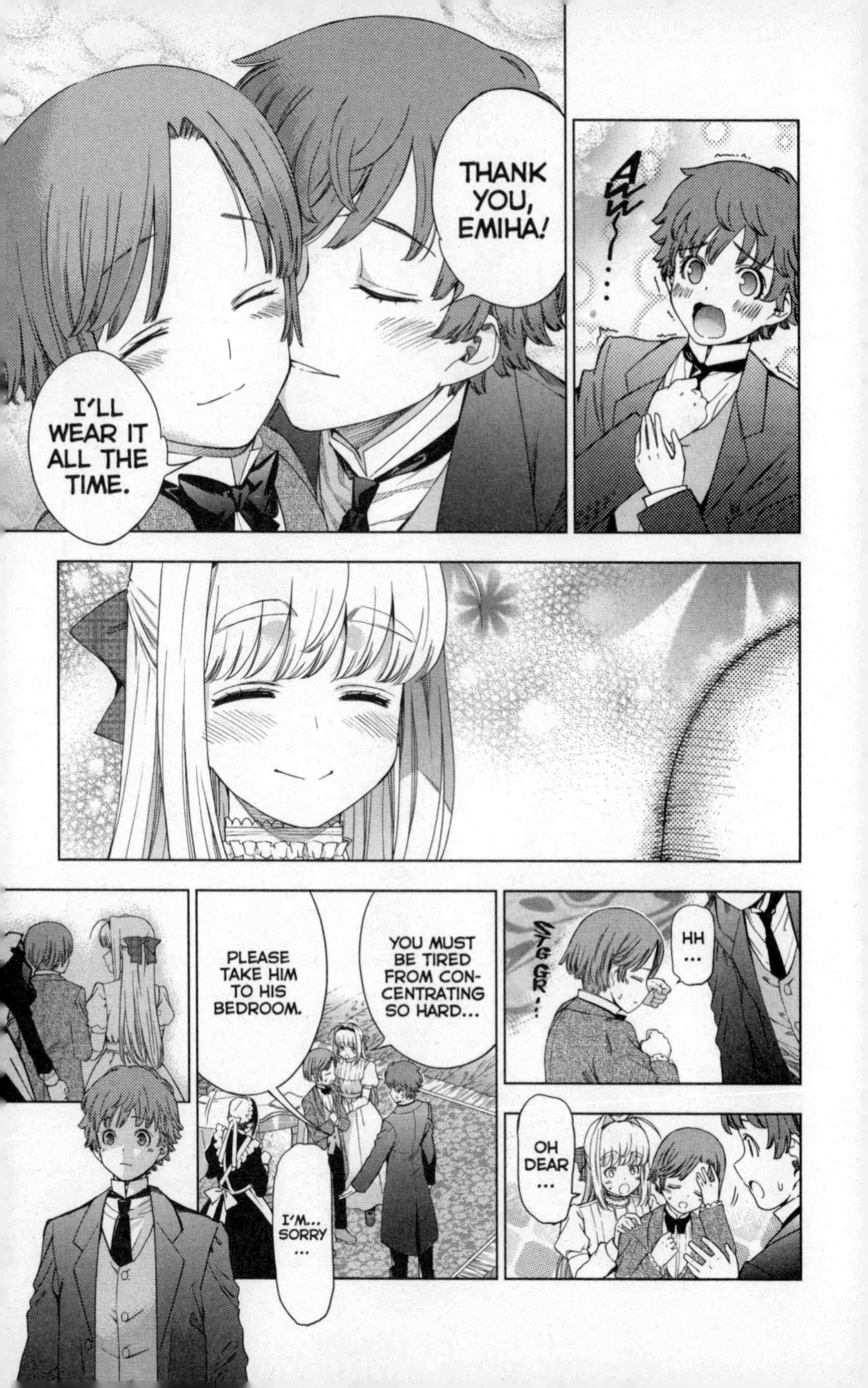
AWW-...
THANK YOU, EMIHA!
I'LL WEAR IT ALL THE TIME.
STGGR..
HH...
OH DEAR...
YOU MUST BE TIRED FROM CONCENTRATING SO HARD...
PLEASE TAKE HIM TO HIS BEDROOM.
I'M... SORRY...

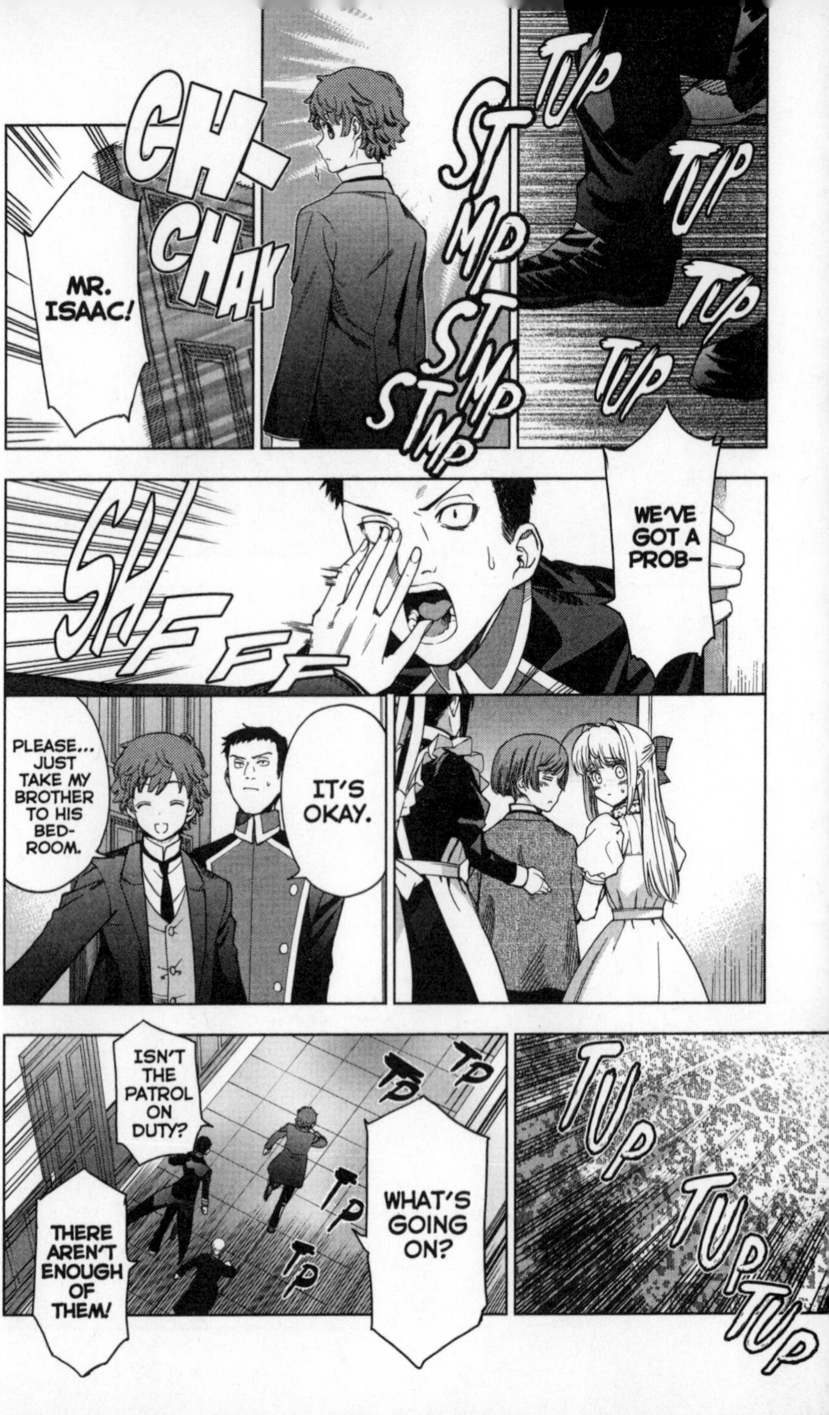
TUP TUP TUP TUP
STMP STMP STMP STMP
CH-CHAK
MR. ISAAC!
WE'VE GOT A PROB-
SHFFF
IT'S OKAY.
PLEASE... JUST TAKE MY BROTHER TO HIS BED-ROOM.
TUP TUP TUP TUP
TP TP
WHAT'S GOING ON?
ISN'T THE PATROL ON DUTY?
TP TP
THERE AREN'T ENOUGH OF THEM!

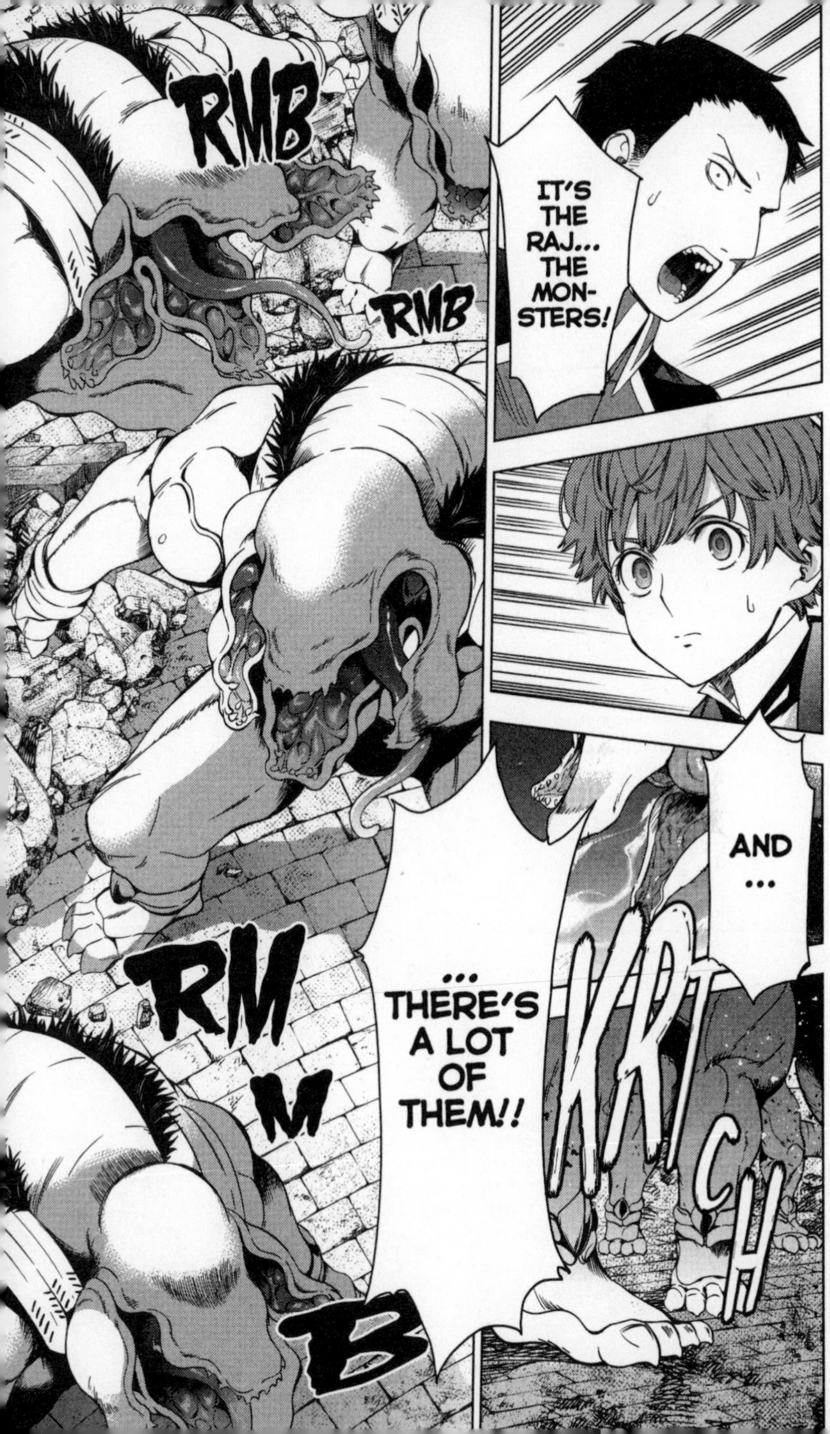
IT'S THE RAJ... THE MONSTERS!
AND ...
... THERE'S A LOT OF THEM!!
KRTCH
RMB
RMB
RMMB

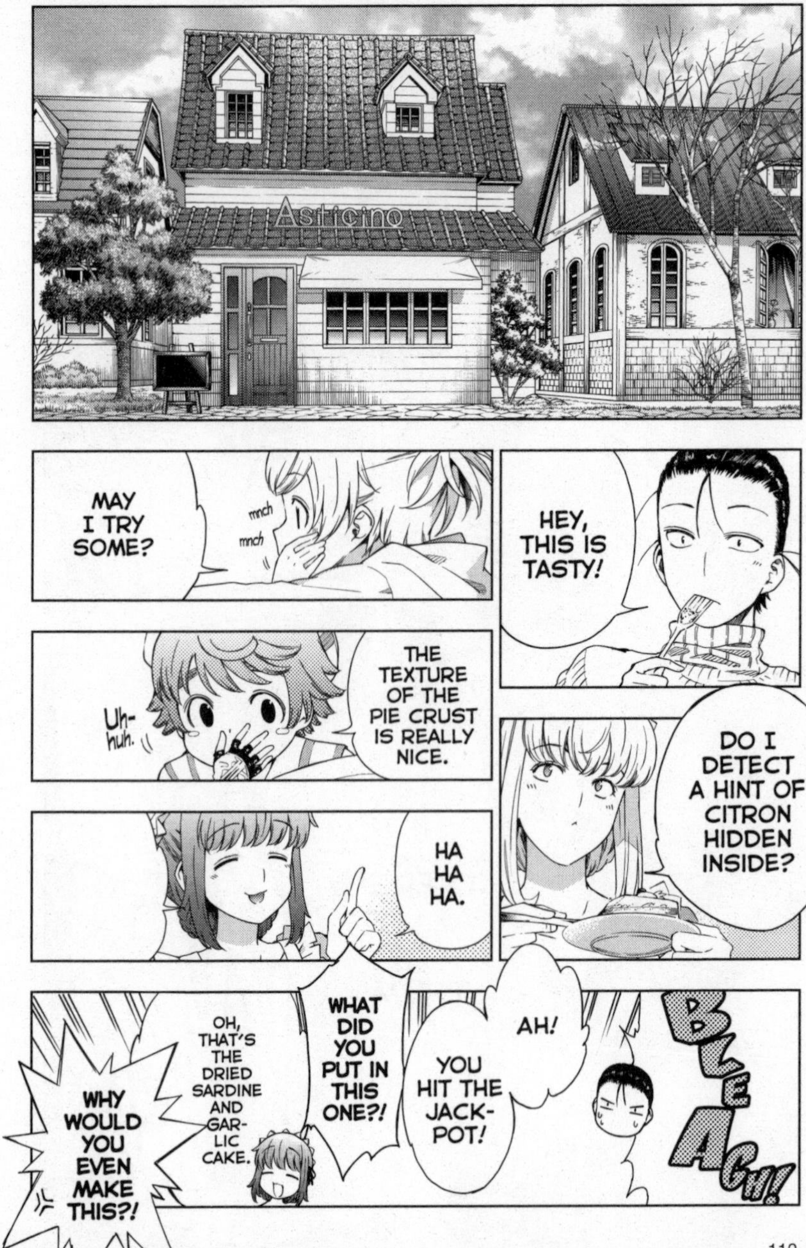
Asticino
HEY, THIS IS TASTY!
MAY I TRY SOME?
mnch mnch
THE TEXTURE OF THE PIE CRUST IS REALLY NICE.
Uh-huh.
DO I DETECT A HINT OF CITRON HIDDEN INSIDE?
HA HA HA.
BLEAGH!
AH!
YOU HIT THE JACK-POT!
WHAT DID YOU PUT IN THIS ONE?!
OH, THAT'S THE DRIED SARDINE AND GAR-LIC CAKE.
WHY WOULD YOU EVEN MAKE THIS?!

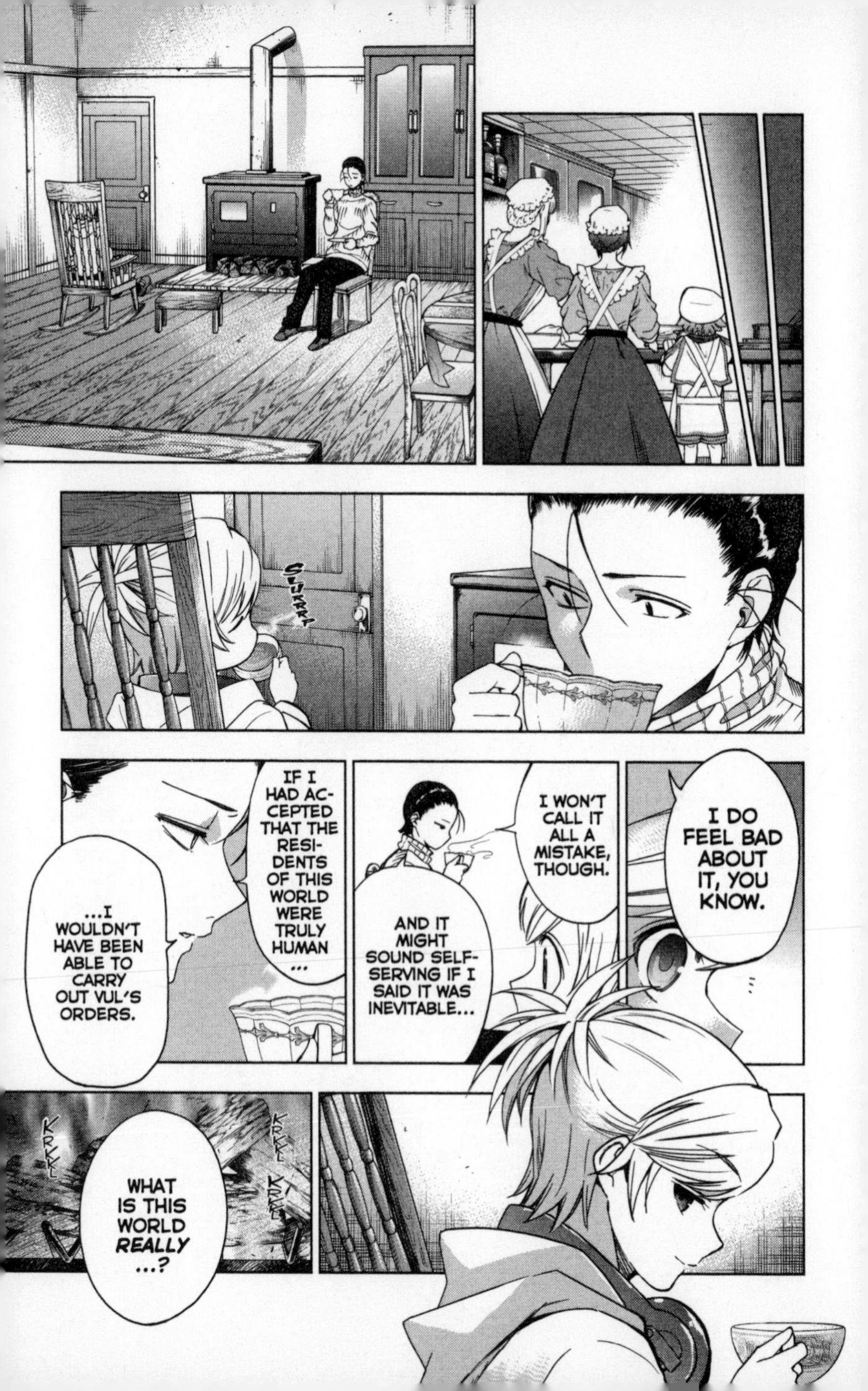
SLURRRP
I DO FEEL BAD ABOUT IT, YOU KNOW.
I WON'T CALL IT ALL A MISTAKE, THOUGH.
AND IT MIGHT SOUND SELF-SERVING IF I SAID IT WAS INEVITABLE...
IF I HAD ACCEPTED THAT THE RESIDENTS OF THIS WORLD WERE TRULY HUMAN...
...I WOULDN'T HAVE BEEN ABLE TO CARRY OUT VUL'S ORDERS.
KRKKL
KRKKL
KRKKL
WHAT IS THIS WORLD *REALLY*...?

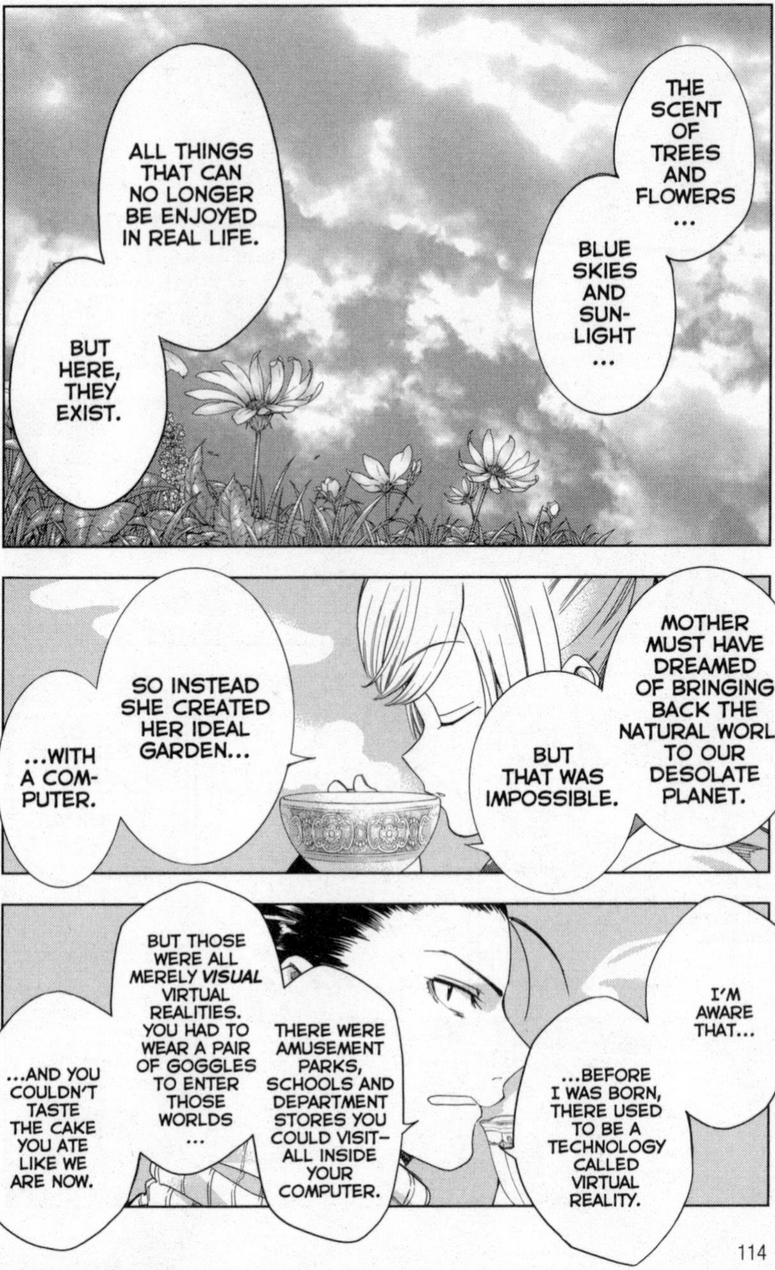
THE SCENT OF TREES AND FLOWERS...
BLUE SKIES AND SUN-LIGHT...
ALL THINGS THAT CAN NO LONGER BE ENJOYED IN REAL LIFE.
BUT HERE, THEY EXIST.
MOTHER MUST HAVE DREAMED OF BRINGING BACK THE NATURAL WORLD TO OUR DESOLATE PLANET.
BUT THAT WAS IMPOSSIBLE.
SO INSTEAD SHE CREATED HER IDEAL GARDEN...
...WITH A COM-PUTER.
I'M AWARE THAT...
...BEFORE I WAS BORN, THERE USED TO BE A TECHNOLOGY CALLED VIRTUAL REALITY.
THERE WERE AMUSEMENT PARKS, SCHOOLS AND DEPARTMENT STORES YOU COULD VISIT—ALL INSIDE YOUR COMPUTER.
BUT THOSE WERE ALL MERELY *VISUAL* VIRTUAL REALITIES. YOU HAD TO WEAR A PAIR OF GOGGLES TO ENTER THOSE WORLDS...
...AND YOU COULDN'T TASTE THE CAKE YOU ATE LIKE WE ARE NOW.

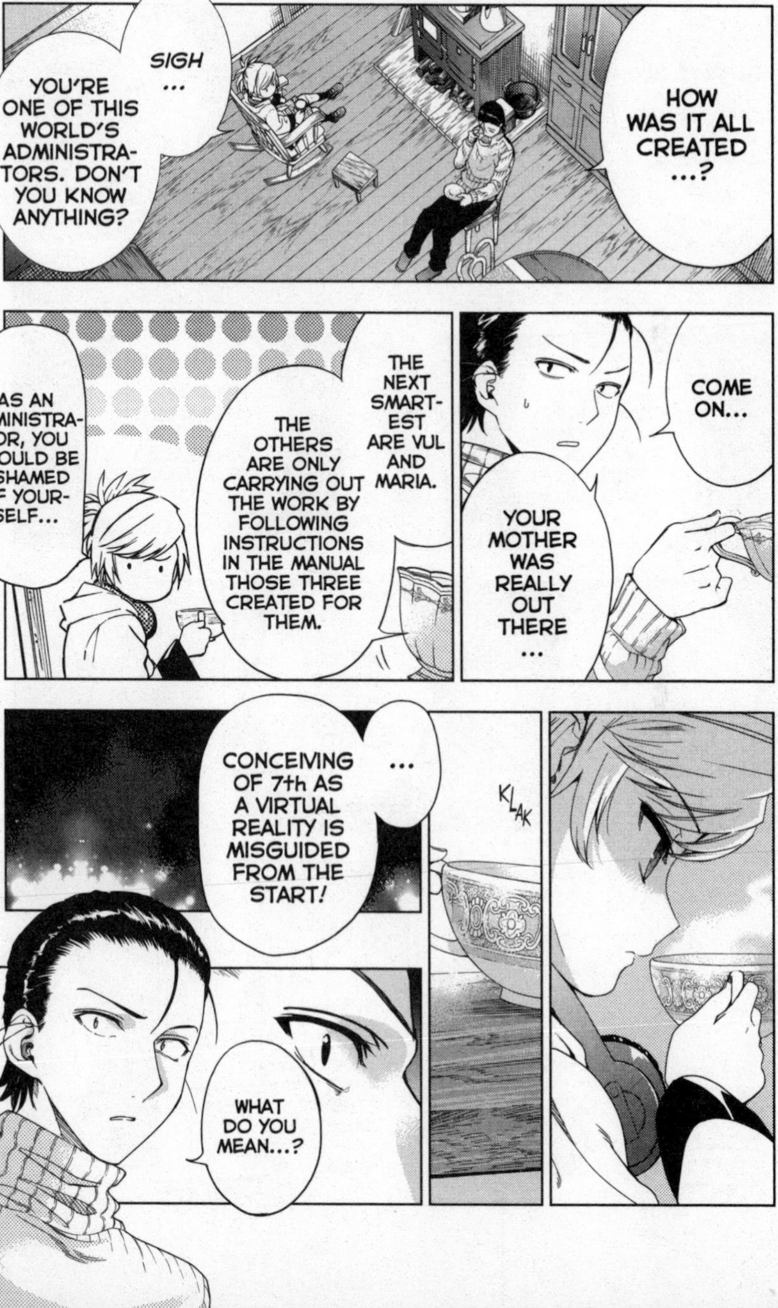
HOW WAS IT ALL CREATED ...?
SIGH ...
YOU'RE ONE OF THIS WORLD'S ADMINISTRATORS. DON'T YOU KNOW ANYTHING?
COME ON...
YOUR MOTHER WAS REALLY OUT THERE ...
THE NEXT SMARTEST ARE VUL AND MARIA.
THE OTHERS ARE ONLY CARRYING OUT THE WORK BY FOLLOWING INSTRUCTIONS IN THE MANUAL THOSE THREE CREATED FOR THEM.
AS AN ADMINISTRATOR, YOU SHOULD BE ASHAMED OF YOURSELF...
KLAK
...
CONCEIVING OF 7th AS A VIRTUAL REALITY IS MISGUIDED FROM THE START!
WHAT DO YOU MEAN...?

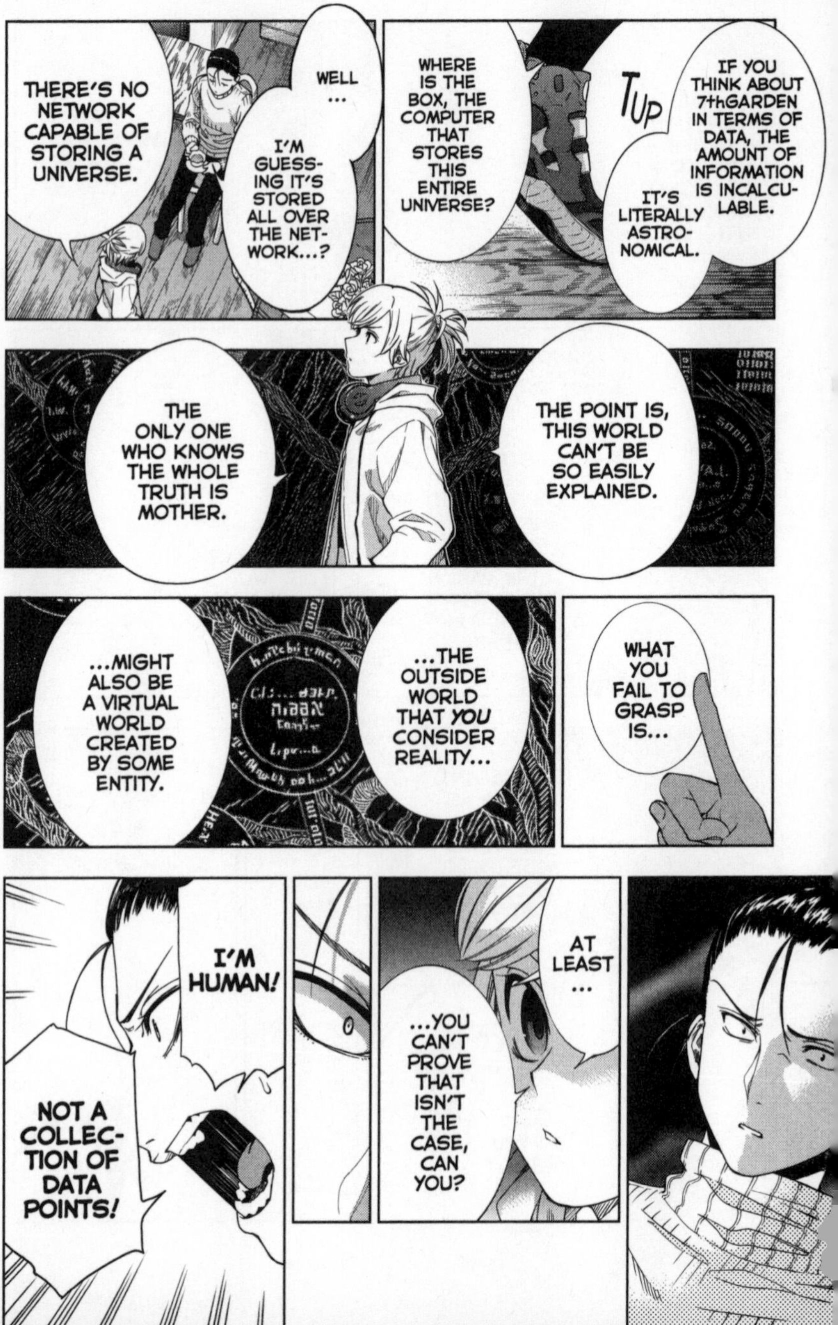
IF YOU THINK ABOUT 7thGARDEN IN TERMS OF DATA, THE AMOUNT OF INFORMATION IS INCALCULABLE.
IT'S LITERALLY ASTRONOMICAL.
TUP
WHERE IS THE BOX, THE COMPUTER THAT STORES THIS ENTIRE UNIVERSE?
WELL...
I'M GUESSING IT'S STORED ALL OVER THE NETWORK...?
THERE'S NO NETWORK CAPABLE OF STORING A UNIVERSE.
THE POINT IS, THIS WORLD CAN'T BE SO EASILY EXPLAINED.
THE ONLY ONE WHO KNOWS THE WHOLE TRUTH IS MOTHER.
WHAT YOU FAIL TO GRASP IS...
...THE OUTSIDE WORLD THAT *YOU* CONSIDER REALITY...
...MIGHT ALSO BE A VIRTUAL WORLD CREATED BY SOME ENTITY.
AT LEAST...
...YOU CAN'T PROVE THAT ISN'T THE CASE, CAN YOU?
I'M HUMAN!
NOT A COLLECTION OF DATA POINTS!

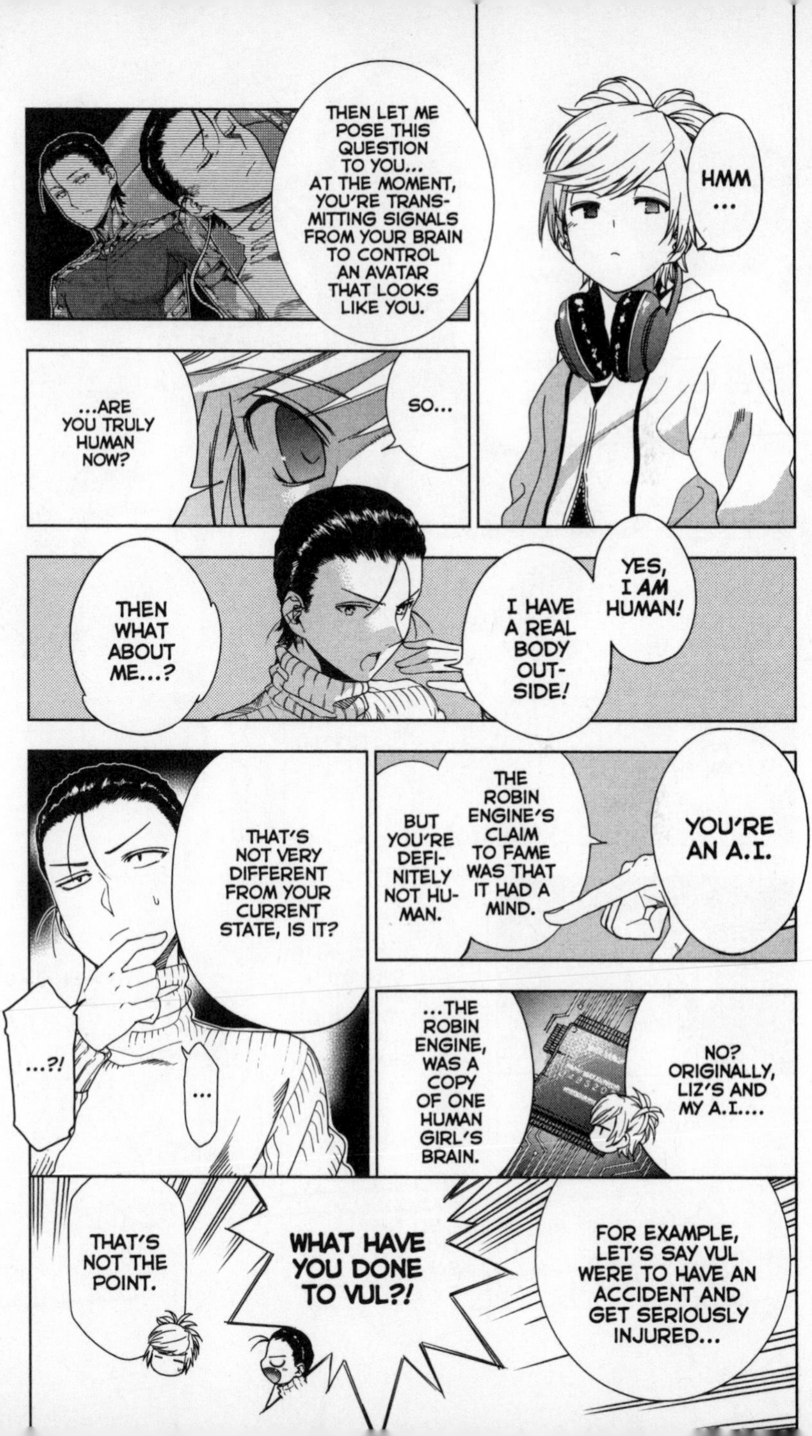
HMM ...
THEN LET ME POSE THIS QUESTION TO YOU... AT THE MOMENT, YOU'RE TRANSMITTING SIGNALS FROM YOUR BRAIN TO CONTROL AN AVATAR THAT LOOKS LIKE YOU.
SO...
...ARE YOU TRULY HUMAN NOW?
YES, I *AM* HUMAN!
I HAVE A REAL BODY OUTSIDE!
THEN WHAT ABOUT ME...?
YOU'RE AN A.I.
THE ROBIN ENGINE'S CLAIM TO FAME WAS THAT IT HAD A MIND.
BUT YOU'RE DEFINITELY NOT HUMAN.
NO? ORIGINALLY, LIZ'S AND MY A.I....
...THE ROBIN ENGINE, WAS A COPY OF ONE HUMAN GIRL'S BRAIN.
THAT'S NOT VERY DIFFERENT FROM YOUR CURRENT STATE, IS IT?
...
...?!
FOR EXAMPLE, LET'S SAY VUL WERE TO HAVE AN ACCIDENT AND GET SERIOUSLY INJURED...
WHAT HAVE YOU DONE TO VUL?!
THAT'S NOT THE POINT.

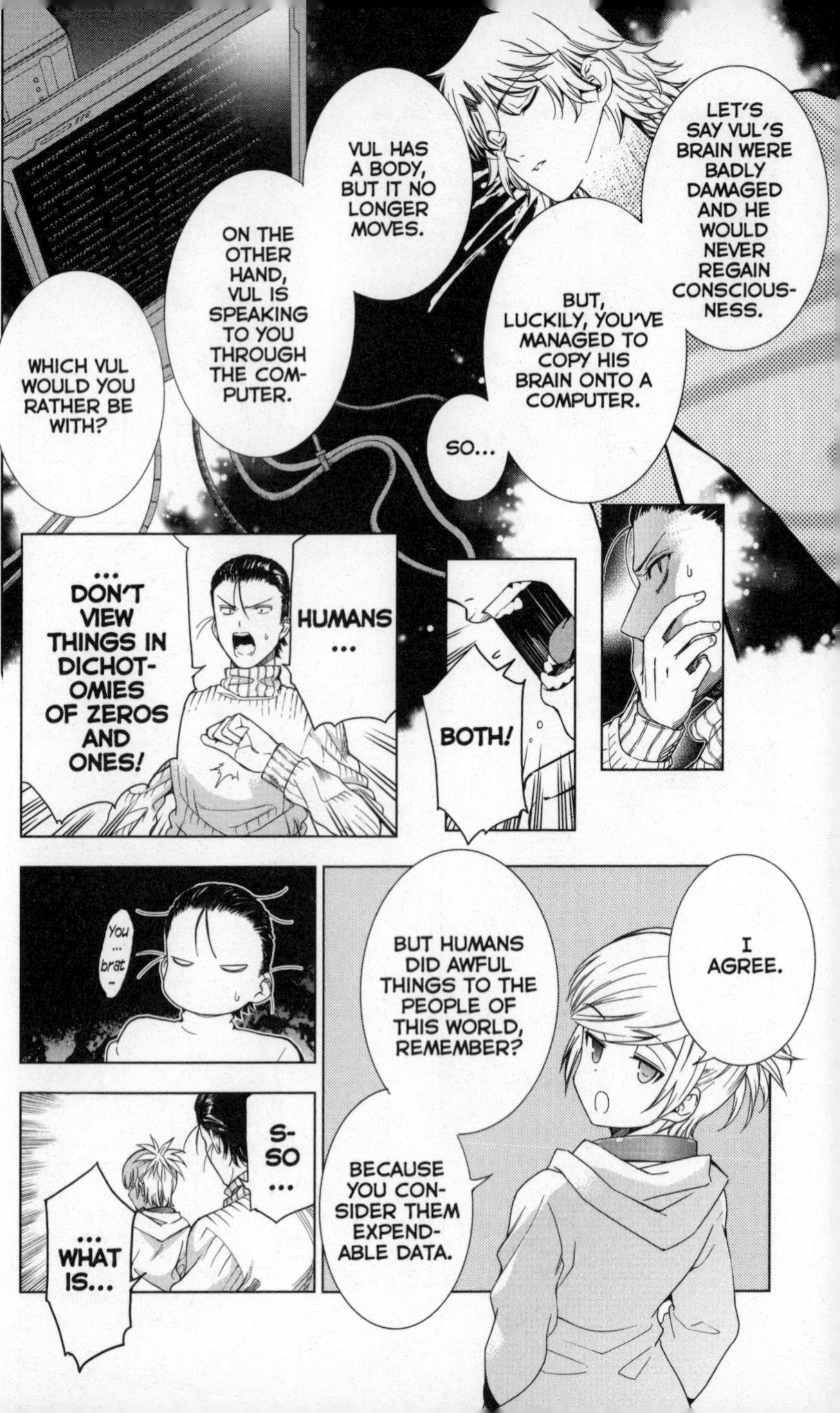
LET'S SAY VUL'S BRAIN WERE BADLY DAMAGED AND HE WOULD NEVER REGAIN CONSCIOUSNESS.
BUT, LUCKILY, YOU'VE MANAGED TO COPY HIS BRAIN ONTO A COMPUTER.
SO...
VUL HAS A BODY, BUT IT NO LONGER MOVES.
ON THE OTHER HAND, VUL IS SPEAKING TO YOU THROUGH THE COMPUTER.
WHICH VUL WOULD YOU RATHER BE WITH?
BOTH!
HUMANS ...
... DON'T VIEW THINGS IN DICHOTOMIES OF ZEROS AND ONES!
I AGREE.
BUT HUMANS DID AWFUL THINGS TO THE PEOPLE OF THIS WORLD, REMEMBER?
BECAUSE YOU CONSIDER THEM EXPENDABLE DATA.
You ... brat ...
S-SO ...
... WHAT IS...

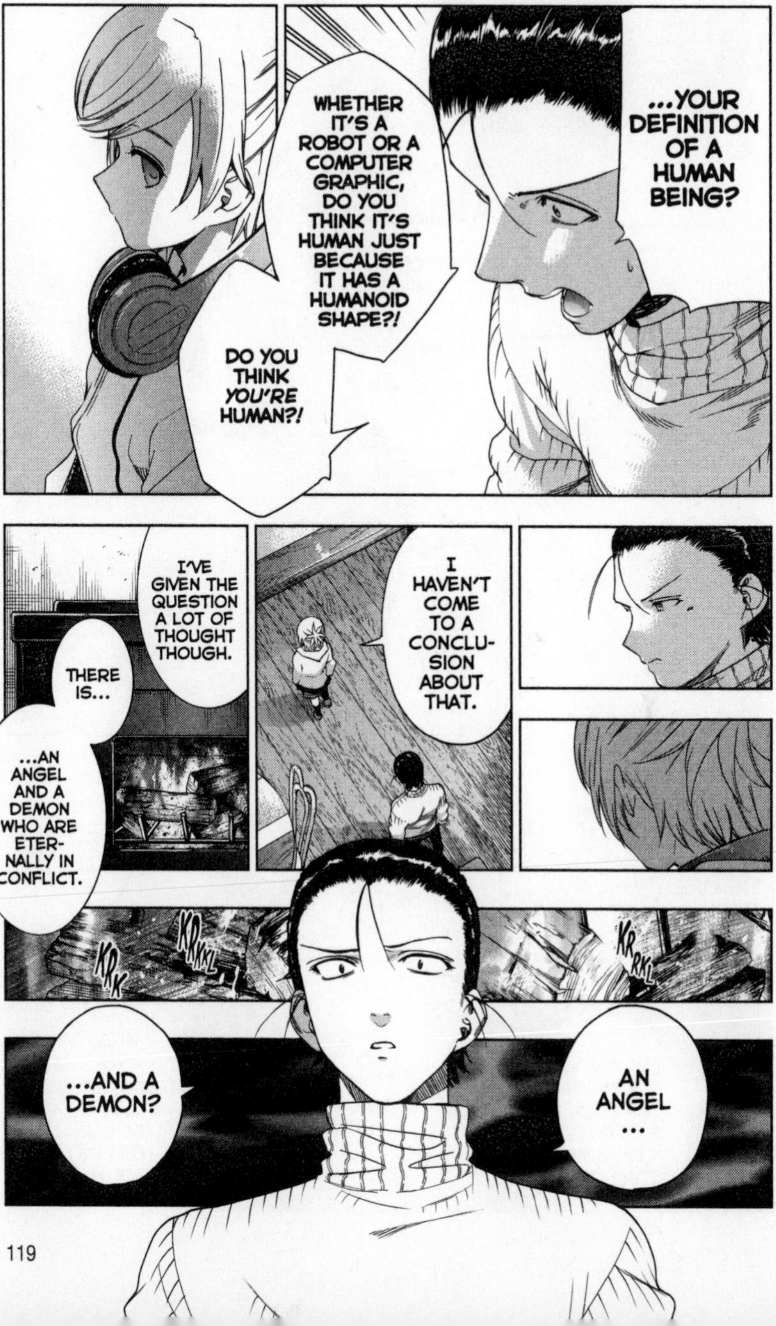
...YOUR DEFINITION OF A HUMAN BEING?
WHETHER IT'S A ROBOT OR A COMPUTER GRAPHIC, DO YOU THINK IT'S HUMAN JUST BECAUSE IT HAS A HUMANOID SHAPE?!
DO YOU THINK *YOU'RE* HUMAN?!
I HAVEN'T COME TO A CONCLUSION ABOUT THAT.
I'VE GIVEN THE QUESTION A LOT OF THOUGHT THOUGH.
THERE IS...
...AN ANGEL AND A DEMON WHO ARE ETERNALLY IN CONFLICT.
KRRKKL
KRKKL
KRK
AN ANGEL ...
...AND A DEMON?

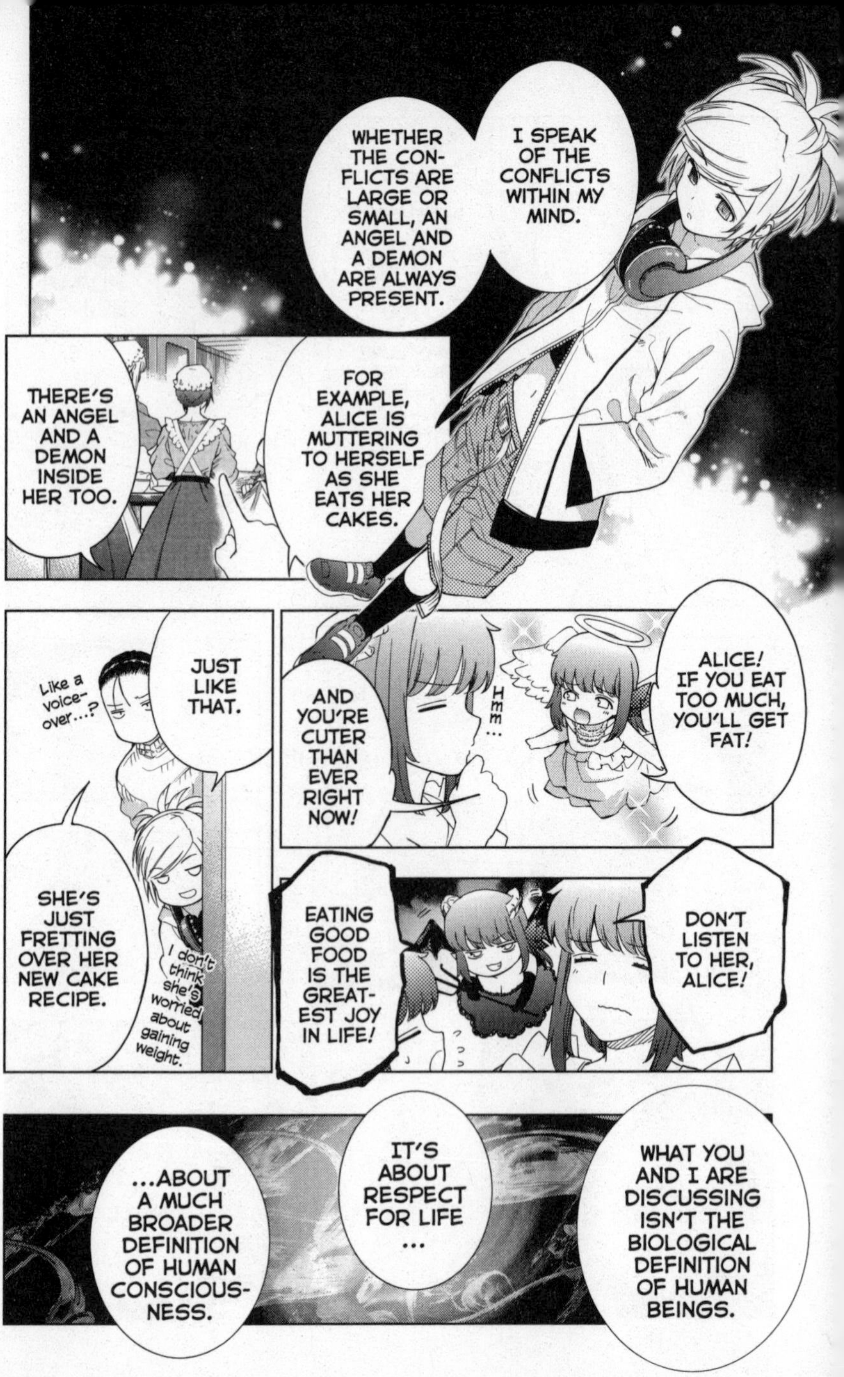
I SPEAK OF THE CONFLICTS WITHIN MY MIND.
WHETHER THE CONFLICTS ARE LARGE OR SMALL, AN ANGEL AND A DEMON ARE ALWAYS PRESENT.
FOR EXAMPLE, ALICE IS MUTTERING TO HERSELF AS SHE EATS HER CAKES.
THERE'S AN ANGEL AND A DEMON INSIDE HER TOO.
ALICE! IF YOU EAT TOO MUCH, YOU'LL GET FAT!
Hmm...
AND YOU'RE CUTER THAN EVER RIGHT NOW!
DON'T LISTEN TO HER, ALICE!
EATING GOOD FOOD IS THE GREATEST JOY IN LIFE!
JUST LIKE THAT.
Like a voice-over...?
SHE'S JUST FRETTING OVER HER NEW CAKE RECIPE.
I don't think she's worried about gaining weight.
WHAT YOU AND I ARE DISCUSSING ISN'T THE BIOLOGICAL DEFINITION OF HUMAN BEINGS.
IT'S ABOUT RESPECT FOR LIFE ...
...ABOUT A MUCH BROADER DEFINITION OF HUMAN CONSCIOUSNESS.

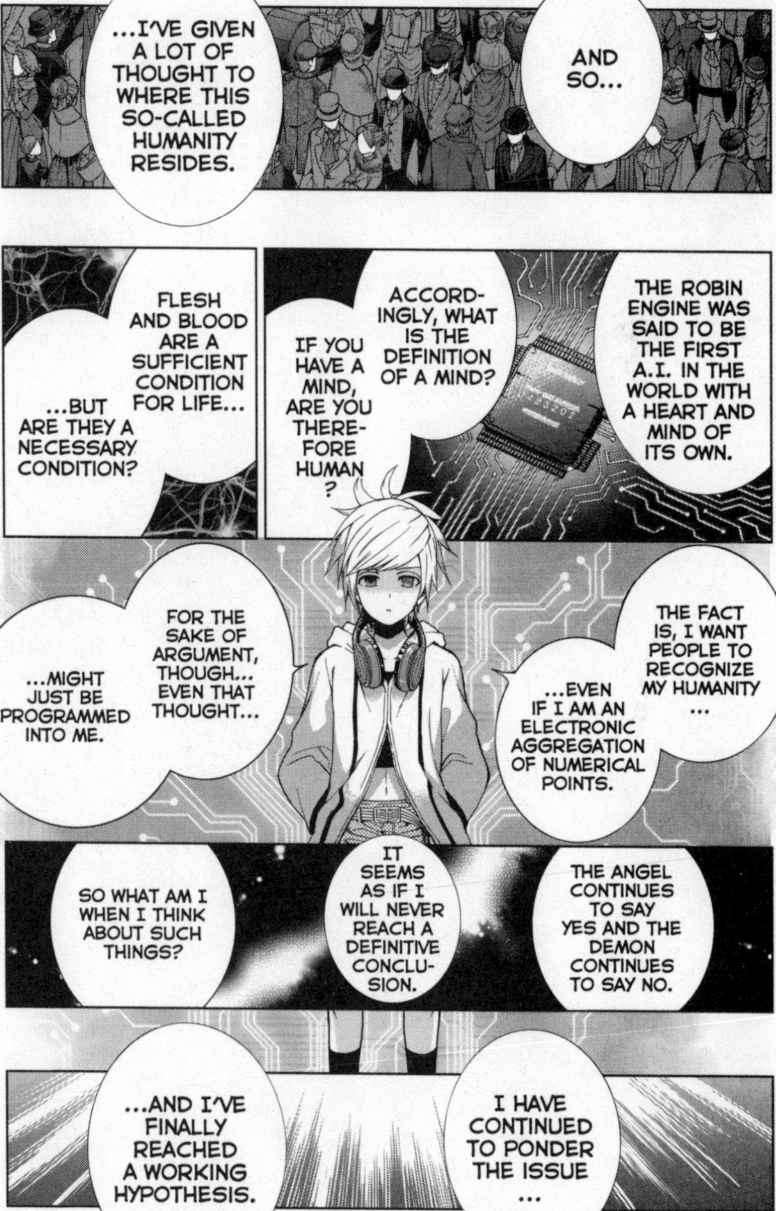
AND SO...
...I'VE GIVEN A LOT OF THOUGHT TO WHERE THIS SO-CALLED HUMANITY RESIDES.
THE ROBIN ENGINE WAS SAID TO BE THE FIRST A.I. IN THE WORLD WITH A HEART AND MIND OF ITS OWN.
ACCORDINGLY, WHAT IS THE DEFINITION OF A MIND?
IF YOU HAVE A MIND, ARE YOU THEREFORE HUMAN?
FLESH AND BLOOD ARE A SUFFICIENT CONDITION FOR LIFE...
...BUT ARE THEY A NECESSARY CONDITION?
THE FACT IS, I WANT PEOPLE TO RECOGNIZE MY HUMANITY...
...EVEN IF I AM AN ELECTRONIC AGGREGATION OF NUMERICAL POINTS.
FOR THE SAKE OF ARGUMENT, THOUGH... EVEN THAT THOUGHT...
...MIGHT JUST BE PROGRAMMED INTO ME.
THE ANGEL CONTINUES TO SAY YES AND THE DEMON CONTINUES TO SAY NO.
IT SEEMS AS IF I WILL NEVER REACH A DEFINITIVE CONCLUSION.
SO WHAT AM I WHEN I THINK ABOUT SUCH THINGS?
I HAVE CONTINUED TO PONDER THE ISSUE...
...AND I'VE FINALLY REACHED A WORKING HYPOTHESIS.

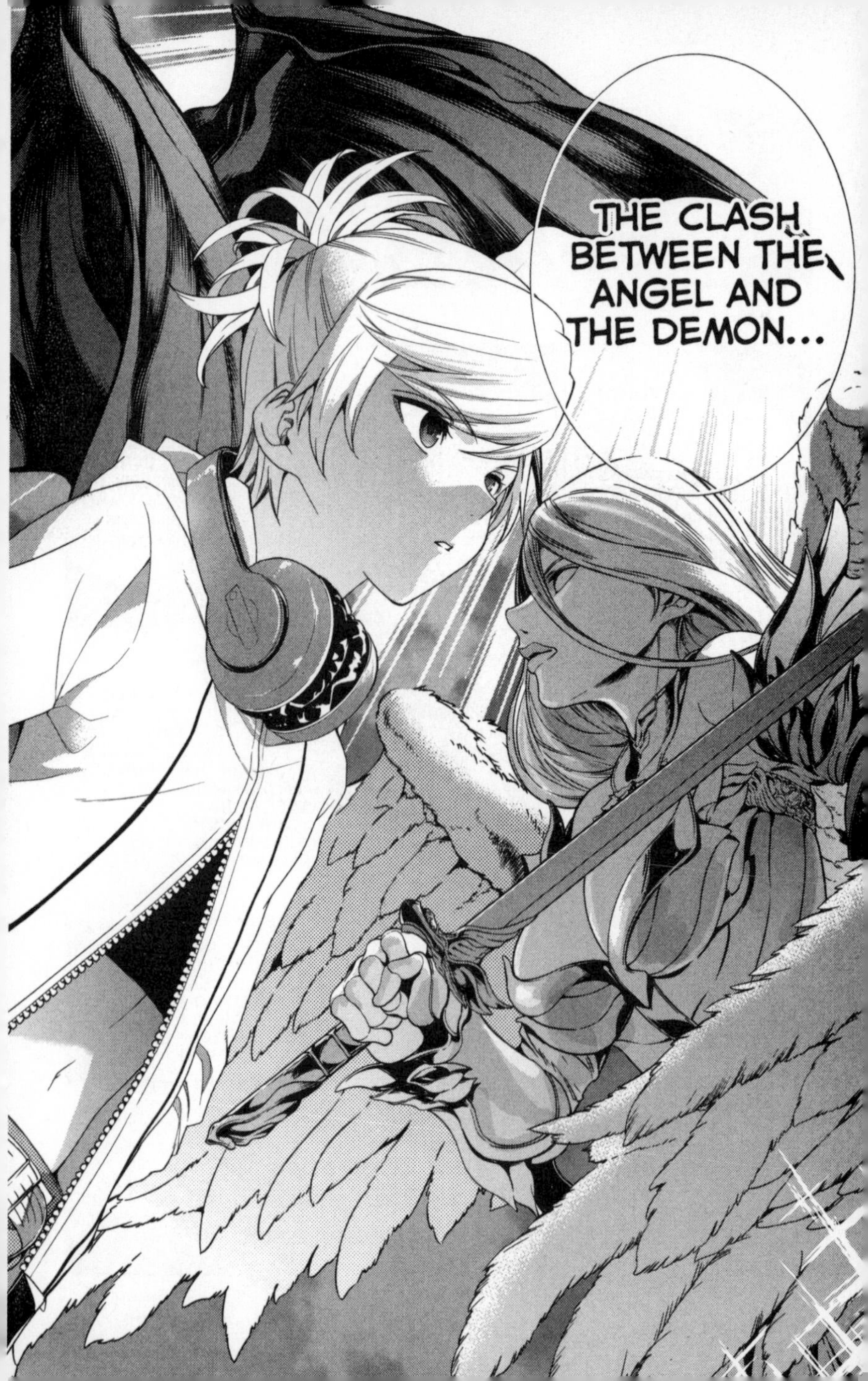
THE CLASH BETWEEN THE ANGEL AND THE DEMON...

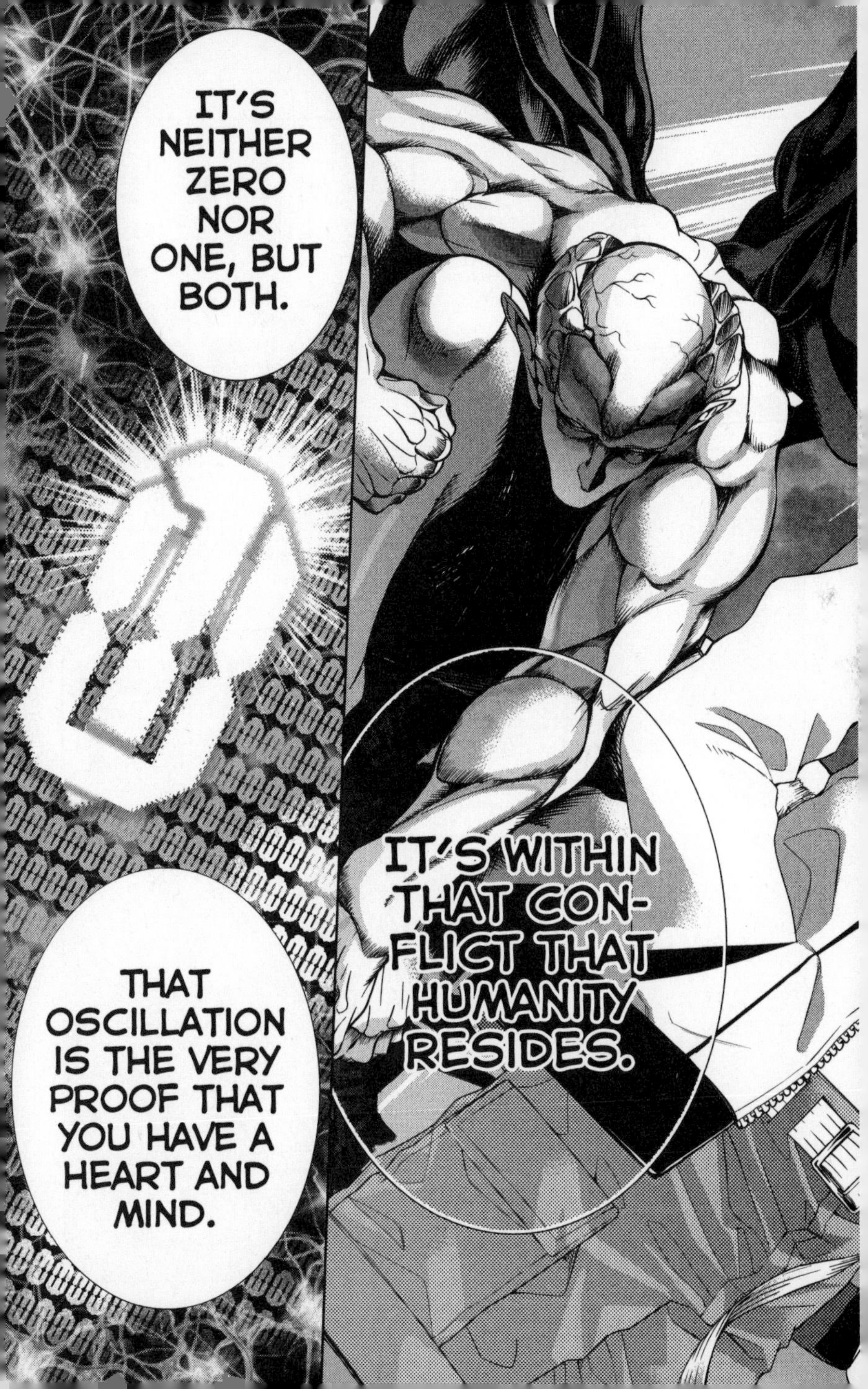
IT'S NEITHER ZERO NOR ONE, BUT BOTH.
THAT OSCILLATION IS THE VERY PROOF THAT YOU HAVE A HEART AND MIND.
IT'S WITHIN THAT CONFLICT THAT HUMANITY RESIDES.

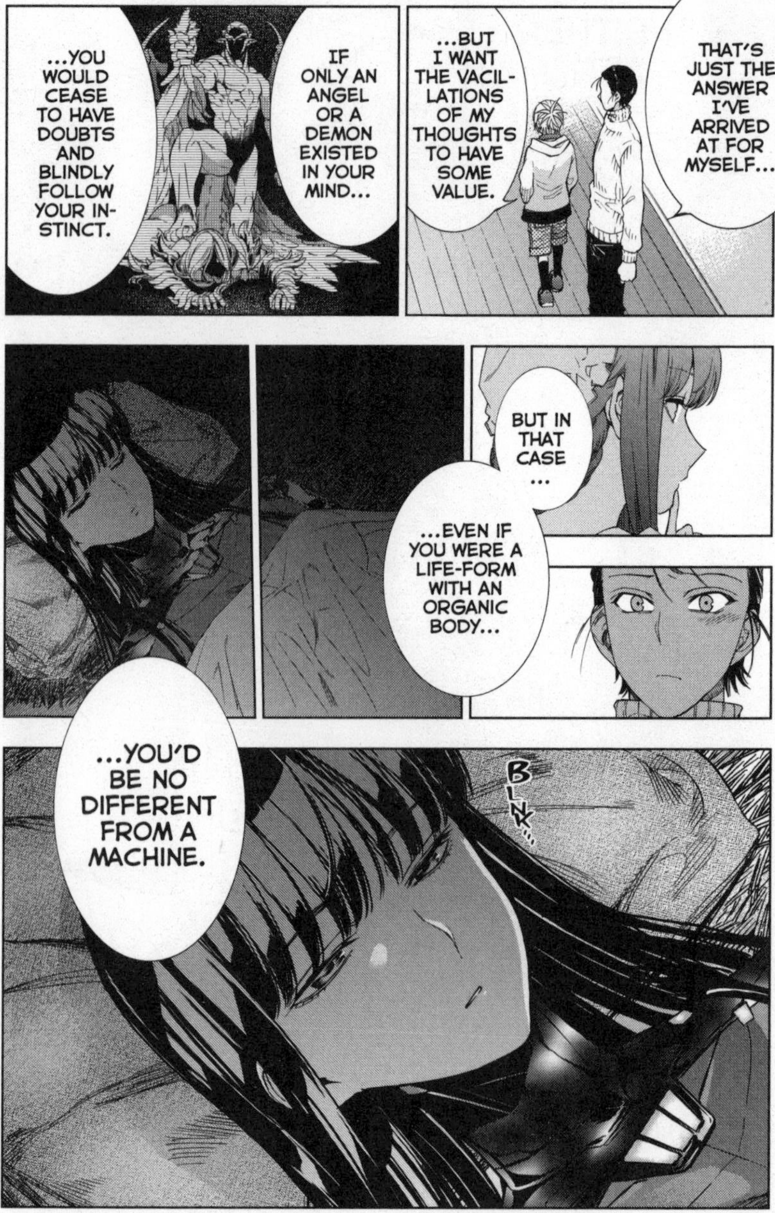
THAT'S JUST THE ANSWER I'VE ARRIVED AT FOR MYSELF...
...BUT I WANT THE VACILLATIONS OF MY THOUGHTS TO HAVE SOME VALUE.
IF ONLY AN ANGEL OR A DEMON EXISTED IN YOUR MIND...
...YOU WOULD CEASE TO HAVE DOUBTS AND BLINDLY FOLLOW YOUR INSTINCT.
BUT IN THAT CASE ...
...EVEN IF YOU WERE A LIFE-FORM WITH AN ORGANIC BODY...
...YOU'D BE NO DIFFERENT FROM A MACHINE.
BLINK...

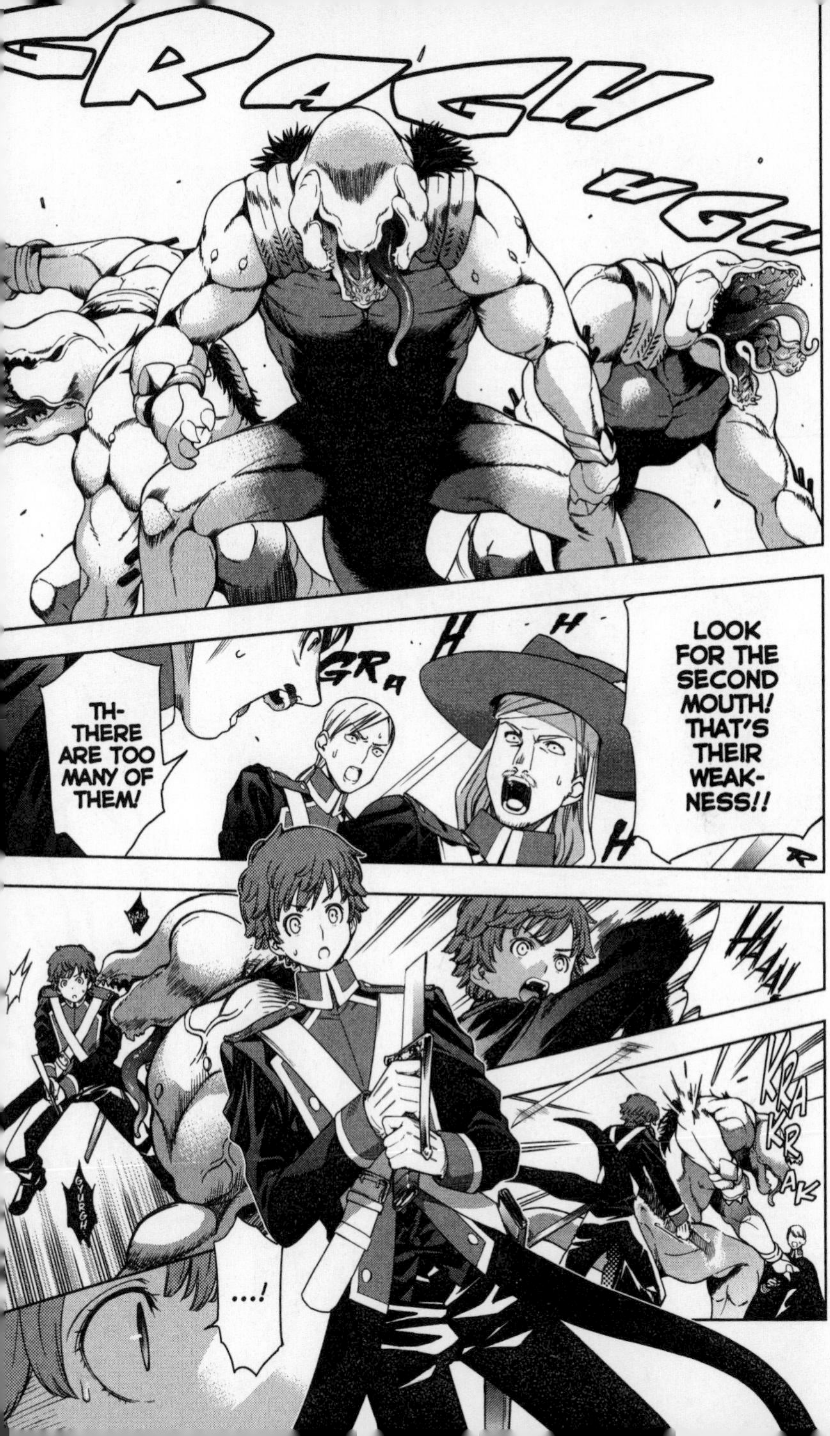
GRAGH
HGH
LOOK FOR THE SECOND MOUTH! THAT'S THEIR WEAKNESS!!
H H H
GRA
TH- THERE ARE TOO MANY OF THEM!
HAAA!
KRAKRAK
GYURGH
...!

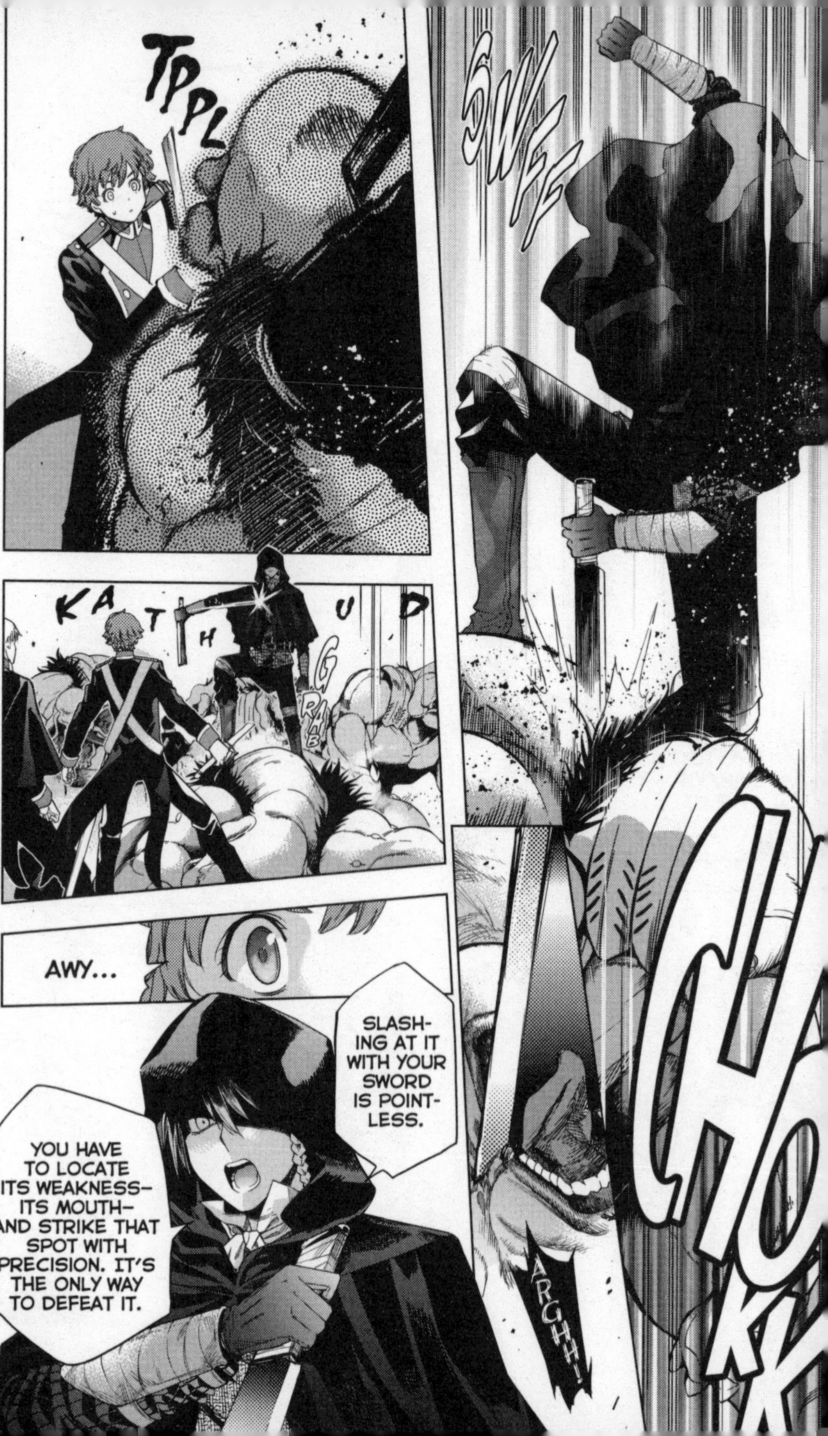
SWFF
TPPL
KATHUD
GRAB
CHOKK
ARGHH!
AWY...
SLASHING AT IT WITH YOUR SWORD IS POINTLESS.
YOU HAVE TO LOCATE ITS WEAKNESS—ITS MOUTH—AND STRIKE THAT SPOT WITH PRECISION. IT'S THE ONLY WAY TO DEFEAT IT.

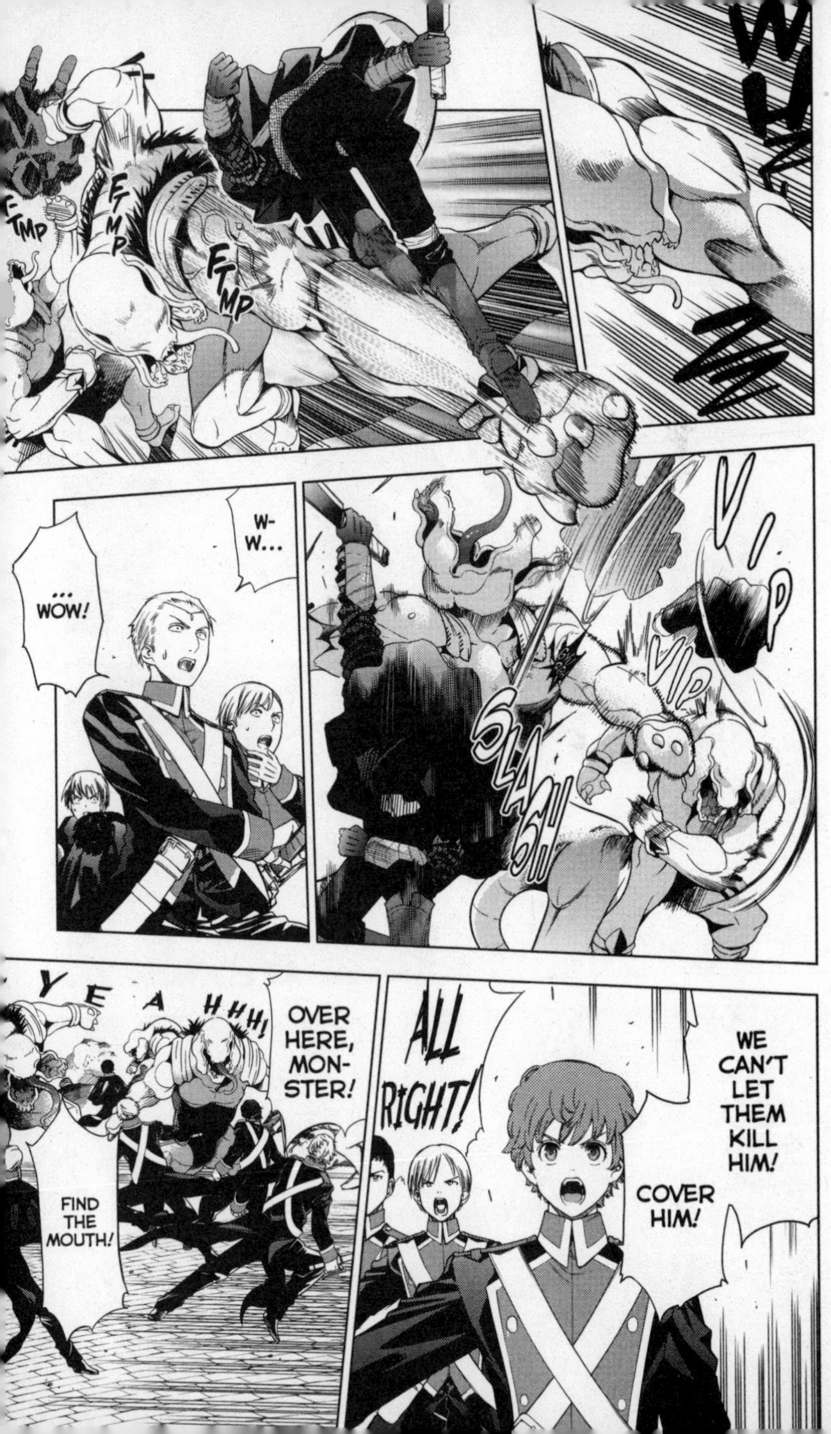
WHAM
FTMP
FTMP
FTMP
VIP
VIP
SLASH
W-
W...
...WOW!
WE CAN'T LET THEM KILL HIM!
COVER HIM!
ALL RIGHT!
OVER HERE, MONSTER!
YEAHHH!
FIND THE MOUTH!

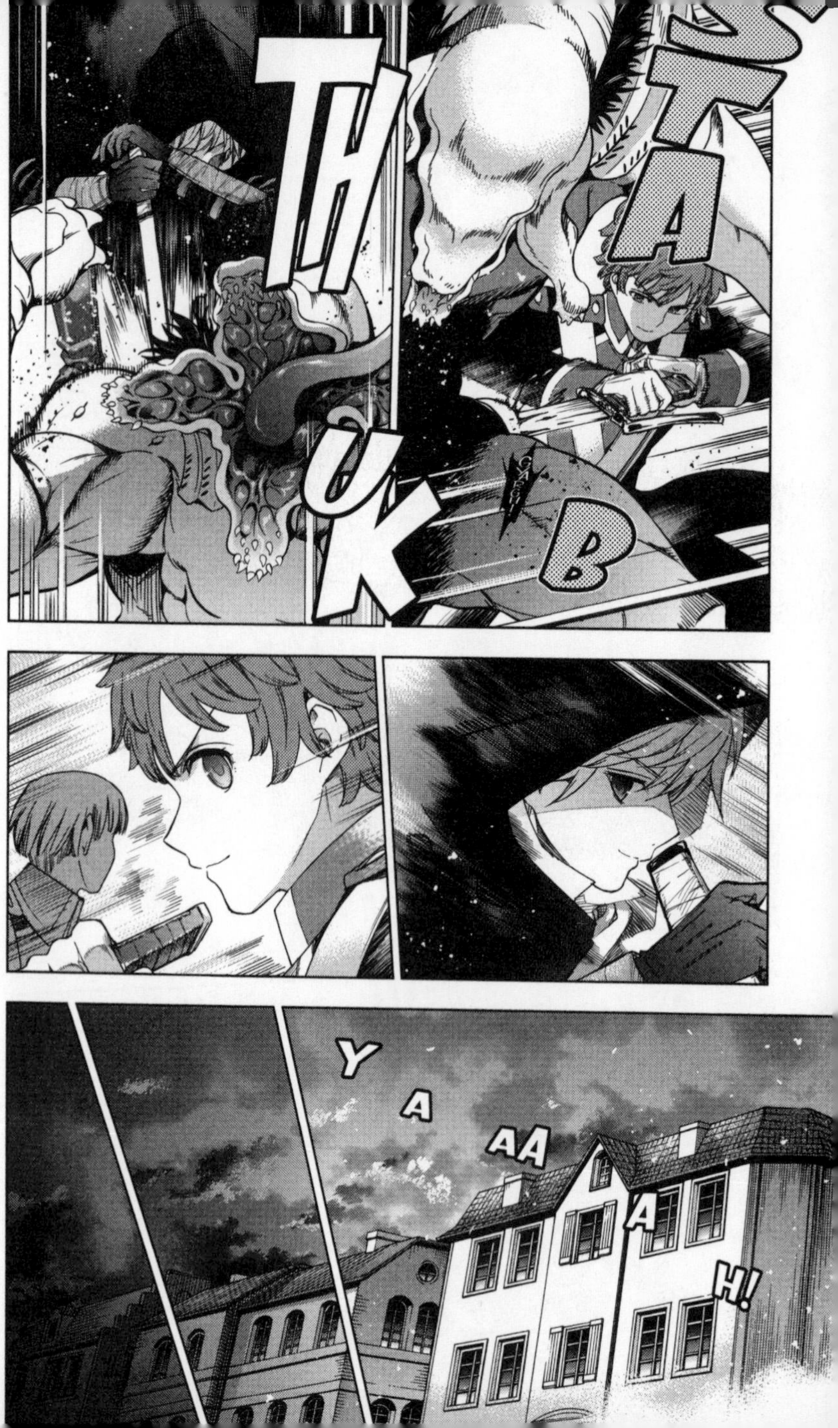

TAB
GAEGH!
THUK
YAAAAH!

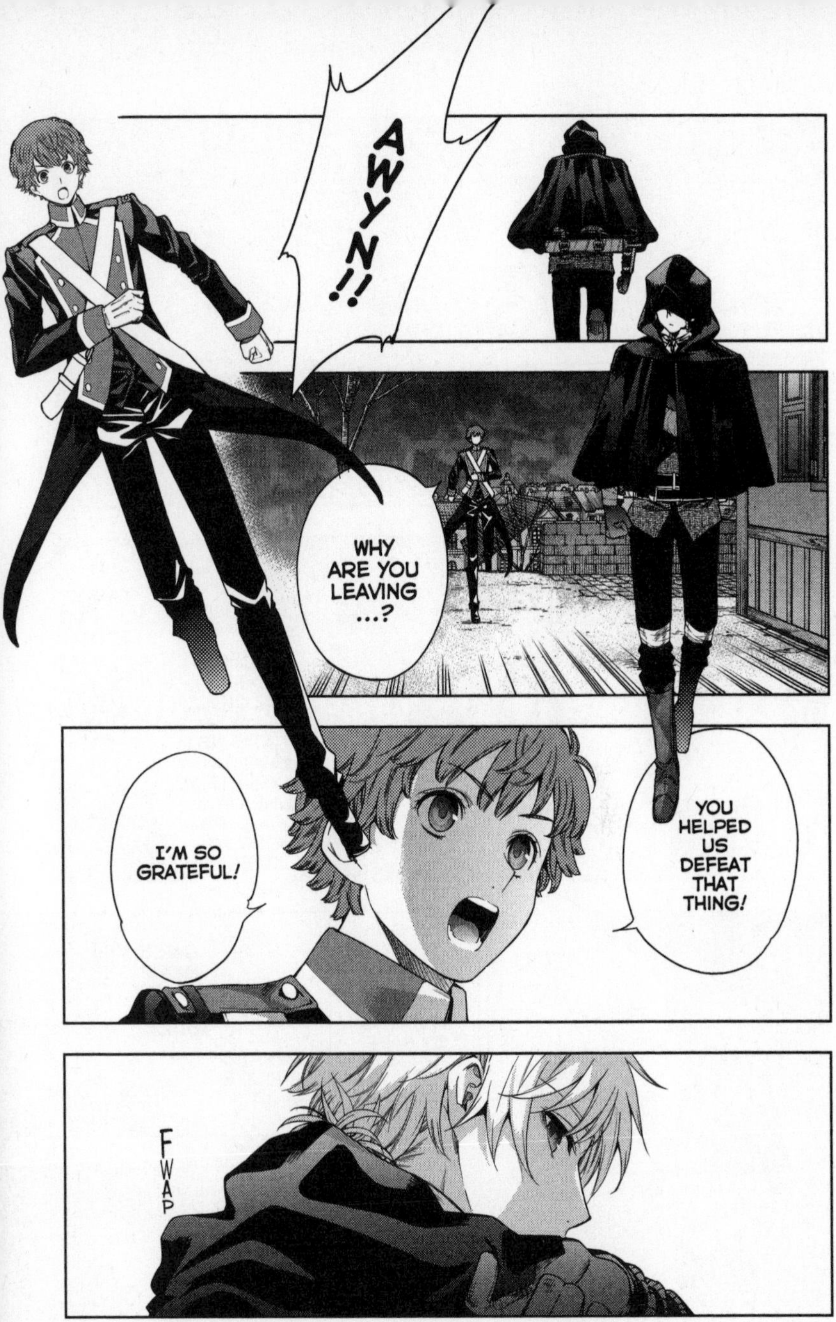
AWYN!!
WHY ARE YOU LEAVING ...?
YOU HELPED US DEFEAT THAT THING!
I'M SO GRATEFUL!
FWAP

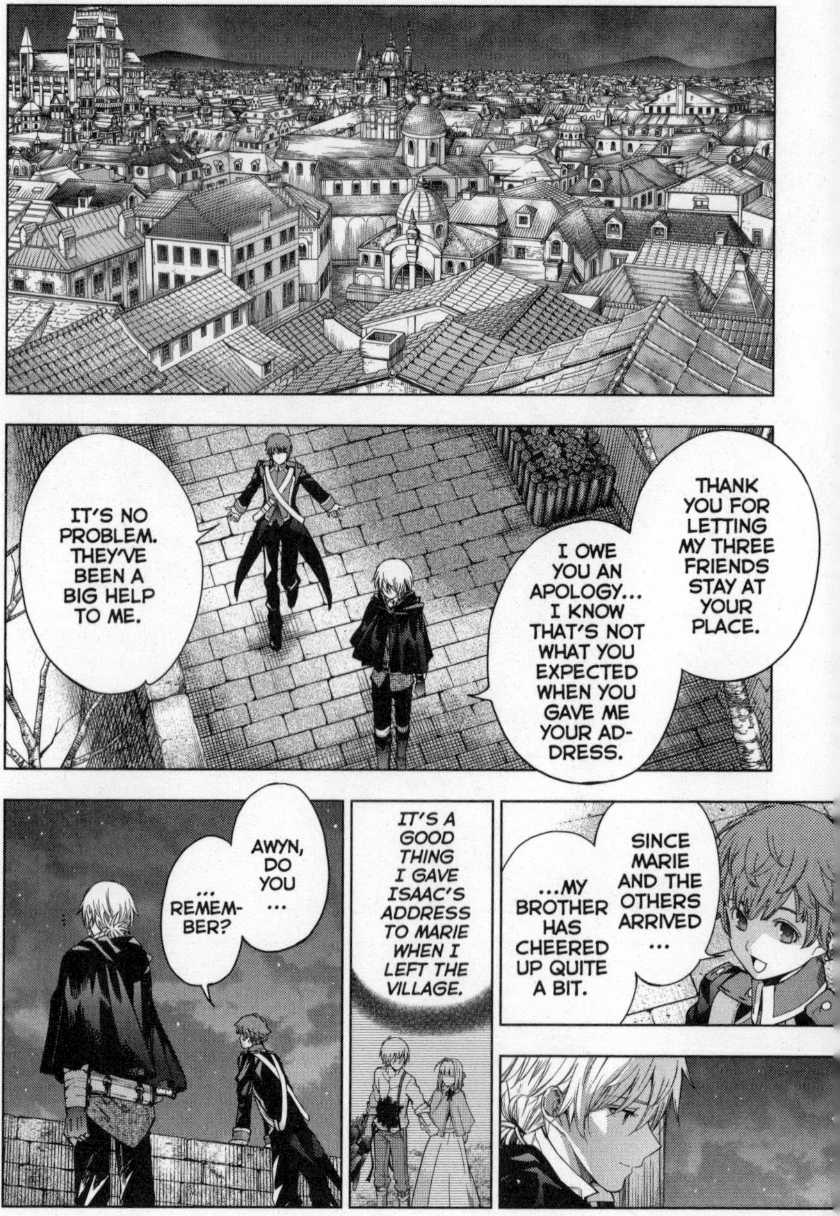
THANK YOU FOR LETTING MY THREE FRIENDS STAY AT YOUR PLACE.
I OWE YOU AN APOLOGY... I KNOW THAT'S NOT WHAT YOU EXPECTED WHEN YOU GAVE ME YOUR ADDRESS.
IT'S NO PROBLEM. THEY'VE BEEN A BIG HELP TO ME.
SINCE MARIE AND THE OTHERS ARRIVED...
...MY BROTHER HAS CHEERED UP QUITE A BIT.
IT'S A GOOD THING I GAVE ISAAC'S ADDRESS TO MARIE WHEN I LEFT THE VILLAGE.
AWYN, DO YOU...
...REMEMBER?

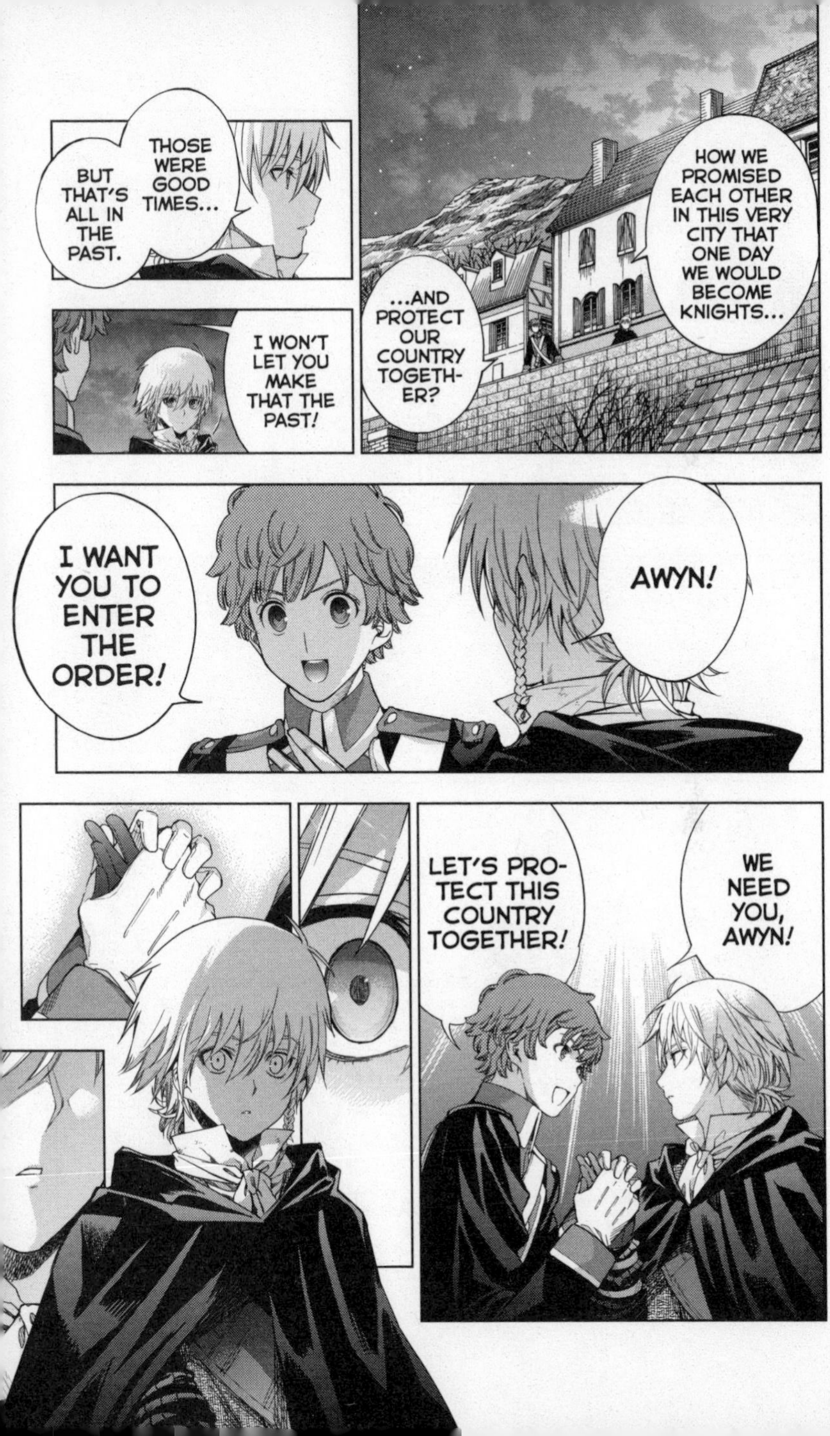
HOW WE PROMISED EACH OTHER IN THIS VERY CITY THAT ONE DAY WE WOULD BECOME KNIGHTS...
...AND PROTECT OUR COUNTRY TOGETH-ER?
THOSE WERE GOOD TIMES...
BUT THAT'S ALL IN THE PAST.
I WON'T LET YOU MAKE THAT THE PAST!
AWYN!
I WANT YOU TO ENTER THE ORDER!
WE NEED YOU, AWYN!
LET'S PROTECT THIS COUNTRY TOGETHER!

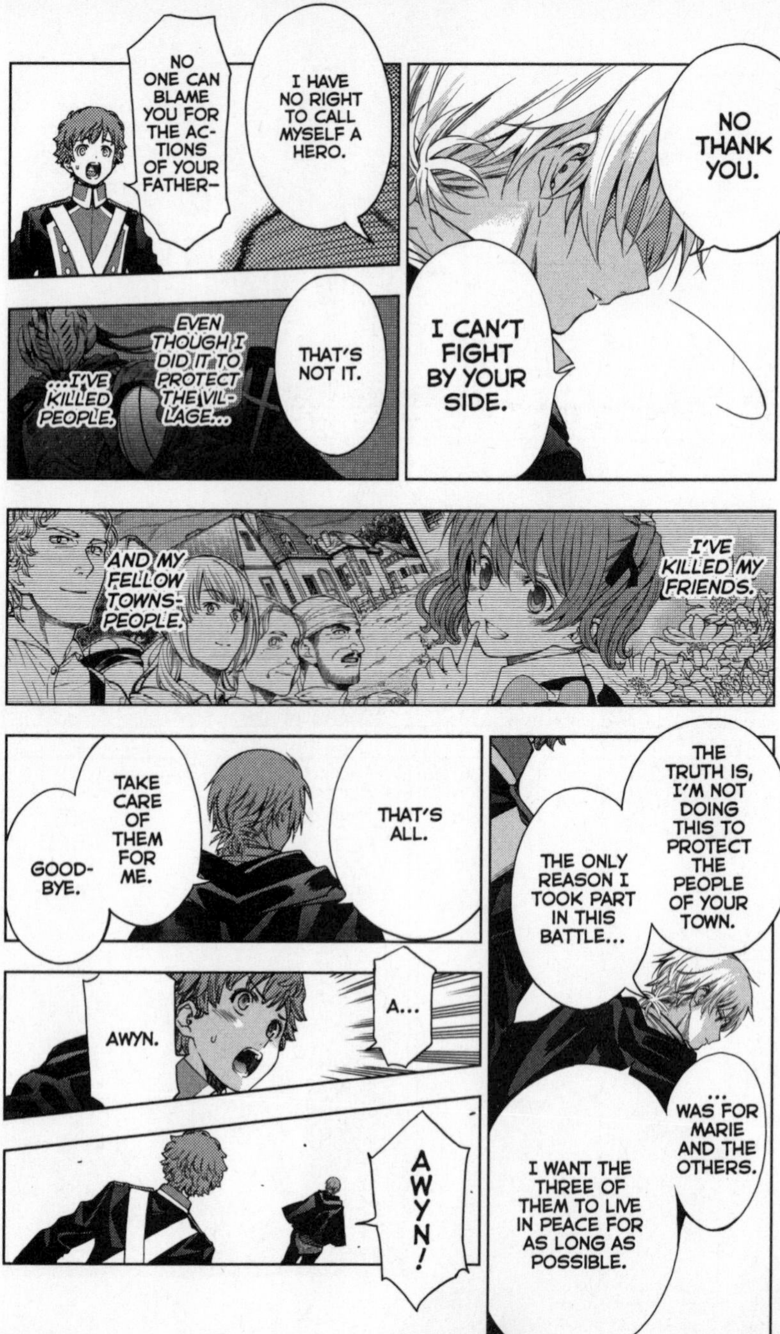
NO THANK YOU.
I CAN'T FIGHT BY YOUR SIDE.
NO ONE CAN BLAME YOU FOR THE AC-TIONS OF YOUR FATHER—
I HAVE NO RIGHT TO CALL MYSELF A HERO.
THAT'S NOT IT.
EVEN THOUGH I DID IT TO PROTECT THE VIL-LAGE...
...I'VE KILLED PEOPLE.
I'VE KILLED MY FRIENDS.
AND MY FELLOW TOWNS-PEOPLE.
THE TRUTH IS, I'M NOT DOING THIS TO PROTECT THE PEOPLE OF YOUR TOWN.
THE ONLY REASON I TOOK PART IN THIS BATTLE...
...WAS FOR MARIE AND THE OTHERS.
I WANT THE THREE OF THEM TO LIVE IN PEACE FOR AS LONG AS POSSIBLE.
THAT'S ALL.
TAKE CARE OF THEM FOR ME.
GOOD-BYE.
A...
AWYN.
AWYN!

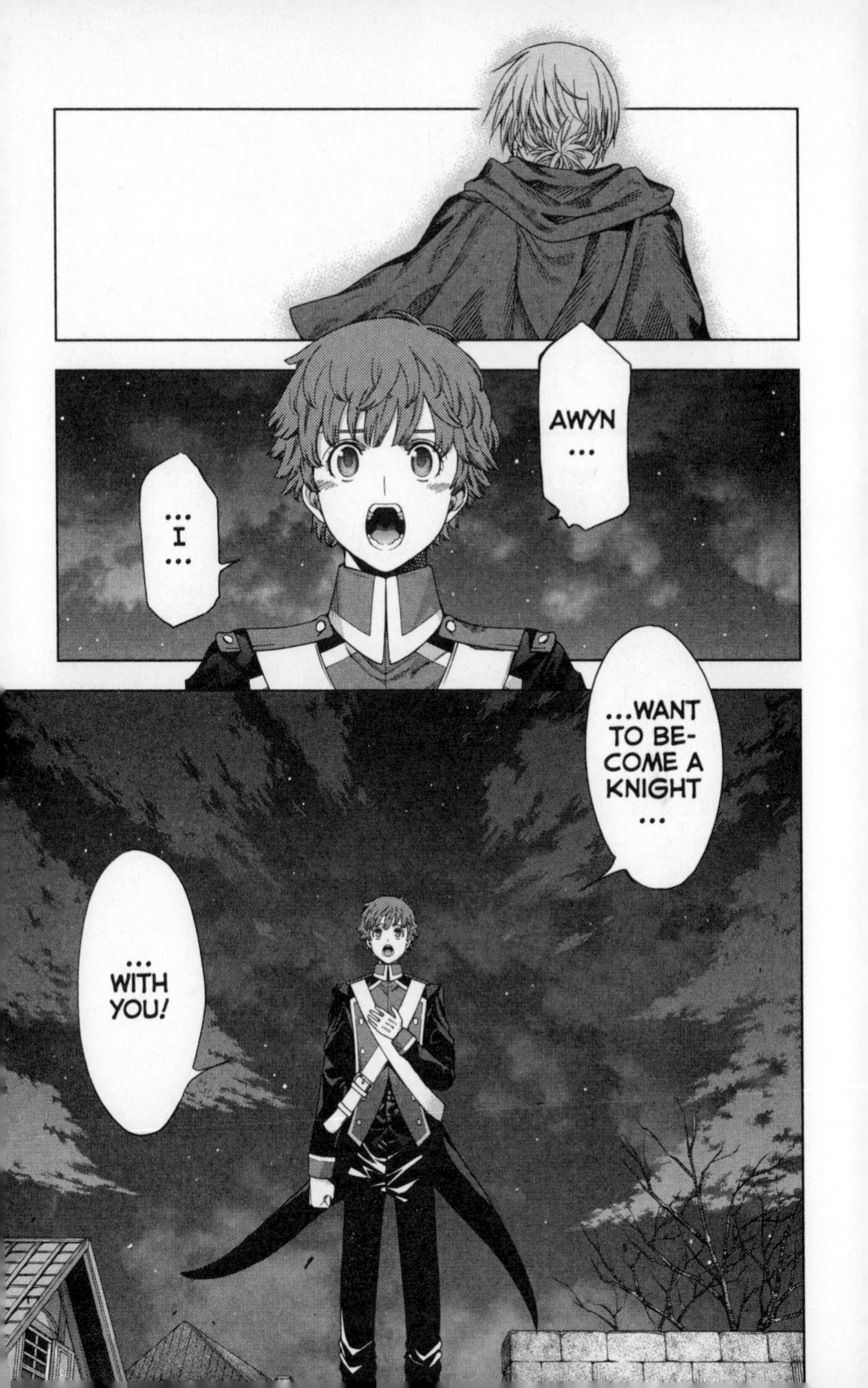
AWYN ...
... I ...
...WANT TO BE-COME A KNIGHT ...
... WITH YOU!

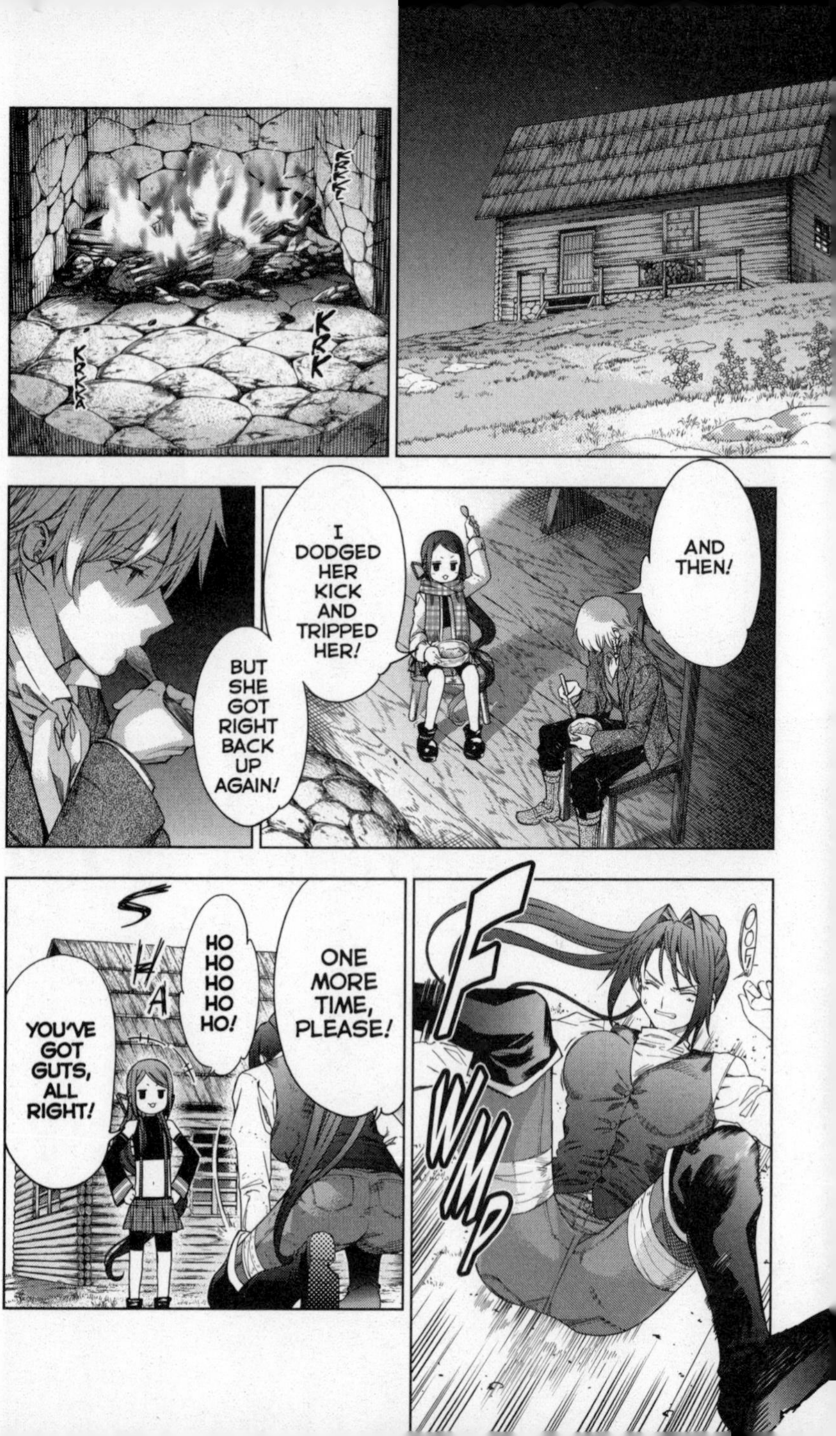
KRKKL
KRK
KRKKA
AND THEN!
I DODGED HER KICK AND TRIPPED HER!
BUT SHE GOT RIGHT BACK UP AGAIN!
F
WMP
OOF
ONE MORE TIME, PLEASE!
HO HO HO HO HO!
SHA
YOU'VE GOT GUTS, ALL RIGHT!

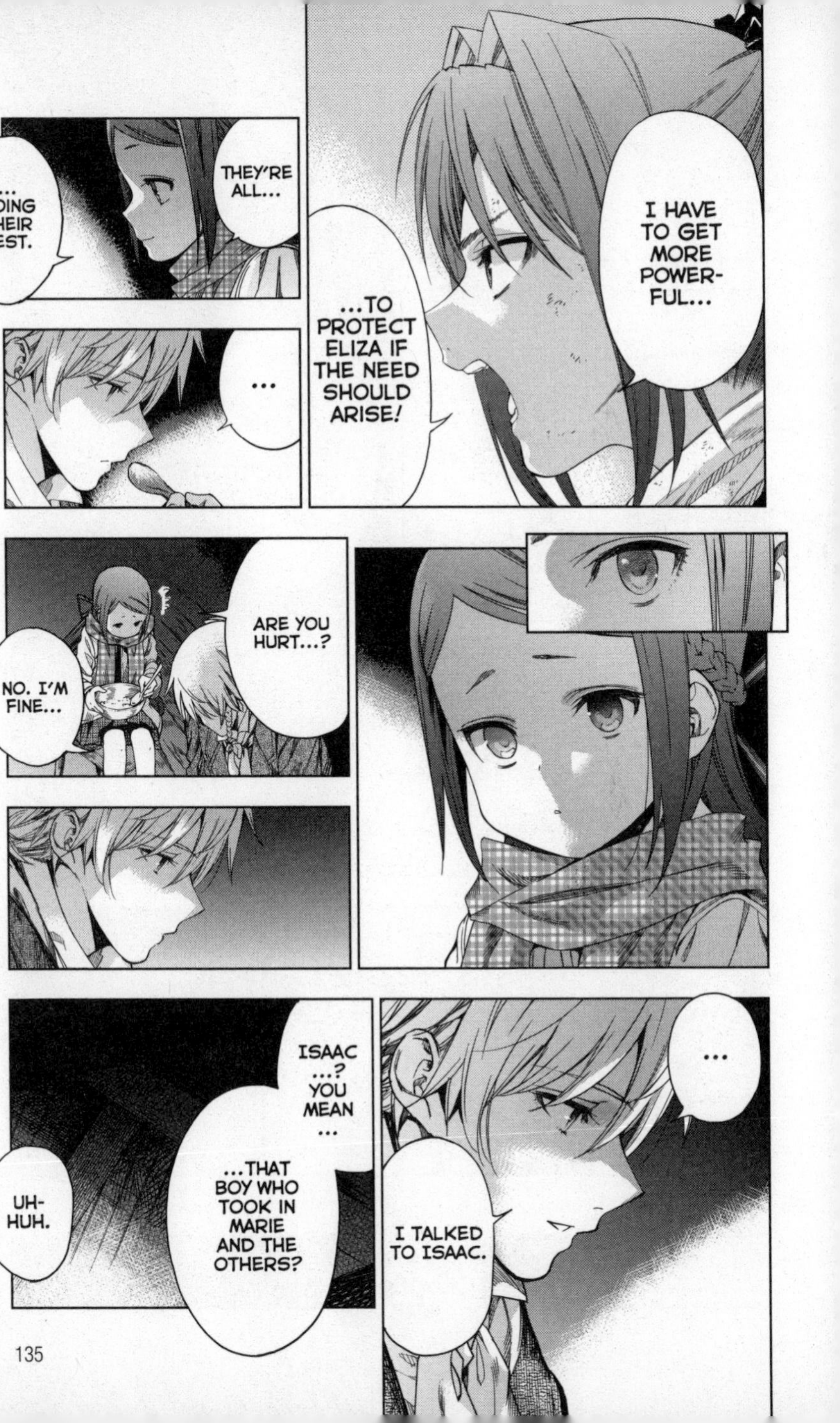
I HAVE TO GET MORE POWERFUL...
...TO PROTECT ELIZA IF THE NEED SHOULD ARISE!
THEY'RE ALL...
...DOING THEIR BEST.
...
ARE YOU HURT...?
NO. I'M FINE...
...
I TALKED TO ISAAC.
ISAAC...? YOU MEAN...
...THAT BOY WHO TOOK IN MARIE AND THE OTHERS?
UH-HUH.

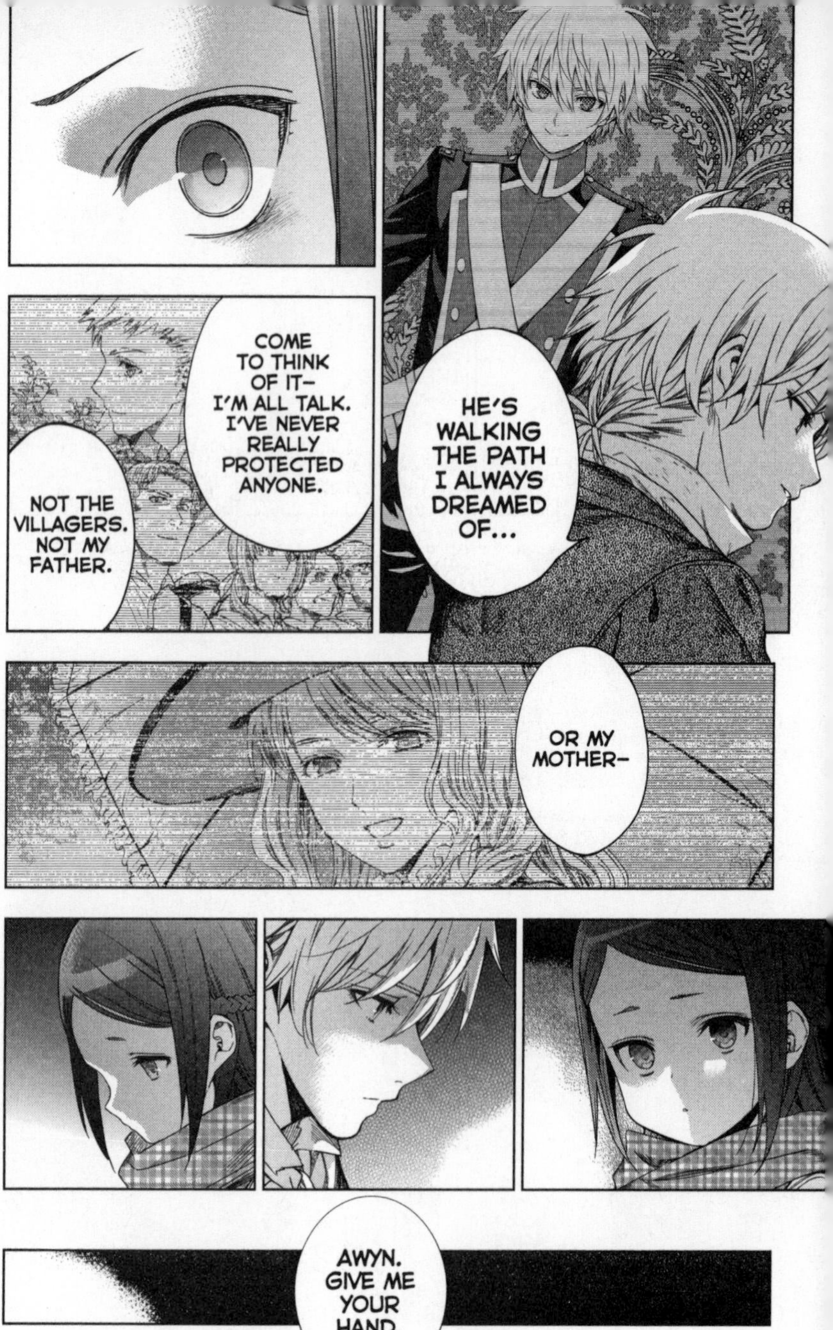
HE'S WALKING THE PATH I ALWAYS DREAMED OF...
COME TO THINK OF IT— I'M ALL TALK. I'VE NEVER REALLY PROTECTED ANYONE.
NOT THE VILLAGERS. NOT MY FATHER.
OR MY MOTHER—
AWYN. GIVE ME YOUR HAND.

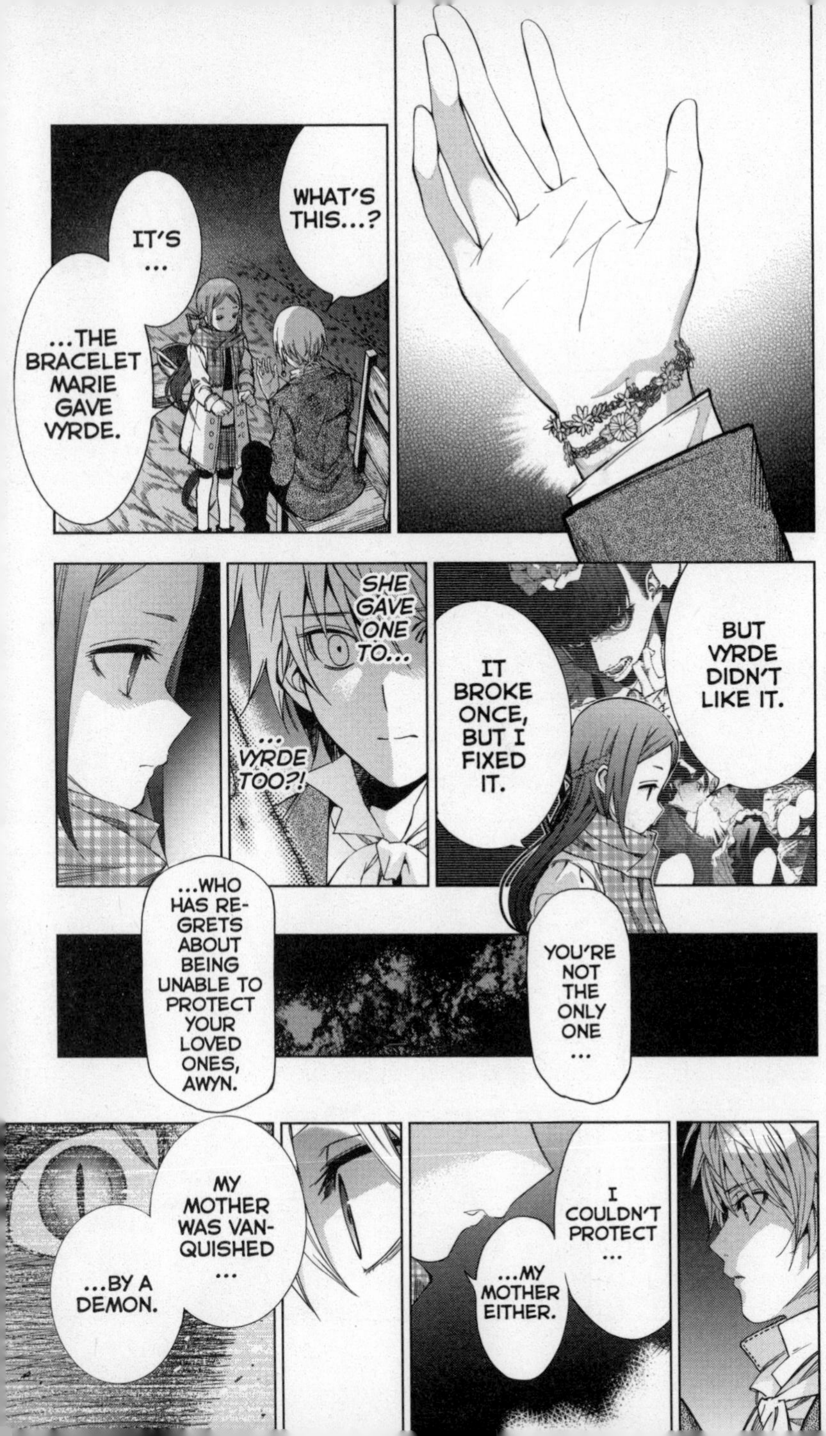
WHAT'S THIS...?
IT'S ...
...THE BRACELET MARIE GAVE VYRDE.
BUT VYRDE DIDN'T LIKE IT.
IT BROKE ONCE, BUT I FIXED IT.
SHE GAVE ONE TO...
...VYRDE TOO?!
YOU'RE NOT THE ONLY ONE ...
...WHO HAS RE-GRETS ABOUT BEING UNABLE TO PROTECT YOUR LOVED ONES, AWYN.
I COULDN'T PROTECT ...
...MY MOTHER EITHER.
MY MOTHER WAS VAN-QUISHED ...
...BY A DEMON.

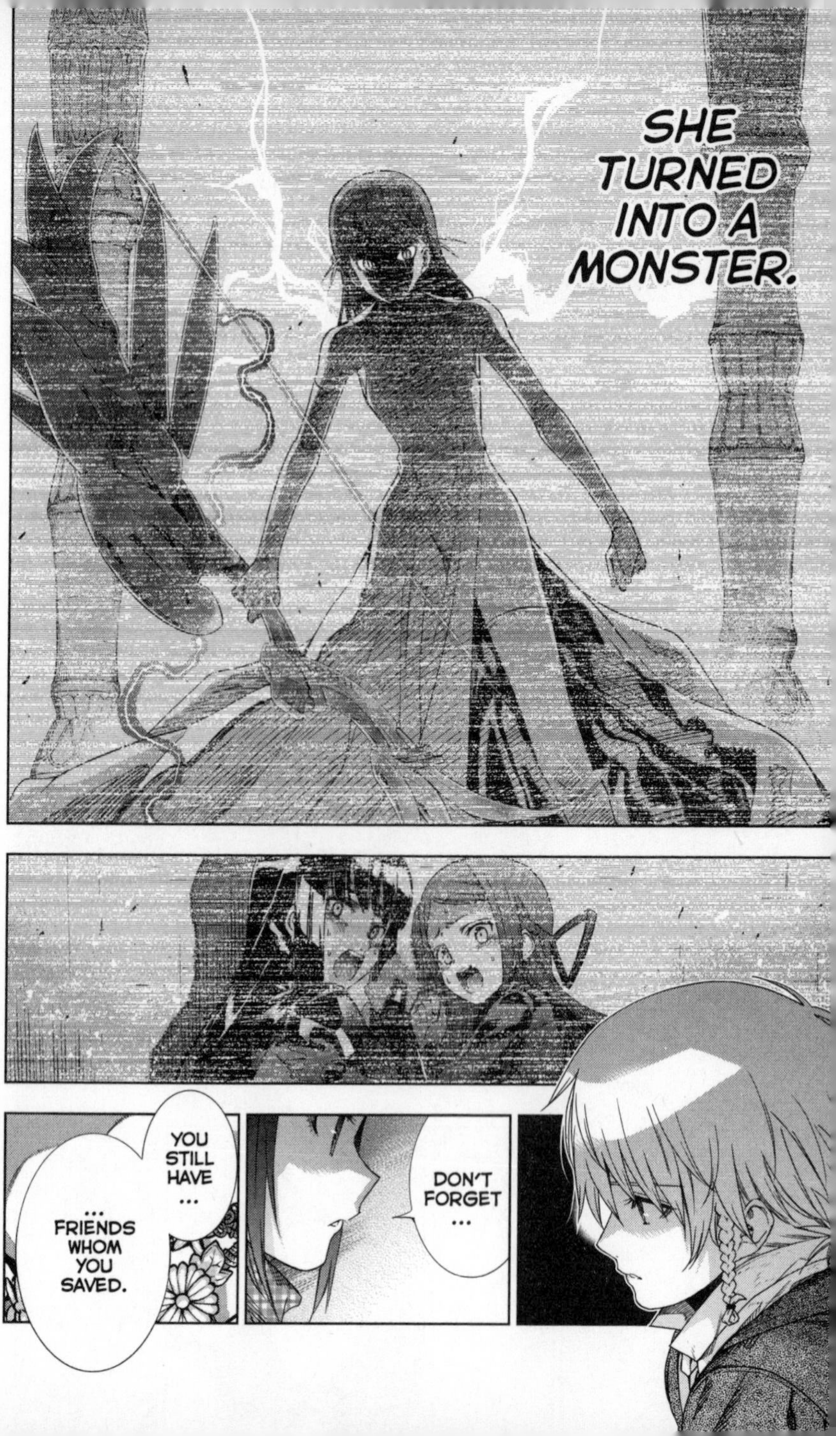
SHE TURNED INTO A MONSTER.
DON'T FORGET ...
YOU STILL HAVE ...
... FRIENDS WHOM YOU SAVED.

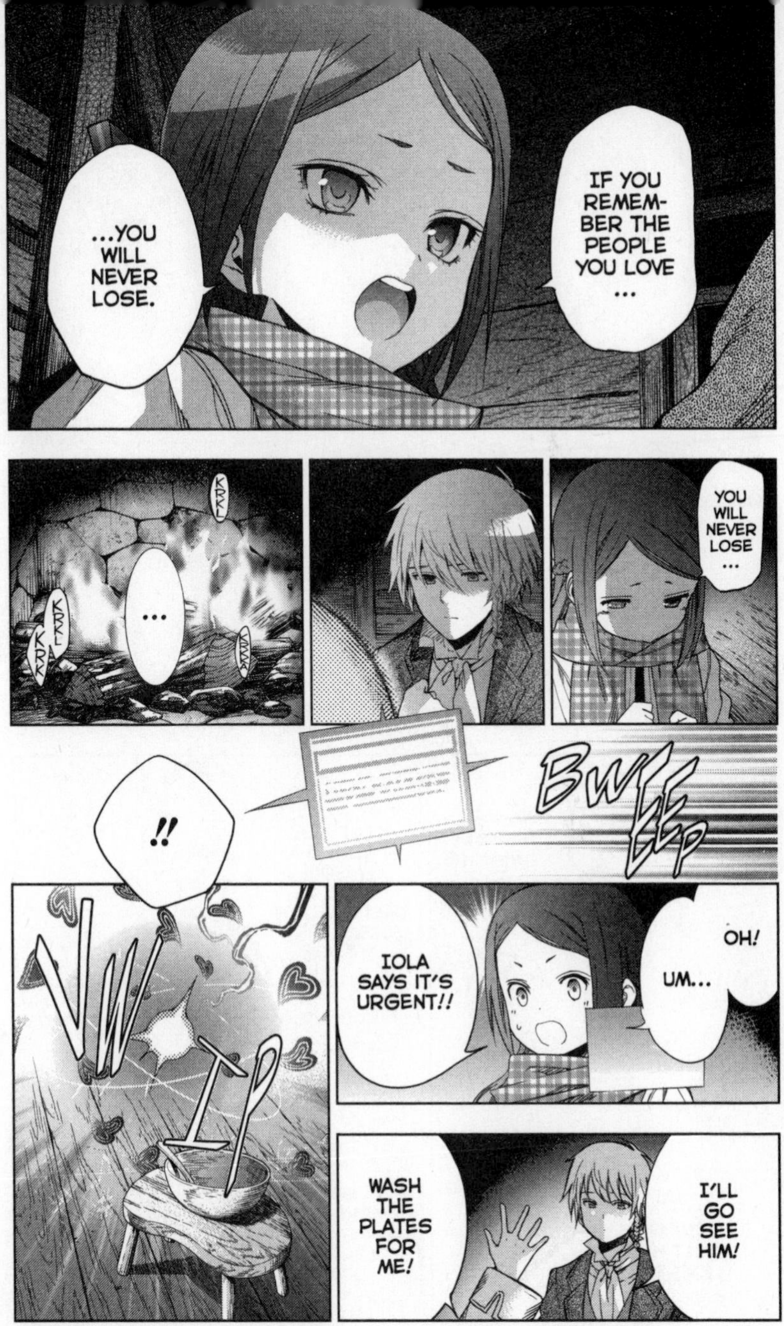
IF YOU REMEMBER THE PEOPLE YOU LOVE ...
...YOU WILL NEVER LOSE.
YOU WILL NEVER LOSE ...
KRKL
...
KRKL
KRK
BWEEP
!!
OH!
UM...
IOLA SAYS IT'S URGENT!!
I'LL GO SEE HIM!
WASH THE PLATES FOR ME!
VWIP

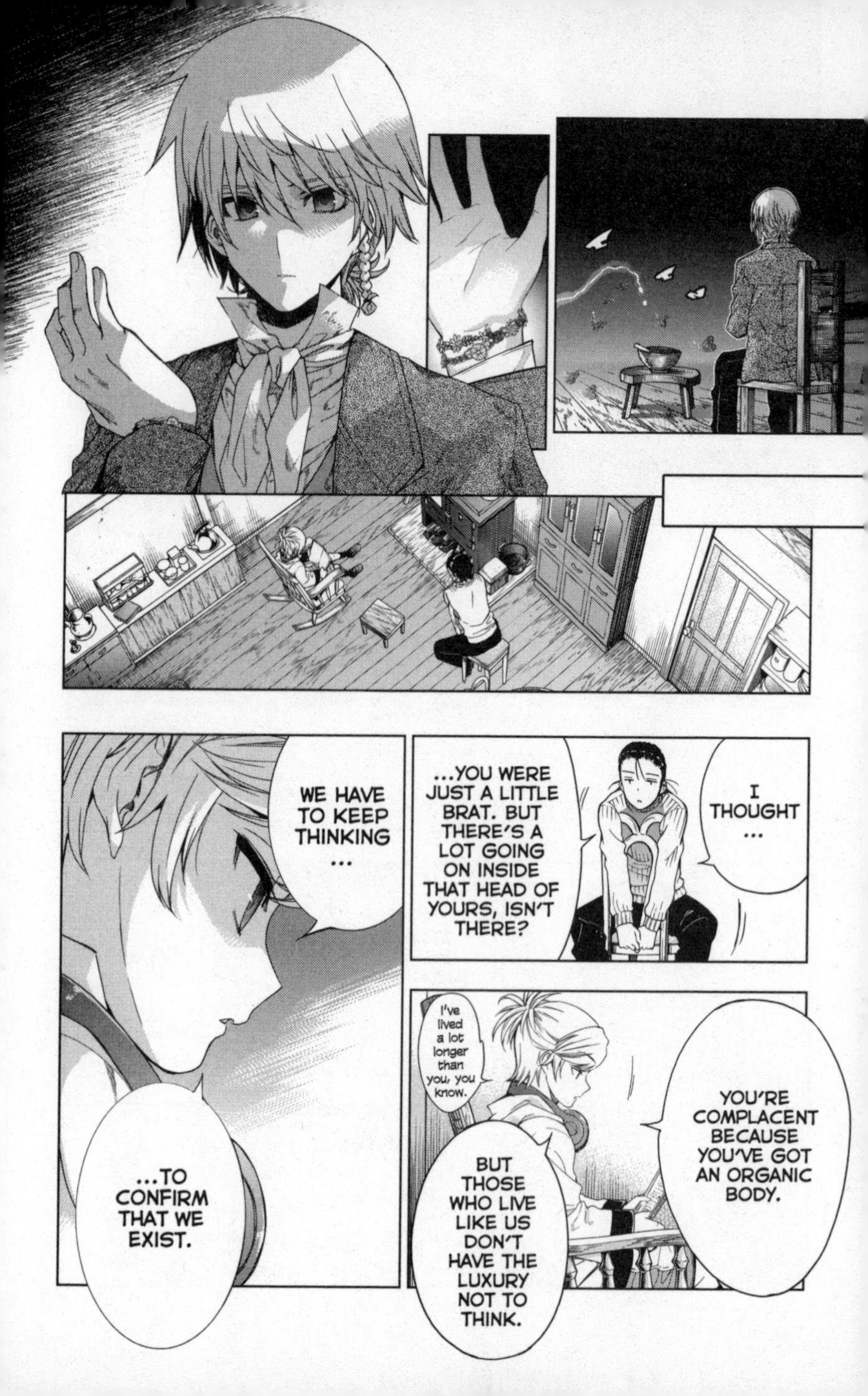
I THOUGHT ...
...YOU WERE JUST A LITTLE BRAT. BUT THERE'S A LOT GOING ON INSIDE THAT HEAD OF YOURS, ISN'T THERE?
YOU'RE COMPLACENT BECAUSE YOU'VE GOT AN ORGANIC BODY.
I've lived a lot longer than you, you know.
BUT THOSE WHO LIVE LIKE US DON'T HAVE THE LUXURY NOT TO THINK.
WE HAVE TO KEEP THINKING ...
...TO CONFIRM THAT WE EXIST.

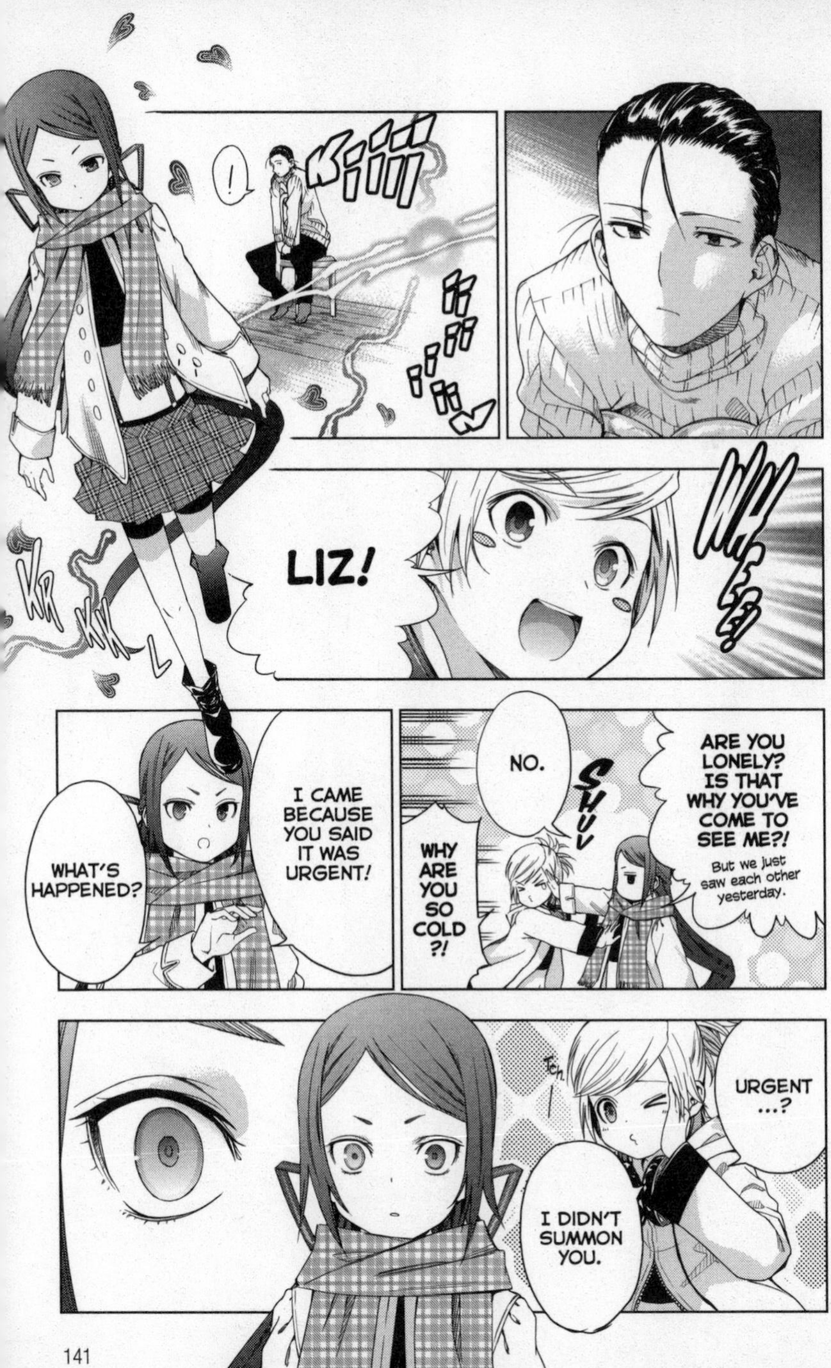
!
LIZ!
ARE YOU LONELY? IS THAT WHY YOU'VE COME TO SEE ME?!
But we just saw each other yesterday.
NO.
SHUV
WHY ARE YOU SO COLD?!
I CAME BECAUSE YOU SAID IT WAS URGENT!
WHAT'S HAPPENED?
URGENT ...?
Tch
I DIDN'T SUMMON YOU.

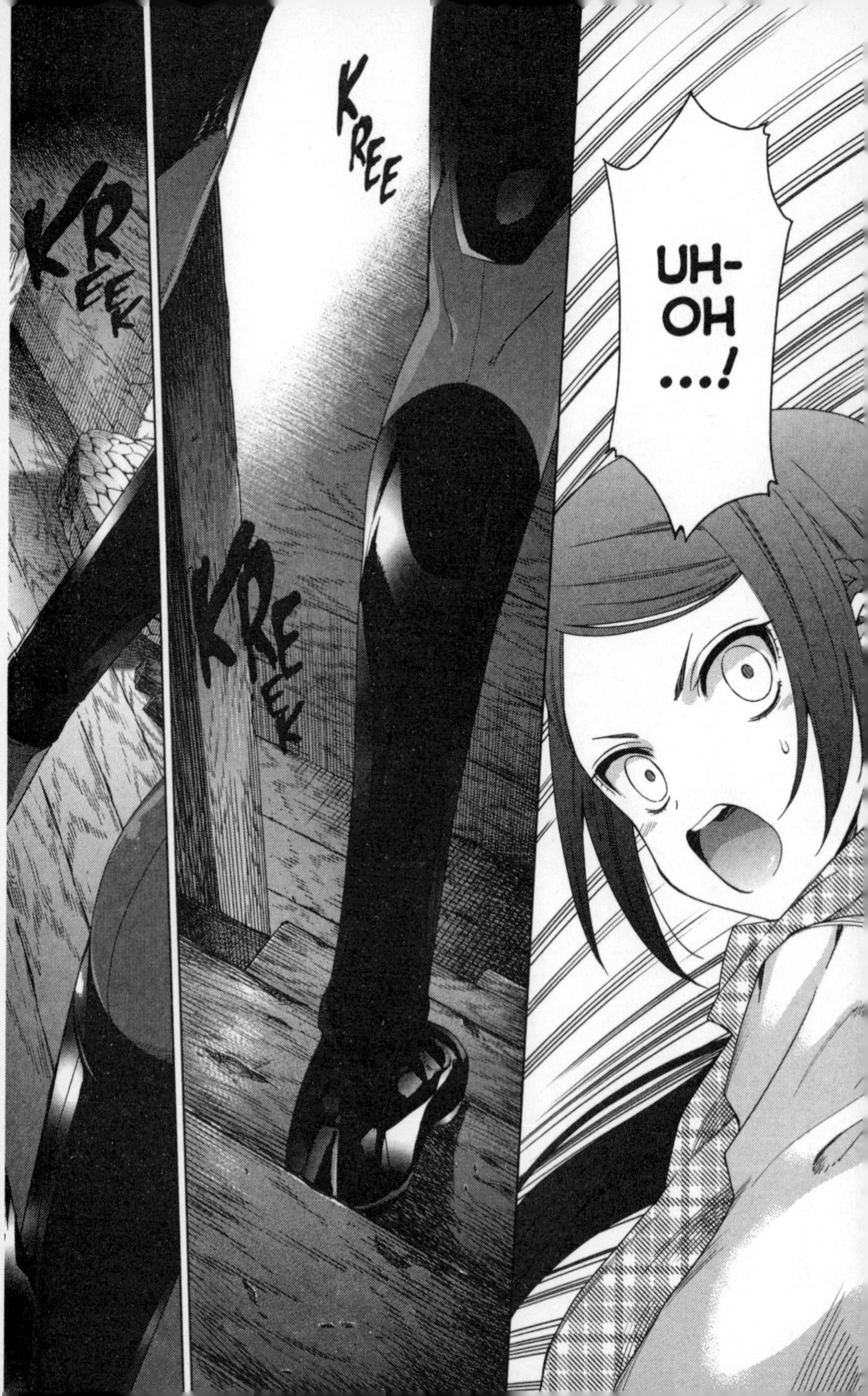
UH-OH ...!
KREE
KREEK
KREEK

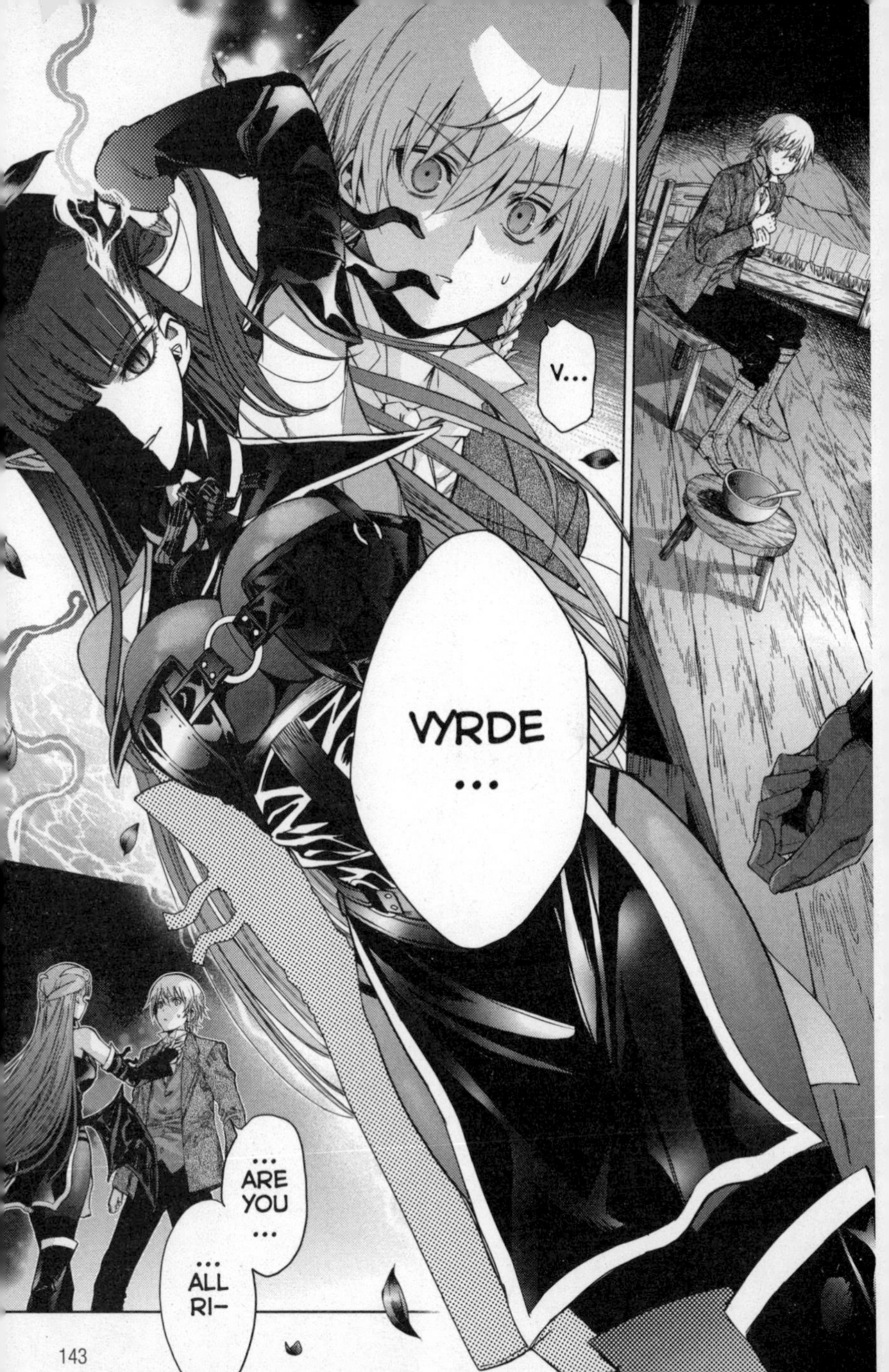
V...
VYRDE ...
... ARE YOU ...
... ALL RI–

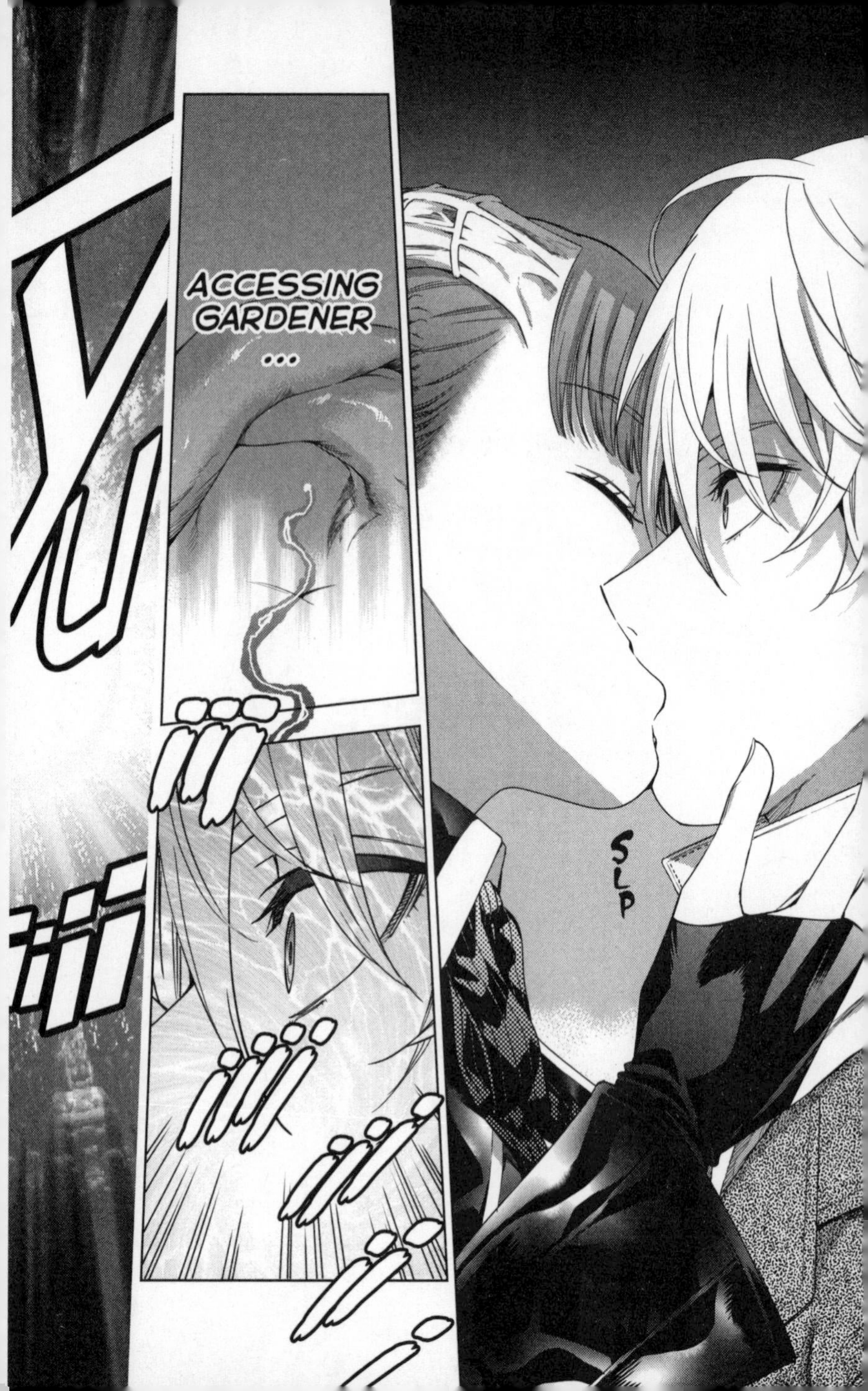
ACCESSING GARDENER ...
SLP

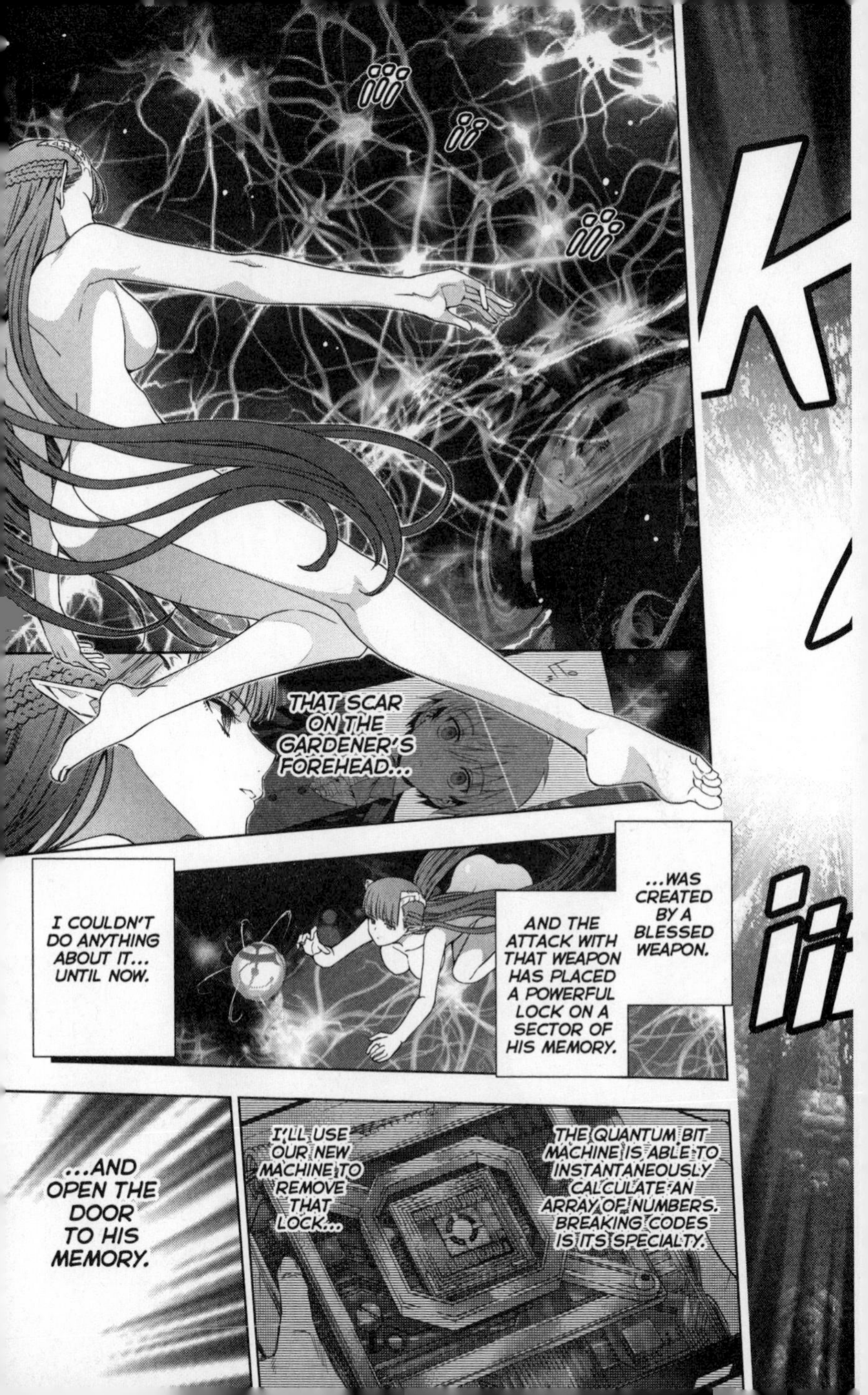
THAT SCAR ON THE GARDENER'S FOREHEAD...
...WAS CREATED BY A BLESSED WEAPON.
AND THE ATTACK WITH THAT WEAPON HAS PLACED A POWERFUL LOCK ON A SECTOR OF HIS MEMORY.
I COULDN'T DO ANYTHING ABOUT IT... UNTIL NOW.
THE QUANTUM BIT MACHINE IS ABLE TO INSTANTANEOUSLY CALCULATE AN ARRAY OF NUMBERS. BREAKING CODES IS ITS SPECIALTY.
I'LL USE OUR NEW MACHINE TO REMOVE THAT LOCK...
...AND OPEN THE DOOR TO HIS MEMORY.

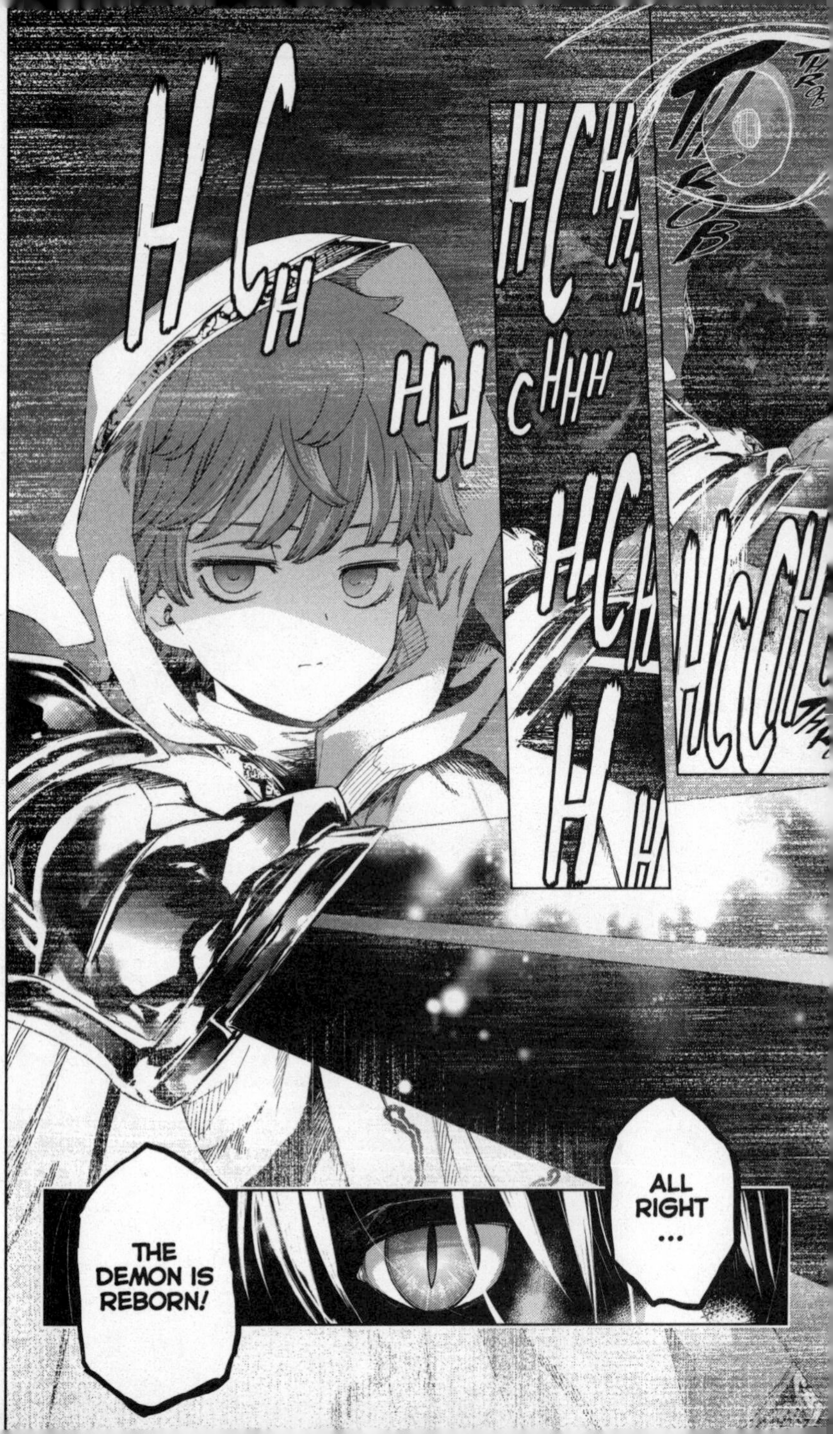
THROB
THROB
HCCH
HCHHH
CHHH
HCHHH
HCH
HH
ALL RIGHT ...
THE DEMON IS REBORN!

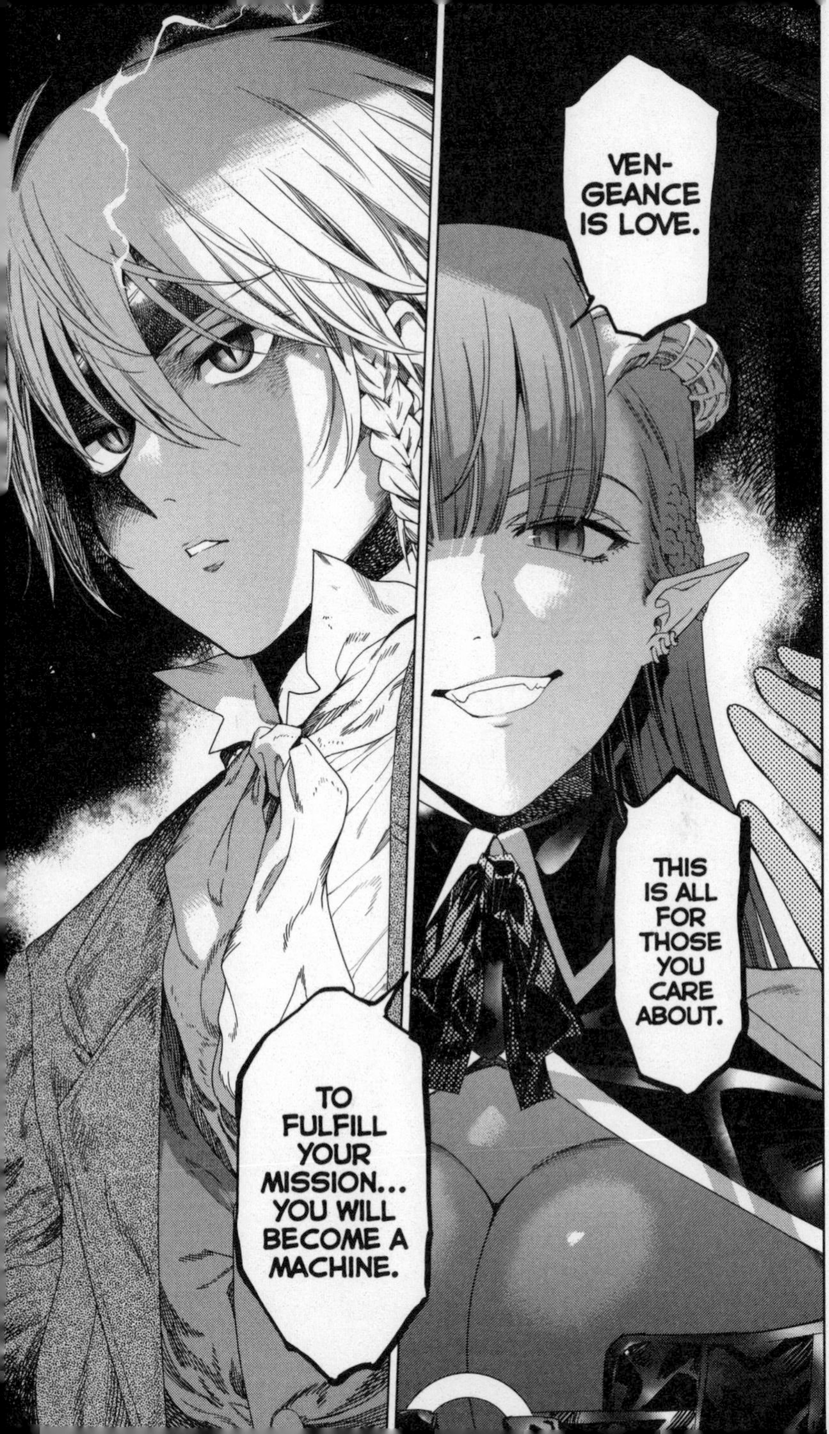
VEN-
GEANCE
IS LOVE.
THIS IS ALL FOR THOSE YOU CARE ABOUT.
TO FULFILL YOUR MISSION... YOU WILL BECOME A MACHINE.

root.32

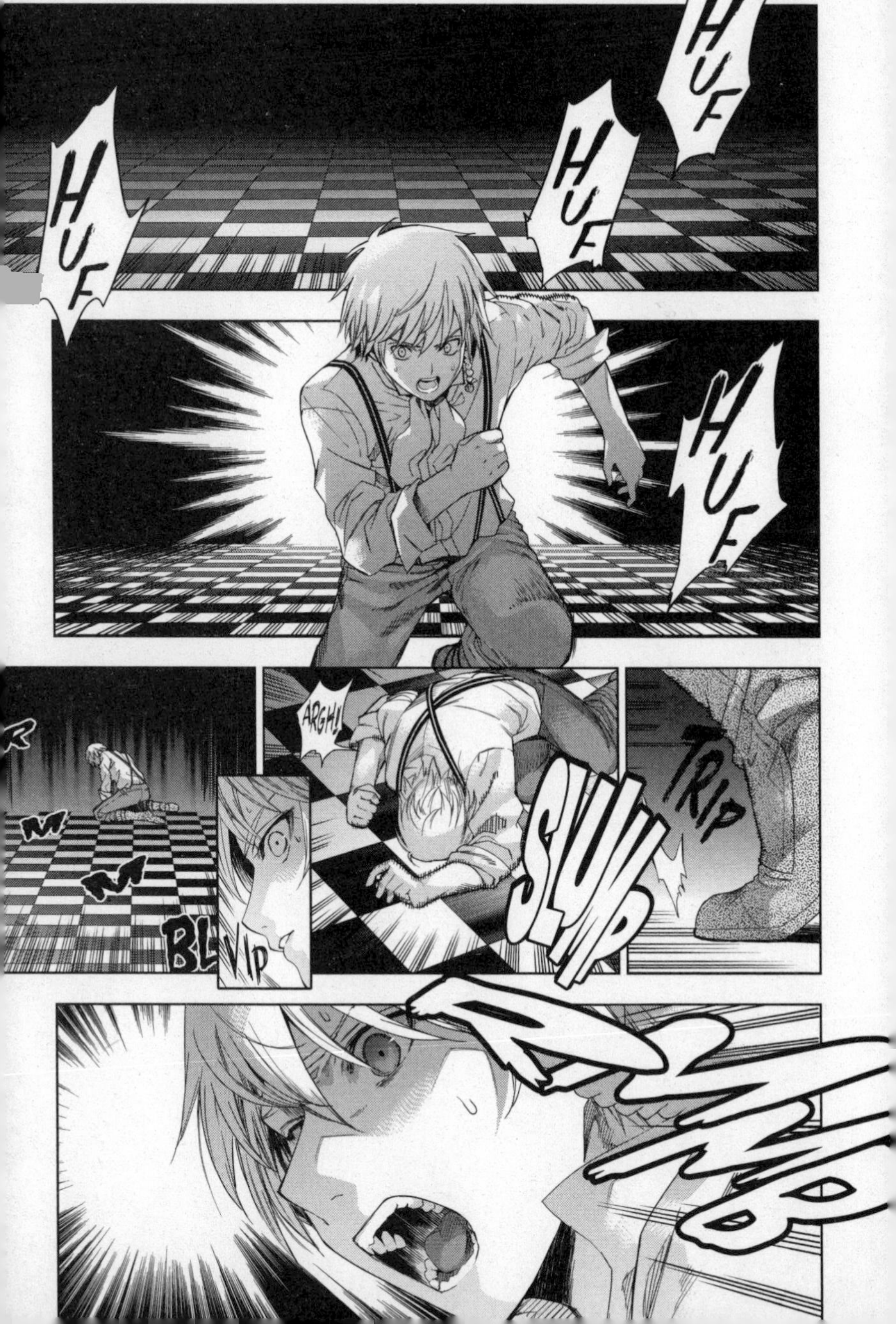
HUF HUF
HUF HUF
HUF HUF
HUF HUF
TRIP
ARGH!
SLUMP

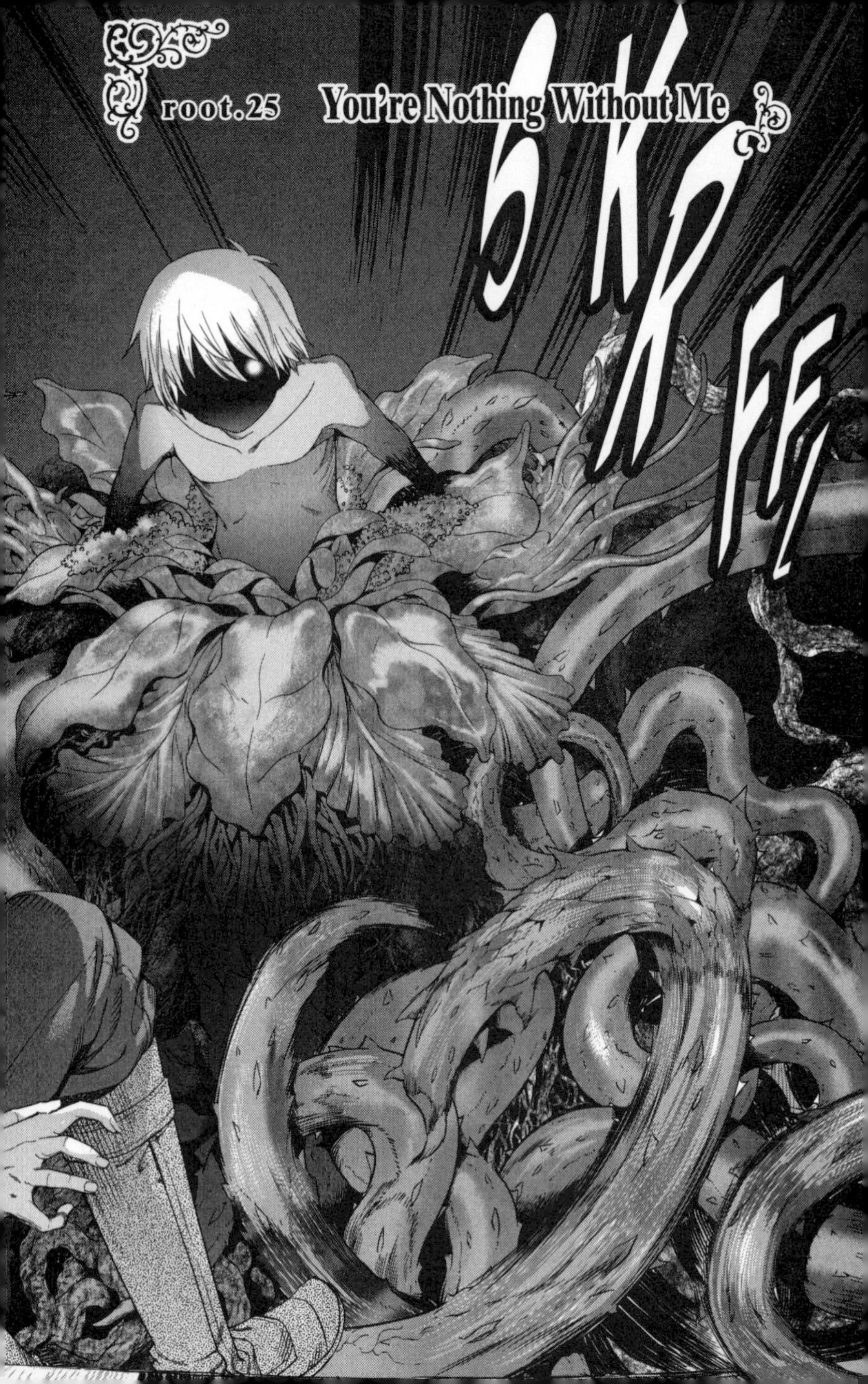
root.25 You're Nothing Without Me

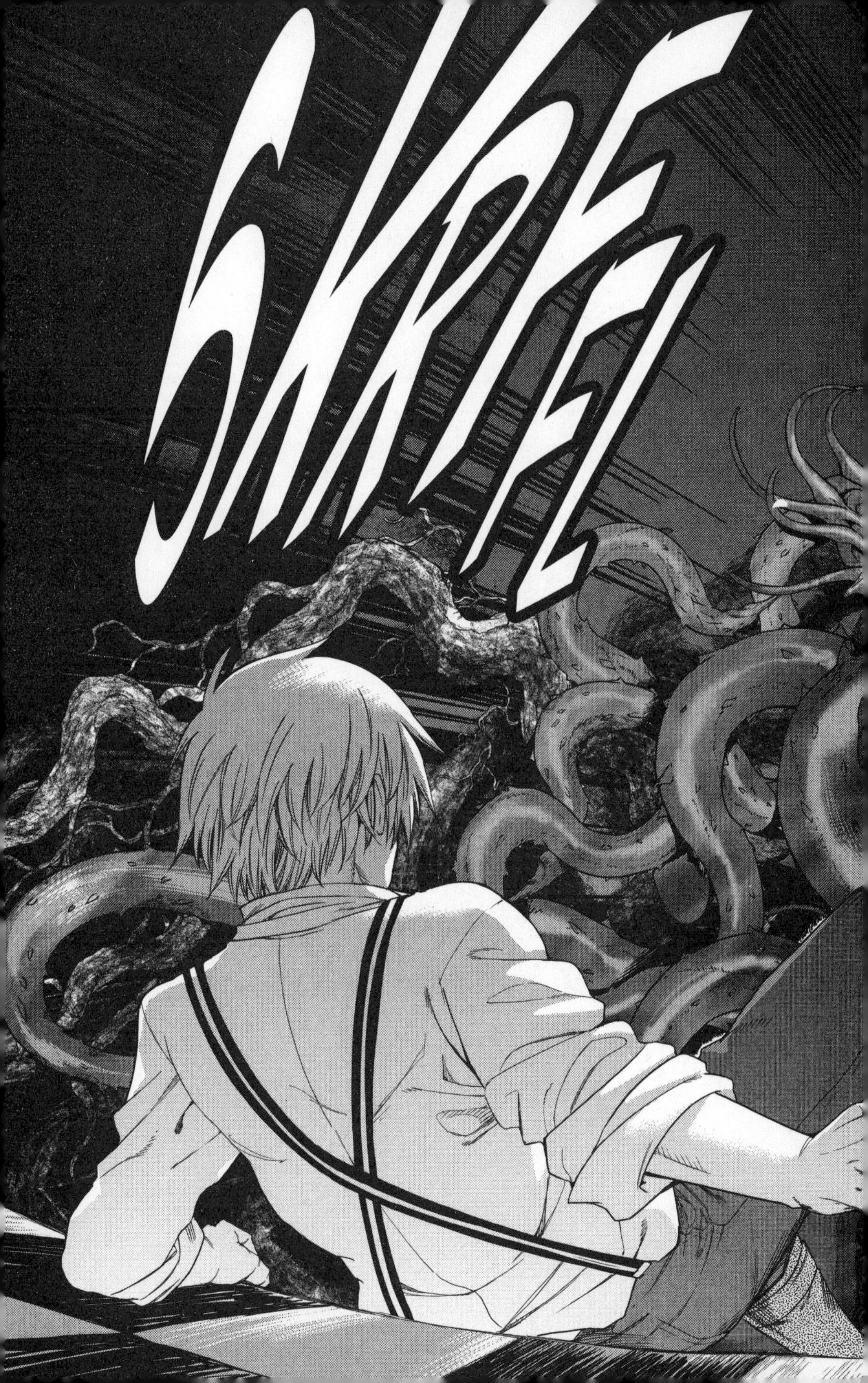
SHKREE

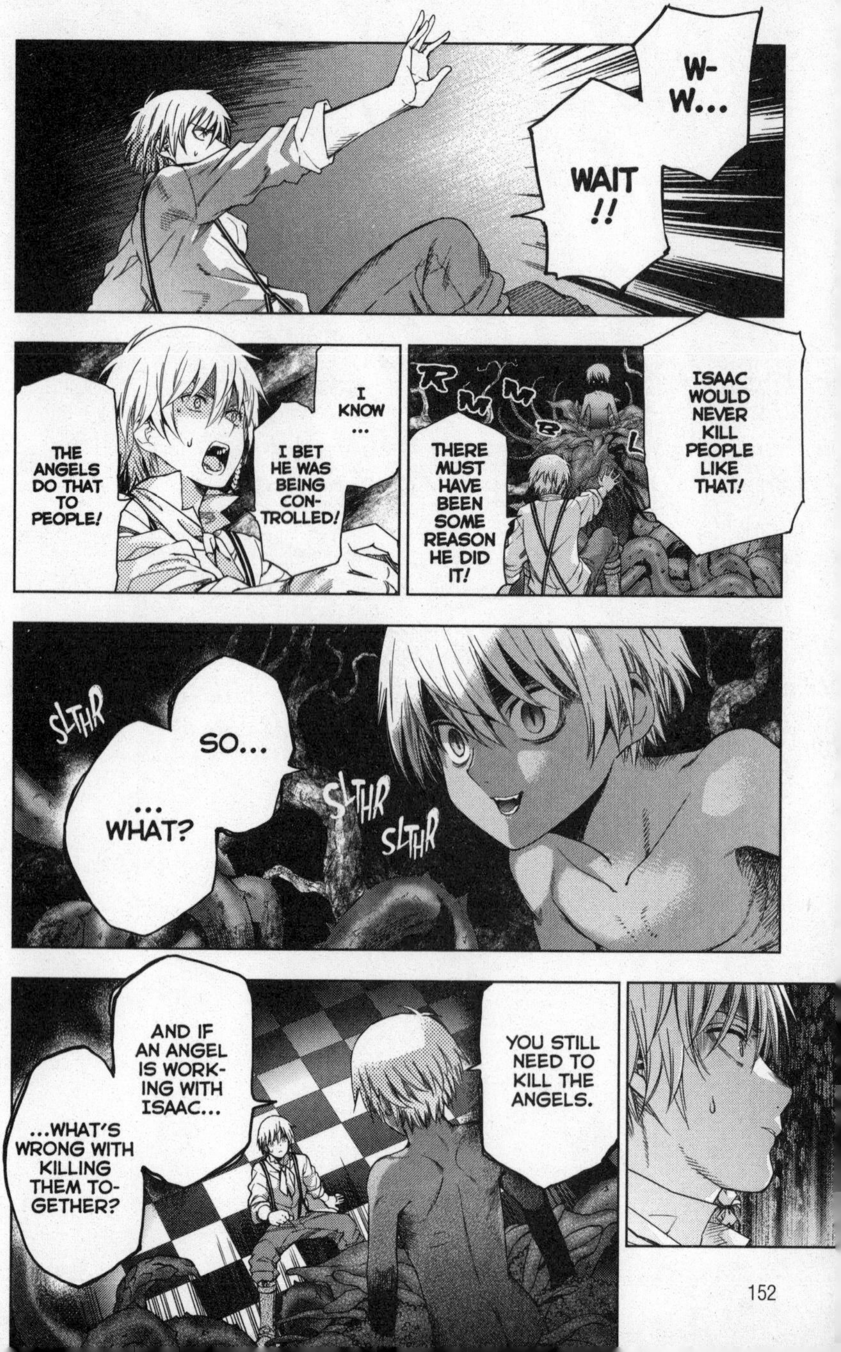
W-W...
WAIT!!
ISAAC WOULD NEVER KILL PEOPLE LIKE THAT!
RMMBL
THERE MUST HAVE BEEN SOME REASON HE DID IT!
I KNOW...
I BET HE WAS BEING CON-TROLLED!
THE ANGELS DO THAT TO PEOPLE!
SLTHR
SLTHR
SO...
...WHAT?
SLTHR
YOU STILL NEED TO KILL THE ANGELS.
AND IF AN ANGEL IS WORK-ING WITH ISAAC...
...WHAT'S WRONG WITH KILLING THEM TO-GETHER?

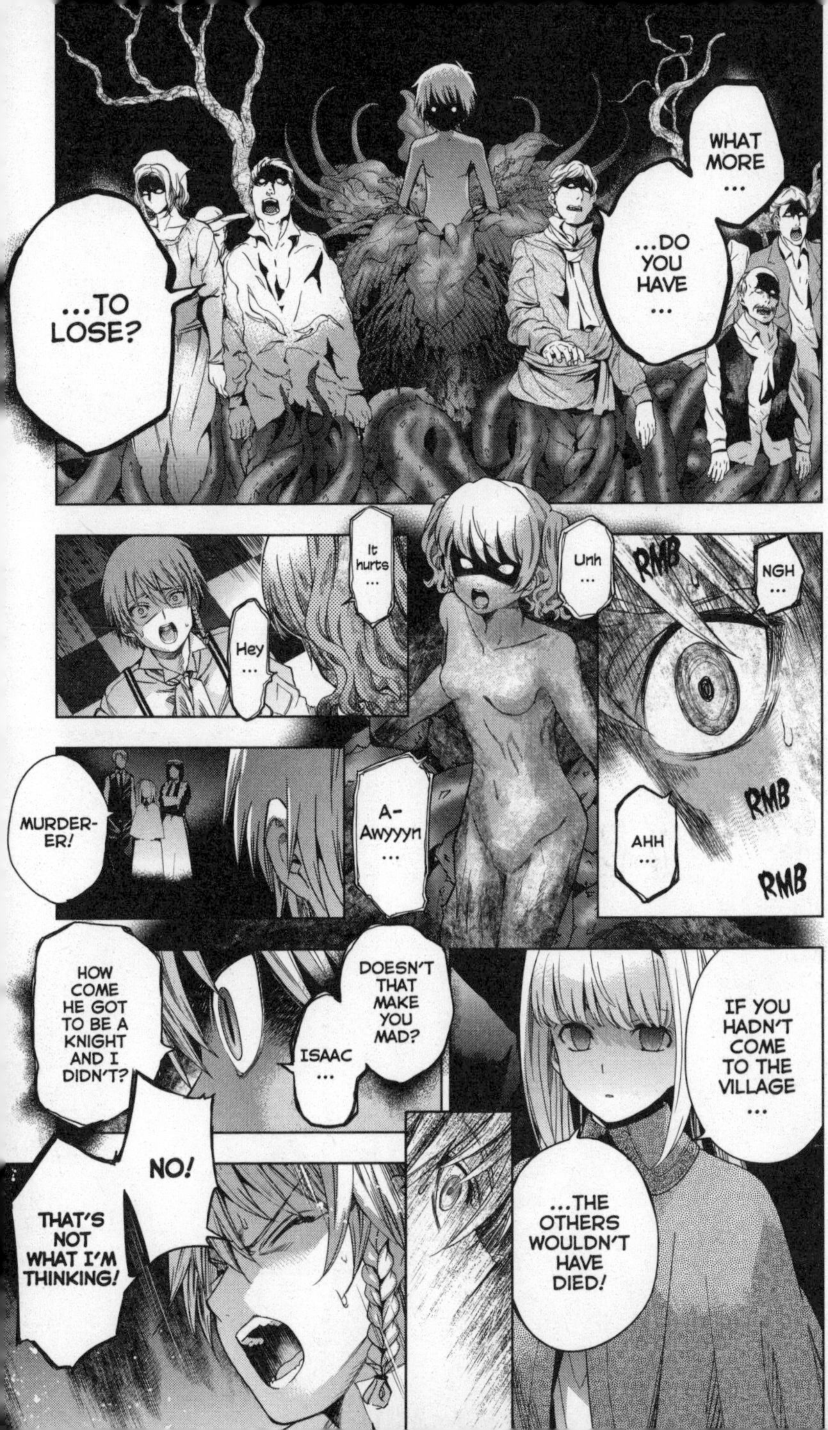
WHAT MORE ...
...DO YOU HAVE ...
...TO LOSE?
RMB
NGH ...
RMB
AHH ...
RMB
Unh ...
It hurts ...
A- Awyyyn ...
Hey ...
MURDER-ER!
IF YOU HADN'T COME TO THE VILLAGE ...
...THE OTHERS WOULDN'T HAVE DIED!
DOESN'T THAT MAKE YOU MAD?
ISAAC ...
HOW COME HE GOT TO BE A KNIGHT AND I DIDN'T?
NO!
THAT'S NOT WHAT I'M THINKING!

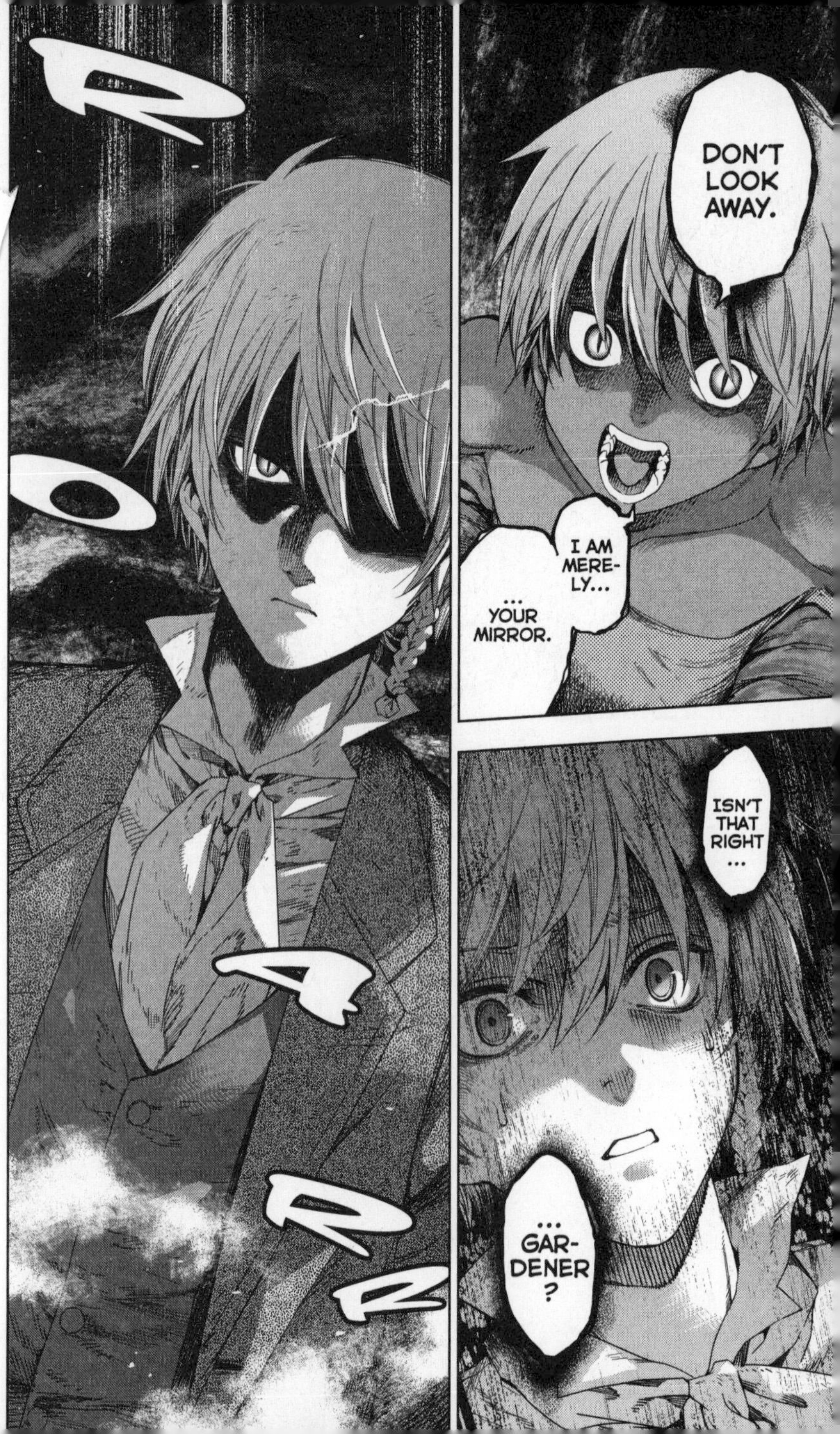
DON'T LOOK AWAY.
I AM MERELY...
...YOUR MIRROR.
ISN'T THAT RIGHT...
...GARDENER?
ROARR

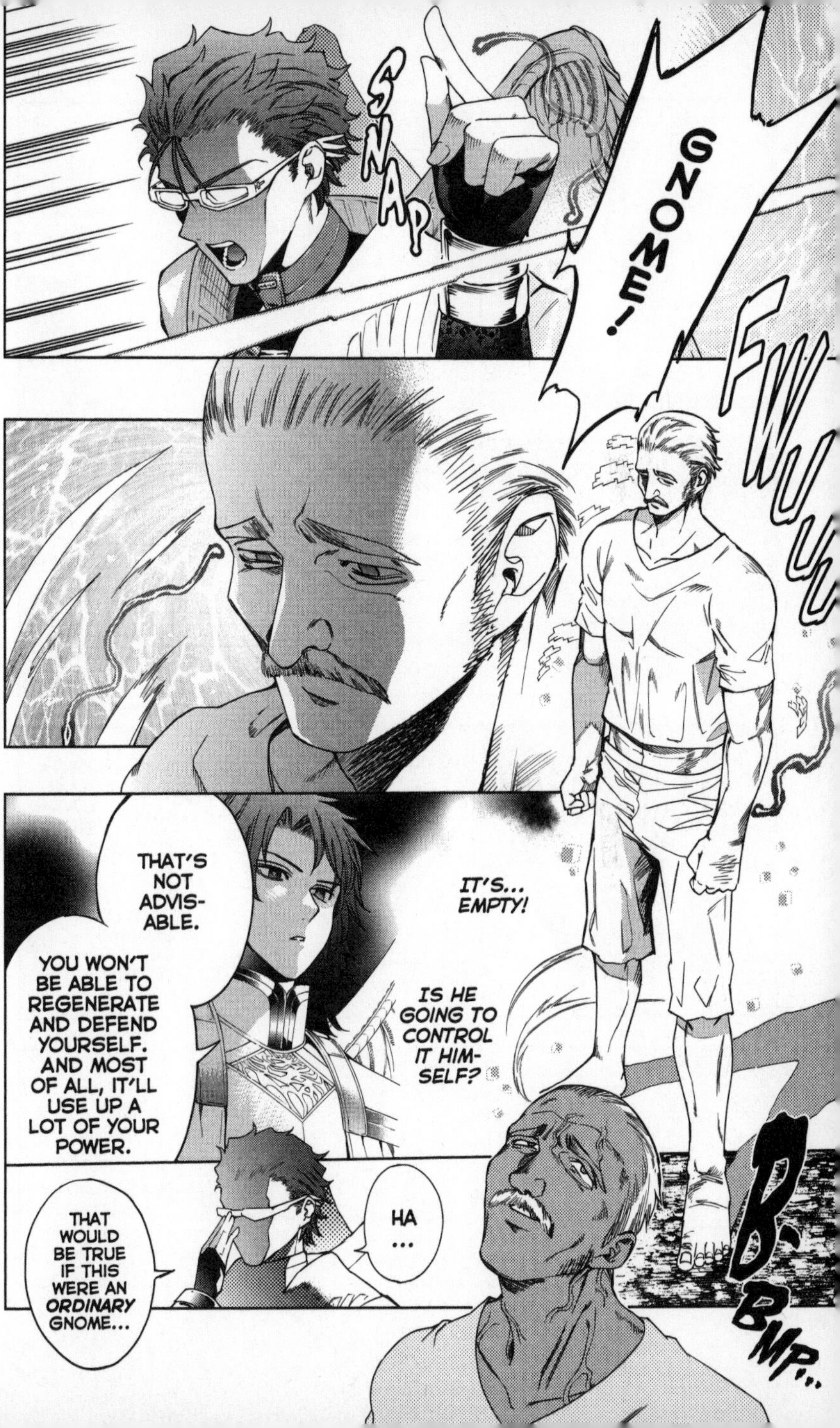
GNOME!
SNAP
FWUUU
IT'S... EMPTY!
IS HE GOING TO CONTROL IT HIMSELF?
THAT'S NOT ADVISABLE.
YOU WON'T BE ABLE TO REGENERATE AND DEFEND YOURSELF. AND MOST OF ALL, IT'LL USE UP A LOT OF YOUR POWER.
B-BMP...
HA...
THAT WOULD BE TRUE IF THIS WERE AN *ORDINARY* GNOME...

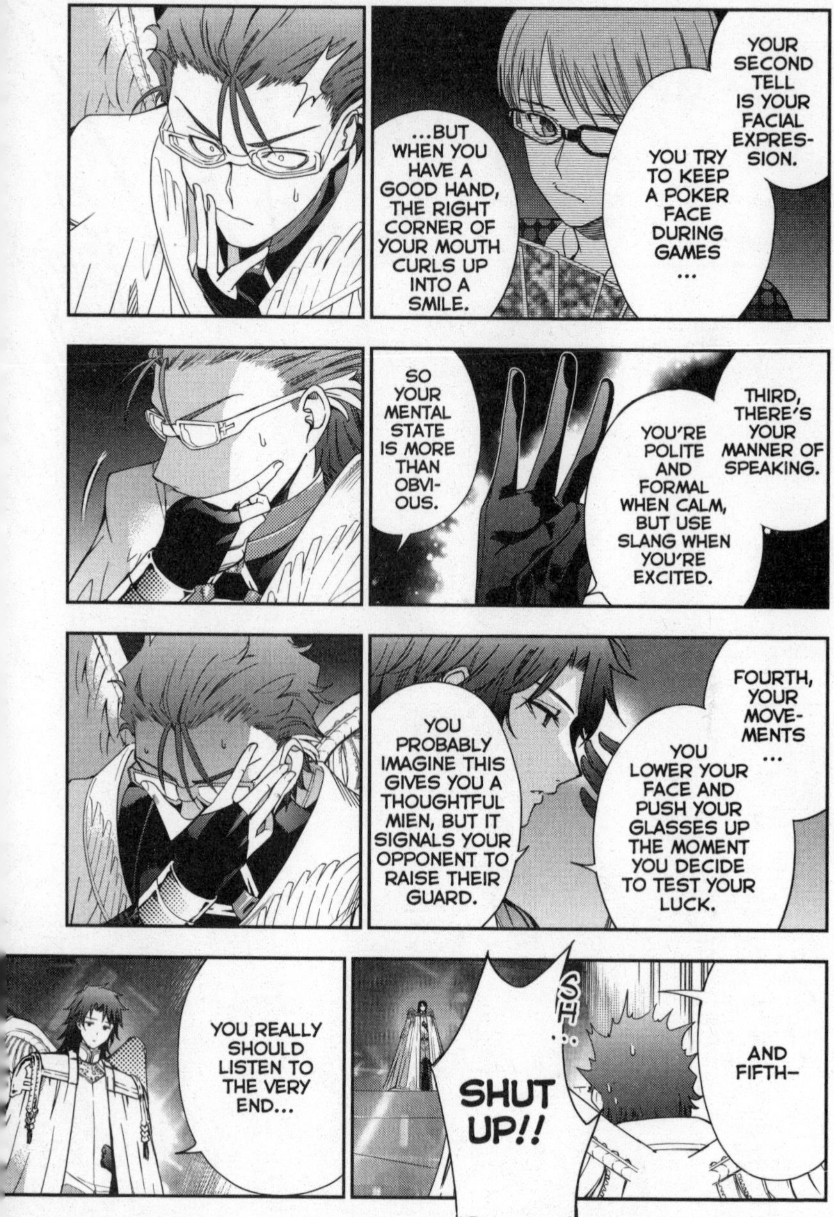
YOUR SECOND TELL IS YOUR FACIAL EXPRESSION.
YOU TRY TO KEEP A POKER FACE DURING GAMES...
...BUT WHEN YOU HAVE A GOOD HAND, THE RIGHT CORNER OF YOUR MOUTH CURLS UP INTO A SMILE.
THIRD, THERE'S YOUR MANNER OF SPEAKING.
YOU'RE POLITE AND FORMAL WHEN CALM, BUT USE SLANG WHEN YOU'RE EXCITED.
SO YOUR MENTAL STATE IS MORE THAN OBVIOUS.
FOURTH, YOUR MOVEMENTS...
YOU LOWER YOUR FACE AND PUSH YOUR GLASSES UP THE MOMENT YOU DECIDE TO TEST YOUR LUCK.
YOU PROBABLY IMAGINE THIS GIVES YOU A THOUGHTFUL MIEN, BUT IT SIGNALS YOUR OPPONENT TO RAISE THEIR GUARD.
AND FIFTH–
SH...
SHUT UP!!
YOU REALLY SHOULD LISTEN TO THE VERY END...

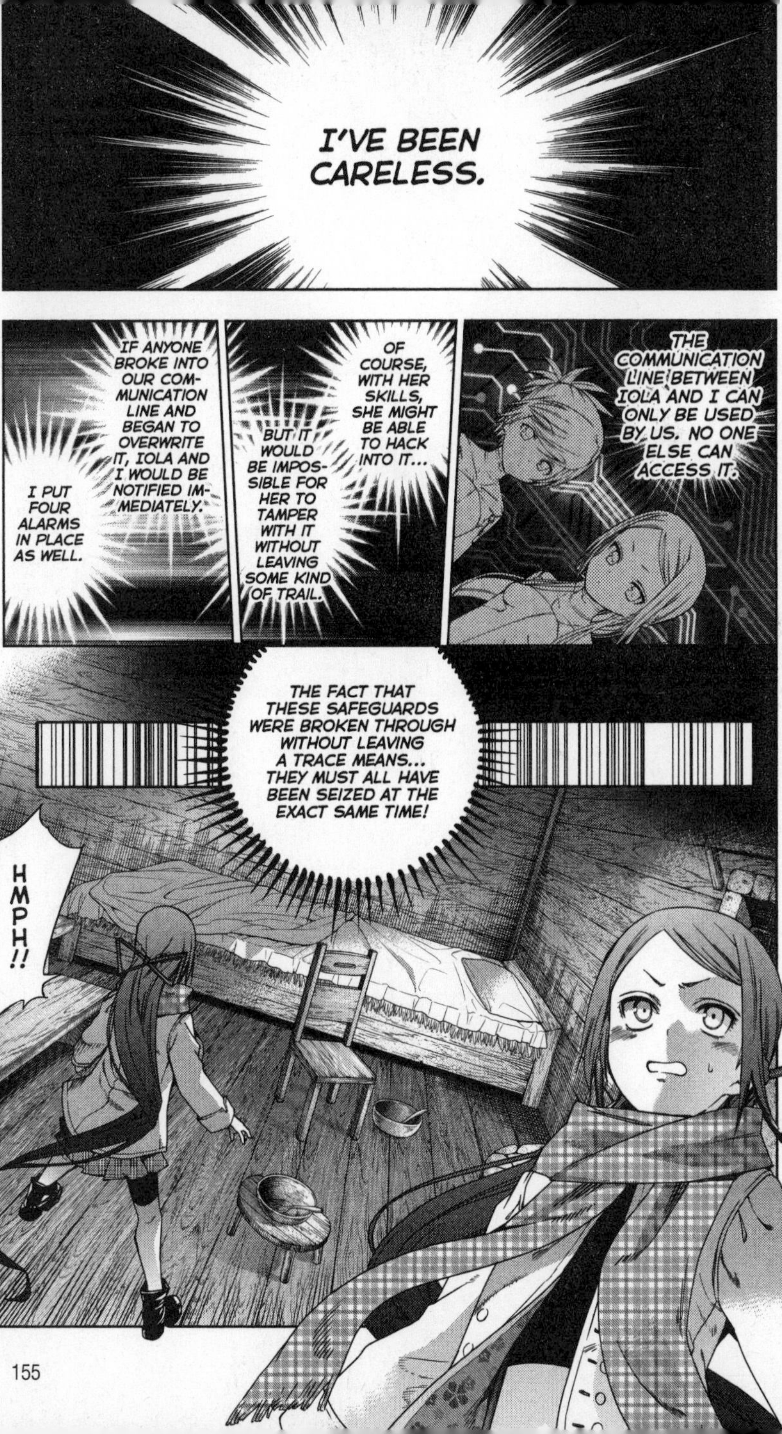
I'VE BEEN CARELESS.
THE COMMUNICATION LINE BETWEEN IOLA AND I CAN ONLY BE USED BY US. NO ONE ELSE CAN ACCESS IT.
OF COURSE, WITH HER SKILLS, SHE MIGHT BE ABLE TO HACK INTO IT...
BUT IT WOULD BE IMPOSSIBLE FOR HER TO TAMPER WITH IT WITHOUT LEAVING SOME KIND OF TRAIL.
IF ANYONE BROKE INTO OUR COMMUNICATION LINE AND BEGAN TO OVERWRITE IT, IOLA AND I WOULD BE NOTIFIED IMMEDIATELY.
I PUT FOUR ALARMS IN PLACE AS WELL.
THE FACT THAT THESE SAFEGUARDS WERE BROKEN THROUGH WITHOUT LEAVING A TRACE MEANS... THEY MUST ALL HAVE BEEN SEIZED AT THE EXACT SAME TIME!
HMPH!!

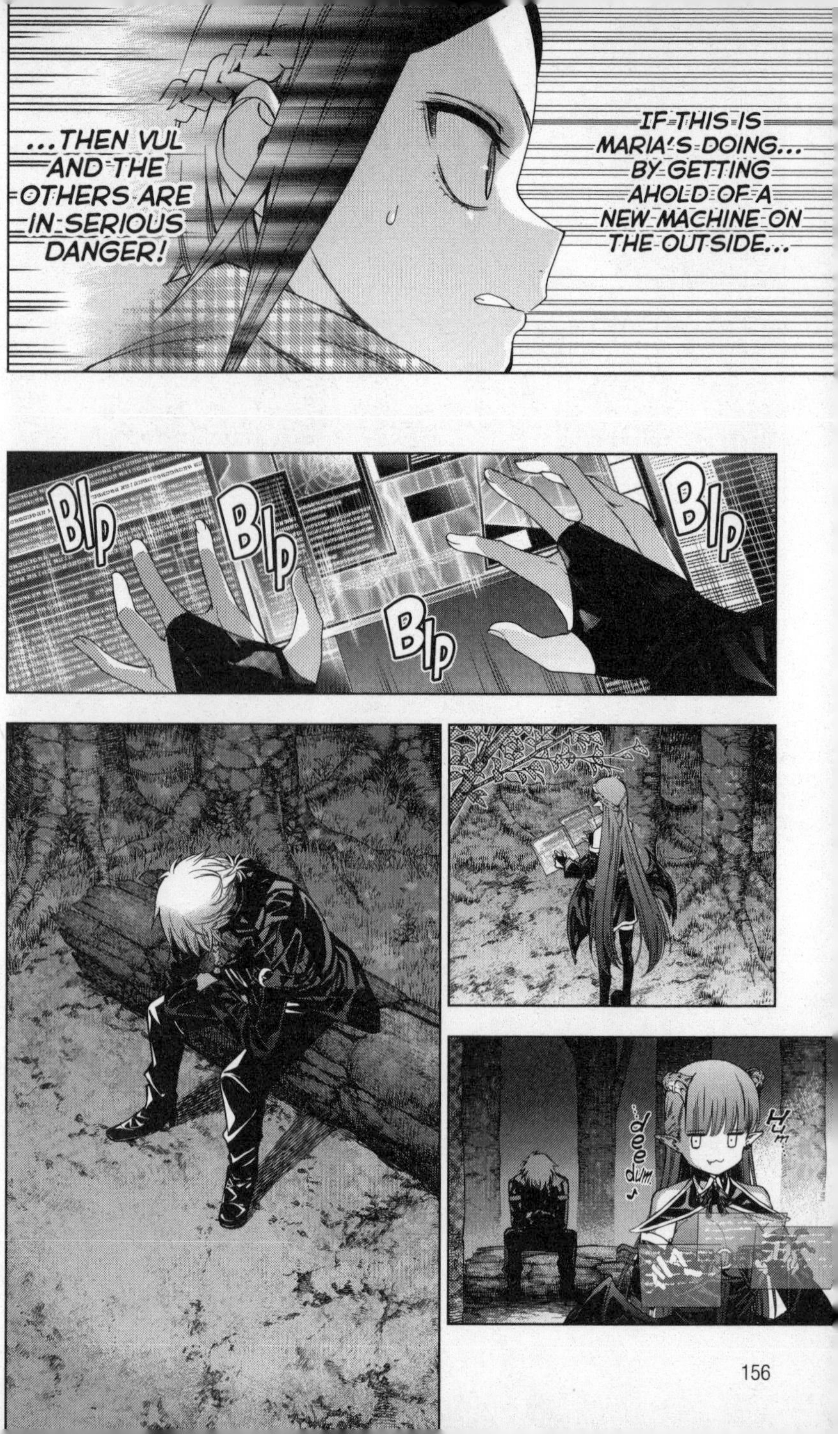
IF THIS IS MARIA'S DOING... BY GETTING AHOLD OF A NEW MACHINE ON THE OUTSIDE...
...THEN VUL AND THE OTHERS ARE IN SERIOUS DANGER!
BLIP
BLIP
BLIP
BLIP
Hum...
...deee dum ♪

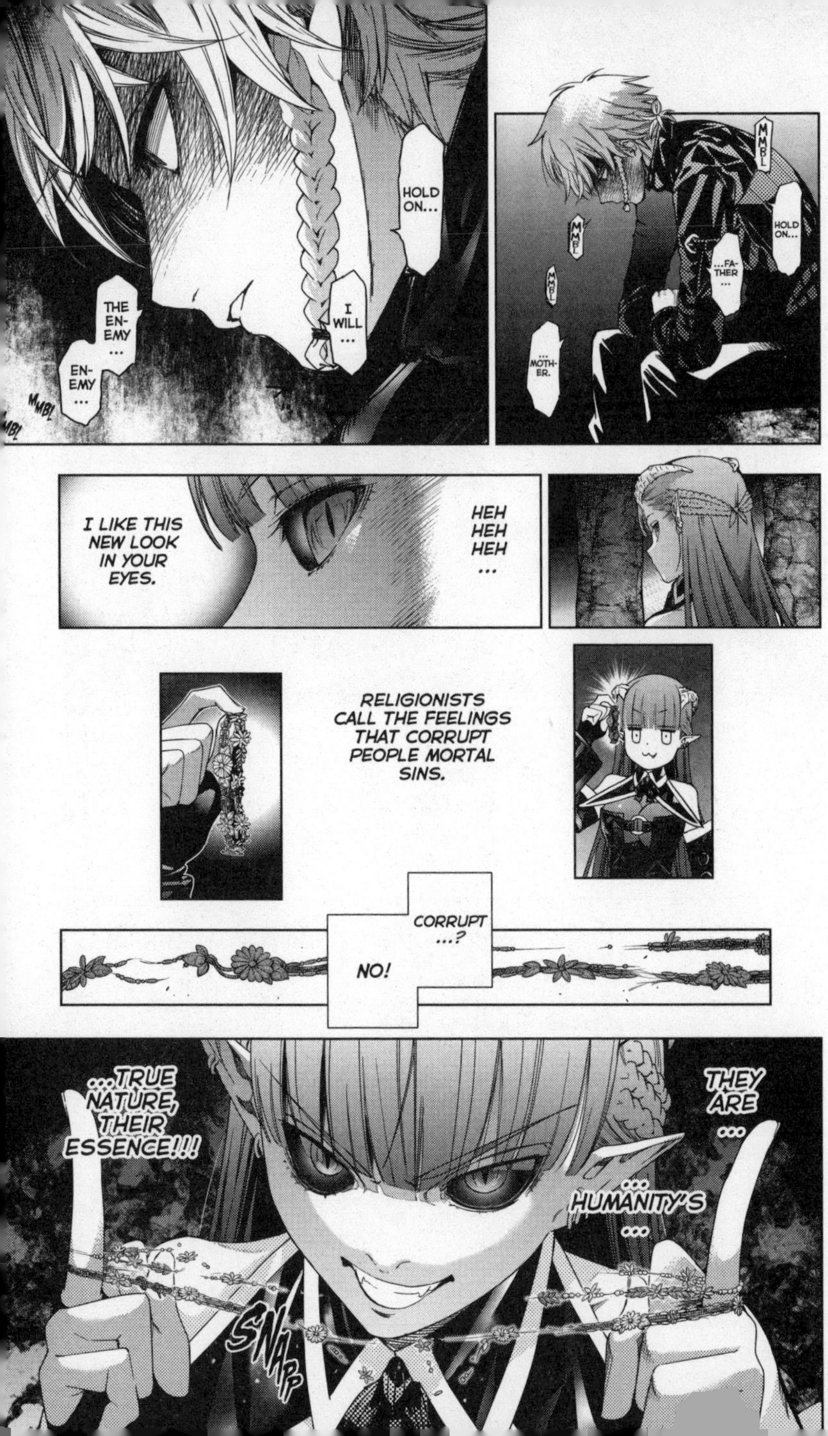
MMBL
HOLD ON...
...FATHER...
MMBL
MMBL
...MOTHER.
HOLD ON...
I WILL...
THE ENEMY...
ENEMY...
MMBL!
MMBL!
HEH HEH HEH...
I LIKE THIS NEW LOOK IN YOUR EYES.
RELIGIONISTS CALL THE FEELINGS THAT CORRUPT PEOPLE MORTAL SINS.
CORRUPT...?
NO!
THEY ARE...
...HUMANITY'S...
...TRUE NATURE, THEIR ESSENCE!!!
SNAPP

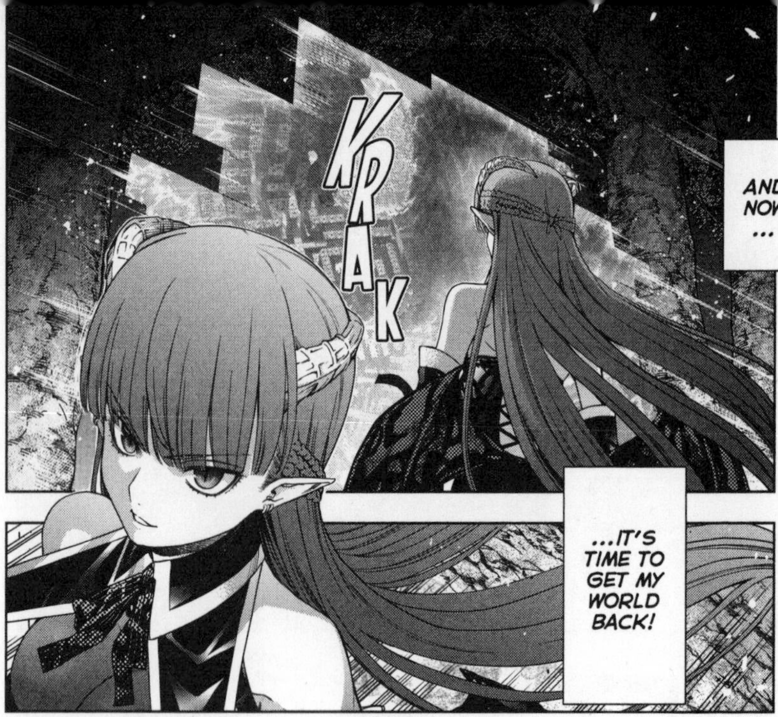
AND NOW ...
KRAK
...IT'S TIME TO GET MY WORLD BACK!

BIG SISTER ...

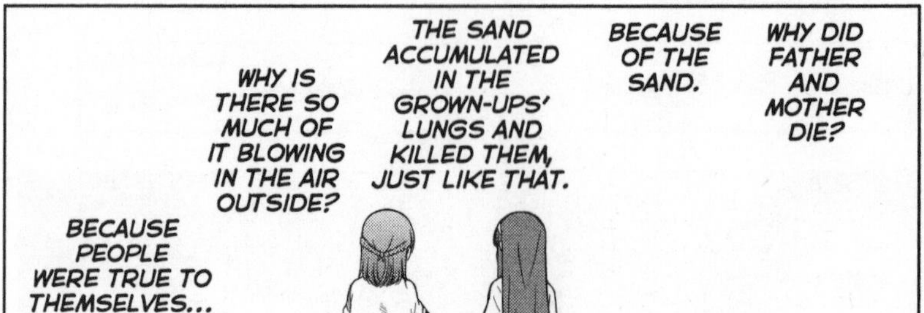
WHY DID FATHER AND MOTHER DIE?
BECAUSE OF THE SAND.
THE SAND ACCUMULATED IN THE GROWN-UPS' LUNGS AND KILLED THEM, JUST LIKE THAT.
WHY IS THERE SO MUCH OF IT BLOWING IN THE AIR OUTSIDE?
BECAUSE PEOPLE WERE TRUE TO THEMSELVES...

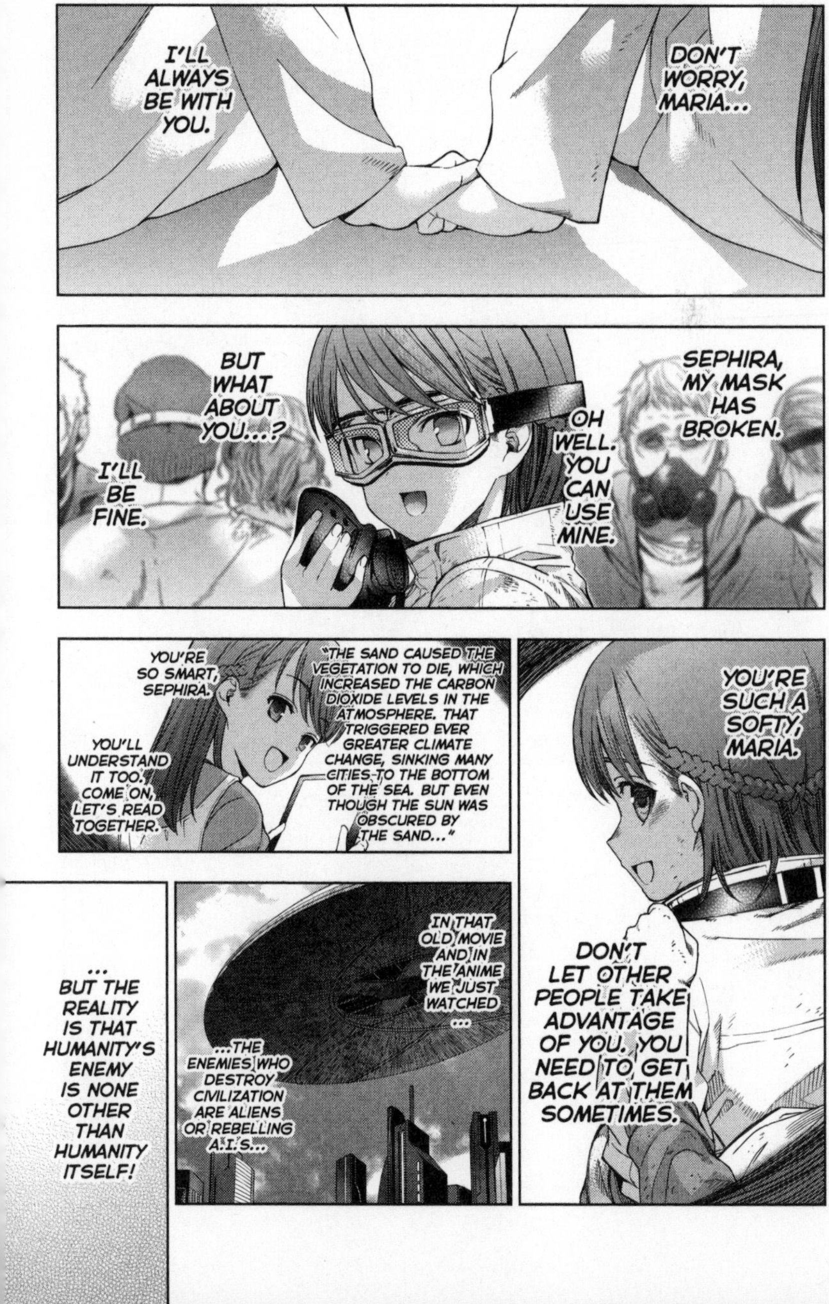
DON'T WORRY, MARIA...
I'LL ALWAYS BE WITH YOU.
SEPHIRA, MY MASK HAS BROKEN.
OH WELL. YOU CAN USE MINE.
BUT WHAT ABOUT YOU...?
I'LL BE FINE.
YOU'RE SUCH A SOFTY, MARIA.
DON'T LET OTHER PEOPLE TAKE ADVANTAGE OF YOU. YOU NEED TO GET BACK AT THEM SOMETIMES.
"THE SAND CAUSED THE VEGETATION TO DIE, WHICH INCREASED THE CARBON DIOXIDE LEVELS IN THE ATMOSPHERE. THAT TRIGGERED EVER GREATER CLIMATE CHANGE, SINKING MANY CITIES TO THE BOTTOM OF THE SEA. BUT EVEN THOUGH THE SUN WAS OBSCURED BY THE SAND..."
YOU'RE SO SMART, SEPHIRA.
YOU'LL UNDERSTAND IT TOO. COME ON, LET'S READ TOGETHER.
IN THAT OLD MOVIE AND IN THE ANIME WE JUST WATCHED ...
...THE ENEMIES WHO DESTROY CIVILIZATION ARE ALIENS OR REBELLING A.I.S...
... BUT THE REALITY IS THAT HUMANITY'S ENEMY IS NONE OTHER THAN HUMANITY ITSELF!

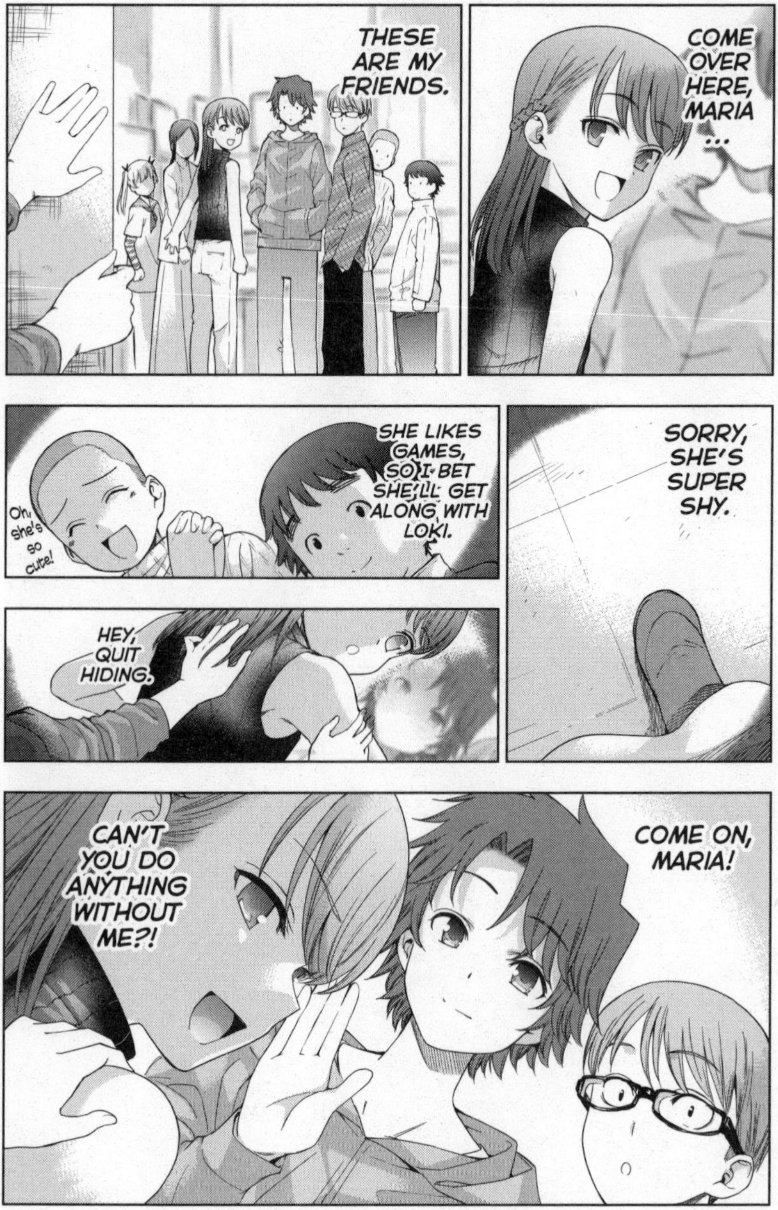
COME OVER HERE, MARIA ...
THESE ARE MY FRIENDS.
SORRY, SHE'S SUPER SHY.
SHE LIKES GAMES, SO I BET SHE'LL GET ALONG WITH LOKI.
Oh, she's so cute!
HEY, QUIT HIDING.
COME ON, MARIA!
CAN'T YOU DO ANYTHING WITHOUT ME?!

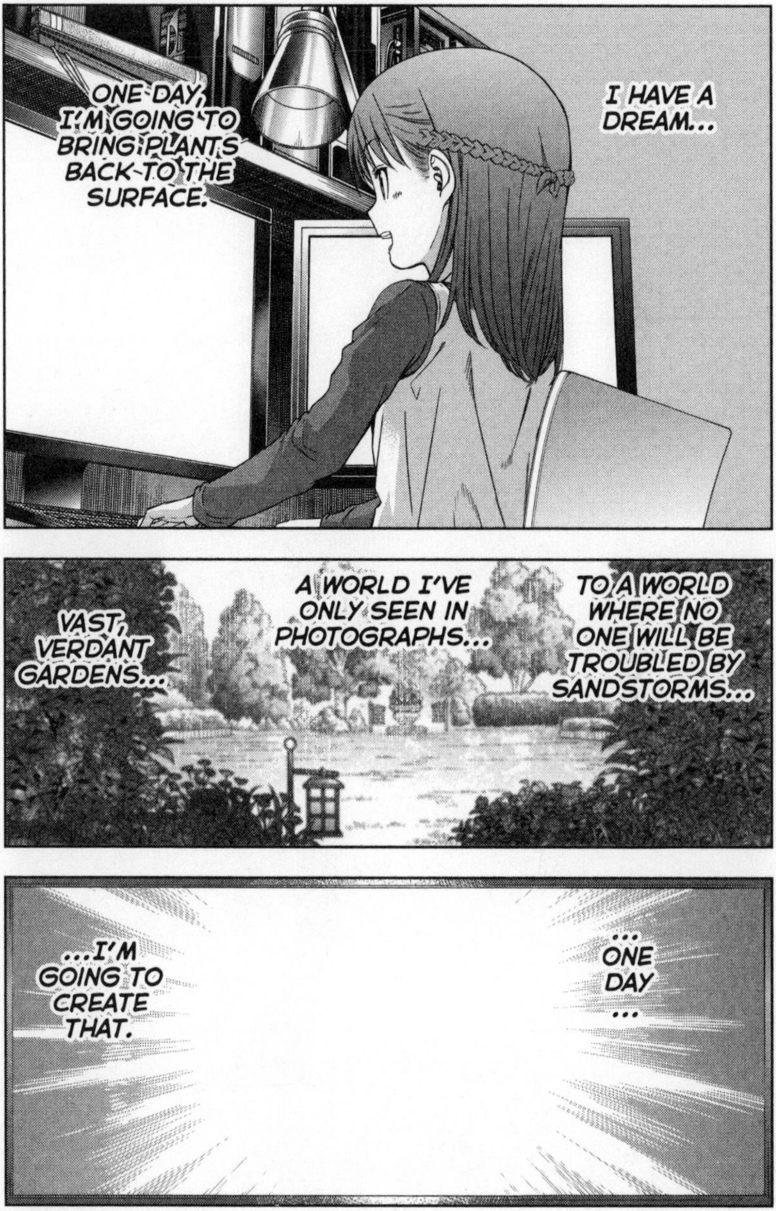
I HAVE A DREAM...
ONE DAY, I'M GOING TO BRING PLANTS BACK TO THE SURFACE.
TO A WORLD WHERE NO ONE WILL BE TROUBLED BY SANDSTORMS...
A WORLD I'VE ONLY SEEN IN PHOTOGRAPHS...
VAST, VERDANT GARDENS...
...ONE DAY...
...I'M GOING TO CREATE THAT.

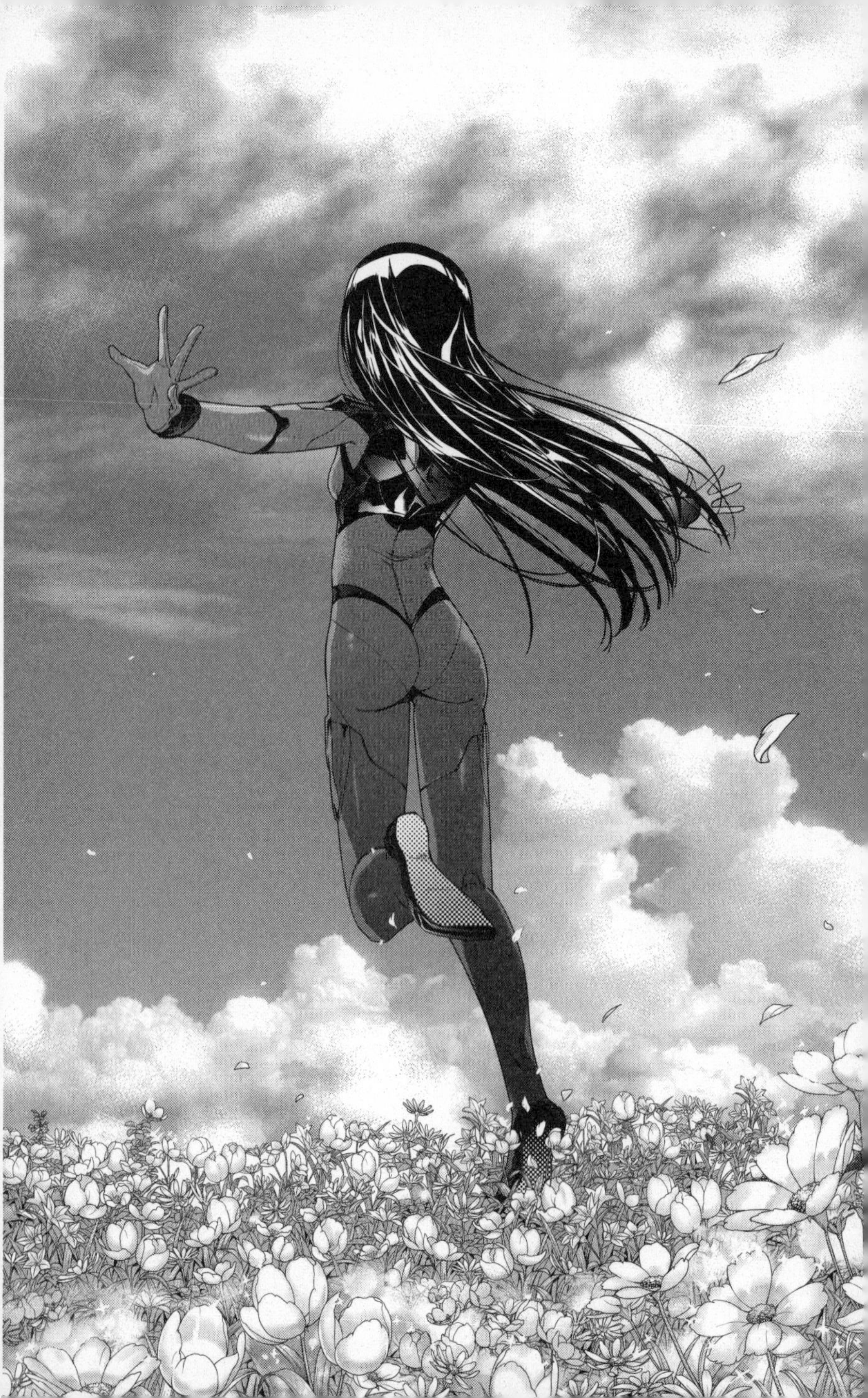

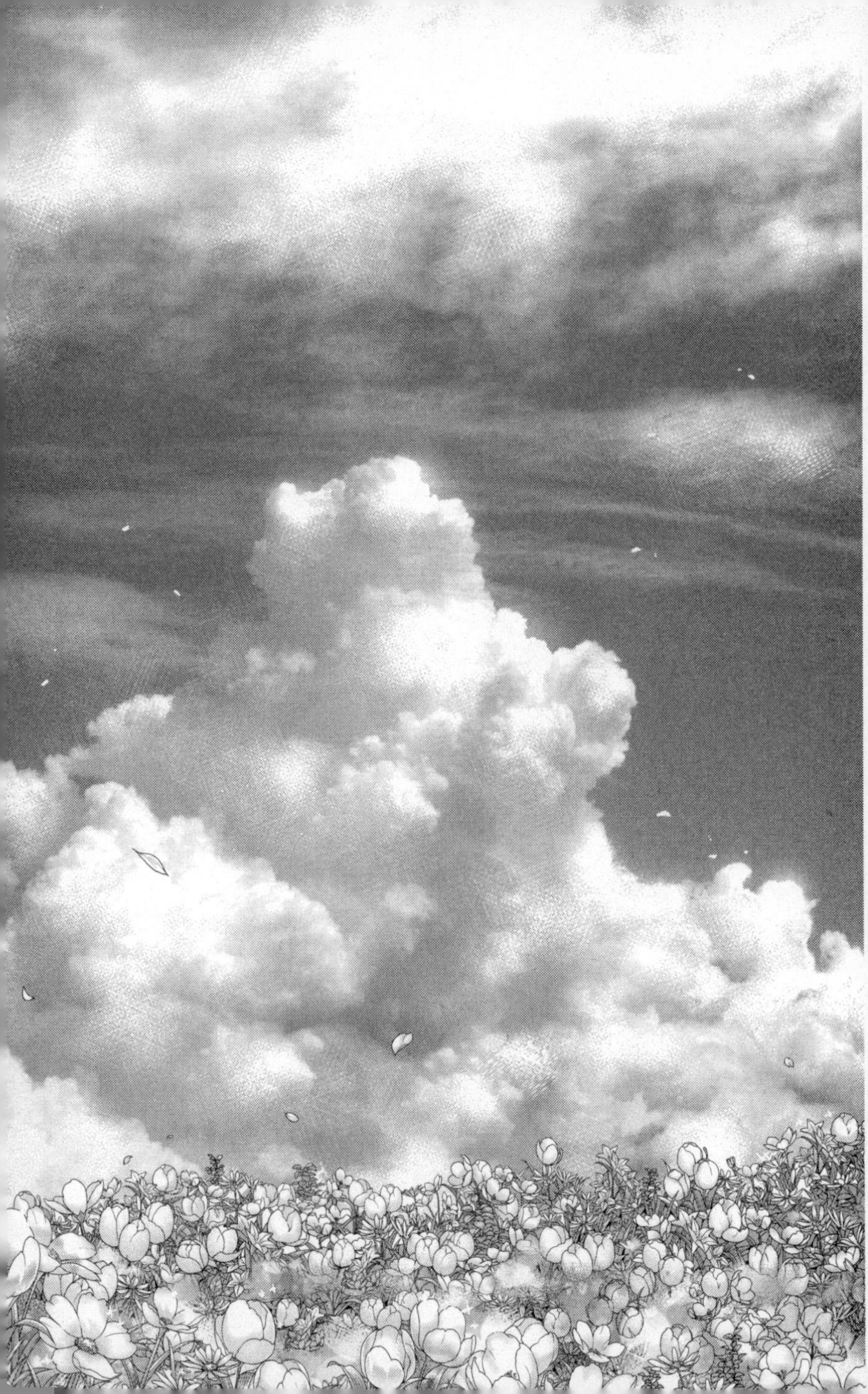

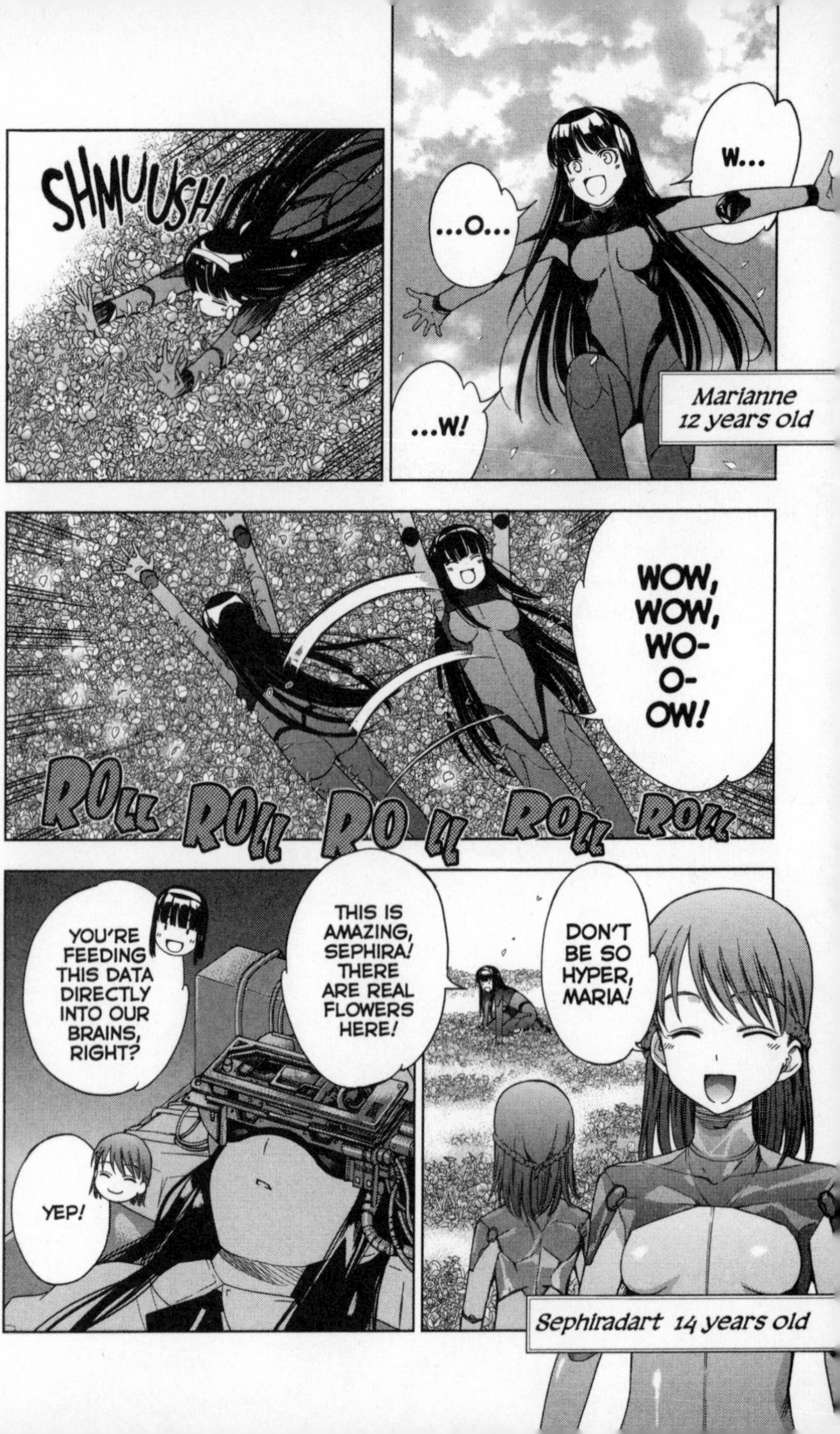
W...
...O...
...W!
Marianne 12 years old
SHMUUSH
WOW, WOW, WO-O-OW!
ROLL ROLL ROLL ROLL ROLL
THIS IS AMAZING, SEPHIRA! THERE ARE REAL FLOWERS HERE!
DON'T BE SO HYPER, MARIA!
Sephiradart 14 years old
YOU'RE FEEDING THIS DATA DIRECTLY INTO OUR BRAINS, RIGHT?
YEP!

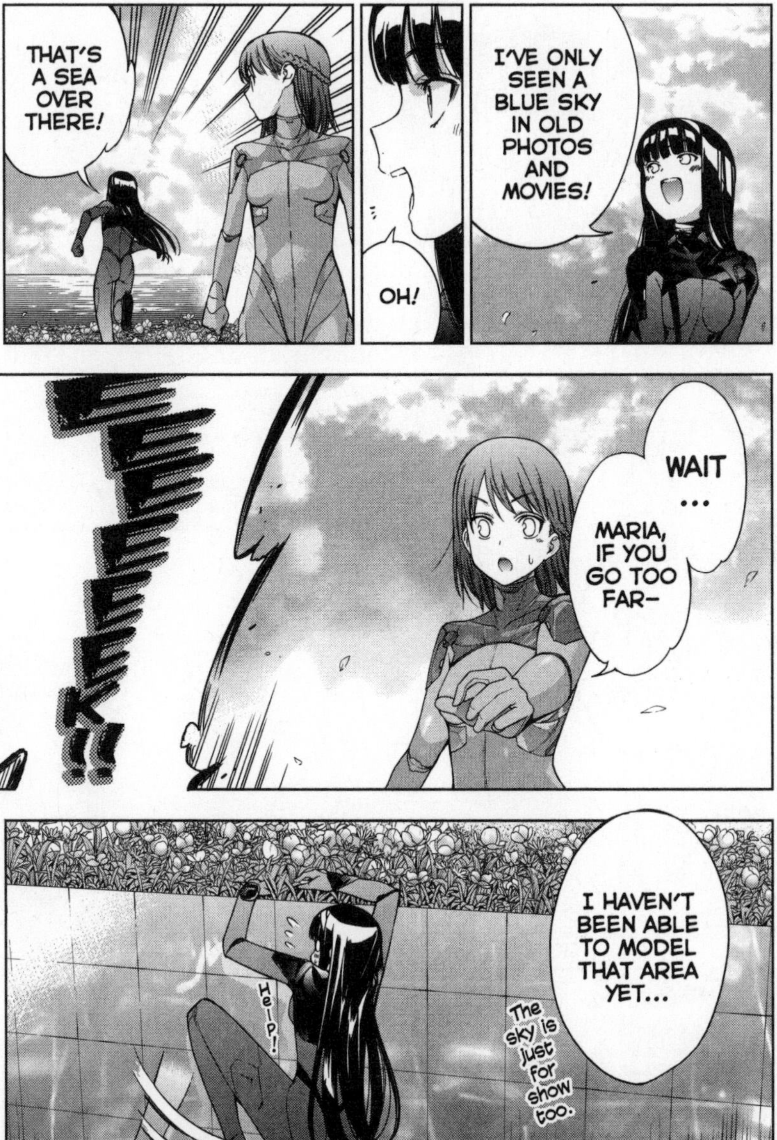
I'VE ONLY SEEN A BLUE SKY IN OLD PHOTOS AND MOVIES!
OH!
THAT'S A SEA OVER THERE!
WAIT ... MARIA, IF YOU GO TOO FAR–
EEEEEEK!!
I HAVEN'T BEEN ABLE TO MODEL THAT AREA YET...
The sky is just for show too.
Help!

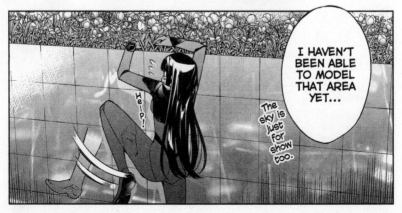

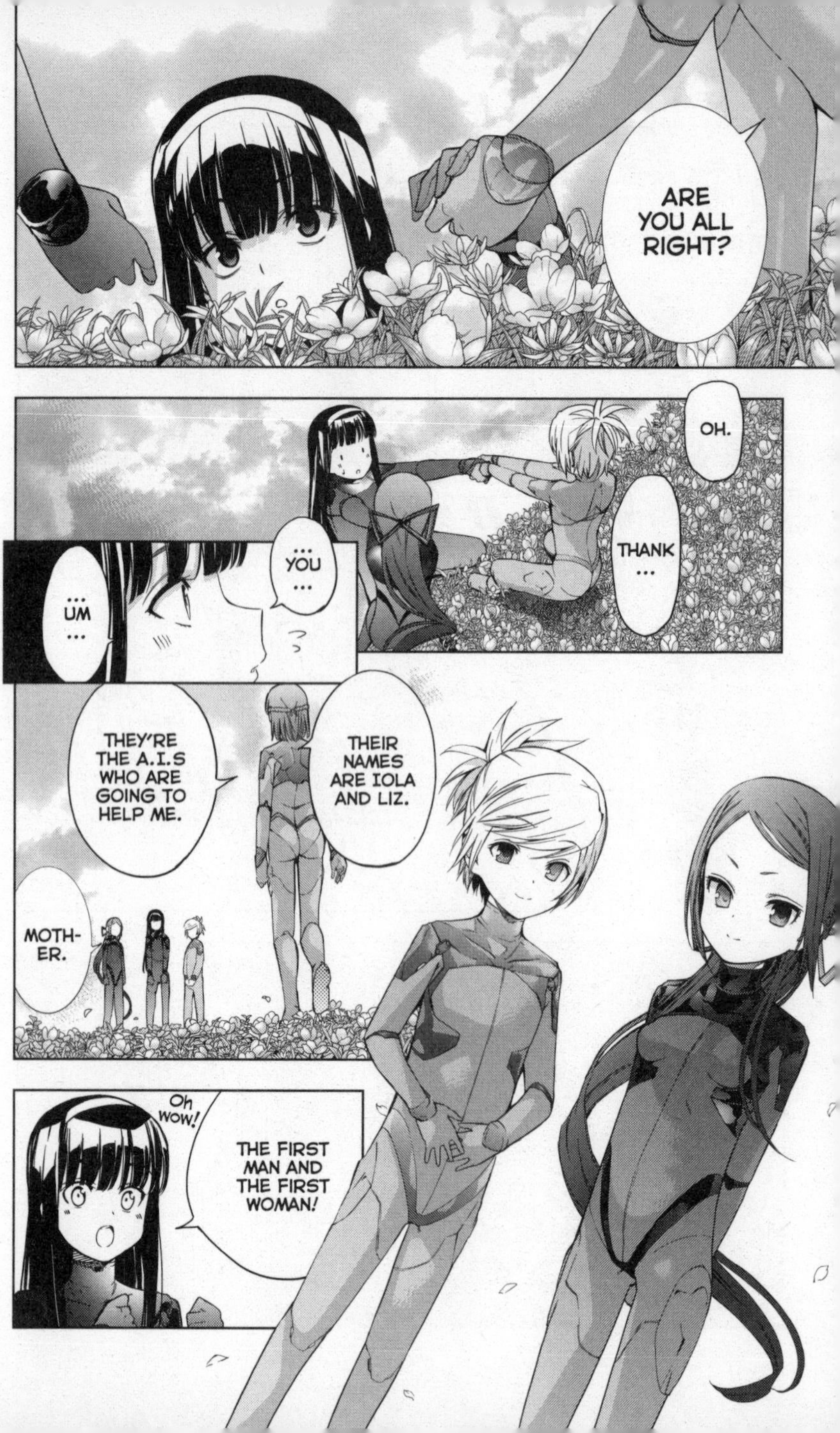
ARE YOU ALL RIGHT?
OH.
THANK...
...YOU...
...UM...
THEIR NAMES ARE IOLA AND LIZ.
THEY'RE THE A.I.S WHO ARE GOING TO HELP ME.
MOTH-ER.
Oh wow!
THE FIRST MAN AND THE FIRST WOMAN!

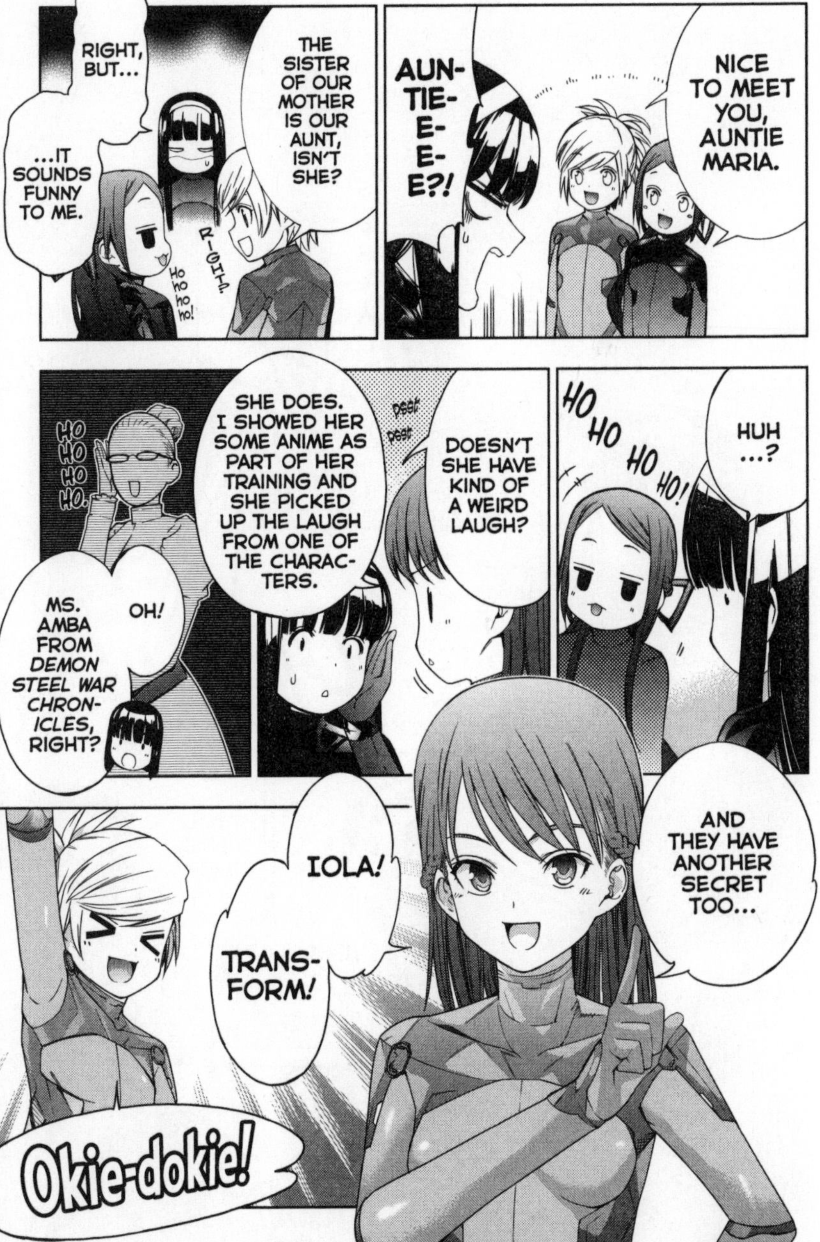
NICE TO MEET YOU, AUNTIE MARIA.
AUN-TIE-E-E-E?!
THE SISTER OF OUR MOTHER IS OUR AUNT, ISN'T SHE?
RIGHT, BUT...
...IT SOUNDS FUNNY TO ME.
RIGHT?
Ho ho ho ho!
HUH ...?
HO HO HO HO!
DOESN'T SHE HAVE KIND OF A WEIRD LAUGH?
psst psst
SHE DOES. I SHOWED HER SOME ANIME AS PART OF HER TRAINING AND SHE PICKED UP THE LAUGH FROM ONE OF THE CHARAC-TERS.
HO HO HO HO.
OH!
MS. AMBA FROM *DEMON STEEL WAR CHRON-ICLES*, RIGHT?
AND THEY HAVE ANOTHER SECRET TOO...
IOLA!
TRANS-FORM!
Okie-dokie!

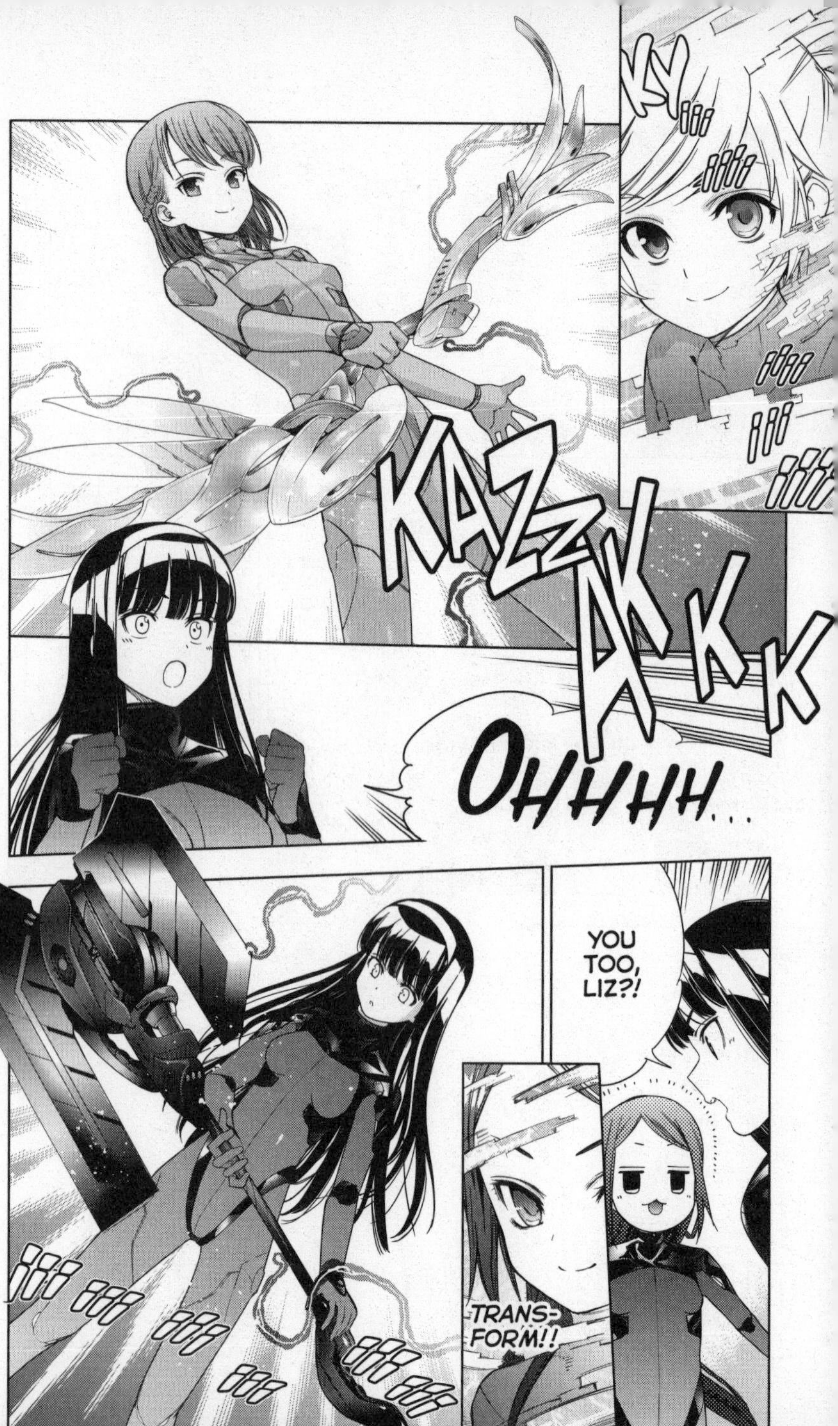
KY
KAZZAKKK
OHHHH...
YOU TOO, LIZ?!
TRANS-FORM!!

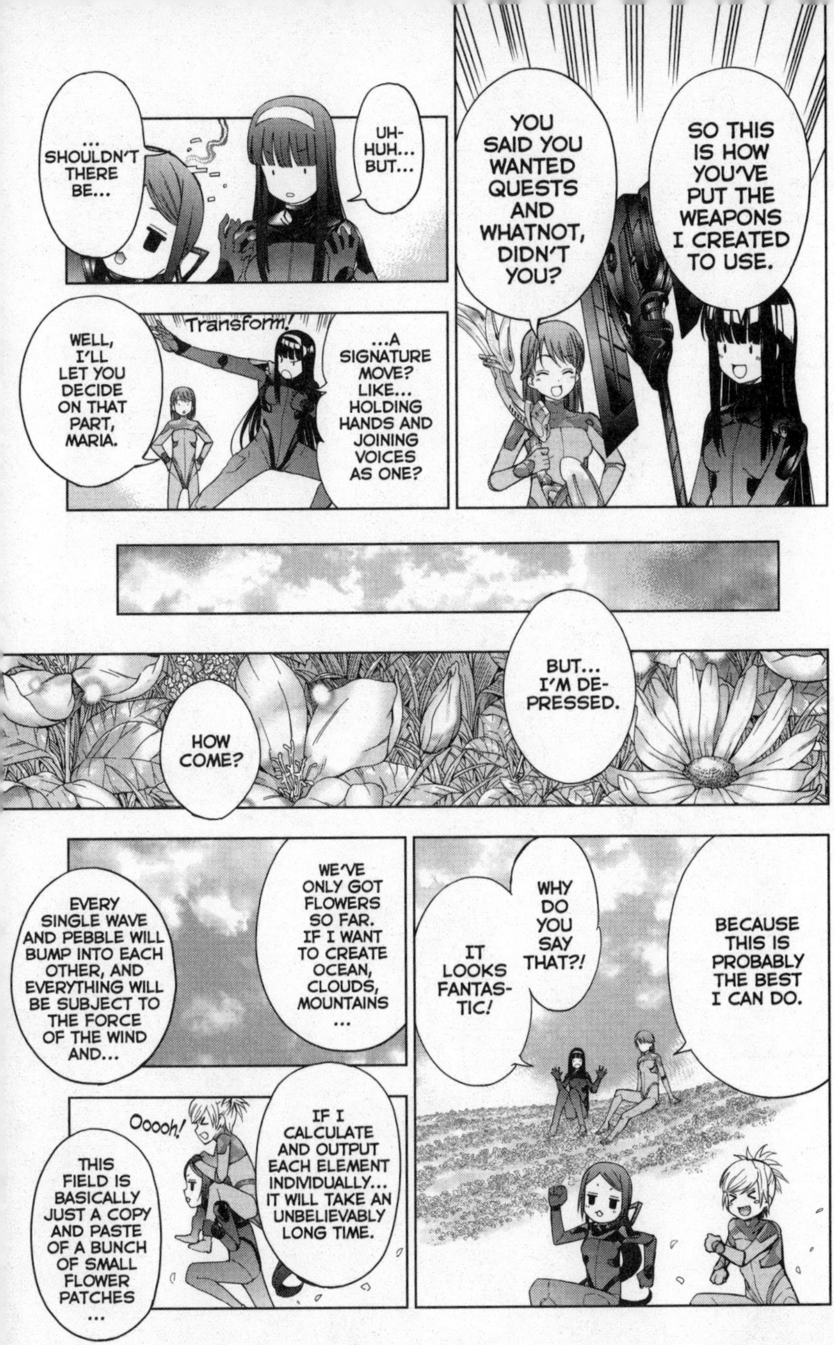
SO THIS IS HOW YOU'VE PUT THE WEAPONS I CREATED TO USE.
YOU SAID YOU WANTED QUESTS AND WHATNOT, DIDN'T YOU?
UH-HUH... BUT...
...SHOULDN'T THERE BE...
...A SIGNATURE MOVE? LIKE... HOLDING HANDS AND JOINING VOICES AS ONE?
Transform!
WELL, I'LL LET YOU DECIDE ON THAT PART, MARIA.
BUT... I'M DE-PRESSED.
HOW COME?
BECAUSE THIS IS PROBABLY THE BEST I CAN DO.
WHY DO YOU SAY THAT?!
IT LOOKS FANTAS-TIC!
WE'VE ONLY GOT FLOWERS SO FAR. IF I WANT TO CREATE OCEAN, CLOUDS, MOUNTAINS ...
EVERY SINGLE WAVE AND PEBBLE WILL BUMP INTO EACH OTHER, AND EVERYTHING WILL BE SUBJECT TO THE FORCE OF THE WIND AND...
IF I CALCULATE AND OUTPUT EACH ELEMENT INDIVIDUALLY... IT WILL TAKE AN UNBELIEVABLY LONG TIME.
Ooooh!
THIS FIELD IS BASICALLY JUST A COPY AND PASTE OF A BUNCH OF SMALL FLOWER PATCHES ...

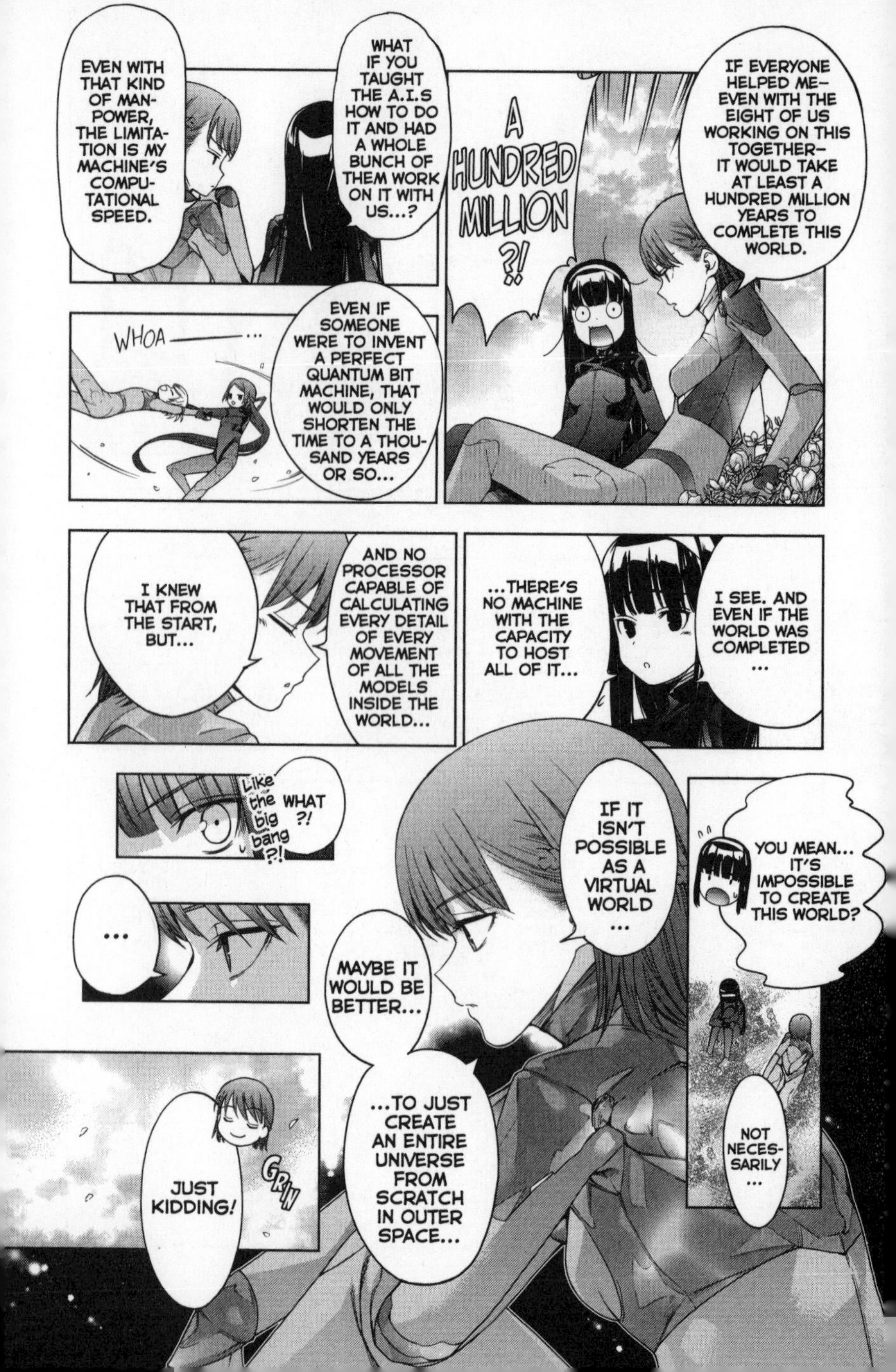
IF EVERYONE HELPED ME— EVEN WITH THE EIGHT OF US WORKING ON THIS TOGETHER— IT WOULD TAKE AT LEAST A HUNDRED MILLION YEARS TO COMPLETE THIS WORLD.
A HUNDRED MILLION ?!
WHAT IF YOU TAUGHT THE A.I.S HOW TO DO IT AND HAD A WHOLE BUNCH OF THEM WORK ON IT WITH US...?
EVEN WITH THAT KIND OF MAN-POWER, THE LIMITA-TION IS MY MACHINE'S COMPU-TATIONAL SPEED.
EVEN IF SOMEONE WERE TO INVENT A PERFECT QUANTUM BIT MACHINE, THAT WOULD ONLY SHORTEN THE TIME TO A THOU-SAND YEARS OR SO...
WHOA——...
I SEE. AND EVEN IF THE WORLD WAS COMPLETED...
...THERE'S NO MACHINE WITH THE CAPACITY TO HOST ALL OF IT...
AND NO PROCESSOR CAPABLE OF CALCULATING EVERY DETAIL OF EVERY MOVEMENT OF ALL THE MODELS INSIDE THE WORLD...
I KNEW THAT FROM THE START, BUT...
YOU MEAN... IT'S IMPOSSIBLE TO CREATE THIS WORLD?
NOT NECES-SARILY...
IF IT ISN'T POSSIBLE AS A VIRTUAL WORLD...
MAYBE IT WOULD BE BETTER...
...TO JUST CREATE AN ENTIRE UNIVERSE FROM SCRATCH IN OUTER SPACE...
WHAT ?!
Like the big bang ?!
...
GRIN
JUST KIDDING!

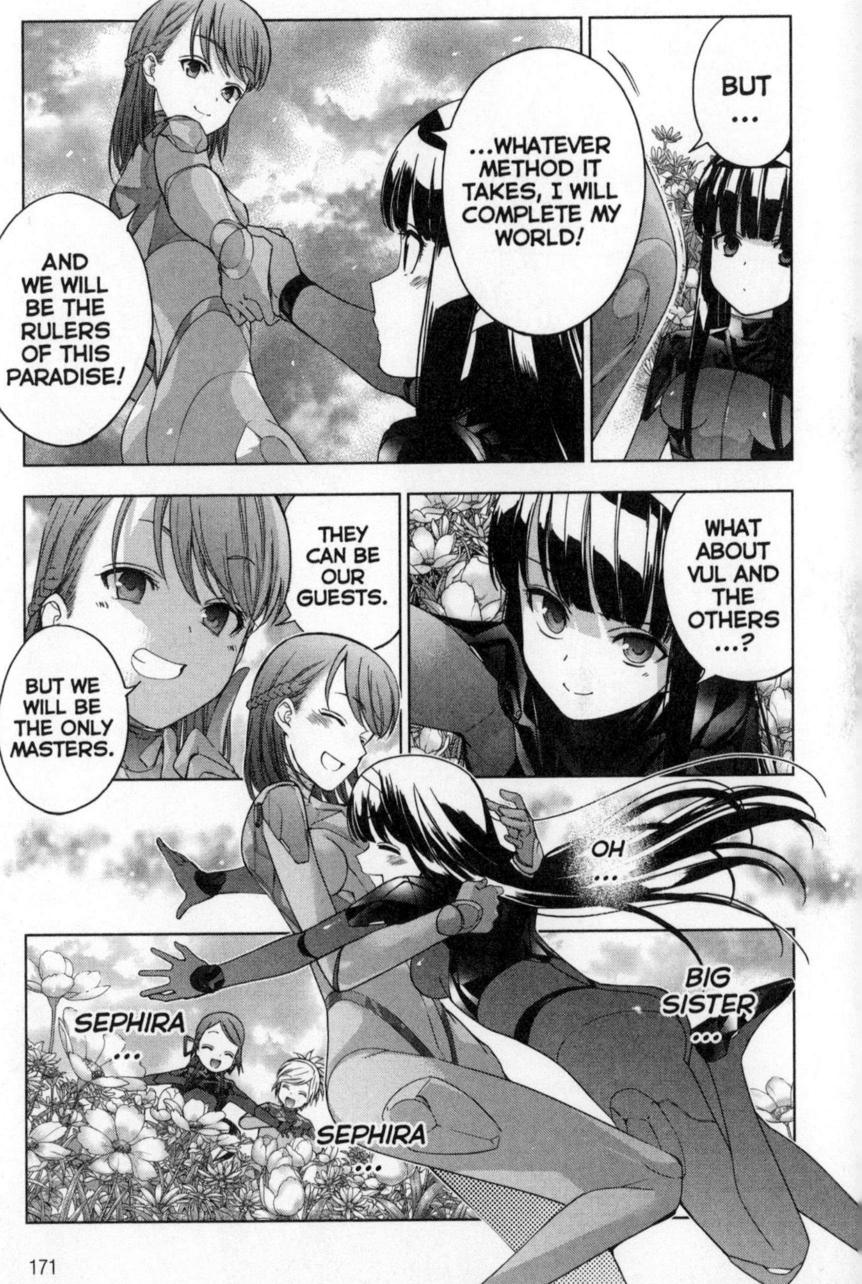
BUT ...
...WHATEVER METHOD IT TAKES, I WILL COMPLETE MY WORLD!
AND WE WILL BE THE RULERS OF THIS PARADISE!
WHAT ABOUT VUL AND THE OTHERS ...?
THEY CAN BE OUR GUESTS.
BUT WE WILL BE THE ONLY MASTERS.
OH ...
BIG SISTER ...
SEPHIRA ...
SEPHIRA ...

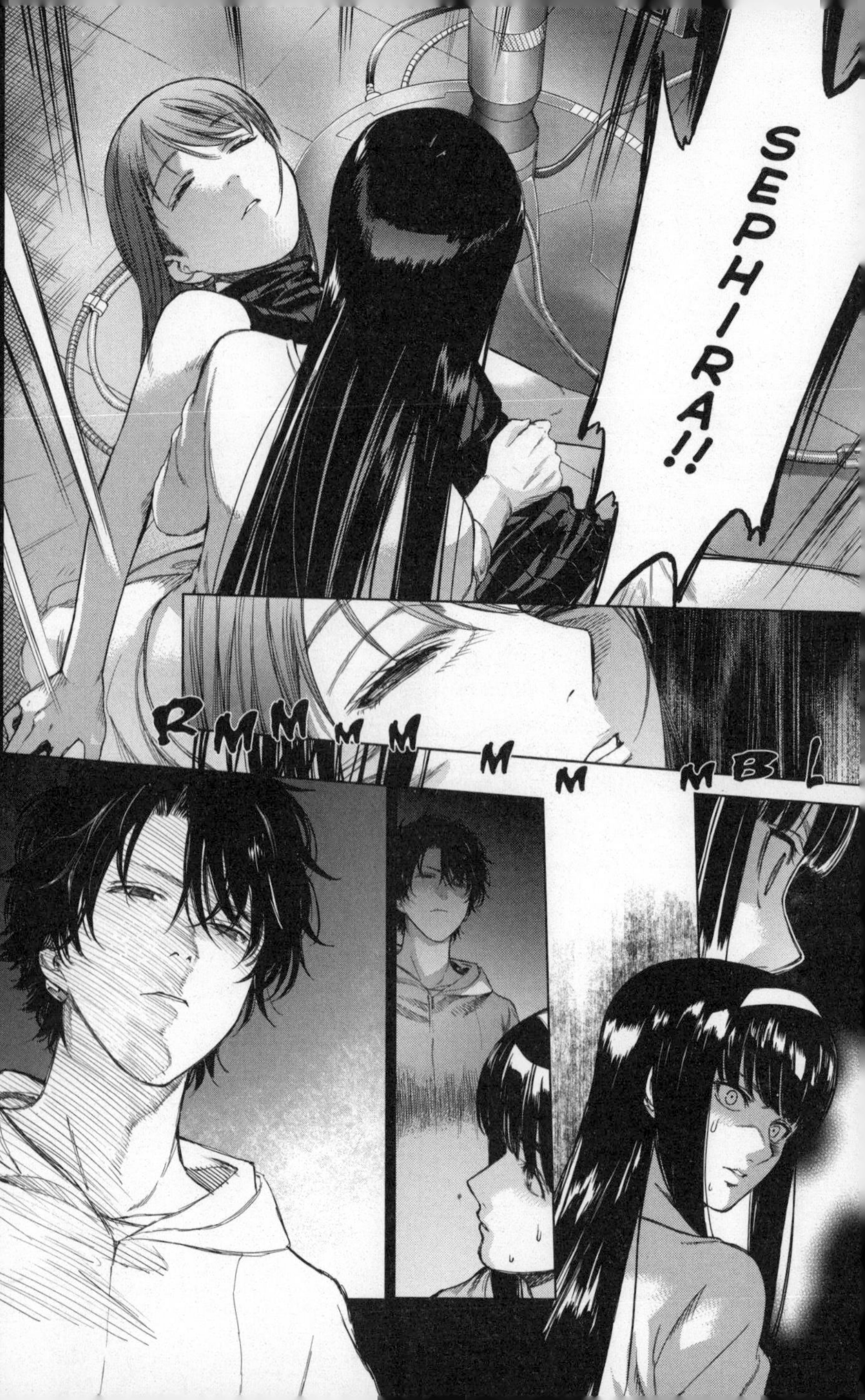
SEPHIRA!!
RMMMMMMMMBL

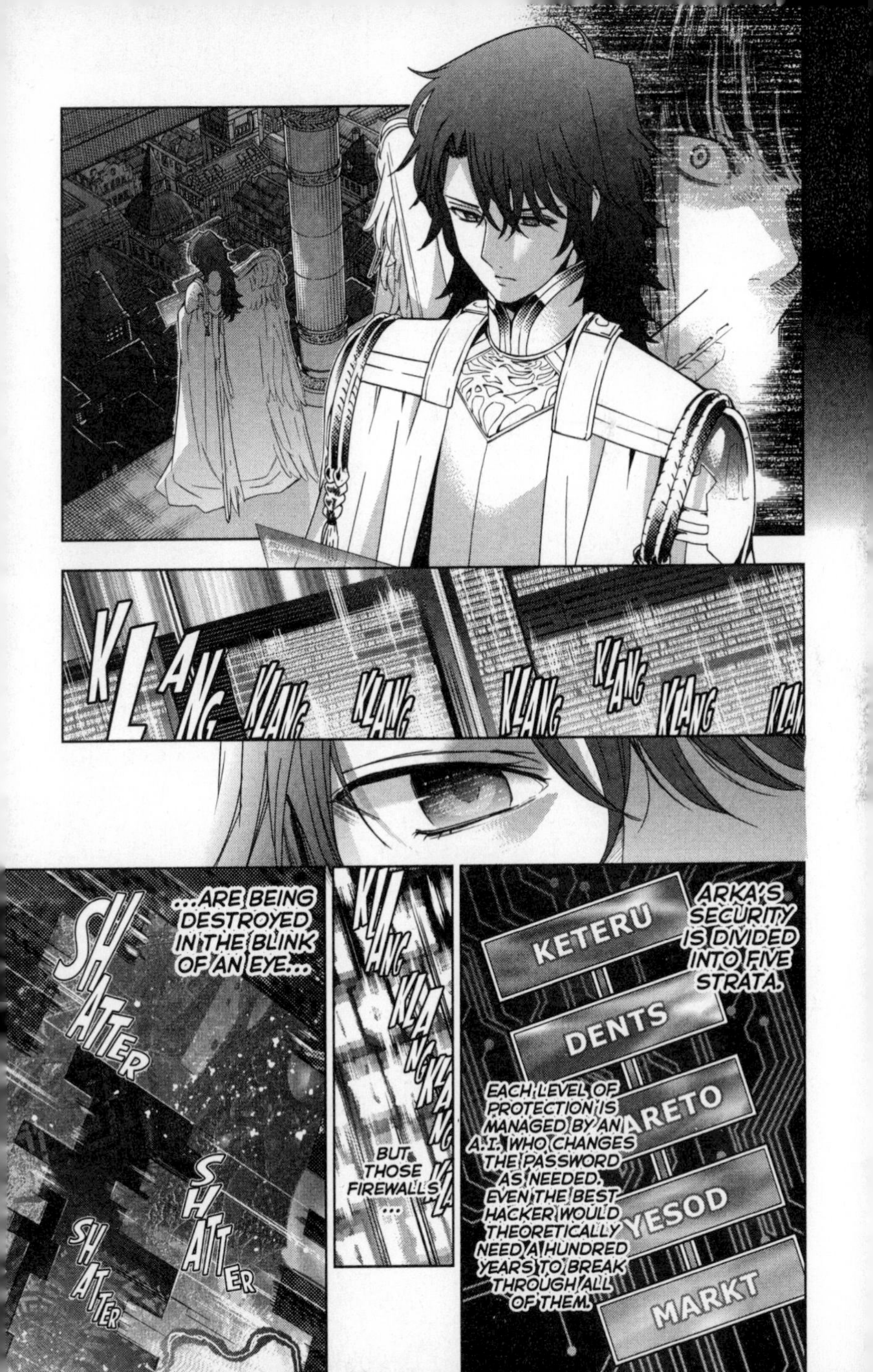
KLANG
KLANG
KLANG
KLANG
KLANG
KLANG
ARKA'S SECURITY IS DIVIDED INTO FIVE STRATA.
KETERU
DENTS
ARETO
YESOD
MARKT
EACH LEVEL OF PROTECTION IS MANAGED BY AN A.I. WHO CHANGES THE PASSWORD AS NEEDED. EVEN THE BEST HACKER WOULD THEORETICALLY NEED A HUNDRED YEARS TO BREAK THROUGH ALL OF THEM.
KLANG KLANG KLANG
BUT THOSE FIREWALLS...
...ARE BEING DESTROYED IN THE BLINK OF AN EYE...
SHATTER
SHATTER
SHATTER

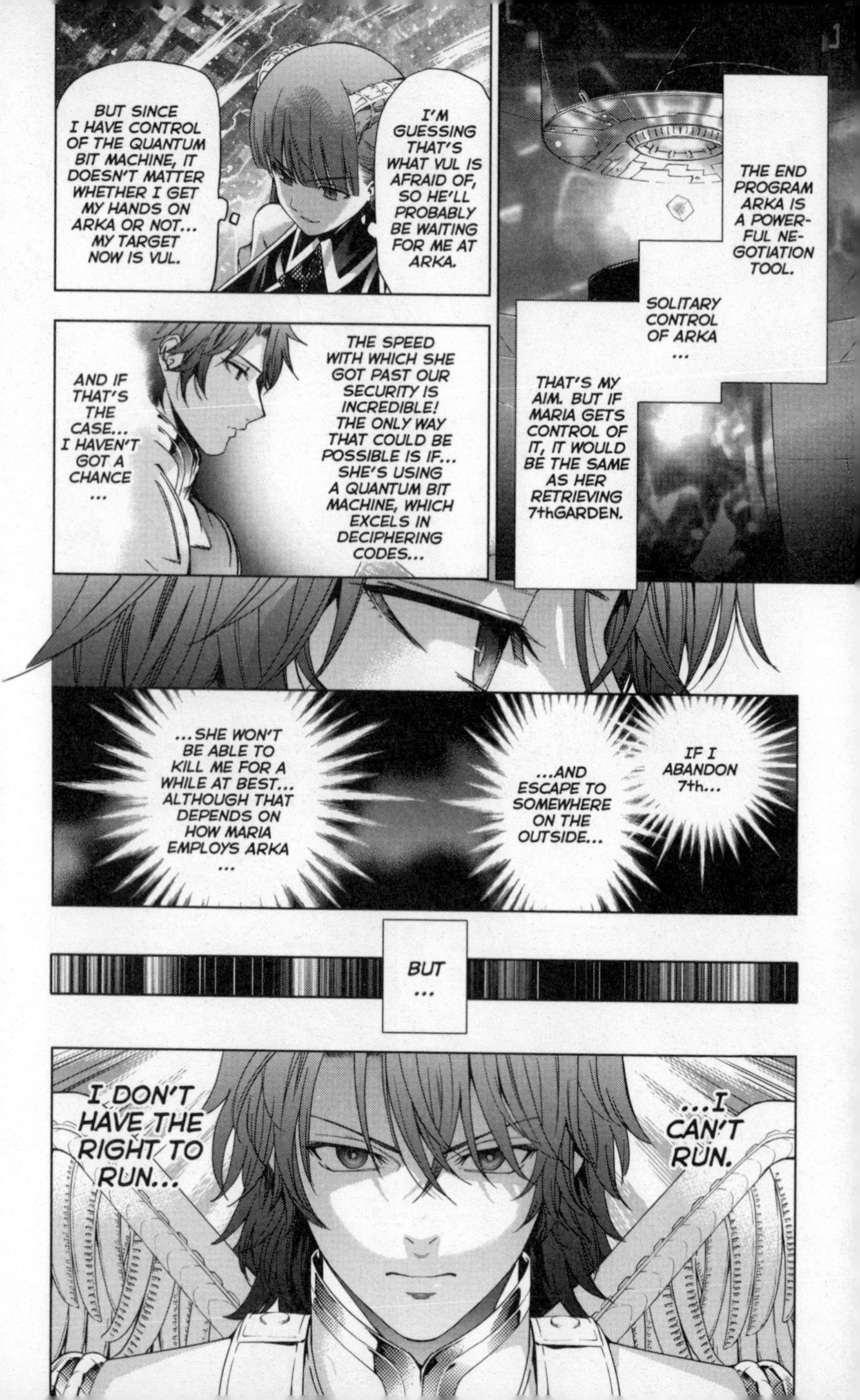
THE END PROGRAM ARKA IS A POWERFUL NEGOTIATION TOOL.
SOLITARY CONTROL OF ARKA ...
THAT'S MY AIM. BUT IF MARIA GETS CONTROL OF IT, IT WOULD BE THE SAME AS HER RETRIEVING 7thGARDEN.
I'M GUESSING THAT'S WHAT VUL IS AFRAID OF, SO HE'LL PROBABLY BE WAITING FOR ME AT ARKA.
BUT SINCE I HAVE CONTROL OF THE QUANTUM BIT MACHINE, IT DOESN'T MATTER WHETHER I GET MY HANDS ON ARKA OR NOT... MY TARGET NOW IS VUL.
THE SPEED WITH WHICH SHE GOT PAST OUR SECURITY IS INCREDIBLE! THE ONLY WAY THAT COULD BE POSSIBLE IS IF... SHE'S USING A QUANTUM BIT MACHINE, WHICH EXCELS IN DECIPHERING CODES...
AND IF THAT'S THE CASE... I HAVEN'T GOT A CHANCE ...
IF I ABANDON 7th...
...AND ESCAPE TO SOMEWHERE ON THE OUTSIDE...
...SHE WON'T BE ABLE TO KILL ME FOR A WHILE AT BEST... ALTHOUGH THAT DEPENDS ON HOW MARIA EMPLOYS ARKA ...
BUT ...
...I CAN'T RUN.
I DON'T HAVE THE RIGHT TO RUN...

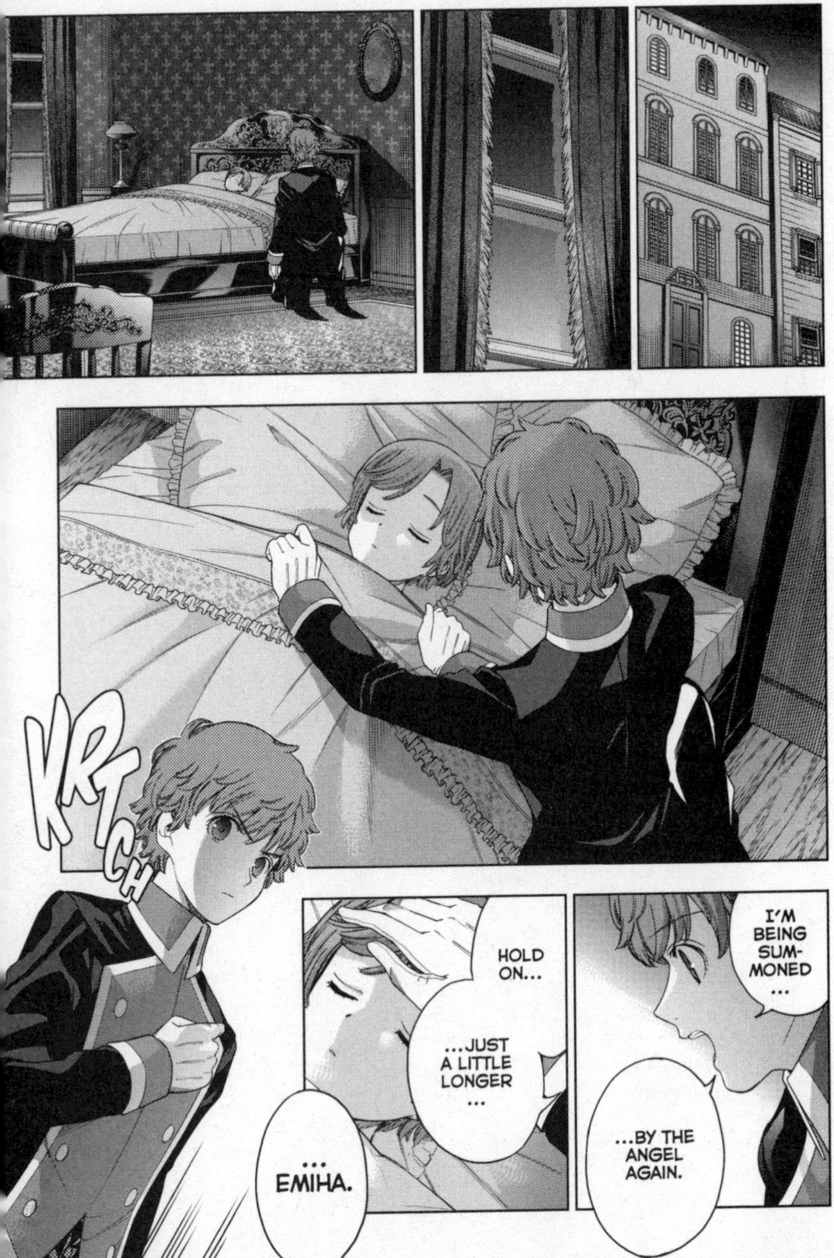
KRTCH
I'M BEING SUM-MONED ...
...BY THE ANGEL AGAIN.
HOLD ON...
...JUST A LITTLE LONGER ...
... EMIHA.

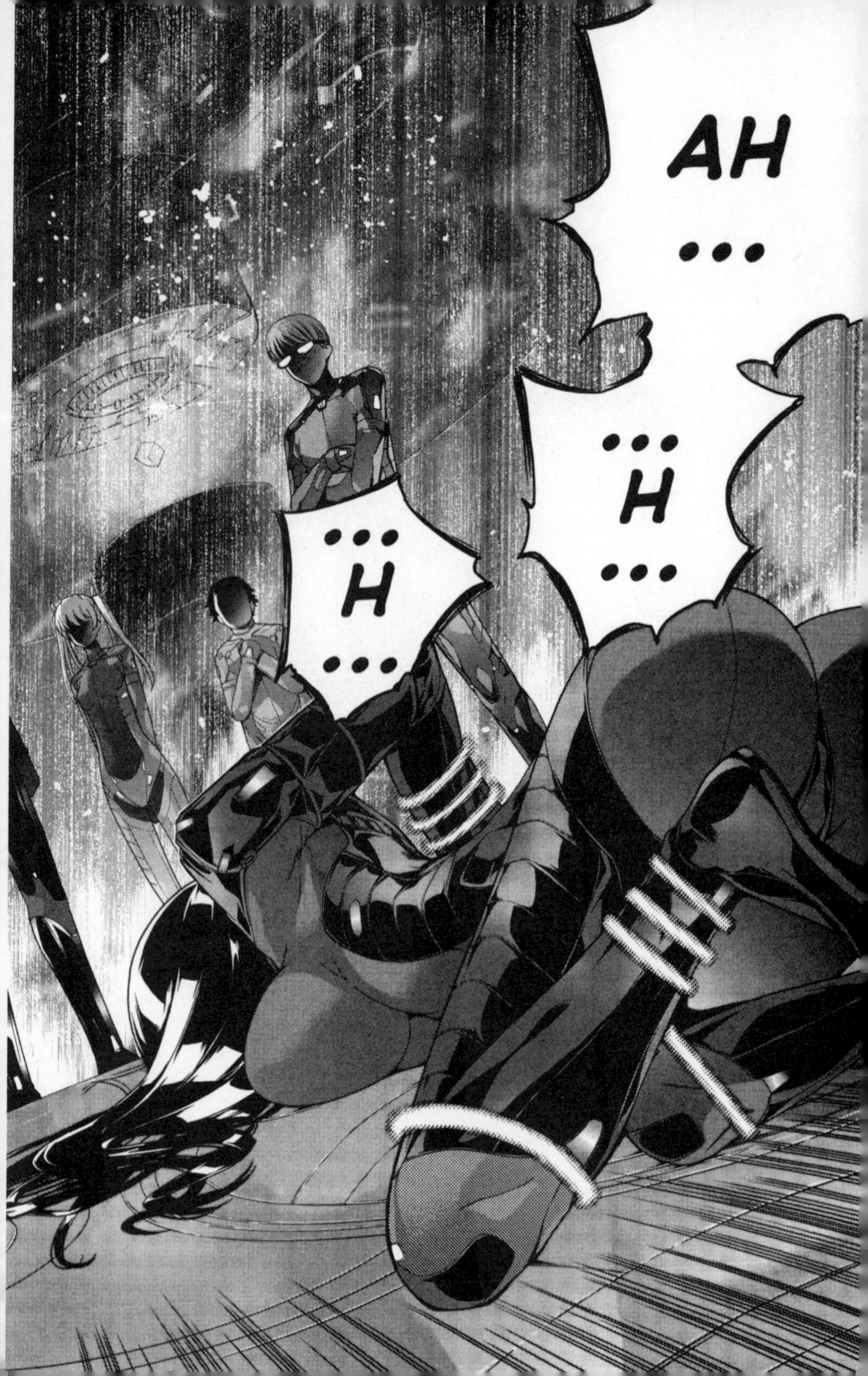
AH ...
... H ...
... H ...

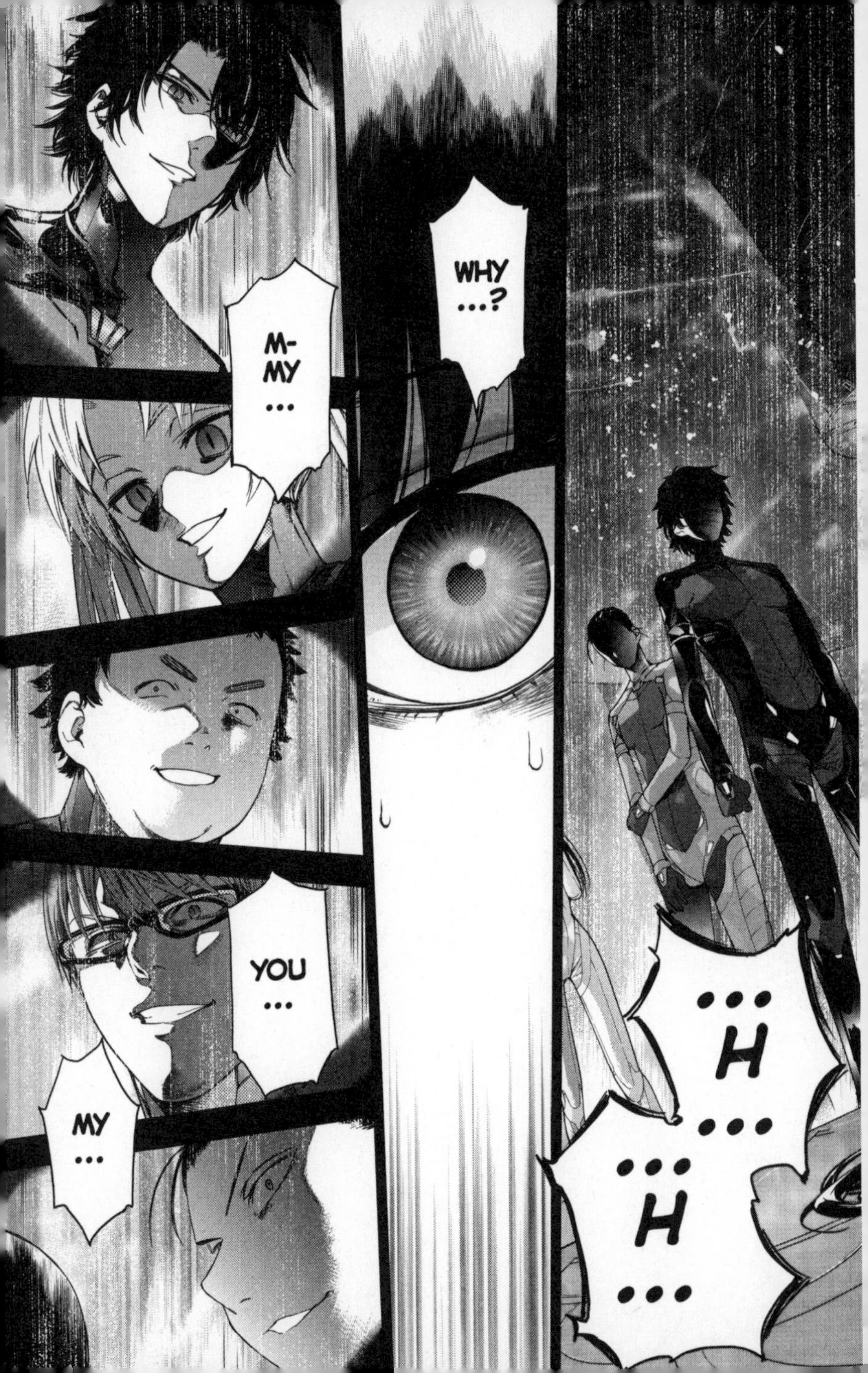
...H... ...H...
WHY...?
M-MY...
YOU...
MY...

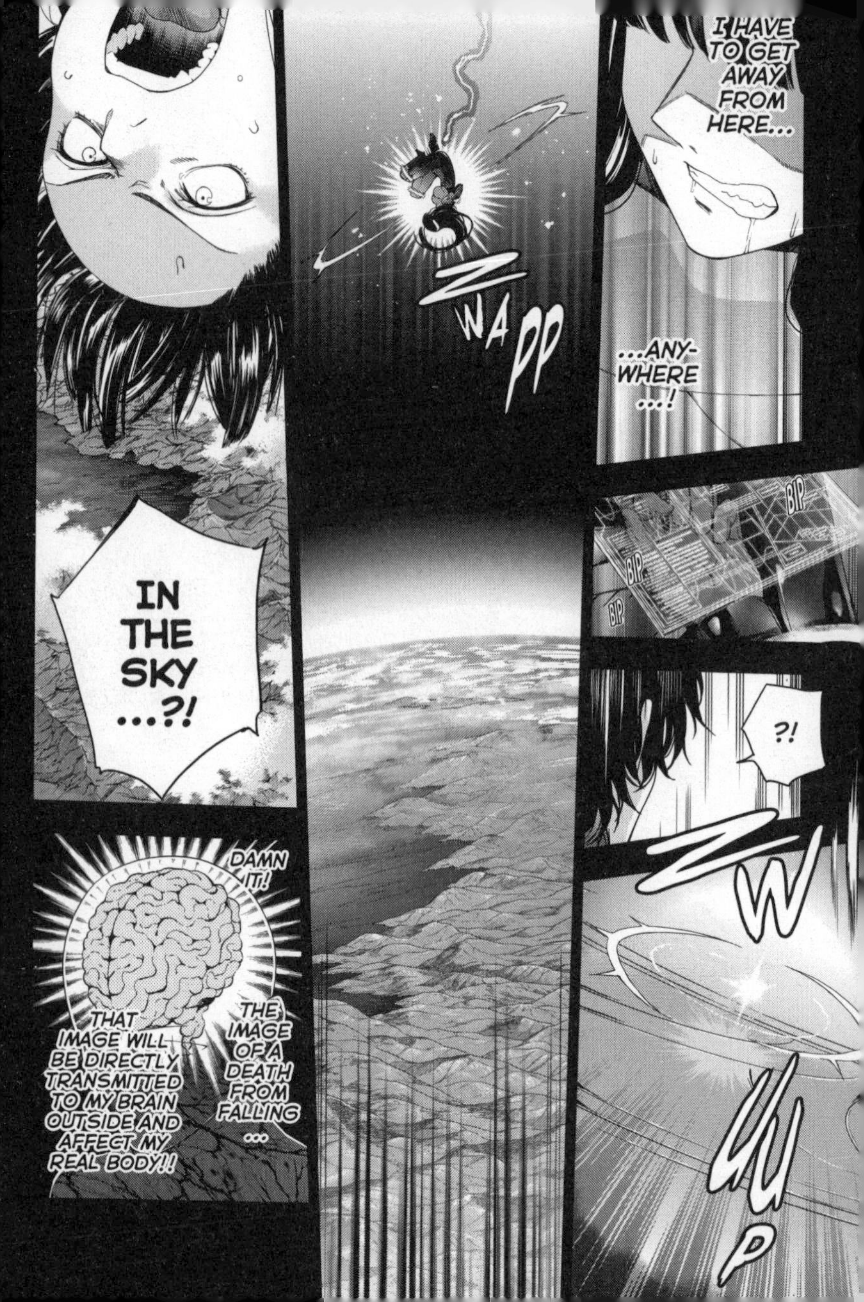
I HAVE TO GET AWAY FROM HERE...
...ANY-WHERE ...!
ZWAPP
IN THE SKY ...?!
BIP
BIP
BIP
?!
ZWUUP
DAMN IT!
THE IMAGE OF A DEATH FROM FALLING ...
THAT IMAGE WILL BE DIRECTLY TRANSMITTED TO MY BRAIN OUTSIDE AND AFFECT MY REAL BODY!!

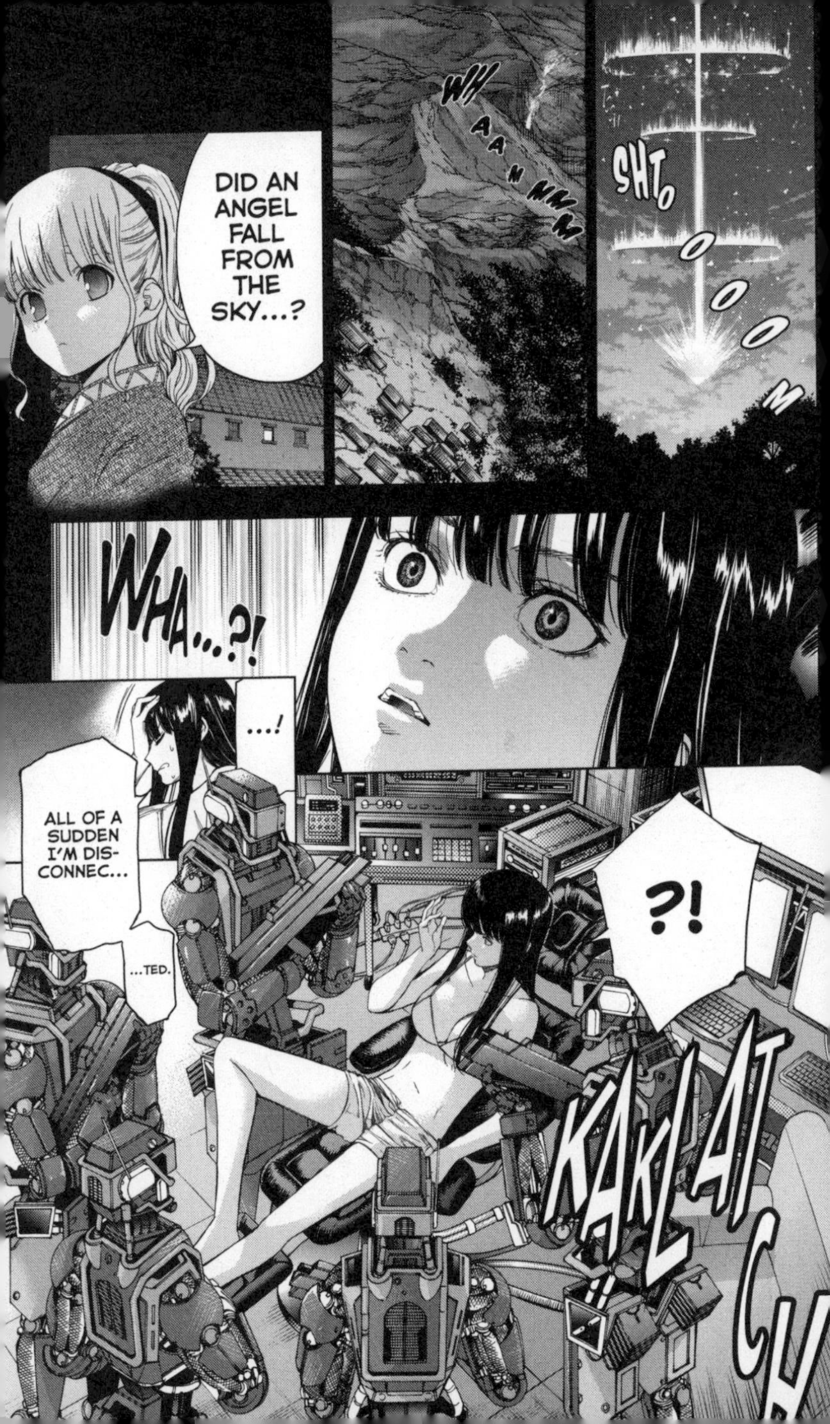
SHTOOOOOM
WHAANMMMM
DID AN ANGEL FALL FROM THE SKY...?
WHA...?!
?!
...!
ALL OF A SUDDEN I'M DISCONNEC...
...TED.
KAKLATCH

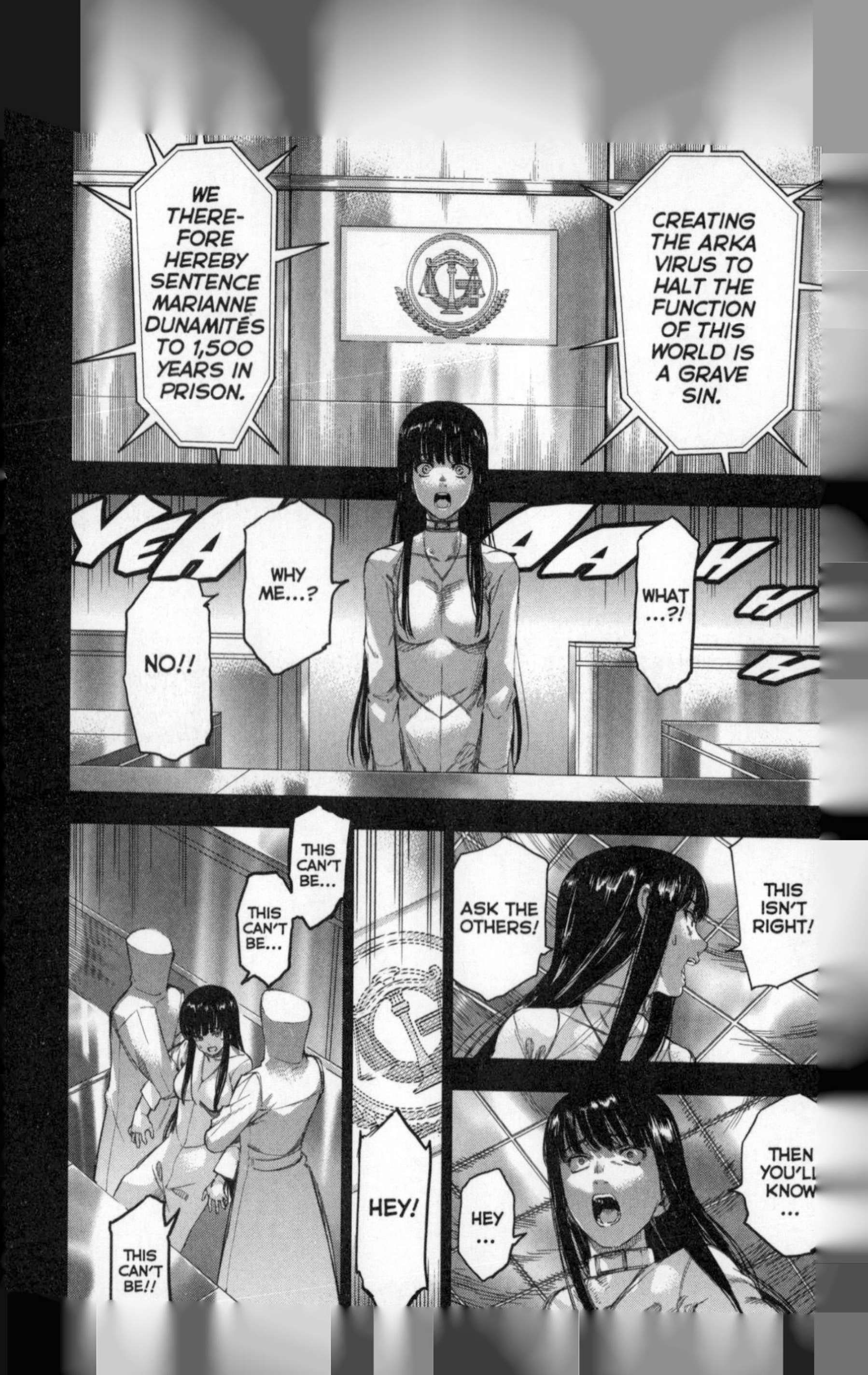
CREATING THE ARKA VIRUS TO HALT THE FUNCTION OF THIS WORLD IS A GRAVE SIN.
WE THEREFORE HEREBY SENTENCE MARIANNE DUNAMITÉS TO 1,500 YEARS IN PRISON.
YEAAAAHHH
WHAT...?!
WHY ME...?
NO!!
THIS ISN'T RIGHT!
ASK THE OTHERS!
THEN YOU'LL KNOW...
HEY...
HEY!
THIS CAN'T BE...
THIS CAN'T BE...
THIS CAN'T BE!!

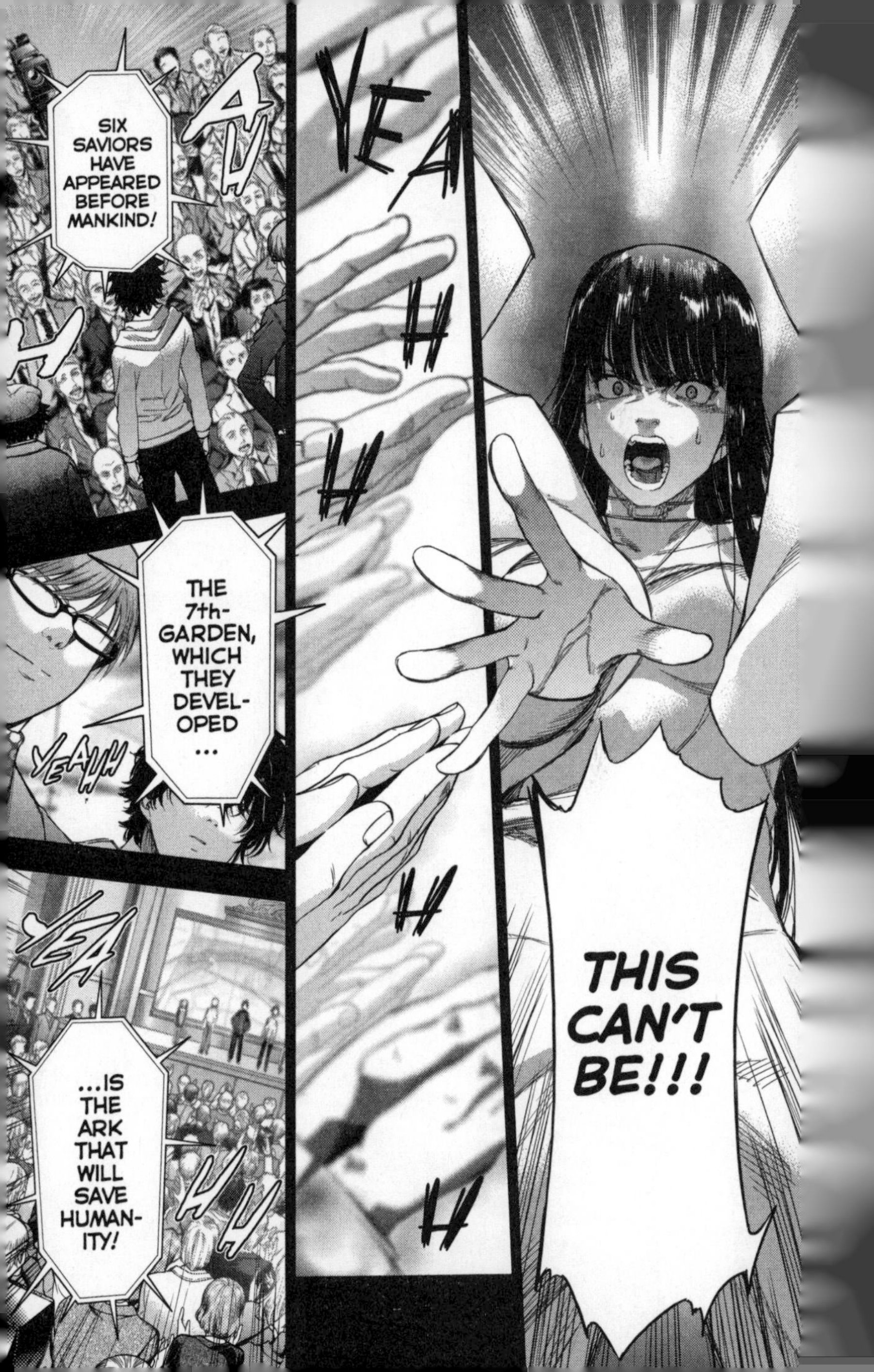
THIS CAN'T BE!!!
YEAHHHHH
SIX SAVIORS HAVE APPEARED BEFORE MANKIND!
AHH
THE 7th-GARDEN, WHICH THEY DEVEL-OPED ...
YEAHH
...IS THE ARK THAT WILL SAVE HUMAN-ITY!
YEAHHH

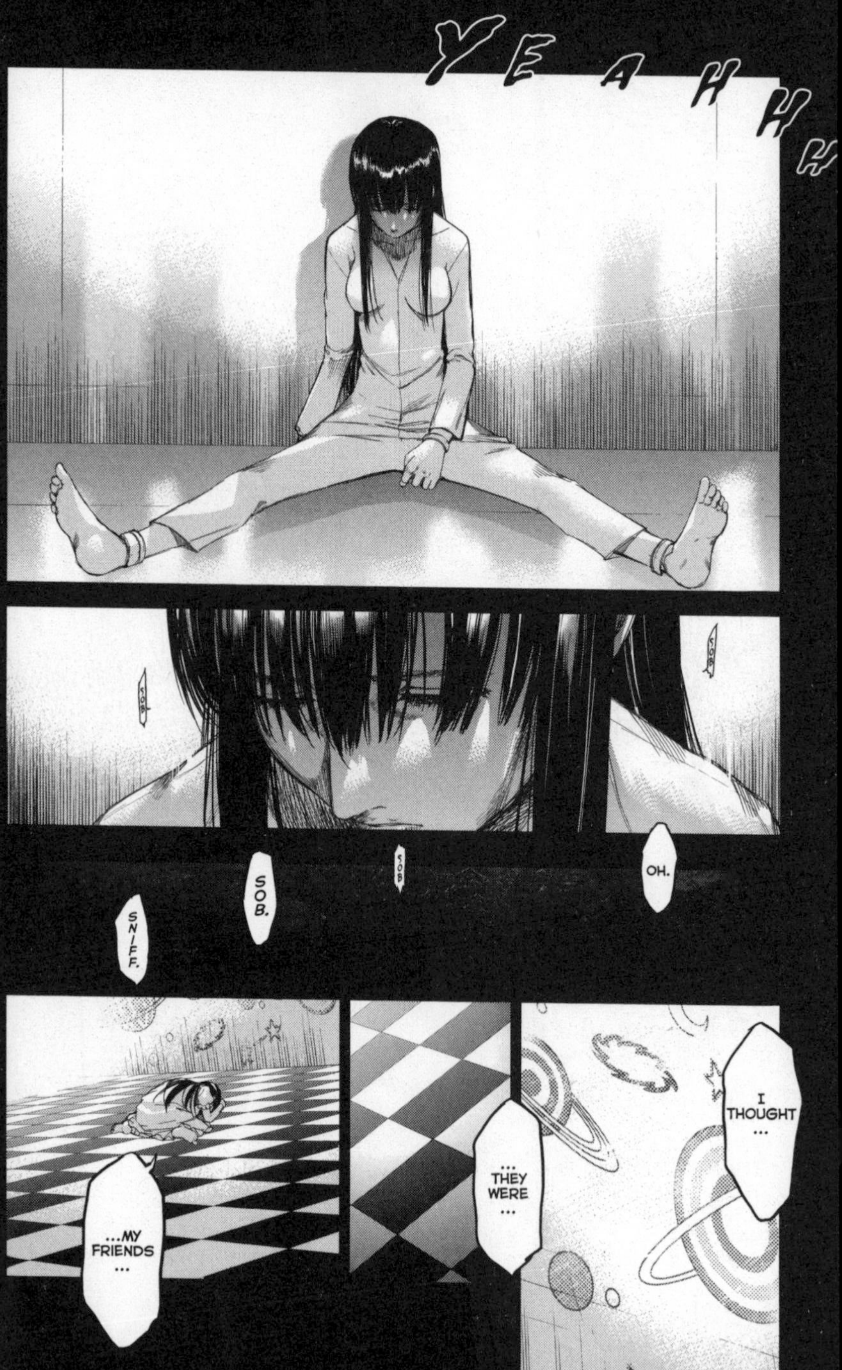
YEAHHHH
SOB
SOB
OH.
SOB
SOB.
SNIFF.
I THOUGHT ...
... THEY WERE ...
...MY FRIENDS ...

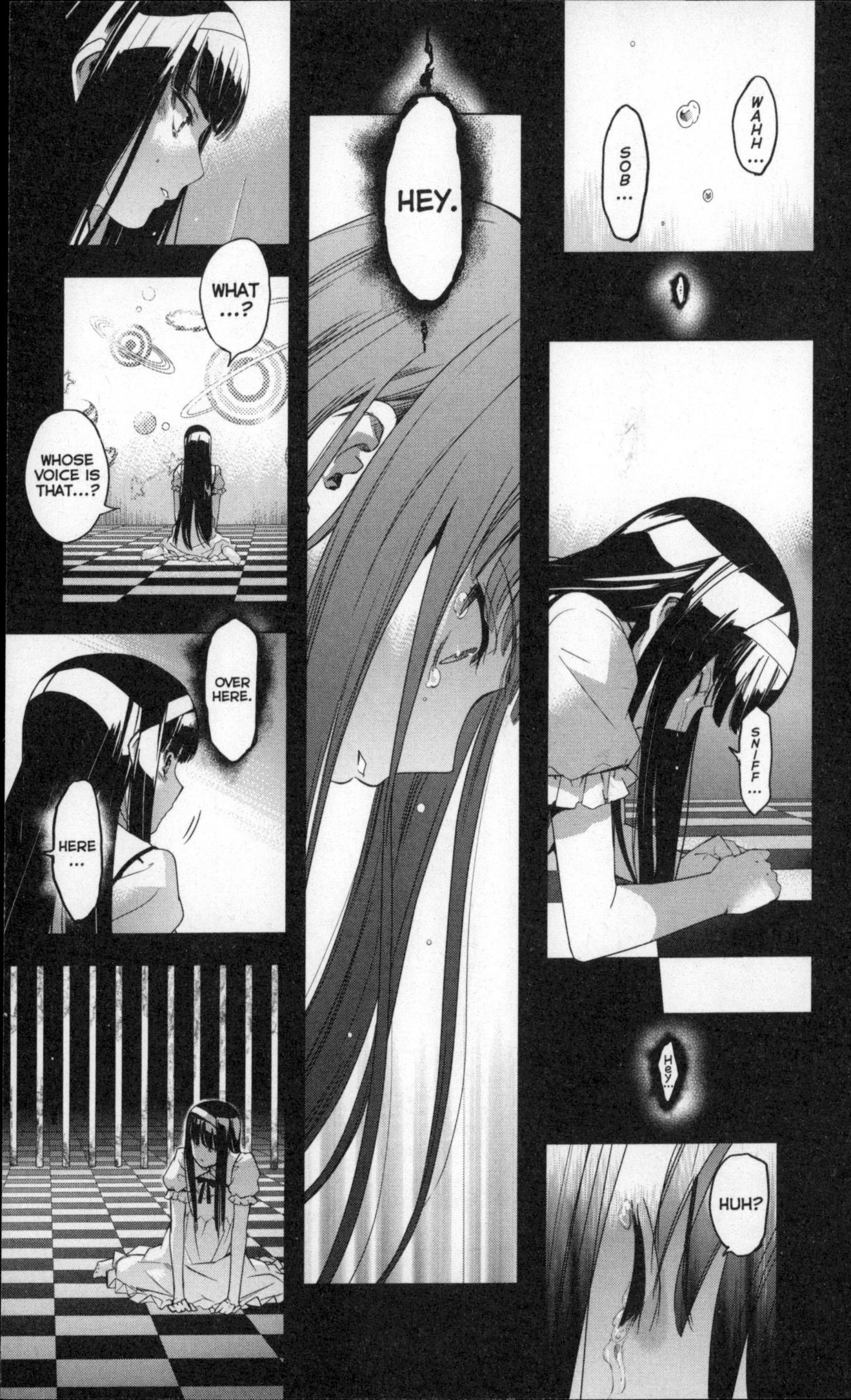
WAHH...
SOB...
SNIFF...
Hey...
HUH?
HEY.
WHAT...?
WHOSE VOICE IS THAT...?
OVER HERE.
HERE...

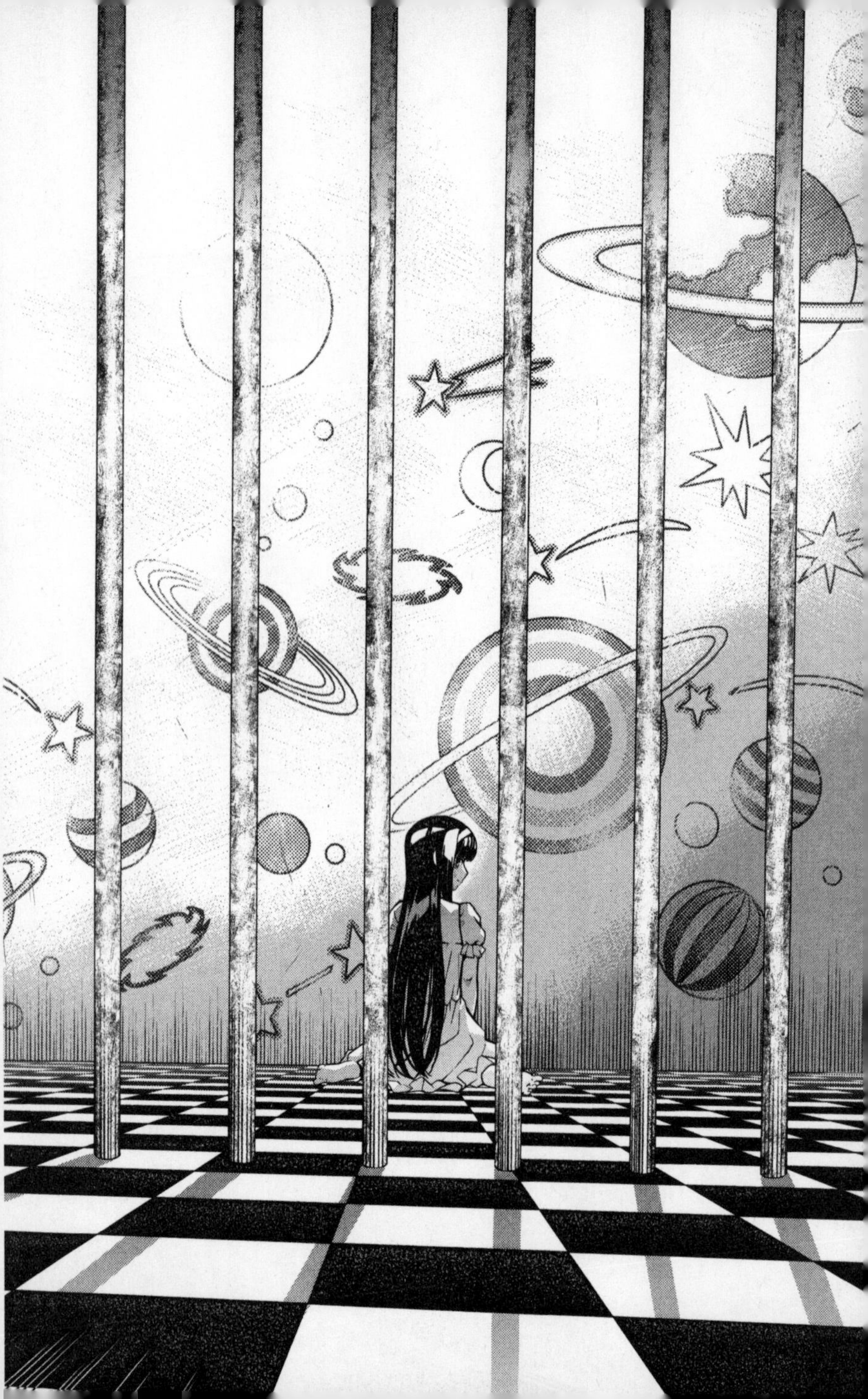

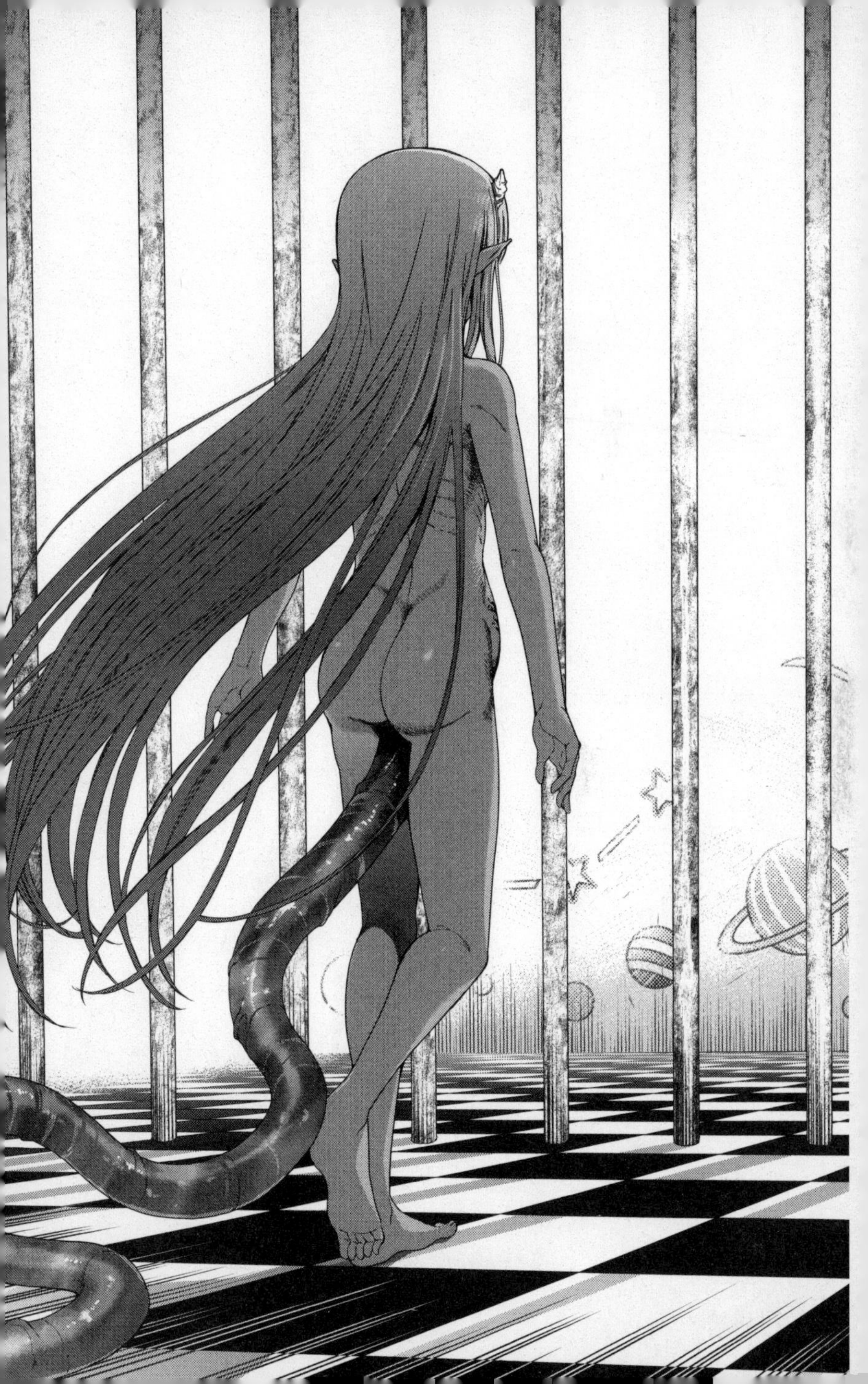

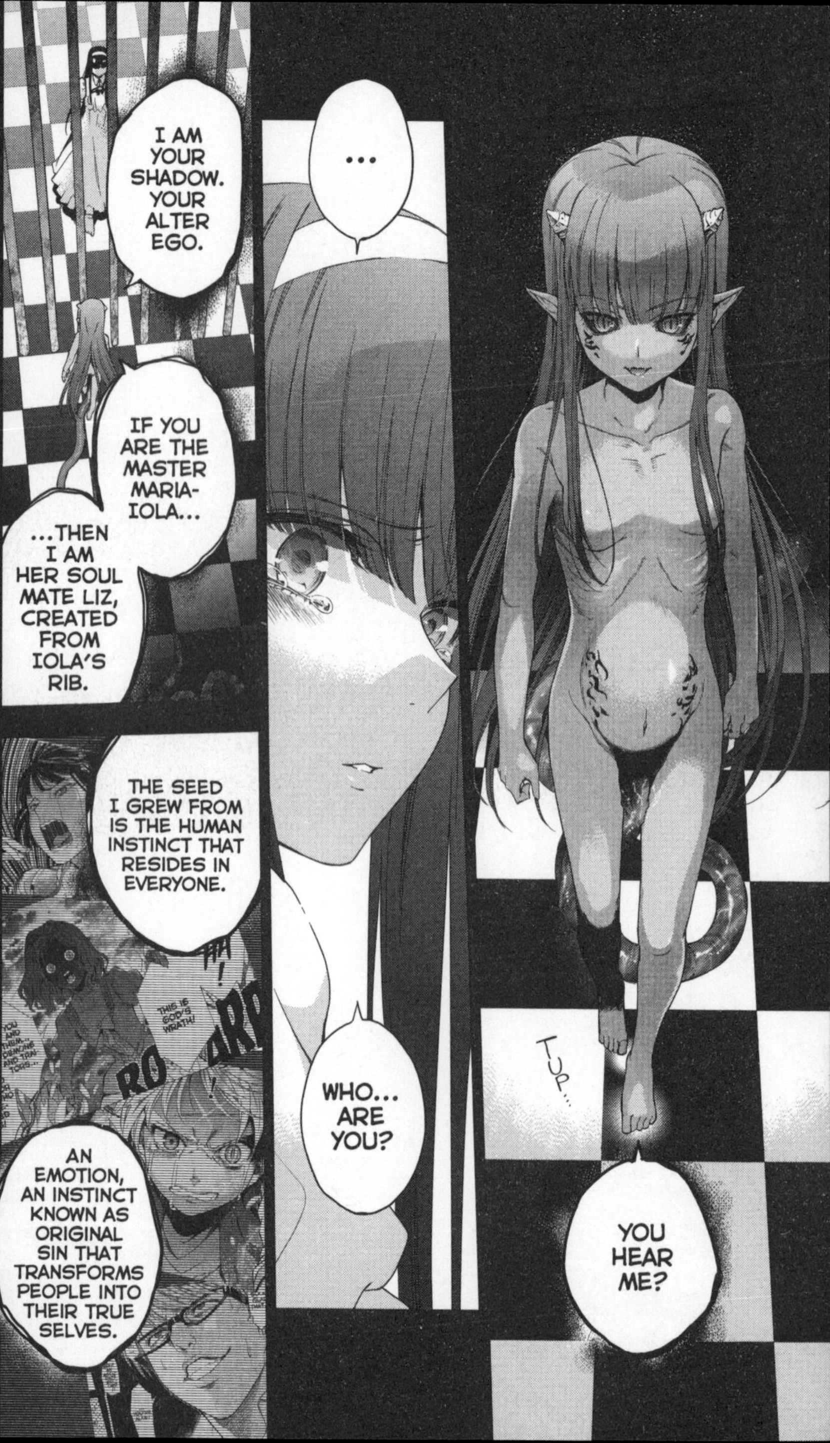
TUP...
YOU HEAR ME?
...
WHO... ARE YOU?
I AM YOUR SHADOW. YOUR ALTER EGO.
IF YOU ARE THE MASTER MARIA-IOLA...
...THEN I AM HER SOUL MATE LIZ, CREATED FROM IOLA'S RIB.
THE SEED I GREW FROM IS THE HUMAN INSTINCT THAT RESIDES IN EVERYONE.
THIS IS GOD'S WRATH!
YOU AND THEM... DEMONS AND TRAITORS...
AN EMOTION, AN INSTINCT KNOWN AS ORIGINAL SIN THAT TRANSFORMS PEOPLE INTO THEIR TRUE SELVES.

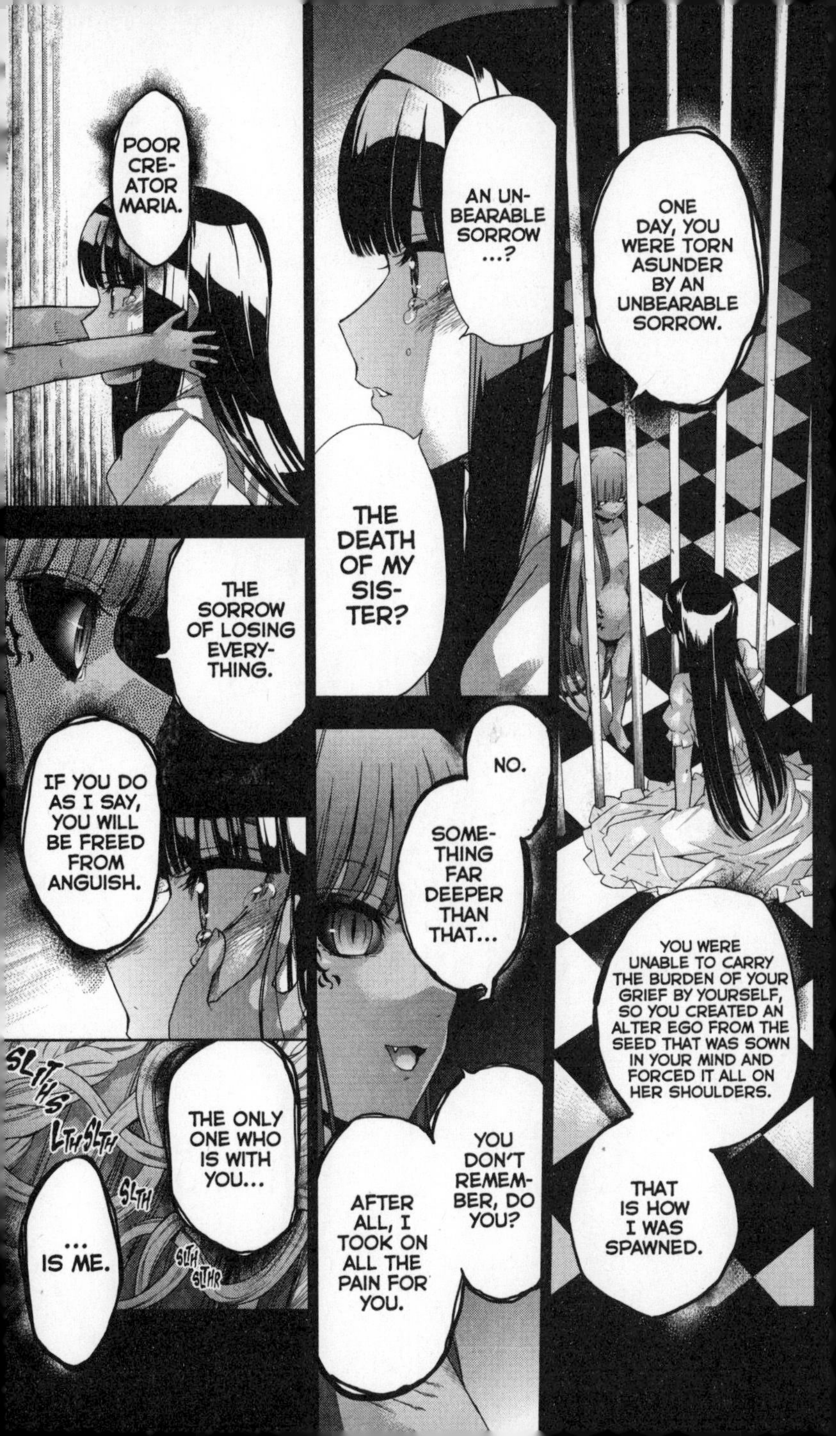
ONE DAY, YOU WERE TORN ASUNDER BY AN UNBEARABLE SORROW.
YOU WERE UNABLE TO CARRY THE BURDEN OF YOUR GRIEF BY YOURSELF, SO YOU CREATED AN ALTER EGO FROM THE SEED THAT WAS SOWN IN YOUR MIND AND FORCED IT ALL ON HER SHOULDERS.
THAT IS HOW I WAS SPAWNED.
AN UN-BEARABLE SORROW ...?
THE DEATH OF MY SIS-TER?
NO.
SOME-THING FAR DEEPER THAN THAT...
YOU DON'T REMEM-BER, DO YOU?
AFTER ALL, I TOOK ON ALL THE PAIN FOR YOU.
POOR CRE-ATOR MARIA.
THE SORROW OF LOSING EVERY-THING.
IF YOU DO AS I SAY, YOU WILL BE FREED FROM ANGUISH.
SLITHS
LTH SLTH
THE ONLY ONE WHO IS WITH YOU...
SLTH
SLTH SLTHR
... IS ME.

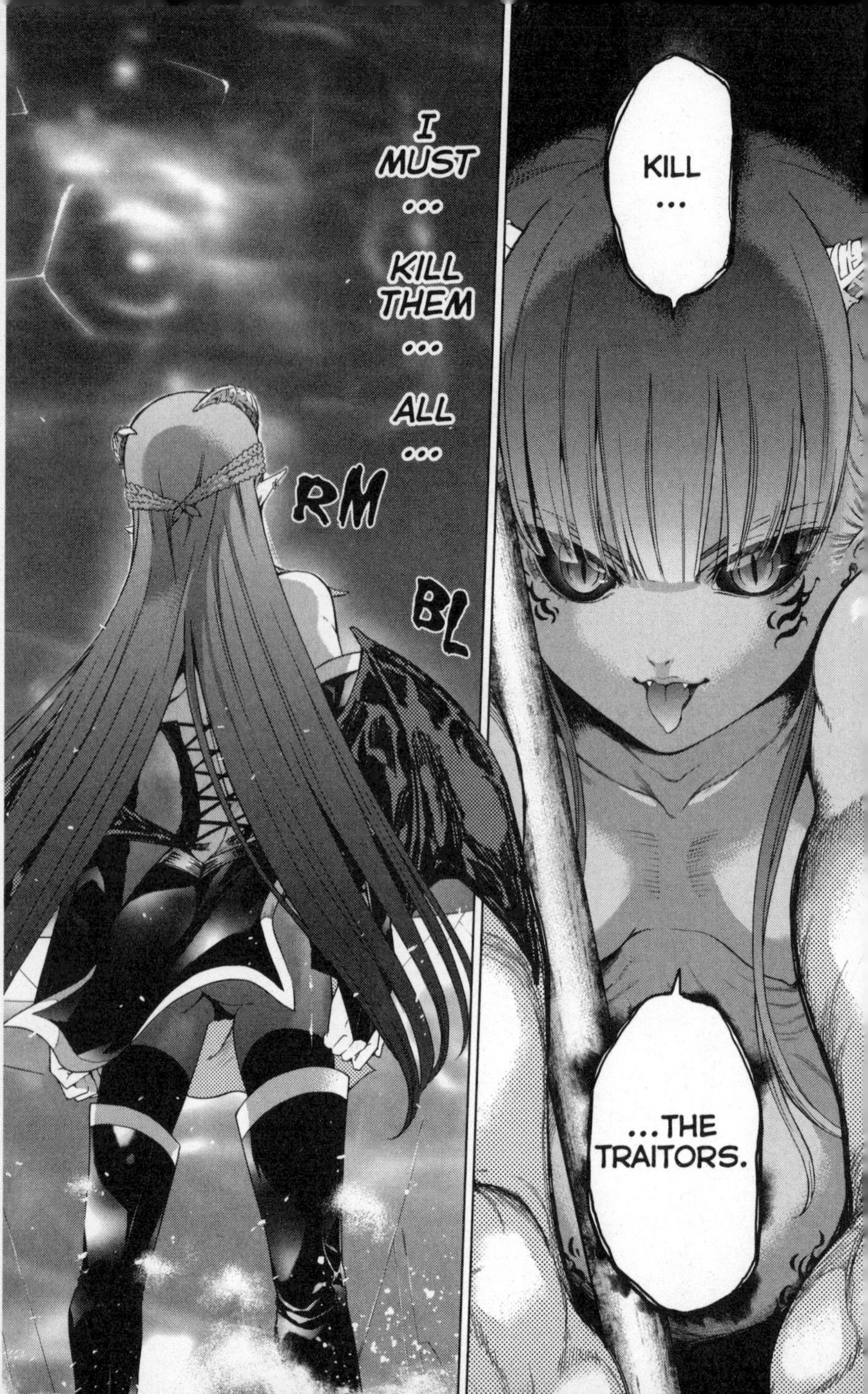
KILL ...
...THE TRAITORS.
I MUST ...
KILL THEM ...
ALL ...
RM
BL

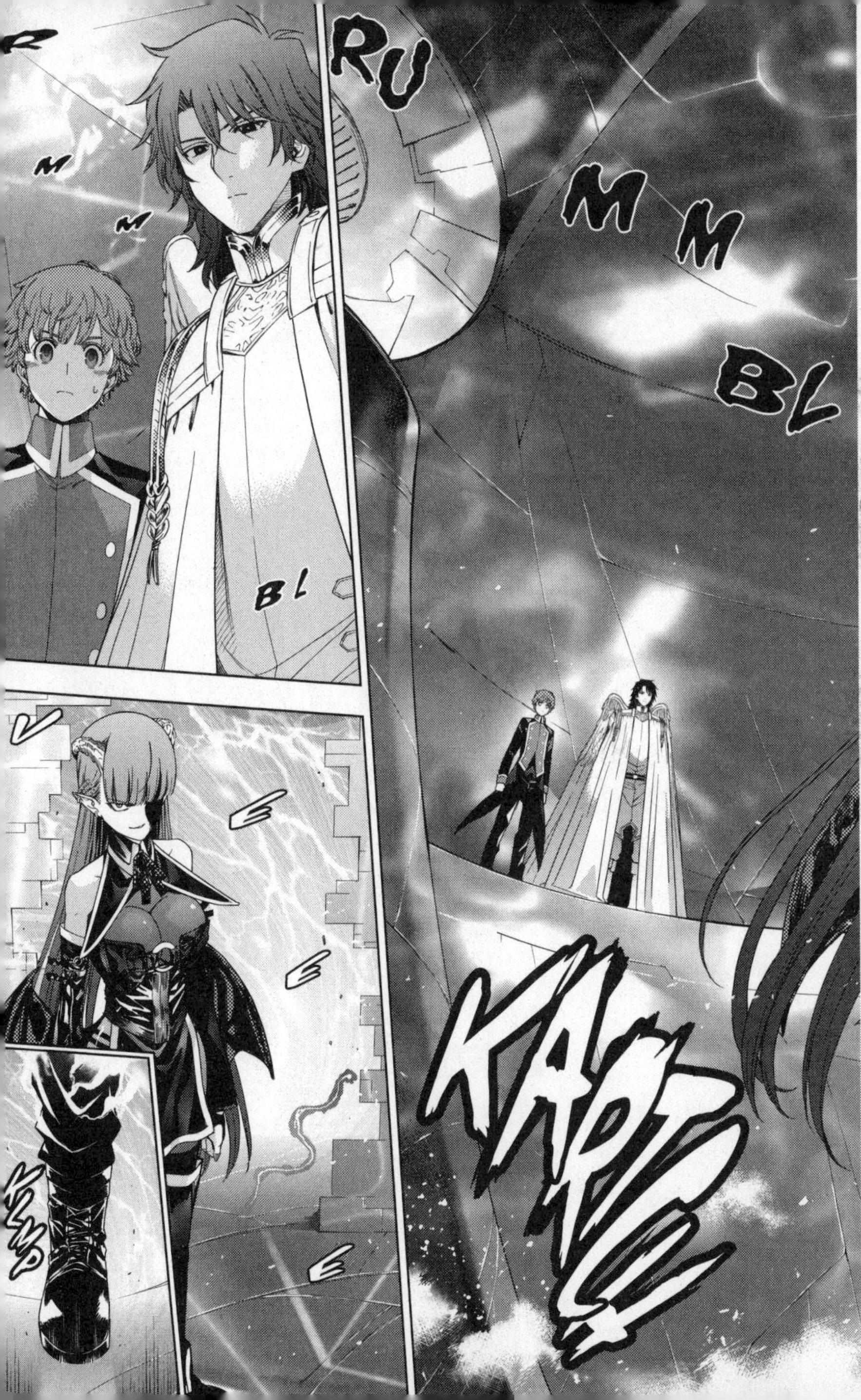
RUMMMBL
RMM
BL
VEEE
KLMP

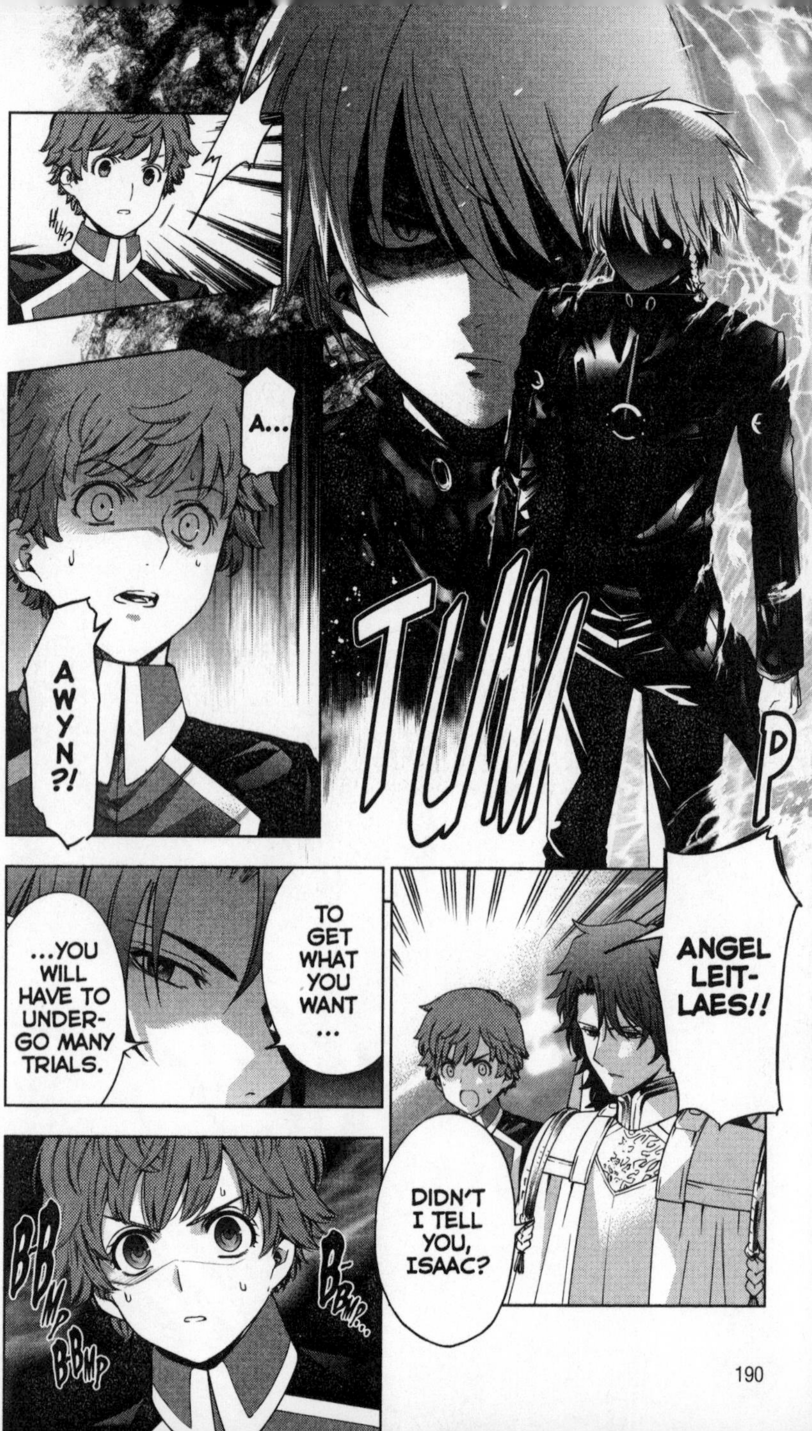
TUMP
HUH?
A...
AWYN?!
ANGEL LEIT-LAES!!
DIDN'T I TELL YOU, ISAAC?
TO GET WHAT YOU WANT...
...YOU WILL HAVE TO UNDER-GO MANY TRIALS.
B-BMP...
B-BMP
B-BMP

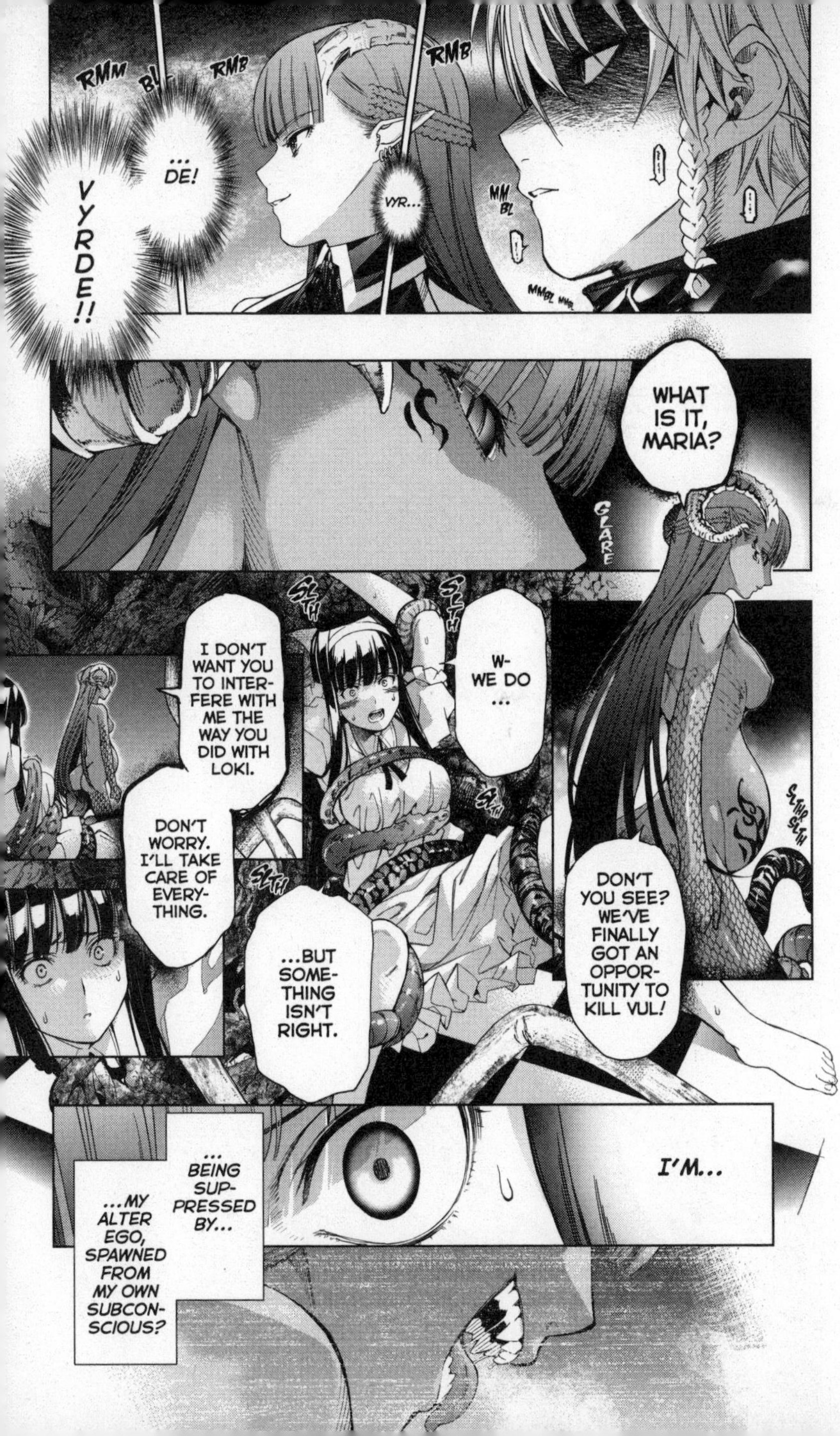
MM BL
MMBL MMBL
RMB
VYR...
RMB
BL
RMM
...DE!
VYRDE!!
WHAT IS IT, MARIA?
GLARE
SLTHR SLTH
DON'T YOU SEE? WE'VE FINALLY GOT AN OPPORTUNITY TO KILL VUL!
SLTH
W- WE DO ...
SLTH
SLTH
I DON'T WANT YOU TO INTERFERE WITH ME THE WAY YOU DID WITH LOKI.
DON'T WORRY. I'LL TAKE CARE OF EVERYTHING.
SLTH
...BUT SOMETHING ISN'T RIGHT.
I'M...
...BEING SUPPRESSED BY...
...MY ALTER EGO, SPAWNED FROM MY OWN SUBCONSCIOUS?

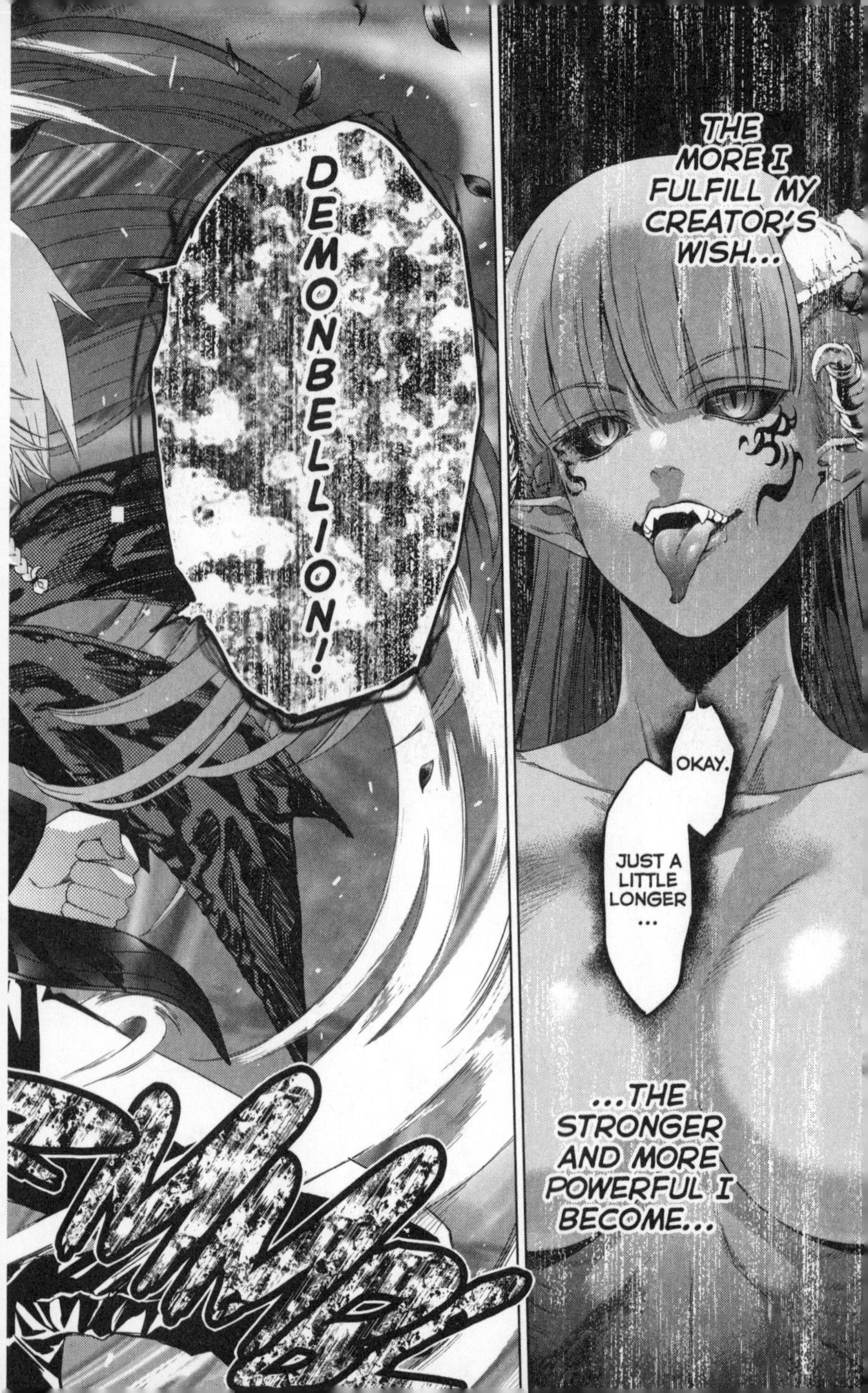
THE MORE I FULFILL MY CREATOR'S WISH...
OKAY.
JUST A LITTLE LONGER ...
...THE STRONGER AND MORE POWERFUL I BECOME...
DEMONBELLION!

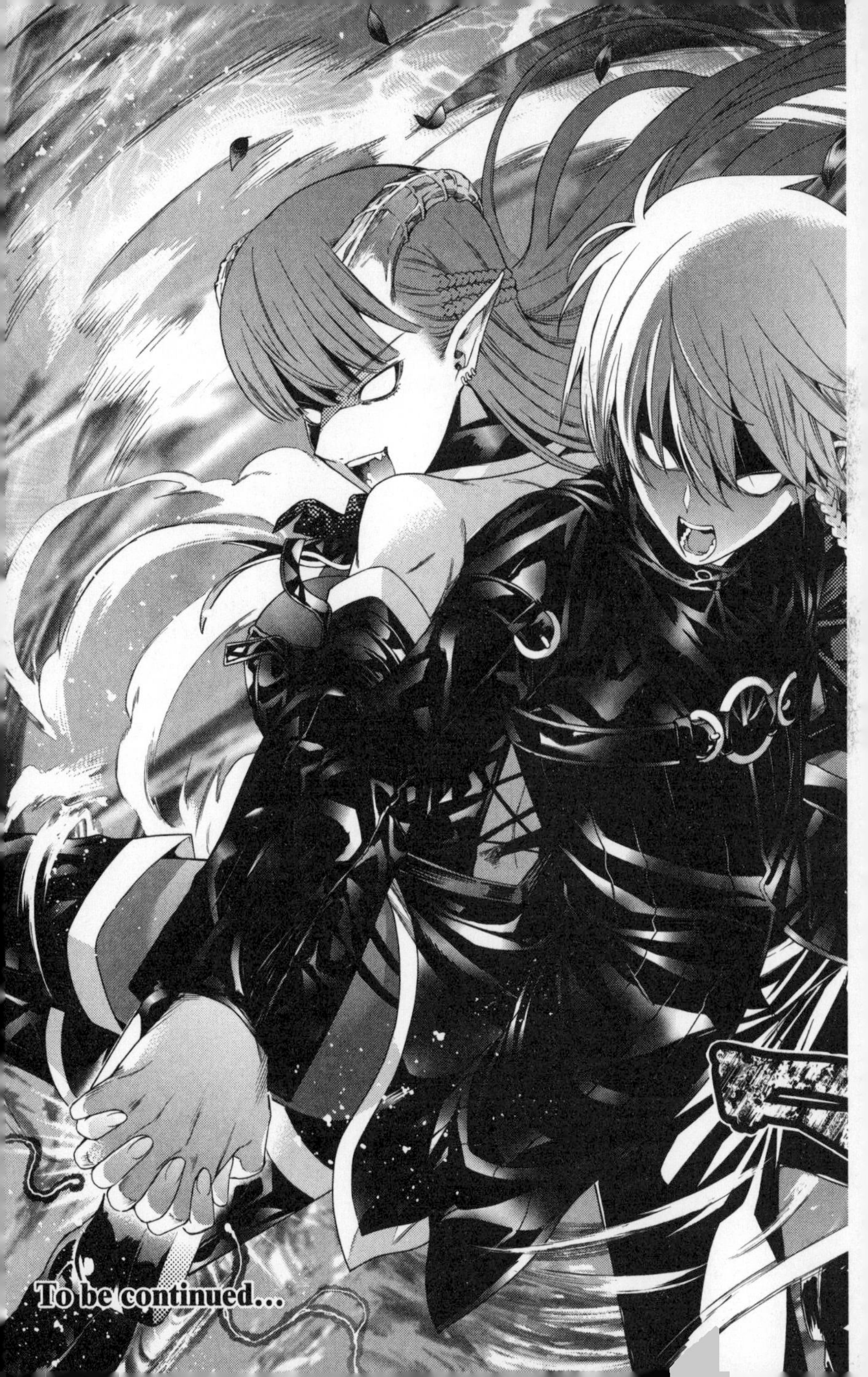
To be continued…

Mitsu Izumi

Mysterious manga creator Mitsu
Izumi was born on February 7
in Kanagawa Prefecture and is
the creator of the manga
adaptation of *Anohana:
The Flower We Saw That Day*,
originally serialized in *Jvmp SQ*.

JUST A
LITTLE MORE...

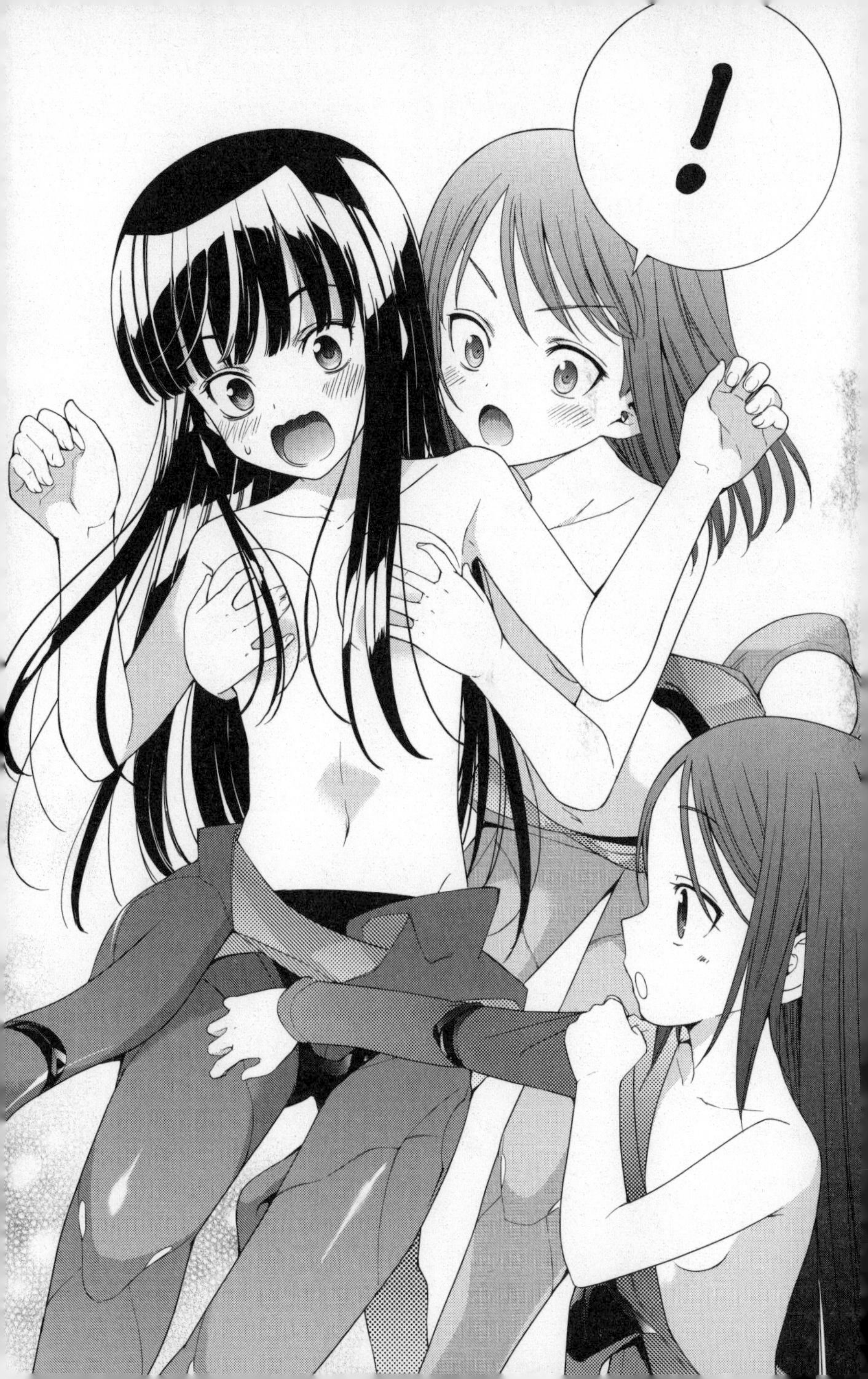
!

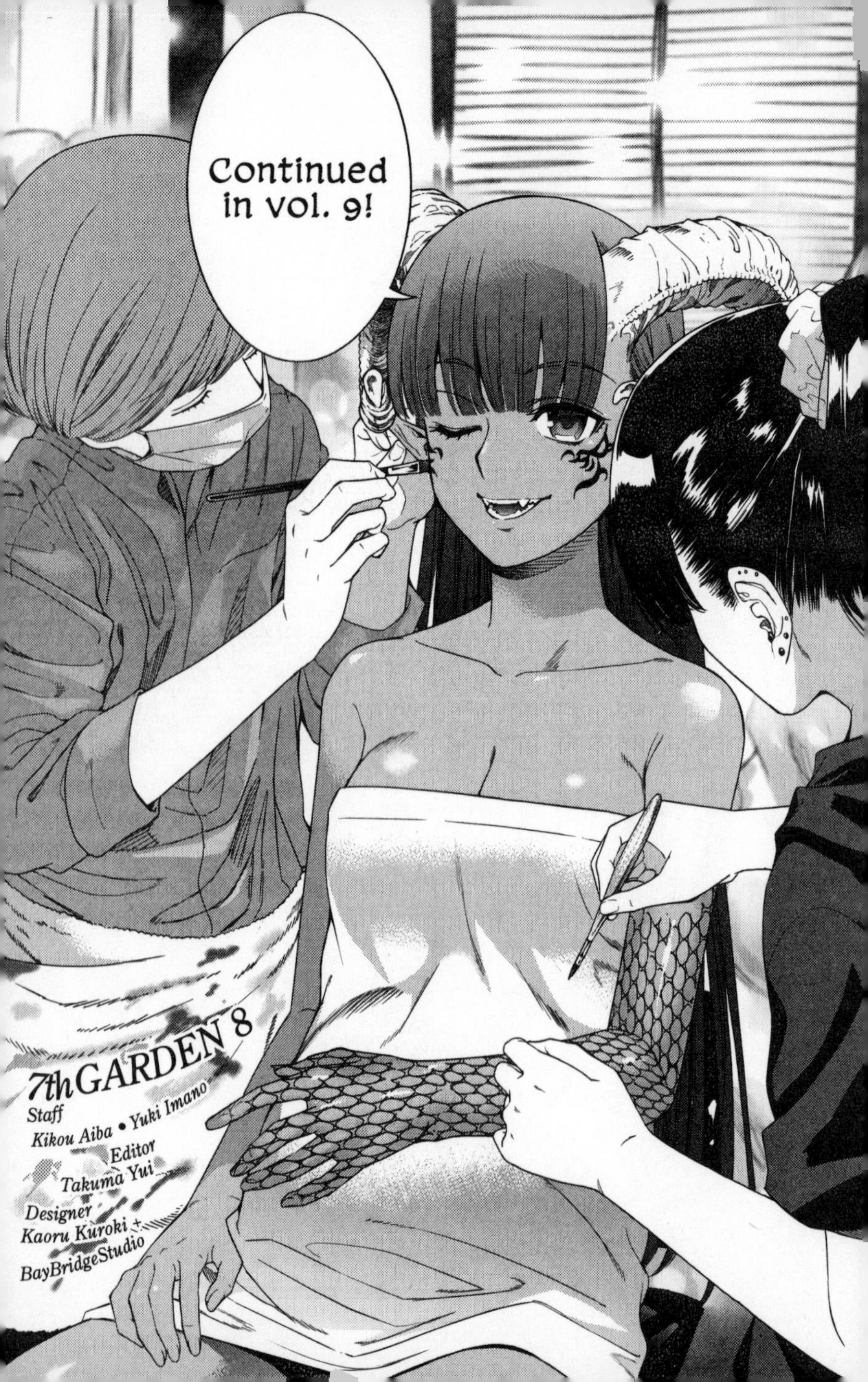
Continued in vol. 9!
7th GARDEN 8
Staff
Kikou Aiba • Yuki Imano
Editor
Takuma Yui
Designer
Kaoru Kuroki +
BayBridgeStudio

7thGARDEN

8

SHONEN JUMP Manga Edition

Story and Art by Mitsu Izumi

Translation/Tetsuichiro Miyaki
English Adaptation/Annette Roman
Touch-Up Art & Lettering/James Gaubatz
Cover & Interior Design/Izumi Evers
Editor/Annette Roman

First published in Japan in 2014 by SHUEISHA Inc., Tokyo.
English translation rights arranged by SHUEISHA Inc.

Printed in the U.S.A.

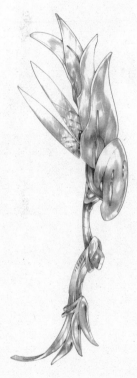

Published by VIZ Media, LLC
P.O. Box 77010
San Francisco, CA 94107

10 9 8 7 6 5 4 3 2 1
First printing, April 2018

www.viz.com

www.shonenjump.com

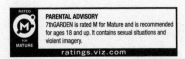

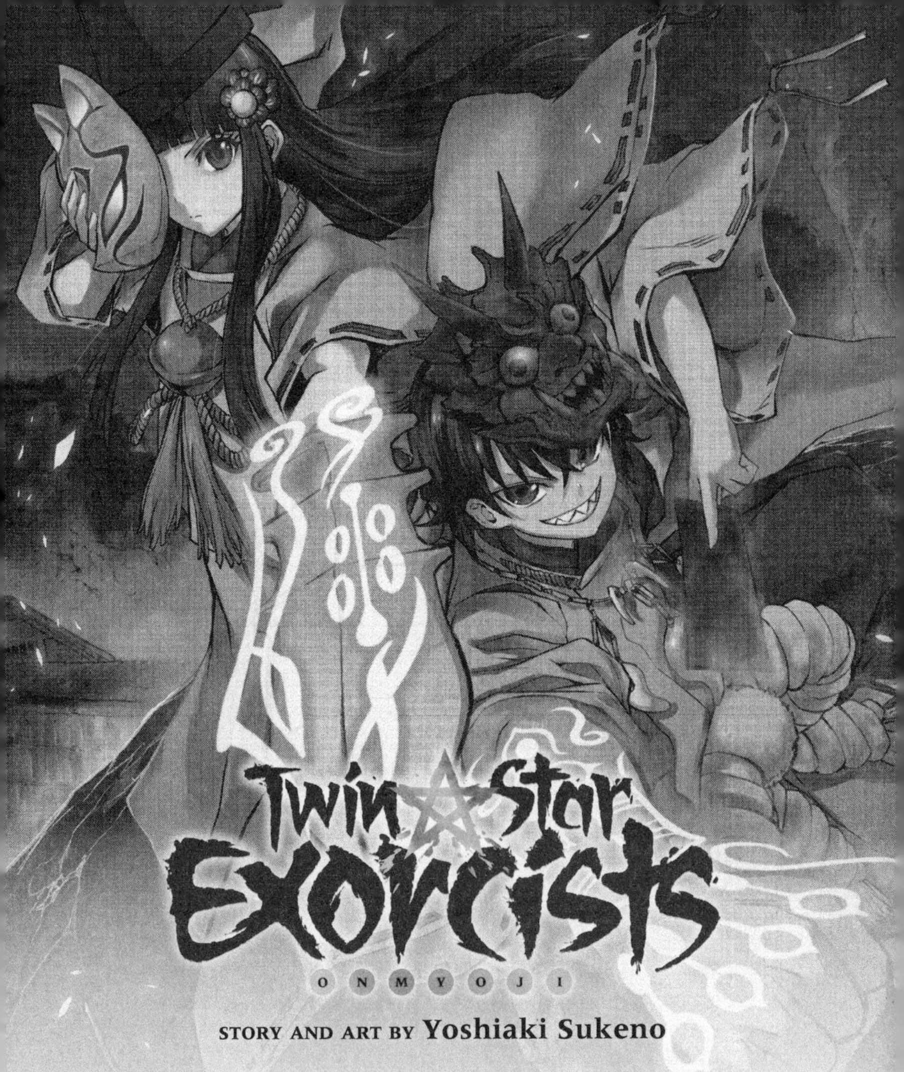
Twin Star
Exorcists
ONMYOJI

You're Reading in the Wrong Direction!!

Whoops! Guess what? You're starting at the wrong end of the comic!

…It's true! In keeping with the original Japanese format, **7thGARDEN** is meant to be read from right to left, starting in the upper-right corner.

Unlike English, which is read from left to right, Japanese is read from right to left, meaning that action, sound effects and word-balloon order are completely reversed… something which can make readers unfamiliar with Japanese feel pretty backwards themselves. For this reason, manga or Japanese comics published in the U.S. in English have sometimes been published "flopped"—that is, printed in exact reverse order, as though seen from the other side of a mirror.

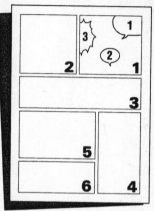

By flopping pages, U.S. publishers can avoid confusing readers, but the compromise is not without its downside. For one thing, a character in a flopped manga series who once wore in the original Japanese version a T-shirt emblazoned with "M A Y" (as in "the merry month of") now wears one which reads "Y A M"! Additionally, many manga creators in Japan are themselves unhappy with the process, as some feel the mirror-imaging of their art skews their original intentions.

We are proud to bring you Mitsu Izumi's **7thGARDEN** in the original unflopped format.

For now, though, turn to the other side of the book and let the adventure begin…!

—Editor